Last Train from Atlanta

Other Books by A. A. Hoehling

The Last Voyage of the Lusitania
A Whisper of Eternity
Lonely Command

LAST TRAIN FROM ATLANTA

by A. A. Hoehling

BONANZA BOOKS
NEW YORK

To the memory of the
little girl who fell
at the corner of Ivy
and East Ellis streets,
July 20, 1864

CONTENTS

ILLUSTRATIONS

9

DRAMATIS PERSONAE

Those Who Have Helped Recount
the Story of Atlanta

ARCHER, W. P.—a Confederate soldier, defender of Atlanta.

BEATTY, COLONEL TAYLOR—General Hardee's military lawyer, from Thibodaux, Louisiana.

BEERS, MRS. FANNIE A.—a nurse from Richmond whose husband fought in defense of Atlanta.

BERRY, CARRIE—little girl of Atlanta, daughter of Maxwell Berry, a contractor.

BRAGG, BRAXTON—General and Chief-of-Staff for Confederate President Jefferson Davis.

BRAUMULLER, O. L.—young boy of Atlanta who lived next door to General Hood's headquarters.

BROWN, JOSEPH E.—Governor of Georgia.

CALHOUN, JAMES—Mayor of Atlanta.

CHAMBERLIN, MAJOR W. H.—Federal infantry officer.

CLARK, WALTER—former Augusta, Georgia, lawyer, Confederate officer.

CLAYTON, "GUSSIE"—a young schoolgirl.

CLEBURNE, PATRICK R. "PAT"—Confederate general.

COBURN, COLONEL JOHN—commanding second brigade, 33rd Indiana Regiment.

CONYNGHAM, DAVID—Federal Captain and correspondent for the *New York Herald*.

COX, JACOB D.—Major General, commanding Federal 23rd Army Corps.

CREW, JAMES—superintendent of West Point Railroad.

CUMMING, KATE—Scottish-born Confederate nurse.

D'ALVIGNY, DR. PETER PAUL NOEL—surgeon of Atlanta Medical College.

11

DYER, PRIVATE JOHN—Confederate soldier from Kentucky who visited Andersonville.

FOARD, A. J.—medical director, Army of Tennessee (Confederate).

FRENCH, SAMUEL—Major General of Atlanta defenders.

GAY, MARY—thirty-six-year-old woman of suburban Decatur.

GEARY, JOHN W.—Major General, civil administrator of Atlanta (for Federal forces).

GRAHAM, SERGEANT WILLIAM—of 53rd Illinois Volunteers.

HARDEE, WILLIAM J.—Confederate General and corps commander.

HEDLEY, FENWICK—Adjutant of 32nd Illinois Infantry.

HILL, JOSHUA—Georgia senator, Unionist.

HITCHCOCK, MAJOR HENRY—St. Louis lawyer and Sherman's assistant Adjutant General of volunteers.

HOOD, JOHN BELL—Confederate General in command of Atlanta's defense.

HOWELL, CAPTAIN EVAN P.—Atlanta resident who evacuated his wife and baby from their Chattahoochee home.

HUBNER, MAJOR CHARLES W.—former Illinois journalist.

HULL, LUCY HARVIE—a child of Atlanta.

JOHNSTON, JOSEPH E.—Confederate Commanding General who was succeeded by Hood.

KEY, CAPTAIN TOM—Confederate Battery Commander and Alabama publisher.

LAY, BISHOP HENRY C.—Bishop of Arkansas.

LUCKIE, SOL—Negro barber of Atlanta.

MEAD, RUFUS—twenty-eight-year-old Sergeant from Redding, Connecticut.

MOORE, J. C.—Federal spy.

MORGAN, IRBY—refugee, with his family, from Tennessee.

NEAL, ANDREW JACKSON—Atlanta lawyer and Lieutenant in the Marion Light Artillery whose house became Sherman's headquarters.

NEWBERRY, THOMAS JEFFERSON—soldier from Mississippi.

NICHOLS, MAJOR WARD—aide-de-camp of Sherman.

O'REILLY, FATHER THOMAS—Atlanta pastor of the Catholic Church of the Immaculate Conception.

PATTEN, DR. JAMES COMFORT—Indiana physician with Federal forces.

PEPPER, CAPTAIN GEORGE—Federal officer from Zanesville, Ohio.

PERKERSON, LIZZIE—sheriff's daughter, living in farm outside of Atlanta.

POE, CAPTAIN ORLANDO M.—Sherman's chief of engineers.

QUINTARD, CHARLES T.—Confederate minister and doctor.

RAWSON, MARY—sixteen-year-old daughter of wealthy merchant, E. E. Rawson, who was also city councilman.

REED, WALLACE P.—Atlanta writer.

RICHARDS, S. P.—English-born bookseller of Atlanta.

ROSE, SERGEANT ANDREW K.—Federal soldier from Dover, Ohio.

RUSHTON, MARY—daughter of William Rushton, superintendent of Georgia Railroad and West Point Railroad shops.

SEMMES, BENEDICT JOSEPH—General Johnston's chief depot commissary in Atlanta; member of old Memphis family and cousin of Raphael Semmes, captain of raider *Alabama*.

SHERMAN, WILLIAM TECUMSEH—Major General, commanding the Federal Military Division of the Mississippi.

SLOCUM, THOMAS W.—Federal General commanding 20th Corps.

SMITH, CHARLES H.—wit from Virginia, refugeeing south with his family.

SMITH, MOLLIE—a young girl of Atlanta.

SMITH, MRS. S. E. D. "Grandma"—nurse from Memphis.

STOKES, TOM—Mary Gay's half-brother, soldier-preacher.

STOUT, DR. SAMUEL H.—medical director of hospitals, Army of Tennessee.

VALE, CAPTAIN JOSEPH G.—Pennsylvania cavalryman.

VAN DUZER, CAPTAIN J. C.—Federal telegraphist.

WATTERSON, HENRY—newspaperman, later spy for Hood, the postwar "Marse Henry" of *Louisville Courier Journal*.

WILLIAMS, NOBLE—a boy of Atlanta.

Note: ▮▮ *Indicates a Northern newspaper source.*
      ▧ *Indicates a Southern newspaper source.*

Last Train from Atlanta

PROLOGUE

"I have hardly felt so profoundly your presence in spirit as I did today . . . though I could not see you in the flesh I felt you were by my side . . . yesterday the enemy shelled us again, heavily and rapidly . . . tearing our houses, burning some, and wounding a number of persons. . . ."

From within beleaguered Atlanta, a Confederate supply officer penned these words to his wife, expressing a loneliness and longing which has spanned time and space in humanity's dreary epic of strife.

Nearly a century ago an American city learned the meaning of total war, and yet found it difficult to comprehend.

Atlanta, Georgia, was young, barely thirty years old. It had become "Gate City" of the South, hub of railroads, factories, foundries, stores, arsenals, government offices, and, inevitably, hospitals for the mounting human wreckage of war. Its population of a few dozen when it was named "Marthasville" and ten thousand at the time of Fort Sumter had been swollen to nearly twenty thousand.

President Jefferson Davis asserted of Atlanta: "Its fall would open the way for the Federal Army to the Gulf on the one hand, and to Charleston on the other, and close up those rich granaries from which Lee's armies are supplied. It would give them control of our network of railways and thus paralyze our efforts."

Like Carthage or Troy of an earlier generation, Warsaw or Manila of a later, Atlanta was doomed by its own desirability. The North sought it with the singleness of purpose of a hawk. Like a "bosom of destruction," Major General William Tecumseh Sherman led an army of one hundred thousand seasoned veterans out of Tennessee, their first and major goal—Atlanta. Hardened by the fury and the disappointments of three years of civil warfare, this huge "Military Division of the Mississippi,"

17

composed of three distinct armies, was perhaps the greatest fighting machine the world had ever seen.

What happened when such a juggernaut reached Atlanta is the subject of this documentary. In a few weeks' time a thriving city, scented with magnolia and echoing with the song of the mule-teamster and the banjo-strummer, was scourged, humbled, and broken.

These events underscore man's inherent inhumanity to his brother, as well as the folly of pride and stubbornness. On the other hand, sin and virtue, heroes and villains, have no place in this chronicle.

While a number of officers and men from both armies, Union and Confederate, help reconstruct the day-by-day scenes of that long-ago summer, the narrative leading up to the departure of the last train from Atlanta is not approached from a military point of view. This, rather, is the recital of little things that transpire in a city under siege, the flickerings that interrupt the monotony of being—the woman who must fall on her face to dodge a shell as she starts for market, the children who hide in backyard dugouts and wonder why others are trying to kill them, the merchants who can find no outlet for their wares, or even the choir singer whose Sundays grow bleak because the churches have been struck so many times that they are locked to their congregations.

The story of Atlanta, however, implies more than mere narration of these "little things." The people are now dust, but their hopes and fears, the mark which privation stamped upon the complex of emotion, as shadows upon a photographic negative, endure in the endless enigma of existence.

It is not easy to stand in downtown Atlanta today and transport oneself back to that hot summer of 1864 when shells struck hit-or-miss. The face of the city is, for the most part, a new face. The earth is paved over, drilled with steel and concrete foundations as though civic fathers wanted to mask even the memory of its mortal scars.

The citizens of Atlanta cannot be dismissed as ghosts out of another realm, distant, improbable people with no present kinship. Children cried out in the night, their parents tasted de-

spair, insecurity, sickness, and hunger. They worried about
food, shelter, the functioning or malfunctioning of their bodies,
and—frequently—about death. Unceasingly, they were tor-
mented by anguish for those separated from them.

This, then, is the simple chronicle of these people, revealed
to the extent that they left testimony behind them. Since this
book is not a work of fiction, no attempt is made to fill in gaps
that may occur in the procession of a day, or of any person's life.

It is the story of how these people—once upon a time—lived,
thought, and felt. In their relation to their descendants, there is
an eloquent timelessness to their lives, particularly in their unhappy fortunes of violence.

Should we conclude that their reward is but a plot in Atlanta's old Oakland Cemetery or that the heritage they be-
queathed is an unrelated sighing out of a yesterday's conflict,
then mankind's hopes for eternity must be as cold as those
graves and this earthly experience a cruel, taunting travesty.

July, 1864

▰ *The Daily Intelligencer* (Atlanta)

"Information from the enemy's lines represent them very despondent and apprehensive of disaster. A prominent officer in Sherman's army is reported to have declared their army whipped, that Johnston had received 25,000 reinforcements and now has overwhelming numbers and that unless the Yankee Government sent them large reinforcements Sherman's army would be cut to pieces. . . .

"Until night, to a very late hour, the Yankees were moving their ambulances along our lines, removing their dead and wounded of the day previous, which appears to be much larger than was at first supposed."

Sunday dawned warm and clear in Atlanta. Church bells tolled a song more reassuring than the battle sounds which had been rumbling from Marietta and Kennesaw Mountain to the north.

Then, as the early morning moisture was consumed by rapidly swelling heat, the air became filled with fine red dust. It was kicked up by wagon wheels, iron-shod hoofs, and the hobnailed boots of soldiers. As on every other day, the smell of horses dominated the city.

It was known that General William T. Sherman was hammering at Marietta, eighteen miles from the center of Atlanta, and that the Military Institute there had already been abandoned. But it appeared unlikely that he could ever ford the Chattahoochee, swollen as it was from June rainfalls.

That summertime Sunday, all access roads except the invasion route remained open. The invasion route was the Western and Atlantic Railroad to Chattanooga, Sherman's "great lever power." Trains moved on the W. & A. tracks out of Atlanta, past Vining's Station, just across the turbulent Chattahoochee, but terminated, perforce, at Marietta.

As the morning wore on and the bells continued to call worshippers to their pews, the various people who called Atlanta home were engaged in characteristically varied activities. A schoolgirl, "Gussie" Clayton, was writing to Mary Lou, her friend:

"As you know, there has been a great deal of excitement in Atlanta that will not be news but a good many persons are packed up who expect to leave if there is any danger of the enemy capturing the city.

"We of course anticipate no such result from the expected battle. Sallie and I packed some bed clothes and curtains and mother had the carpets taken up and fixed, so they could be carried off, but we have done nothing further. If there is any danger we will go immediately to Augusta, tho' I sincerely hope we will not have to leave our homes, as I should not think the life of a refugee was very pleasant. . . . I must close as some French verbs demand my attention."

A younger girl, Lucy Harvie Hull, stood by her fence on Peachtree Street, entertained by the visit of a "cracker" wagon. She watched the familiar "yellow-faced women and children in their long-slatted sun-bonnets and faded calico dresses," and listened to "the bargaining and jesting that passed between buyers and sellers."

It seemed to her that all the neighborhood converged on the rickety provisions cart. From her own house, across the large piazza screened by hop vines and honeysuckle, and over the lawn past the boxwood and flower beds, came "Mammy the cook and Uncle Dick the coachman." They stood by with their bowls and pans ready for the vegetables and eggs, but too proud to join in the homely joking of these strange, gaunt folk from the Georgia hinterlands: "They treated the 'crackers' with distant politeness as 'po' white trash."

Mrs. Hull could not leave the handsome, shaded house this morning. The wife of a railroad superintendent who was almost always away, she was taking care of several wounded soldiers.

Assisted by little Lucy, she rolled bandages and made "beat biscuits by the wheel-barrow full."

Several blocks away, on Washington Street, S. P. Richards
had no interest in food or bartering. The forty-year-old English-
born shopkeeper existed through the tedium of each week for
the Sabbath and the Second Baptist Church, in whose choir he
would raise his voice in throaty hosannas.

S. P. Richards and his brother J. J. were familiar figures in
Atlanta, whether in church, on the street or inside their book,
music, and stationery store. S. P., with his thick hair, his stocky
frame, his never-changing dark clothing, vest, and watch fob,
had been particularly well known ever since he moved from
Macon ten years previously.

He had built a two-story stone house on a large, shaded lot.
Neighbors considered it distinctive with its ceiling-high parlor
mirror, onyx mantel, sliding doors, gold-framed oil paintings,
and "art treasures." His white-sanded paths, magnolias, wisteria,
and snowball bushes so big that their bloom resembled "a whole
week's wash hanging," encompassed half a block.

But, today, neither his residence nor the pamphlet he published, *The Soldier's Friend,* would occupy his mind. This solemn, reserved man was thinking of church and the diary entry
he would make in the afternoon:

"It is a bright and pleasant Sabbath morning and the church
bells are pealing out their call to the sanctuary, while mingling
with their peaceful sound comes the deep booming of the distant cannon telling of War and its dreadful scenes of blood. It
is said that the enemy is very desirous of taking Atlanta by the
Fourth of July, and a battle has been expected to come off today
as the glorious Fourth is so nigh. Our army is still at Kennesaw
Mountain near Marietta about twenty-five miles from here and
several attempts of the enemy to dislodge them have been repulsed, with great loss to the enemy. *Old Abe* has been nominated for re-election by the Baltimore Convention and *Fremont*
by the *other* Abolition party. The Democratic Convention that
was to have met tomorrow at Chicago has been postponed until
August 29th probably to see the result of the present campaign
in Virginia and Georgia. It is hoped that if these great efforts

prove abortive that a peace candidate will be nominated by that assembly. . . .

"Dr. (W. T.) Brantley preached this morning from the text 'Give us this day our daily bread.' This aft. I went to prayer meeting at our church. I have been to such a meeting for prayer for the country almost every day for nearly two months. It would seem as if all Christians in this extremity would be both ready and anxious to seek a throne of Grace to implore God's protection from our cruel foes, but alas! how few there are who evince any such desire.

"It seems to be pretty certain now that our army has again *fallen back* nearer to Atlanta since two o'clock this morning. I was in hopes that this would not be necessary."

Men like Major General "Pat" Cleburne were contemplating neither church nor diaries, but the swarming problems that plagued the military. Pat, famed for his stand at Chickamauga, was looking for his horse. The much-valued steed had strayed in the direction of Lieutenant General John B. Hood's corps in a recent skirmish.

Notices published by Cleburne indicated that the horse was sixteen hands high with a white right hind foot and a star on his forehead. He had snapped the tether that held him to a chestnut tree and bolted.

Other men, men whom few persons had ever heard of, were trying to find their mules. J. B. D. Osborne was one. His seven-year-old mule mare, with "a few white spots on the left shoulder," had been tied in front of the Whitehall Building.

Osborne was sure that stragglers had stolen his animal, a species increasingly hard to obtain these days. He offered a liberal reward for her return, no questions asked. By the same token, owners were posting rewards as high as one thousand dollars for runaway slaves, a situation which was reoccurring with disturbing frequency as the Yankee army plunged ever deeper into Georgia.

P. E. McDaniel was such an owner. He would pay, he advertised, five hundred dollars for the return of his Lavonia, "about 23 years of age, dark, copper color, weighs about 120 pounds, with a small foot for a Negro. My overseer suspects that she was

carried off by Wash Stewart who was loitering about my place
on the day before her disappearance."

At noon on that Sunday, a sudden summer thundershower
burst with drenching violence. An *Intelligencer* reporter, soaked
by "drops as large as pint cups," joined the "thousands who
were perambulating the sidewalks" in seeking refuge. Back in
his office, diagonal to the railroad depot, he wrote:

"A sudden fluttering was seen in the immense crowd, then a
general rush was made for shelter. One enormous fat woman
hustled by me puffing and blowing like a porpoise: lame men
took long strides, forgetting their sticks, soldiers on crutches
thumped and plunged along; peanut boys ran shouting to cover;
teamsters whipped their mules and yelled and cursed; beggars
disappeared; a city 'local' rushed his horse furiously over that
abomination, the railroad crossing, seemingly unconscious of
the great danger he ran of having his neck broken by falling
into one of the pitfalls that abounds in it. The last that was seen
of him, his coat tail was flying straight out and his head and
arms engaged in a furious rivalry with the horse's head as to
who should beat in the race. When he disappeared we think the
horse was gaining on the rider and the glorious rain on both."

But there were far more acute problems than rain and mud-
holes worrying Dr. Samuel Hollingsworth Stout, medical director of hospitals for the Army of Tennessee. He had moved his
major medical center from Catoosa Springs before the Union
advance, was now evacuating all hospitals in the Marietta area,
and was faced with the prospect of hustling his labyrinth-like
Atlanta set-up yet farther south. Some had bitterly dubbed this
refugee existence "the dance of the hospitals."

The sick and wounded ached and moaned in many private
homes besides Mrs. Hull's. Permanent structures such as the
Medical College Hospital, famed for its surgeon, Dr. Peter Paul
Noel D'Alvigny, were overflowing, Large buildings like the
Concert Hall, opposite the passenger depot, and the City Hotel
were commandeered but could not alleviate the bed shortage.

Tent cities sprang up in the parks and blotted out the sweet
smells of grass and flowers with their morbid reek of disinfec-
tant, of festering wounds, of sweating, frightened, malfunction-

ing, and shattered bodies. The strange white-gray outcroppings were given names, including Fair Ground Hospital Number 1, Fair Ground Hospital Number 2, Empire Hospital, Institute Hospital, Grant Hospital, Heery Hospital, and Gate City Hospital.

On that day, Dr. Stout ordered new hospitals to be constructed and more churches and public buildings requisitioned in nearby Newnan and Covington to the south, where six large hospitals were already in commission. He contemplated establishing his own headquarters in Macon, one hundred miles from Atlanta.

Foard's Hospital, from Marietta, had just been reopened one mile from Atlanta, close to the rolling mill, and not far from two other hospitals, Gilmer and Academy. The encampment thereby boosted its bed capacity to one thousand.

Day and night the trains were chugging in with more wounded, more sick—boxcars, flatcars, coaches and, infrequently, specially fitted hospital cars. As the long, misery-laden trains rolled into the city, the bells tolled and tolled, as if in requiem. Many of the patients were dead upon arrival. Illness alone had accounted for eight times as many casualties as enemy bullets, shells, or bayonets.

Atlanta was increasingly being looked upon as a somber "charnel house." At Foard's Hospital alone the list of last night's deceased was horrifying. The list began with Jacob Dickerson, Private, Company F, 1st Georgia, and ended with J. T. B. Busi, Hospital Steward, Company B, 18th Alabama.

New signs sprouted like the very tombstones they symbolized —"Embalming—Free From Odor of Infection." The war spawned this gruesome trade. On Luckie Street, near Walton Spring, C. Bohnefield's Coffin Shop became within a few months one of Atlanta's most thriving industries.

J. G. W. Mills, a special postal agent, was hard at work on his new assignment: unraveling the mail of refugees. "Refugee," a new, chilling word in the lexicon of Georgians, referred to a person who had to leave his home, almost all his possessions, and flee before Sherman's "vandal hordes."

Even as far south as Thomasville, fear of invasion gripped the residents. The Reverend J. B. Jackson, for example, asked E. E.

Rawson, member of the Atlanta City Council, to advertise his 1,470-acre estate, ten miles from the railroad, for sale. The preacher, listing himself as a refugee, hoped to realize eight dollars per acre. But land in Georgia was becoming less and less desirable.

Hotels not taken over for hospitals—the Atlanta, Planter's, the Tennessee House, Washington Hall, and the Trout House —could not accommodate the swelling refugee tide, even if the hapless families could afford such an expensive abode.

On the meager ground of City Hall Park not blanketed by hospital tents, the local militia (ages sixteen to sixty) started their daily afternoon drill. They had answered Governor Joseph E. Brown's fervent plea:

"Your state is invaded and a portion of its most valuable territory overrun by a vindictive enemy of great strength who is laying waste and devastating the country behind him. Unless this force is checked speedily, the property and homes of thousands must be destroyed and they driven out as wanderers in destitution and beggary. Our noble army needs further reinforcements."

Mayor James M. Calhoun underscored Georgia's chief executive's proclamation by setting a day of "fasting, humiliation, and prayer."

Sergeant Robert J. Massey ordered all men with certificates of exemption to be "re-examined" at Camp Georgia. In his private opinion much of the home guard was a decrepit, stumbling, tragi-comic assemblage. He knew any additions to the ranks would be of no higher caliber since the army had already skimmed the cream. But he had no choice. The defense of Atlanta would be desperate and people were needed, if only to brandish old flintlocks.

In neighboring Marietta it seemed still less like Sunday. All who could were "refugeeing" before the storming Federals. Their ranks were filled with weary, heartsick families who had already fled once, twice, or even three times in the course of the war, like involuntary gypsies. The Morgans belonged in this category. Irby was forty-two when he left home in Nashville to fight as a private for the Confederacy. His friends told him a man of his age wasn't expected to bear arms. Irby was determined. But neither the older nor younger males of Tennessee could stem the Union tidal wave which engulfed their state.

Mrs. Morgan and her children had lived in Shelbyville, Fayetteville, and upon the very slopes of Lookout Mountain, near Chattanooga, before they finally crossed the Georgia border to settle "far south in safety," in Marietta. On the last and supposedly final move, Julia took her severely wounded husband with her. He had been with the 51st Alabama Regiment of his brother, Brigadier General John T. Morgan.

Irby slowly returned to health. He was resolved to remain on his farm in Marietta with the pleasant view of Kennesaw Mountain. But the echoes of battle thundered nearer and nearer. Julia wrote:

"Our town was almost in a frenzy of excitement. Our house was crowded with soldiers as the army was almost in town. The boys begged Mr. Morgan to take us south and he said he had moved his family so much he didn't see how he could go farther; but that boom, boom, boom, got to be every minute, resounding from hilltop to hilltop. We could see the smoke from the firing. O, it was a grand but awful sight! We could do nothing but walk, talk, and wait, feeling that some great calamity was impending. We could hear nothing from Sister Lucy and family and knew by that time that the enemy were near her house, and we thought of the girls, the old father and daughter in their helpless condition, and we were miserable. We knew the old man could do nothing to protect them and our hands were equally powerless. We were nearly crazy.

"All the information we could glean was that our army was fighting as few ever fought and falling on all sides. About 11 o'clock we saw an ambulance stop at the gate, and my first thought was that some dear one, wounded or dead, had been brought to us. We ran to see who it was, when Sister and girls bounded out, then the old father and three Negroes, all in a pitiful condition.

"Their clothes were muddy, bedraggled and saturated with water. They told us the Federal batteries were planted so that they swept the house, and shell after shell was sent crashing and shrieking through the house. At intervals they tried to get their precious clothes and succeeded and tied them in bundles and then started to run. A shell would burst near them and they would drop their treasures and cry awhile, then at an interval seize them and start running until they got far enough to feel safe from the shells. It commenced raining and they were in a deplorable condition. Gen. John T. Morgan, her brother, with his command had been for several days around and in her house, as she knew many of them; but he had taken part of his troops and gone around in another direction to meet the enemy, leaving part of his command with Wheeler's Brigade. When they returned to where Wheeler's troops were stationed and heard of the sad plight the family were in, the boys were furious, they believed it premeditated cruelty on the part of the Federals. They jumped on their horses and in the midst of flying shells rode up to where the helpless family were in the woods, near their house.

"The enemy in passing had raided the house, and as they could not carry off the things, had deliberately ripped open feather beds and had the contents flying in every direction; they had knocked in the heads of several barrels of molasses and did all the damage they could.

"After they left, our boys went into the house and saved what things they thought most essential for the family and that could be hurriedly moved; brought ambulances enough to carry the family and what was left of their belongings to Marietta. Some of the boys laughed and said the last thing they saw were ducks, chickens and turkeys, struggling in molasses and feathers."

JULY 4

⊠ *The Daily Intelligencer* (Atlanta)

"The object of the enemy seems to be to prevent our men from getting rest. . . .

"The present position is an enormous fortification. The whole country around Kennesaw Mountain and over the whole extent of Noonday Valley is burrowed and ditched with an interminable net of earthworks. Sherman has placed on his farthest right and on the Powder Spring road all the forces he can possibly spare without endangering his communications. He cannot weaken any farther his line that protects the communications of his base at Big Shanty with his army. Herein lies his great danger if he attempts a march on our rear. . . .

"The Army of Tennessee commenced a retrograde movement from the lines of Kennesaw Mountain at midnight on Sunday and by a rapid march retired our right to its present position on the Chattahoochee. Our left fell back slowly before the heavily massed force that Sherman had placed on the Powder Spring and Sand Town roads."

▰ *Frank Leslie's Illustrated Weekly* (New York)

"We took possession of the place (Marietta) and hold it as important. It contained a population of about 3,000 and was a place of great wealth. It was also a place where considerable manufacturing was done for the rebels in the way of shoes, clothing, caps, etc.

"It was noted for its paper manufactory, a large part of the paper used South being manufactured here. Much of the paper on which Confederate money and bonds are printed was manufactured at this place. We captured no commissary stores or supplies here of consequence. Most of the citizens fled at our approach, carrying with them their effects."

On that Monday, the North observed Independence Day. Fourth of July in Atlanta infused no desire for celebration. The merchants were concerned with matters of liquidation—if they could pay the premium prices for what few wagons had not been commandeered by the army. Macon and Columbus were the most frequently mentioned cities of relocation.

W. B. Young's shop in Forsyth's Alley, to the rear of the Masonic Hall and the Trout House on Decatur Street, was overstocked with sewing machines. Young had purchased somewhat improvidently because of the Quartermaster's factories in Atlanta with its need for machines with which to spew unending spates of uniforms and shoes.

He offered over two thousand Singer's "of different sizes for cloth and leather," also Grover & Baker's, Wheeler & Wilson's, and Bartholf's machines, all at reduced prices. Who had time to sew these days? Certainly not the Quartermaster, obsessed with one desire: to get out of Atlanta!

On Whitehall Street, F. M. Fisk's Wholesale Mart was stacked with an assortment of commodities differing in nature, size, and smell—"25 barrels of Tanners Oil, 1,000 pounds of printing ink, 4 iron safes, 50 casks of New Rice and 100 pairs of 'Ladies Bootees.' "

Fisk saw little hope of unloading the ink. The rumors seemed well founded that Atlanta's newspapers would be suspending publication.

Welborn, Taylor & Co. announced an auction for the next day. They would close out such choice merchandise as five sacks of "fine" sugar, a buggy horse, and a Negro with her two children.

Philander P. Pease, on Peachtree Street, another wholesaler, knew that in victory or in defeat an army must eat. He was looking high and low for one hundred head of "good beef cattle."

In Mobile, blockaded and bombarded by Admiral Farragut, there was a potential of many commodities. If one survived the hazards of rail travel, one could attend daily wharf-side auctions of cargoes trapped in port: stationery, shoes, hats, calf skins, coffee, "delicacies," even the rigging and rope of the vessels themselves. Some joked that you could buy everything but the barnacles of the captive ships.

The fever to reduce inventories had infected almost every type of business endeavor: Thomas M. Clarke's, hardware; Silvey, Dougherty & Co., retail drygoods; E. Andrews & Co., saddles and leather; Hunnicutt & Belingrath, major nitre contractors for the Confederacy; Cox & Hill's, liquor store; and Dr. J. S. Pemberton's, pharmacy (whose familiar advertisement now had a hollow ring, "an almost endless list of our modern Pharmacopaea. . . fine chemicals and perfumery. . . not excelled, perhaps, by any in the south. . . . in proprietary medicines, 'Globe Flower Syrup,' 'Compound Extract of Stillingia,' 'Taylor's Antidyspeptic Elixir' ").

But hair still grew and Solomon Luckie, the popular Negro barber, still filled the air outside his little Alabama Street parlor with his steely, snip-snip cadences. Government workers and army officers swelled his clientele hundreds of per cent. He could not keep up with business, even by working late into the evenings.

And trains still ran, even though equipment and personnel was strained to the breaking point. After three depleting years of war, fares had doubled, often tripled, and schedules had ground to a shaky crawl; rolling stock was hauled off to support the armies fighting east and west.

Sherman, to veteran trainmen in Atlanta, was the arch-enemy of railroading. His cavalry would appear like a demon at a lonely stretch of right-of-way, tear up the rails, and heat them over roaring bonfires of ties. The glowing tracks would be twisted around tree trunks and left to cool as neat, but useless bowknots.

Wear and obsolescence caused equal destruction. There was no time for maintenance.

The fare to Macon had soared to seven dollars, almost twice the prewar scale. The train departed from Atlanta daily at 6:30 A.M., and was due at Macon at 12:54 P.M., averaging sixteen miles an hour.

The train from Macon to Atlanta was due at 4:00 P.M. But no one meeting a friend ever arrived at the depot even close to on time, not caring to wait in a miasma of dust, smoke, and wood sparks, or to be jostled by soldiers, stragglers, pitch men, prostitutes, and every species of station loiterer, the chaff and riff raff of a wartime city.

Passengers were more apt to find freight cars than coaches to carry them through the purgatory of their journey.

George Yonge, general superintendent for the Georgia Railroad, published in the *Intelligencer* that Monday:

"The Government calls upon this road for transportation to the full extent of its ability, and the Road is not open for transportation of private freight. Agents cannot give receipts for private freight left at stations for shipment. Shippers leaving freight at stations must take risk of delay, weather, fire, and all other incidental risks."

The Atlantic (telegraph) Office on Alabama Street was posting notices of telegrams which could not be delivered "for want of proper address." The lengthening list seemed to ask what had happened to "W. D. Young, Captain D. H. Fitz-Wilson," and many, many more? What, indeed?

Sometimes the answer was to be found in the obituary columns. Death notices spread over the newspapers like open sores—the daily hospital bulletins, a line, at most two lines; the labored threnodies composed (and paid for) by friends and relatives, such as that of J. J. Morton, twenty-three years old, Company I, 6th Kentucky Regiment:

"His favorite song was 'Sweet Home' and he especially liked the line,

" 'And I know that my mother now thinks of her child.'

"Oh how desolate she will feel when she knows that her dear brave boy is dead! It will be little consolation to her to hear that his Captain said, 'A braver soldier never lived' . . . for she can only think of him in the bright young beauty of his glorious manhood, lying cold and still in death."

For Private G. B. Shivers, Company A, 39th Mississippi Regiment, Sears Brigade, French's Division, the laments were somewhat more restrained:

"He leaves his wife and three lovely children to mourn his loss who in their great grief will be cheered by the fact that previous to his death he had obtained hope in the Redeemer."

Obituaries were so much in the news that sometimes even

happier events were bordered in deep black by the printers, out of pure habit. Such was the fate of the nuptial announcement of Josephine Hanleiter, one of twelve children of C. R. Hanleiter, early resident and publisher, married at Savannah to Henry Gullatt.

Purely local problems continued in the face of war. The *Intelligencer* fumed:

"A most disgraceful mud hole that lies like a festering sore on the face of our city seethes and frets over the track. The mud oh! the mud. Dear city fathers, you wise men on muddy matters, do you hearken unto our supplications and render our ways more pleasant . . . if you don't we'll set on you the hundreds of beautiful ladies that float like mists of glorious clouds in gorgeous colors along our streets this exquisitely lovely day. How they pout, how they flutter when they come to the railroad crossing! They say naughty words, they are sneering at the contemptible parsimony of a city that obliges them to wade through mud up to their ankles. Why, dear dadas, just see what ruin that mudhole produces! . . . We were told that on Wednesday morning whilst trying to run the dangerous crossing . . . a horse and dray and driver sank out of sight, deeper and deeper into the mud until nothing but the driver's whip was seen waving over the place where the trio was imbedded."

In Marietta, General Sherman, a "brute," an "inhuman monster," a "butcher," and "a merciless avenging angel of the Lord," was spared this day. Death passed him by "while reconnoitring in the second story of a house on our picket-line, which was struck several times by cannon-shot, and perfectly riddled with musket-balls."

By late afternoon, the family of Irby Morgan, refugees once more, arrived from Marietta in the Atlanta railroad station, en route to Augusta where Irby had heard of a home for lease. All the way down Julia was plagued with the irrational fear that her seven-year-old son, whom she had dressed in a child's "artilleryman's suit," would be carried away as prisoner should the train be halted by Federal cavalry:

"Pandemonium reigned in streets—soldiers, wagons, artillery wagons, drivers shouting and hurrying, and the 'tramp, tramp,

tramp,' was heard in every direction, all falling back as fast as possible, going to Atlanta to make a stand. We were soon in readiness and all of our small possessions packed in the cars. Mr. Morgan, his father and sister with her family, and the children and myself and our faithful Joe got in the car and started to Atlanta.

"On arriving in that city we were in such a crowd we had to wait some time before we could push through. Every little while some kind friend would come in and speak a word of encouragement and offer to render some assistance. . . .

"We were worn and weak from work and anxiety and so tired waiting, and were almost famished for water. It was very scarce as hundreds of soldiers and people from every direction were thirsty, too, and begging for it on all sides. I don't know when I ever felt so gratified in all my life as when old Dr. Hudson of Nashville came up with a tin bucket of cool, fresh buttermilk. He told me that he had walked for some time trying to find this milk for the children and myself; had offered to buy it, and finally he succeeded in begging this bucketful. I thought it the most delicious milk that I ever tasted."

JULY 5

The Daily Intelligencer (Atlanta)

"Field, Near Ruff's Station—In order to counteract a flank movement made in force by the enemy on our left, the army commenced to withdraw from the neighborhood of Marietta night before last. . . .

"Gen. Hardee's corps, though in some places not more than forty or fifty yards from the enemy's lines, did not begin to move until just before daylight yesterday, and was conducted so quietly the enemy was not aware of it until the evacuation was completed. . . .

"The enemy is now at the doors, as it were, of Atlanta. The movements of both armies since Sunday morning last indicate that Sherman must now fight for the possession of the city, or that, declining a battle, he will continue his flanking operations with the hope of possessing the railroads leading to this point, eventually surrounding and besieging it. In either event Atlanta is in a perilous position. . . . Our advice to all is *stand firm!*"

Welborn, Taylor & Co.'s auction drew a sizable crowd that Tuesday morning. Added to his advertised items were mules, mares, bacon, a wagon and harness, and household and kitchen furniture. Uncle Billy Hill, the veteran auctioneer, kept the bidding going with his croaking, penetrating voice.

Another merchant, Colonel Robert A. Crawford, who operated on Peachtree Street "the most extensive Negro depot in the Confederacy—healthy, safe and comfortable," tried to overcome the shortage of his human wares in Atlanta. Offering "cash advances to regular traders," he advertised that his "old and trusty" porters, Andrew and Antony, would be on trains to meet and care for all shipments of fresh slave stocks.

People like R. Hirsch of Milledgeville, lifted their eyebrows suspiciously at such enticements. His Negro boy, "Aen," was stolen and he would pay one thousand dollars for his return. He wasn't sure whether his "black" was with a Confederate cavalry company south of Marietta, or whether some unscrupulous trader was spiriting him to his mart.

Nor were slaves the only object of theft. Draft dodgers were proportionately as numerous as in the North. For the precious exemption certificates some men would literally commit murder —if simple theft were not sufficient. Jesse Dodds' certificate had been stolen, and he was pouring money into newspaper space to announce that all should be "forewarned from trading on said certificate."

Generals were in the news. From La Grange, there was word that the wife and two daughters of Lieutenant General William J. Hardee were devoting their time to hospital work.

Accompanied by a retinue of servants, they had become familiar sights hurrying to visit bedridden soldiers, "setting an example to women of the south."

Lieutenant General Hood, an old thirty-three, was stumping painfully about Atlanta. He had lost his right leg at Chickamauga and his left arm was paralyzed by wounds from Gettysburg. He had to be strapped to his horse when he rode.

This big man with the flowing beard and deep-set, sad eyes had come to bear little resemblance to the gregarious officer once sought by Richmond belles. His military ambitions had assumed a frantic desperation as though he were obsessed with a feeling that time was running out. In turn, an arrogant, if not ruthless, quality became manifest.

The main obstacle to Hood's coveted personal destiny, General Joseph Eggleston Johnston, had been slowly retreating from winter quarters at Dalton, under the weight and fury of Sherman's might. He was the subject of an article in the *Mobile Advertiser and Register*. It said of the West Point-trained commander of the Army of Tennessee:

"Gen. Johnston is more than a match for Sherman . . . is the bravest and most cool man under fire that I ever saw. He is almost reckless with his own life, but is exceedingly careful with the lives of his men."

From Savannah, however, Bishop Elliott voiced a fear that people were relying on military men alone:

"However brave our soldiers, however skillful our generals, from God's help alone can we look for such successes as will give us peace. He sits in the Throne judging right and therefore does it become us to supplicate him unceasingly to take the cause into his own hand."

Still, the wounded arrived in Atlanta—ranking officers and raw, ignorant, almost infantile privates.

Among the former was Lieutenant Colonel E. M. Seagg, transferred to Institute Hospital after the Battle of the Wilderness in Virginia. His Regiment, the "glorious old 20th Georgia Volunteers," which had always seen him leading in battle, agreed he was a "most gallant officer." The doctors thought that he would recover.

The young girls of Atlanta devoted more and more of their days to meeting the trains of sick and wounded at the depot. Even the wheezing of the locomotives was lugubrious, a harbinger of the wretchedness and abject suffering being borne into Atlanta.

The girls, neat in their plain cotton dresses, their hair always combed and usually braided, afforded the only happy relief to an otherwise dismal scene. Over their arms were baskets containing coffee, cakes, fresh vegetables, and fruit. Peaches and blackberries abounded in peculiar lushness this year, as though nature were defying the devastation which was scourging Georgian earth. Only the desperately wounded or the feverishly sick did not devour the food ravenously.

Mary Rushton, the daughter of William Rushton, superintendent of the Georgia Railroad and West Point Railroad shops, was a faithful visitor to the depot. Atlanta, as it seemed to all of her friends, had completely changed its face and character from prewar days made memorable by "amateur concerts, tackey parties and gaieties of all kinds." Now she thought of the great city as a dreary succession of canteens for soup and coffee, greasy ladles, ever-swarming flies, and bearded, smelly, terribly hurt men.

"Sister Eva and I were going across town to make some visits, the train had just come in with the wounded and dying and these were being carried on litters or stretchers to the hospitals near the square. Just as Sister and I were opposite the depot —it was indeed a heart-rending sight—she fell in a dead faint on the street. But several surgeons from the hospitals came to our relief, soon had her all right, ordered a carriage and took us home."

The volunteers, no matter how devoted, were not sufficient. Professional help had to be borrowed from Dr. Stout's other hospitals. Newnan, now virtually a city of the sick and wounded, had sent up a large contingent of doctors and nurses the night before.

Kate Cumming was among these. Scottish-born, Kate had been nursing the backwash of the carnage since the first days of fighting, and as zealously as though the Confederates were her own countrymen.

"Several ladies and myself went to the train as it steamed in from the scene of conflict, and beheld a woeful sight," Kate wrote. "Train after train, filled outside and inside with hundreds of wounded—the worst cases were on mattresses in box cars. As the men fought behind breastworks, they were chiefly wounded on the head and upper limbs. Old gentlemen and ladies were there to meet the poor fellows with baskets full of edibles and buckets full of milk, coffee and lemonade, and some had wine. I noticed one aristocratic looking old gentleman who wore a large white apron, serving out the rations with as much zest as the youngest there. I was told that this work had been going on ever since the war commenced. Many a time, tables were set at the depot for the benefit of the well soldiers going from and returning to their command.

"Our party went to the Gate City Hospital where we found many ladies dressing wounds. Strange as it may seem, I had never dressed one, having plenty other work to do. I managed to dress the wound on the hand of one poor fellow, and just as I got through Dr. Jackson, who had come with us from Newnan, requested me to come to assist him.

"We were in a large hall, crowded with wounded, some walking about, others sitting on the floor—all waiting to have their wounds dressed. As soon as this was done, they were sent off to make room for others. Surgeons, nurses and ladies were so intently employed that they did not appear to notice each other. I brought the patients to Dr. Jackson and unbound the stiff bandages, making the wounds ready for the doctor to dress. These men were called by the surgeons slightly wounded. One poor fellow from Alabama had both hands disabled, from one he had lost three fingers, and was shot through the wrist of the other. The man was perfectly helpless. Several of the slightly wounded had each lost an eye.

"Dr. Welford was near where we were, as busy as he could possibly be, one of the ladies assisting him as I was Dr. J. After getting nearly through, I went into the rooms which were filled with badly wounded men in bed. I noticed many ladies bathing the men's faces and attending to their wants in other ways.

"While in one of the rooms, a young man called me by name, and told me he had seen my brother the night before, and that he was well. This young man was named Laramar, from Mobile . . . informed me that the Seventeenth and Twenty-ninth Alabama had suffered severely."

On that afternoon, a "Miss Eula" bought newspaper space to promise she would "confer quite a favor upon her friend, Bartow, by addressing him at Atlanta, Ga., care Col. C."

At 5:00 P.M. there was a prayer meeting at Central Presbyterian Church, the church with the high steeple and imposing white columns across from City Hall, close to many of the hospital tents. Services were to be held every afternoon that week at the same time, partly for the benefit of the soldiers.

At the suburban railroad community, Vining's Station, across the Chattahoochee, there was an afternoon visitor—General Sherman.

Past the rough Union Hospital established in a farmhouse, past the shacks of inhabitants, and up a steep hill back of the little station, Sherman walked. There in the woods, pungent with pinesap, he viewed a thrilling sight for the first time, and recorded:

"Houses in Atlanta, nine miles distant, and the whole intervening valley of the Chattahoochee; could observe the preparations for our reception on the other side, the camps of men and large trains of covered wagons."

Kate Cumming continued her nurse's work long after dark. "It was a bright, moonlight night," she wrote, "and there were some folks who came into the hospital with provisions for the men. Dr. Welford and a number of us took them and went all over, to see if we could find any in want, but nearly all had been supplied. The men were lying all over the platform of the depot, preferring to remain there so as to be ready for the train which would take them to other places.

"I was informed that there were about seven or eight hundred wounded who had come in that evening.

"Dr. Pursely is surgeon of the receiving hospital and seemed to be doing all in his power for the sufferers. Every one in it looked weary and worn out with the constant work which they had to do. The matron was very ill.

"Dr. Bemiss, who is assistant medical director, was at the hospital, and going around in his usual kind manner, seeing that the men were attended to. About ten o'clock he took Mrs. Harris and myself to Mrs. Lowenthall's, where he boarded, who received us very kindly.

"There was a young man visiting her, who was dressed in the extreme of fashion, with the addition of a few diamonds. I could not help contrasting him with the men I had just seen, who had been fighting for everything truly noble—wounded, covered with dust, and many of them in rags.

"Foppish dress is bad taste in a man at any time; but if there is one time more than another when it is out of place, it is the present. . . .

"I have heard soldiers (I mean the fighting kind) say that nothing disheartens them so much as to see men so overdressed."

JULY 6

✉ *The Daily Intelligencer* (Atlanta)

"Interminable lines of army wagons are going and coming in a constant stream. Hundreds of horsemen and footmen are dashing hither and thither. Our city is almost exclusively a military camp. The roar of wagons rolling on the streets and the cracking of whips, the screeching and grinding of wheels, the shouts of drivers, the braying of mules and the rapid footfalls of couriers congregate a medley of sounds that seem strange and almost bewildering to the citizen.

"Notwithstanding these exciting scenes and movements, and the fact that an enemy thunders his hostile strokes on our battlements a few miles to the Northwest, yet an unusual calm rests on the surface of the life presented here. An extraordinary tranquility apparently pervades the great heart of the people. They seem to have settled down into a conviction that Atlanta is secure against the enemy that threatens its peace and safety. . . .

"The advance of Sherman to his present position, his almost unchecked, steady march gives us good cause to study well before speculating any farther on his movements. We remember that one of the best military writers of the age said, 'no country in which man can exist can be impenetrable to an invading army.' "

> *Atlanta Register*

"The men worked on the fortifications like beavers. Spades are emphatically trumps in these latter days. We lost on them in the beginning but it is our lucky suit now.

"The cannon would occasionally clear their brazen throats but attracted no special attention, and but few were hurt."

Early that breathlessly hot Wednesday, Atlanta was swept by the rumor that Sherman was a prisoner. In the billiard halls, brothels, and grog houses of Alabama Street and Decatur Street, as well as the elegant lobbies of the Atlanta Hotel and the Trout House, some swore they had seen him being marched under guard into the city.

Everyone in Georgia was certain that he was a "devil incarnate." And he had compounded his malevolence most recently, it was said, by ordering pieces of tin screwed to Minie balls, which would cut arteries and "poison the flesh."

The rejoicing in his "capture" was as profound as it was short lived. A Sherman had been taken prisoner, but he was Colonel Frank Sherman of Chicago, and no relation.

Later, young Sherman confided to his captors that his namesake had been close by the thicket into which the colonel had inadvertently wandered—to meet a nest of enemy pickets face to face.

"Atrocities," however, did not appear wholly confined to the celebrated Tecumseh. As a soldier wrote to the *Intelligencer:*

"I must relate one incident of the battle of the 27th as it illustrates alike the chivalry of a Tennessean and the perfidy of the Yankees. After the terrible repulse of the six lines of battle and while the surviving Federals of the assaulting party were crouching under cover of the hill which slopes down from that part of Cheatham's front—the ground being strewn with Federal dead and wounded—one who was badly mutilated cried out to our boys in great agony, 'For God's sake, boys, bring me a drink of water. I would go to you if I could, but I am disabled—in God's name bring me a drink of water.'

"A noble youth of our State, pitying the miserable wretch, mounted the breastworks and shouted to the Federals, who were in full hearing, 'I am going to take one of your wounded men a drink of water, don't shoot at me!' Whereupon he took the dying Federal the canteen, allowing him to drink, and in retiring was fired at by a dozen Yankees, and instantly killed. Our boys witnessed the act, instantly and without orders fired at the squad before they could conceal themselves and it is said *killed every one of them.*"

Kate Cumming, the Scottish nurse, before returning by train to her Newnan hospital, discovered wounded men even in the hotels.

"I went into the Trout House, in the hall of which I saw a young man lying wounded. I learned he was from Mobile. His name is Leslie, and he is a member of the Seventeenth Alabama Regiment. His wound was not a bad one. He told me that his colonel was in the hotel severely wounded. I paid the latter a visit to see if I could be of any service to him, but found him doing much better than I had expected; his wife was with him. . . .

"I again visited the Gate City Hospital. . . . While standing on the gallery I heard a young man just come from a hospital in Cassville, grumbling very much at some doctor who had made him leave in such a hurry that he had not time to get his clothes. He was giving it to officers in general and spoke as if he was fighting to please them.

"I listened awhile, and then asked him what he was fighting for. He replied for his country. I then told him how he had been talking. He said he knew that it was wrong, but really the men had a great deal to endure from their officers.

"I have heard many complaints of the kind; I think that often the men are to blame; they treat their officers with too much contempt.

"Our officers should be the best of our men; and their rank respected if they are not. . . .

"I visited one of the other hospitals, Dr. C. going with me; I think the name of it was the Medical College. The building is a very handsome one, and had just been fitted up. Everything about it was in perfect order. It is one of the nicest hospitals in which I have ever been. It was filled with badly wounded men, as I am told is the case with every hospital in Atlanta. I find men there from every state in the Confederacy.

"We left Atlanta on the passenger car, and when halfway down had to get out, as the freight train that had left some hours before had met with an accident, and blocked up the road.

"We got into a freight car in front; in it there was a very large man, who had been in the car on which the accident happened; he had got mashed between two beams; his collar-bone was broken and his chest very much bruised, so that it was with difficulty he could breathe. His face was so much bruised that his eyes were closed. There were a number of surgeons on the cars who were very kind to him."

Nightly, as the *Intelligencer* reported, citizens were imperiled, two blocks from Atlanta's common well at Five Points:

"An association of niggers and white boys are in the habit of congregating in large numbers every evening at the corner of Hunter and Pryor Streets. They throw stones there promiscuously at the Martens that roost in the trees thereabouts. These raiders have broken a great many window panes during their battles with the birds and caused several unpleasant accidents to residents in the neighborhood, who are very much annoyed by the operations. We suggest that a policeman be placed there every evening from 6 to 8 o'clock whose duty it shall be to arrest the nuisance and those rascally boys who do the mischief."

Near Vining's, General Sherman started his dispatch to General Henry W. Halleck, Army Chief of Staff in Washington:

"The telegraph is finished to Vining's Station, and the field-wire has just reached my bivouac, and will be ready to convey this message as soon as it is written and translated into cipher.

"I propose to study the crossings of the Chattahoochee, and when all is ready, to move quickly. . . . At present the waters are turbid and swollen from recent rains; but if the present hot weather lasts, the water will run down very fast. We have pontoons enough for four bridges, but, as our crossing will be resisted, we must maneuver some. All the regular crossing places are covered by forts, apparently of long construction; but we shall cross in due time, and, instead of attacking Atlanta direct, or any of its forts, I propose to make a circuit, destroying all its railroads. . . . the weather is intensely hot, and a good many men have fallen, some with sunstroke. The country is high and healthy, and the sanitary condition of the army is good."

JULY 7

✉ *The Daily Intelligencer* (Atlanta)

"*Green's Ferry*—Skirmishing has been almost incessant during the day up to this time. Most of the skirmishing is done across the Chattahoochee . . . it may be that Sherman is massing his forces on Johnston's left, but in that event he would be so far from his base he could scarcely support his Army five days. Campbellton is some thirty-two miles from Marietta and the place at which he is going to attempt to cross with cavalry. . . .

"The enemy cautiously approach and carefully occupy their positions for batteries and lines from which to operate with as much safety as possible to themselves. On Wednesday, they occupied the hills on this side of Vining, and as near the river as they seem to desire for the present. . . . Sherman still masses to our left, and threatens by flank to displace us again.

"His strategy has hitherto evinced an unusual shrewdness in the disposition of his plans for the capture of Atlanta. He must necessarily arrange his movements to engage the attention of our front during a few days, against his feints whilst he secures his positions and repairs the railroad so that he may bring to his immediate rear his railway supply trains . . . thus it will occur that several days must elapse before the enemy can make any advances on this city with such force as to seriously threaten our occupation or cause us to evacuate if battle is not given. . . .

"*Noon*—The enemy this morning made a heavy advance on our extreme left and commenced severe skirmishing with musketry and artillery, exhibiting an intention to cross the river at Green's Ferry. The skirmishing has continued to increase in intensity and rapidity up to this hour, but without any advantage being secured by either party. It is evident that the enemy is making this sudden and persistent demonstration for the purpose of attracting attention away from their operations in some other important quarter."

The previous night Atlanta had rung with the music of the most famous military band in the South. The musicians of the late Stonewall Jackson's cavalry had arrived in the city for several concerts. Its leader, Henry Farmer, gave flute and piano solos and Charley Ford, the composer, sang *The Old Play Ground,* his "sweetest and most beautiful."

The city had been treated to few such recitals since the Concert Hall was converted into a hospital. The Athenaeum, in its second-story quarters on Decatur Street, opposite the Atlanta Hotel ("up-to-date" and with the added extravagance of scenery), had become the only decent place of entertainment.

Lieutenant Andrew Jackson Neal, Marion Light Artillery, son of a well-known Atlantan, John Neal, wrote to his mother, temporarily living in Zebulon. Twenty-six-year-old "Andy" had practiced law after graduating from the University of Virginia. Both Andrew and his brother, James, joined the army at the outbreak of hostilities. The handsome Neal residence, at the

corner of Washington and Mitchell streets, was used by the
Atlanta Female Institute in 1863, after its own quarters on Ivy
Street were requisitioned for a hospital, and now was occupied
by Judge R. F. Lyon. Neal wrote:

"It is really refreshing to be relieved after sixty-eight days
continuous marching, fighting and entrenching. Since Gen.
Bragg has visited the Army I think something may be accomplished. I do pray we may never move with our faces turned
Southward again.

"While we were on picket our Battery was distant from the
Yankee pickets only the width of the river. Our men talked all
the time as a truce was made. The Yankees asked us why we conscripted all their deserters that came into our lines. All the prisoners taken say this is the universal belief in their army and say
many of their men would desert were it not for this impression.
Hooker's Corps are by no means anxious to cross the Chattahoochee and pretend to believe their Army will march back.
Our scouts report the enemy is tearing up the track and shipping troops off. . . .

"There was not an officer or man in this Army ever dreamed
of Johnston falling back this far or ever doubted he would attack when the proper time came. But I think he has been woe-
fully outgeneraled and though he has inflicted losses on the
enemy only (surpassed) by Grant's losses in Virginia, has made
a losing bargain."

His envelope bore an engraving of a cannon firing and the
rallying verse:

> To arms! to arms, ye brave,
> The avenging sword unsheath;
> March on! march on! all hearts resolved
> On victory or death.

Nearby, above the same swamp-smelling banks of the Chattahoochee, another officer, Captain Benedict Joseph Semmes, General Johnston's Chief Depot Commissary, was writing home.
Now forty-one, he was once a wholesaler in groceries, wines,
and liquor in Washington, D.C., and in Memphis, Tennessee,
his home.

Joe Semmes was ordered into the duty more closely related to his civilian occupation as merchant after being seriously wounded at Shiloh. His wife, the former Jorantha Jordan, of New York, and his old servant, Mack, had helped carry him, bleeding, from the battlefield, and placed him on a flatcar from Corinth.

Jorantha, sometimes addressed as "Eo," personally nursed Joe back to life. She was living temporarily in Gainesville, Georgia, when he wrote from his bivouac on a hill, in sight of the enemy's batteries:

"The railroad bridge, the truss bridge and the pontoon bridge are all just under and crowded with the passing trains of rations and ordnance, etc.—on each side of me are two forts but no troops in them as our army is still on the opposite bank in plain view in the breastworks. The enemy are moving to the left trying to flank Atlanta without a battle. Our guns and men are moving away to the left which here appears to be far in our rear as the river winds in that direction. Should the enemy succeed in flanking us it is likely they will get possession of our cut off the West Point Road and thus temporarily cut off communication between us. I tell you this to prepare you and prevent you from feeling any alarm; it is just such a move as Grant has made on the south side of Richmond. Do not then worry if you should fail to hear from me regularly. I will try to get letters to you however by hand should my expectations be realized. It is possible that Atlanta may be evacuated but do not be discouraged. Remember Moscow and Napoleon's splendid advance and miserable retreat. We are all in fine spirits, tho we hated to fall back from Marietta. Our losses so far, trifling. I send you notices of poor Tom's death. Send them to Cousin Jake. . . . The sun is terrible in these hills with no shade. You have never mentioned the receipt of the fine candles sent you. . . . God bless and protect you my precious wife and little ones.

Your devoted husband,

B. J. Semmes"

In Atlanta there was growing irritation over passes. Citizens complained that sentries spat tobacco juice in their faces as they

demanded "pass"; that some days they could not walk two blocks
without being challenged again. At night the sentries were removed, just when people felt they were needed most, the soldiers filling up on corn whiskey and stragglers boasting they
would "take the town."

Authorities repeated that Atlanta was known to harbor Union
spies. They would not alter the pass system for personal identification. The fact that every male over the age of sixteen required a pass caused strange complications. An Atlanta youth,
fifteen and a half and tall for his age, was sent by his parents to
Alabama though Georgia authorities would not issue him a pass;
he was nearly arrested on two different trains.

Rather than risk the return journey without a pass, he lied
about his age and obtained a certificate before boarding the
train back to Atlanta. In Montgomery, he was taken off his car
by the provost marshal's office, where it was a toss up as to
whether he should be shot as a deserter or given a uniform and
rifle. Finally, a friend of his father's who happened to be in
Montgomery on business recognized him and returned the youth
to his home.

Off the presses came the latest issue of the *Camp Follower*.
Priced at two dollars and fifty cents a copy (postage paid), it
featured these stories: "The Cock Fight," "The Wife's Strata-
gem," "How I Coated Sal," and "The Champion."

Literature of another type was printed in the *Intelligencer*—
for example, the musings of "J. R. B." following a walk in
Woodland Cemetery:

> . . . The Hero of the field,
> With his battles lost or won,
> Here doffs in the dust his shield,
> The track of his glory won;
> The humblest soldier here,
> With him of the high command,
> Finds berth in a quarter near, . . .
> Where each on a level stand . . .
> The babe, the prattling child,
> The maiden in bloom of life,
> The form on whom beauty smiled,

The mother, the sister, the wife,
Here find alike repose
Where the dream of earth is past,
And each as a pilgrim goes
To the land of heaven at last.

Word was flashed to Atlanta of two soldiers who were home under false pretenses. Captain R. B. Hogan advised from Gaines Mill, Virginia:

"As Privates J. C. Hardin and T. F. Rainey, of Co. C, 19th Georgia Volunteers, are at home in Campbell County, Ga., at this time, deriving the sympathies of the people as being wounded soldiers from the late Battle of Drewry's Bluff, I wish it distinctly understood and known that they skúlked out of said battle and inflicted their wounds upon their own persons themselves in order to avoid further danger of battle."

JULY 8

✠ *Southern Confederacy* (Atlanta)

"There is no material change in the situation on the Chattahoochee. The army is in an immensely strong position north of the bridge, while proper steps have been taken to anticipate the designs of the enemy on our left.

"A small squad of Federal cavalry took possession of Roswell factory, on our right, day before yesterday morning. They told the operatives to continue their work and trade for provisions, but to furnish no supplies south of the river.

"The enemy on the left are said to be in force at Baker's Ferry and in the neighborhood of Cambellton. Doubtless, they will attempt the crossing at this point, and will endeavor to repeat the maneuver of the Etowah, flanking back to the State Road, with the design of pressing our army back.

"There is some little uneasiness manifested on the part of the

civilians, but the military are more than confident, knowing
and plucky. . . . 12 noon."

■ *The New York Times*

"The situation in Georgia is considered to be on the whole
both strong and hopeful. If Gen. Sherman can bring the army
of Johnston to a general battle before the close of the month
there is confidence that he will succeed in practically breaking
it up.

"(1:30 P.M.) Sherman has several good roads converging at
Atlanta, which is not over 12 to 15 miles distant from the river.
We have no positive assurance of the passage of the Chattahoochee by either army. . . . Probably the first that will be heard
positively of this will be from Gen. Sherman himself."

The capture of Roswell, eighteen miles north of Atlanta,
plunged its big neighbor into gloom, while underscoring the
urgent need to defend the "Gate City" if it was not to go the
way of Dalton, Resaca, Marietta, and now Roswell. The latter,
populated by French and English mill workers, was owned
mainly by foreign interests. Its international character cloaked
it with no immunity, but tended to infuriate the Federal troops
further.

An interview published on that Friday morning with Captain
Will Clark, of Missouri, who commanded the Roswell battalion
—hardly more than a token one—supplied some details of Sherman's lightning swoop on the factory:

"Roswell was evacuated at 8 A.M. yesterday, and the bridge
on the Chattahoochee River burned at 11 when a brigade of
the Yankee General Wilder's cavalry occupied the post after a
heavy cavalry skirmish with the 4th Tenn. Cavalry. The Yankees will keep the Cotton and Woolen mills in operation.

"Capt. Clark brought down with him, as prisoner, the Yankee
Capt. Austin, of the 8th Kansas Infantry, captured by his command near the Paper Mills, between Roswell and Marietta.

"Gen. Phillips' Paper Mill, at Roswell, was burned on Tuesday morning. The General sent them word that 'the mill belonged to a man who had fought them from the beginning of

the war, and who would continue to fight them to the bitter end; that he had been taught from childhood to hate them as enemies to him and his, and that he would die hating them; that he did not ask any favor from them; and they might burn to their hearts' content. These bold words of defiance, as a matter of course, did not have any influence in protecting the property. It was dismantled completely before the proprietor retreated. He remained in sight of the place until he saw the flames consume it.' "

Death in Atlanta found a snug dwelling place. Many wondered if it would ever depart. The daily newspapers read more and more like the "memory" plaques upon the walls of churches or the tombstones in church cemeteries.

This day, for example, some mourned Thomas W. Cox, a first sergeant with the 6th Kentucky Regiment, among the many who had fallen, and inserted their grief in the newspapers:

"Here, as on other fields, he was conspicuous for bravery, and volunteered to go in dangerous positions, where he died at the post of honor. . . . He was the hope of a fond mother and the idol of affectionate sisters. We can only tender them our heartfelt sympathy in their irreparable loss, and point them to Him who doeth all things well, and who alone is able to comfort the widow and wipe away the tears of a weeping Mary."

Civilians also died and—too often—very young ones. A burial was scheduled for later in the day: "The members of St. Philip's Church and the friends of the family are invited to attend the funeral of Mary Graham, infant daughter of Mr. and Mrs. John Henderson, from their residence, next the African Church, on this afternoon at 5 o'clock."

At the same time, men and women of Atlanta redoubled their efforts to help Dr. Stout in his monumental task of providing even minimum hospital facilities and care. One organization, the Soldiers Executive Aid Association for the Relief of the Army of Tennessee, through its "Daily Committee from the Passenger Depot," served soldiers arriving from the fighting in Virginia as well as from the Atlanta area with food and "refreshments."

The committee, after consulting with Dr. J. P. Logan, the

overworked surgeon in charge of Atlanta's General Hospital and well-known Georgia physician, made recommendations aimed at easing delays:—efficient registration of patients upon arrival, more ambulances and faster turn-around of ambulances from the hospitals, more clerks, litter-bearers and litters, and better coordination of the large number of furloughs being granted for recuperating patients.

Special field orders were issued to hasten ambulatory soldiers to their homes. The "probability of a general engagement" was openly admitted by the provost marshal and other ranking officers in Atlanta.

Mrs. J. G. W. Mills, wife of the postal agent, formed the Ladies 5th Ward Relief Association "for the purpose of affording all the relief possible to the wounded heroes of General Johnston's Army, who are daily arriving from the battlefield and being assigned quarters at the Erwin and Kingston Hospitals, located one and a half miles on the Western & Atlantic Railroad. Contributions of vegetables and such other food as is best conducive to the health of the sick and wounded are earnestly solicited."

Dr. Joseph Groves, surgeon-in-charge of the Erwin Hospital, appealed for more Negroes immediately—at least twenty men and women to clean, cook and assist the nurses.

Colonel Taylor Beatty, General Hardee's military lawyer, arrived in Atlanta after trouble in obtaining a pass. Writing home to Thibodaux, Louisiana, he remarked at "quite a bustle as the government stores, etc., are all being sent off."

It appeared that the government was pulling out of Atlanta —commissaries, storekeepers, engineers, quartermasters, paymasters, "nitre and mining" engineers, and purchasers of all types of ordnance, even Navy representatives and a few military observers from foreign countries. Only the unpopular conscription officer promised to remain.

No one knew what would become of Atlanta's vast production of pistols, mortar shells, saddles, brass buttons, clothing, torpedo fuses and such at the naval laboratory, or whether the bulging warehouses could be emptied in time.

Lewis Schofield's rolling mill, beside the railroad tracks east of the city, had brewed hundreds of thousands of tons of steel for the war effort. Here was forged armor plate for ironclads. People asked: "Will the fires be banked? Will the mill be scuttled?"

Schofield was nearly horsewhipped once for avowed Union sympathies. Now it was gossiped that he and his partner, William Markham, also a Unionist, might attempt to flee north to make steel for the "murderer" Lincoln.

The exodus of civilians followed the pattern set by the Confederate government. Mr. and Mrs. Cohen, for example, who recently moved to Atlanta from Augusta, told their friend Colonel Beatty that they were packing to return to their old home.

William Rushton, because of his position with the railroad shops, obtained space to send his daughter Mary away. He loaded her first on a train to Stone Mountain.

"Finally father managed to get hold of an engine not being used for other purposes," she wrote in a letter, "and he put Eva and me in the cab with the engineer and fireman, piled our trunks on the tender, and sent us off down the road to Madison, while he went back to Atlanta. Before we left Stone Mountain, as we were laughing and talking with some of the young officers who perhaps laughed and talked no more after that day, we could hear the cannonading in the distance and the gun shots of the pickets and outposts who were falling back."

Philander P. Pease's largest ad in the history of his wholesale business offered half-a-million-dollar inventory at reduced prices —clothing materials, English prints and "mourning" prints, hats, sole leather, tobacco, salt, knives, tallow, sugar, cotton and wool, oil and vinegar, corn sacks—an almost endless list.

One wagon, believed to be carrying the stock of J. M. Holbrook's hat store (Atlanta's first established), was being driven pell mell out of the city when it collided with a train. The locomotive was moving slowly in toward the water tower to replenish its tanks, so the wagon was not "much injured." What happened to the thousands of hats was not known.

A reporter for the *Southern Confederacy*, who witnessed the accident, expressed the belief that the teamster became "somewhat demoralized."

The confusion within Atlanta became a signal for excessive drinking. On Marietta Street a fight occurred at 7:00 A.M. between two soldiers, both of Irish lineage. An officer was carried off "in a beastly state of intoxication." His arrest, especially, sparked renewed appeals to close the whiskey shops.

JULY 9

✖ *Southern Confederacy* (Atlanta)

"8:00 A.M.—The thunder sound of war has not come to our ears this morning. The voice that speaks from the throat of cannon preaches not.

"12:00 noon—We still hold our position on the right, the earthworks in front and north of the river, where our lines on this side are being prolonged towards the left to anticipate the enemy's flank in that direction. The echo of a few heavy guns has been heard in the city during the morning. There is a little skirmishing, but no general fighting yet. This is all that is occurring and our readers may rest assured we shall keep them daily posted of further developments of the enemy and such disposition of our own troops as may not betray the movements and designs of the Commander-in-Chief.

"Later, from Turner's Ferry—The usual skirmishing and cannonading which have characterized the retrograde of our army since it left Dalton is progressing with no great damage to either side. Our army is in entrenchments beyond the river, and will repulse any attack made by the enemy. . . .

"So far as I can learn, the enemy has not crossed the river at any point and my information is that every ford place possible for him to cross is well guarded on both sides."

At a crucial position on the northerly banks of the Chattahoochee, Andy Neal seized a few precious minutes to write "Dear Ma." The enemy and the uncertainties of wartime living were not a fighter's only concerns. There were continual lesser annoyances which had a way of magnifying themselves far beyond the proportions of normal times:

"After an immense deal of trouble I succeeded in getting my box this morning. It had been opened and robbed of everything except two bottles and one small jar of preserves. I was surprised after hearing of the direction to find it at all. I sent two of my Sergeants to look everywhere for it and finally found it in an old shanty on the Rail Road. Never send anything in charge or care of any relief committee for even if they take any care of it, it is impossible to find their quarters and when you do they are off where you cannot get the wagons except by making a special trip. . . .

"I have no time to write now and send this letter and the mail carrier is waiting on me. . . . Gen. Johnston has just published an order to his troops saying we must now fight the enemy and can fall back no more. I have not seen it."

Up the river from Neal, Union cavalrymen of the Second Division, Army of the Cumberland, were fording the Chattahoochee under heavy fire.

"The brigade," penned Captain Joseph G. Vale, a Pennsylvanian, "in fact the whole division, was armed with the Spencer repeating rifle and carbine, using a metallic waterproof cartridge. The river was very rocky, and in many places the channels between the rocks were found to be 'over head' in depth. As the rebel bullets began to splash around pretty thick, the boys sought to keep in this deep water with only the head exposed; they soon discovered that they could throw the cartridges from the magazine into the chamber of the piece, by working the lever, as well under water as in the air; hence, all along the line you could see the men bring their guns up, let the water run from the muzzle a moment, then taking a quick aim fire his piece and pop down again, with only his head exposed. Now, the rebels had never seen anything of this kind before, nor, for that matter, had we, and their astonishment knew no bounds. We could hear them calling to each other.

" 'Look at them Yankee ——— ——— ———, loading their guns under water!'

'What sort of critters be they, anyhow?'

' 'It's no use to fit agin fellus that'll dive down to the bottom of the rivah an git that powdah and ball! . . .'

"Something over two hundred in number remained on the bank, quit firing and surrendered as soon as we got on the south side, anxious only to see the guns that could be loaded and fired under water."

In Atlanta, people wondered if there would be any classrooms when school time came around again in the fall. The teachers were in the army. The women were rolling bandages, or were far away in some field or base hospital.

The blackboards were dusty and bare. School bells had long since been taken down to be melted into guns and bullets.

The Female Institute at Collins and Ellis streets had been used as a hospital for almost a year. The school moved to Andy Neal's home and continued classes until spring, when—largely for lack of faculty—it disbanded for the duration of the war.

Such signs of privation were both evil auguries of the disintegration of the Confederacy and its social structure as well as sources of further embitterment and disillusionment to Southerners already classed as "Unionists." Senator Joshua Hill of Madison, was among their number. He had not favored secession, but because of his stature was still a respected leader, though a group of drunken Kentucky soldiers had sought, abortively, to lynch him.

Now, his teen-age son had fallen in recent skirmishing, a tragedy which drove deeper his personal sorrows and dissatisfaction for a cause he believed lost. However, his immediate concern was the recovery of the boy's body, and to this end he had written James R. Crew, superintendent of the West Point Railroad:

"You have doubtless heard of the cruel affliction this abominable war has brought to my hearthstone. I can't help thinking this was more than I merited. My poor boy met his death on Thursday morning the 19th of May, as I am informed, about 2½ miles above Cass Station beyond Ben Johnson's house on the road leading from Cassville to Kingston, about ½ mile from the R. road. He is said to have been brought by some comrades nearer the R. R. and left by the side of the public road, somewhere about or near a deserted cabin or perhaps nearer still to a small frame house near the R. R. *No one else was killed.* His name was Hugh Legare Hill, age 18 years—Complexion fair & ruddy. Light brown hair thick & inclined to curl a little—but was thin, rather short height about 5 ft. 8½ in. trim, erect figure eye-lashes long and dark. Had been sick and was rather thin in flesh, clothing all marked with his initials & name, thus 'H. L. Hill," pants dark grey Janes—new (nearly) & lighter grey jacket, plaid domestic shirt—name on the front. His death wound was received in a retreat and entered at the back of the head. I write these particulars in the hope that with the shifting scenes through which we are passing you may see some chance to ascertain the fate of the poor boy's body—whether it was interred by some kind human or was left to waste away by the action of the elements. My object is to recover his remains—as perfectly as may be. Should any opportunity offer for you to obtain me this coveted information I know you will take pleasure in receiving it for me. . . .

"I forgot to state that my son had a beautiful set of regular and white teeth."

There was tragedy of many cruel hues. Women, living in relatively deserted locations, were too often the victims of both Northern and Southern soldiers. Southeast of Marietta, the countryside was feeling the scourge of war.

Major General Jacob Dolson Cox, commanding the 23rd Army Corps, was himself appalled at the needless cruelty and wantonness of "professional stragglers and skulkers." As he noted:

"Some soldiers went to a house occupied only by a woman and her children and, after robbing it of everything which they wanted, they drove away the only milch cow the woman had. She pleaded that she had an infant which she was obliged to bring up on the bottle and that it could not live unless it could have the milk. They had no ears for the appeal and the cow was driven off. In two days the child died of starvation chiefly, though the end was hastened by disease induced by the mother's trying to keep it alive with food it could not digest."

General Cox, a former Ohio businessman, learned of the tragedy in an indirect fashion. One of the woman's neighbors, an elderly farmer, asked permission to bury the child, while admitting a grave was already "stealthily" dug. He feared the funeral gathering might be interpreted as "hostile" to the Federal army.

"The old man was abject in his solicitude not to seem to be complaining, and did not give the worst of the story till my hot indignation at what I heard assured him of sympathy and of a desire to punish the crime.

"A woman came to me the same morning and said the cavalry had taken the last mouthful from her, telling her they were marching and hadn't time to draw their rations, but that she would be fed by applying to us of the infantry column. The robbers well knew that we were forbidden to issue rations to citizens. They sacked the house of an old man with seven daughters by a second wife, all young things. He came to me in utter distress—not a mouthful in that house for 24 hours, their kitchen garden and farm utterly ruined, the country behind in the same condition, and he without means of travelling or of carrying anything if he tried to move away.

"I added, of course in such extreme cases I try to find some way of keeping the people from death, and usually send them to the rear in our empty wagon trains going back for supplies, but their helpless condition is very little bettered by going."

In a long proclamation, under preparation at Milledgeville, Governor Brown called for more volunteers.

"Sherman," he warned, "will drive you back in the Atlantic, burn your cities and your public buildings, destroy your property, and devastate the fair fields of your noble State. . . .

"If Gen. Johnston's army is destroyed, the Gulf States are thrown open to the enemy, and we are ruined."

In the evening, the skies to the north flamed red. Joe Johnston had fired the Chattahoochee railroad bridge as he fell back.

JULY 10

✉ *The Daily Intelligencer* (Atlanta)

"*Chattahoochee*—There was heavy firing last night along General Hood's front caused by an attempt of the enemy to plant a battery and cross the river. Our artillery opened upon them and theirs replied but were soon silenced. . . . One regiment of the enemy's cavalry endeavored to cross the Chattahoochee yesterday at Roswell. Our cavalry pickets waited until they got halfway across, when they opened on them and drove them back in great confusion, wounding many horses."

✉ *Southern Confederacy* (Atlanta)

"We shall not attempt to lull to a fancied security the readers of the *Confederacy* by the declaration that Atlanta is not in immense peril. Its capture, however, cannot be considered a foregone conclusion. The withdrawal of stores from the city may appear ominous, but the activity and vigilance of Gen. Johnston, as at present displayed along the Chattahoochee, indicates at least a determination to hold it at all hazards. Save the rumble and dust of wagons upon her pavements, Atlanta appears today as quiet as if there was not a Yankee in North Georgia. There is no panic or any existing excuse for it."

Henry Watterson, who had written for the *Confederacy* after leaving the *Chattanooga Rebel,* was planning to enter another profession: spying. He confided to a very few that he would join General Hood's staff as a "scout."

Watterson's stocky figure was familiar in Atlanta although his unpredictable explosive temper had kept him securely immune to close friendships. He had criticized the South's prosecution of the war so sharply while on the *Rebel* that he had alienated both the military and civilians. He was well accustomed to threats of physical violence.

George W. Adair and J. Henley Smith, publishers of the *Con-*

federacy, were already packing for Columbus. The *Confederacy* was not setting precedent in its contemplated evacuation. The *Gate City Guardian* and the *Reveille* had already ceased publication. Colonel Jared I. Whitaker, publisher of the *Intelligencer,* continued to offer "a large lot of old newspapers for sale"; while he stoutly denied any such intent, most businessmen in Atlanta assumed his newspaper would soon join its late competitors in retreat.

It would leave Atlanta with one paper, the emaciated but dogged *Appeal,* which had refugeed through several adopted cities after fleeing from Memphis. It was a foregone conclusion that another, the *Register,* of Knoxville, would go.

Most publishers and editors had little heart to meet the generals who had been for so long the target of their best-polished invective and vituperation—especially Sherman. For the citizens who remained in Atlanta, a complete news blackout loomed.

Hospitals, too, were hastening this latest phase of their "dance." Foard's Hospital proved that its relocation in Atlanta, after being pulled out of Marietta, was but a temporary roosting spot. By noon of that July Sunday, the last of its tents and cots had been stowed on wagons and in box cars, headed for Americus. The correspondent for the *Daily Sun* of Columbus, filed a story that all hospitals would be rushed from Atlanta before the week was out. He believed the precipitate action reflected a bleak conclusion by General Johnston—that Atlanta itself was doomed.

Even the more intelligent citizens, S. P. Richards, for example, shared the unhappy belief. Sitting in his garden house Sunday afternoon, surrounded by the bloom of the canna, zinnia, and larkspur, he could not easily be cheered by their pastel colors or fragrance as he put his thoughts into writing:

"This has been a sad day in our city, for it has been quite evident for some days past that there is a great probability of Atlanta falling into the hands of the enemy and the city has been in a complete swarm all day and for several days. All the Govt. stores and Hospitals are ordered away and of course the citizens are alarmed and many have left and others are leaving. Dr. Brantley preached for us this morning to a small congregation, and requested the members of the Church to remain after service to determine whether we would have the communion in the afternoon, which was decided affirmatively. Only about a dozen members were present at the ordinance, those from the immediate neighborhood, but it was quite a touching session. Dr. B. was so affected that he could hardly speak. The Church gave him liberty to go when it became necessary. His family have already left for Augusta. I took the pulpit Bible and Hymn Book home with me as it seemed almost certain that it would not be again needed there for the present. Alas! these dreadful times of war! When will they be ended? If Atlanta falls, I fear it will be a long, long time. Charlie DuBose and his son Charles came today and tonight Mary Brown has decided to go to Sparta with mother and Annie and Ethel who go in 'little' Charlie's care. Mary did not much want to go. Sallie and I have about decided to stay at home, Yankees or no Yankees. We hear and read terrible tales of them, but I don't think they are as bad as they are said to be. We hear of a good many who are going to remain in the city if the enemy gets possession."

Bishop Henry C. Lay of Arkansas, preached at St. Luke's. This church, on Walton Street, but two blocks from Five Points, built by soldiers' contributions, was consecrated on April 22. Since then, sorrow dogged it.

On June 16, the body of Bishop General Leonidas Polk lay in state in St. Luke's. The fifty-eight-year-old fighting clergyman fell at Pine Mountain. On his chest was a cross of white roses. In his pocket at the time of his death was the first copy off the presses of *Balm for The Weary and Wounded,* by Dr. Charles Todd Quintard, rector of St. Luke's and also Chaplain of the First Tennessee Regiment. One of its selections, which ran to many stanzas, began:

> There is an unseen battle-field
> In every human breast
> Where two opposing forces meet
> And where they seldom rest. . . .

Scarcely a week after the rites for Bishop Polk, there was another funeral in St. Luke's—for eleven-month-old Stephen Elliott Peters, son of Richard Peters, railroad executive and one of the city's early (and richest) citizens. Stephen was named for the first bishop of Georgia who, in fact, had consecrated St. Luke's.

There had been but five baptisms at the church. Most of the week the minister was with the army, as its chaplain.

Colonel Beatty, Hardee's lawyer, ate Sunday dinner with his friends, the Cohens. They hoped to leave for Augusta in the evening, abandoning home and furniture to whatever fate might befall the city.

"Stay at least a few days longer," the Colonel advised, "as I think we will hold this place at least a week—if the enemy succeed in getting it at all."

In Decatur, six miles east of Atlanta, Elizabeth S. Wiggins wrote to her mother:

"There is a great many refugees from above gone down the railroad and there is a heap in Atlanta just in tents. It is frightful times on every side. Everything is so high that people can't buy much: corn is 13 dollars a bushel, meat four dollars and a half a pound, flour 80 cents per pound and everything in proportionate . . . it has been raining here for 10 days nearly every day . . . we have a nice garden but we don't get a drop of milk . . . Mr. Wiggins works at the mountain in the shop.

"He makes a heap of money, but it takes a heap to buy a little."

JULY 11

Knoxville Register

"We cannot say that 'all is quiet along the Chattahoochee today,' but we know of no movements that it would be prudent to chronicle. The report of cannon was heard down the river this morning, but it was very light.

"Some very agreeable rumors are abroad today. Let us wait and see what comes of them."

The *Register,* a refugee newspaper, announced it would leave Atlanta with only one paper, the *Appeal.* On Saturday, a newspaper that few citizens even saw, the *Commonwealth,* finally conceded defeat. It strove vainly to beat the paper shortage by printing on wallpaper, book paper, wrapping paper, heavy manila wrappers, even colored, scented correspondence paper, placed laboriously in the presses by frustrated, incredulous printers. Its editor, J. S. Peterson, gave notice that he could "improvise" no more. He had penned some harsh remarks about the apparent conqueror from the North.

The *Intelligencer,* too, would leave for Macon. None had really expected the old standby to desert the city, even though its publisher, Colonel Whitaker, was desperately busy with his duties as commissary officer.

Tucked on the last page of the final edition, among the ads was this verse:

> Hoot away despair,
> Never Yield to sorrow,
> The blackest sky may wear
> A sunny face tomorrow.

Sherman, thus, had accomplished what a printer's strike some weeks back had failed to do. Since newspaper employees had been exempt from military service, the editors concluded the way to break the strike was to request the conscription officer to end this exemption.

The officer quickly agreed. He added, however, that the editors must also be drafted since, without printers, there could be no newspapers. The differences, one publisher recorded, "were speedily settled."

Now, the worst had come. The emaciated *Appeal,* with minuscule circulation, hardly counted as a metropolitan daily. The Gate City was virtually without news.

A drooping overcast sky blanketing the city at dawn, soon worsened to heavy rain. It was refreshing to parched skins and throats. It settled the dust and washed away garbage and other litter that lay putrefying and repugnant along the streets. Steam rose from the baked earth and from board and tin roofs of dwellings and stores. At the same time, the rain, with its tropical-drenching quality, served to deepen the depression that weighted everyone's spirits.

Sodden in the rain, one of Atlanta's defenders, Private Robert J. Wood, wrote a letter home. Seated on a tree stump beside the Marietta Road, Wood scrawled slowly on the mussed paper he carried in his pocket, pausing to scratch himself.

"We have not tents and it rains almost every day or night," he wrote. "We are the dirtiest set you ever saw, and lice is getting very common. I count two off me yesterday but I think I can keep clean of them if I can get my clothes washed . . . there is a great revival of religion moving on around here—I saw twenty-three baptised at one time yesterday and there is preaching every day and almost every nite."

Captain Vale, just decamped with his Pennsylvania cavalrymen from south of the Chattahoochee near Cross Keys, was troubled with bees:

"Some of the Seventh Pennsylvania boys contrived to get a forage bag over one of the hives, thus securing both bees and honey for future use, smuggled it into the column, and by supporting it on the horse in front, relieving each other in turns, and having it covered with an overcoat or something of the kind, carried it along until well in the forenoon. Somehow, in the march, the bag worked off the end of the hive, and the bees maddened by the jolting and confinement, rushed out in any angry swarm, attacking indiscriminately officers, men and horses . . . it looked for a time as though . . . the division (would be) scattered all over the Southern Confederacy. But by getting far enough away from the hive, now left by the purloiners in the middle of the road, after a good deal of scare, and a good many 'stings and arrows of outraged fortune' the column renewed its march in pretty fair order. The only casualties noted, and that on the quartermaster's report of Company G, Seventh Pennsylvania cavalry, was 'one horse stung to death by bees.' This was the literal fact. The bees seemed to center on one particular horse of that company, and absolutely stung him to death."

It was learned that some four hundred factory girls from Roswell were sent to Indiana by orders of "Sherman, the unfeeling beast, penniless and friendless, to seek a livelihood among a strange and hostile people."

A Union spy, J. C. Moore, completed his mission in Atlanta and returned to his own 4th Army Corps in the vicinity of Turner's Ferry. He had loitered, undetected, in the neighborhood of General Johnston's headquarters, a two-story, small white house on Marietta Road, fronting on the W. & A. tracks and about three miles from the center of Atlanta.

He noticed a woman he identified as Mrs. Johnston at the six-room dwelling, as well as "other ladies" on Saturday night. To Moore, their activities suggested a "jollification."

JULY 12

◢ Southern Press Association

"*Atlanta, July 12*—There has been no change in the position of affairs during the past few days. The enemy are in position on the northside of the river. There is some firing between sharpshooters, with occasional artillery firing by the enemy, without damage to us.

"A small force is reported on this side of the river, about 8 miles above the railroad bridge. They keep very close to the fort.

"The Governor arrived here last evening and is urging forward everything for the defence of Atlanta."

◢ Nashville Times

"Our army rests its wings on the Chattahoochee above and below the bridge. The main rebel army is across—only one corps (Hardee's) remains on this side, occupying the tete-dupont. The weather is very bad. We have driven the enemy from

the strong positions at Kennesaw and Smyrna and camp five
miles south of Marietta. We have taken some 2000 prisoners.
Our pickets are on the river bank at Price's Ferry and at the
mouth of Nickajack."

Governor Brown conferred with Mayor Calhoun, members of
the City Council, and local militia until after midnight. The
men agreed, a "crisis" was at hand. Every male citizen, short of
complete senility and infirmity, was to be forcibly called to arms.
The very fact that Georgia's Governor had deemed it necessary
to rush to Atlanta was considered a dire omen.

Meanwhile, in rustic Decatur, a thirty-six-year-old woman,
Mary Ann Harris Gay, was preparing to bring food to the Empire Hospital on Whitehall Street in Atlanta. Mary, small,
brunette, moderately attractive, was her twice-widowed mother's
sole companion, aside from slaves. Her half-brother, Tom
Stokes, who had been fighting the Union forces as a soldier-
preacher ever since she could remember, rarely came home.

By mid-morning, Mary took her fifteen-year-old Negro, Toby,
in tow. They hurried out of the low, one and one-half-story
frame house, across their acreage of lawns and woods toward
the railroad station. The Gay residence was but three blocks
from the center of town and about nine from the station.

She passed the court house, the square, the shaded grounds
of her neighbors and, then, was at the Augusta Railroad station.
Several days ago she had brought food to the Fair Ground Hospital, where she had met wounded comrades of Tom whom she
loved and admired far more deeply than she could have her own
brother.

Finally, the train, made up only of box cars, and spewing
wood cinders like some mechanized arsonist, ground and wheezed
its way into the small station. In another hour, Mary and the
provisions-loaded Toby were in Atlanta:

"Taking one of the baskets we had brought with us from
Decatur, and which contained biscuits, rusks, broiled and fried
chicken, ground coffee, and blackberry wine, I handed it to him
and we wended our way to the hospital. Things were not in as
good shape there as at the Fair Ground Hospital. I perceived

this at a glance, and upon asking and receiving permission from the Superintendent, I soon tidied up things considerably. Toby brought pails of fresh water, and aided in bathing the faces, hands, and arms of the convalescing soldiers, while I hunted up the soldier lads who ought to have been at home with their mothers, and bestowed the tender loving service that woman only can give to the sick and suffering.

"Entering one of the wards I perceived a youth, or one I took to be a youth, from his slender fragile figure, and his beardless face, lean and swarthy in sickness, but beautiful in its fine texture, and the marble-like whiteness of the brow. That he was of French extraction there could be no doubt. Quietly kneeling by the side of his cot, I contemplated his face, his head, his figure —I listened to his breathing, and watched the pulsations of his heart, and knew that his days, yeah, his hours, were numbered. Taking his hand in mine, I perceived that the little vitality that remained was fast burning up with fever. Putting back the beautiful rings of raven hair that lay in dishevelled clusters over his classic head, and partly concealed his white brow, I thought of his mother, and imprinted upon his forehead a kiss for her sake. The deep slumber induced by anodynes was broken by that touch, and a dazed awakening ensued. 'Mother,' was his pathetic and only utterance.

" 'What can I do for you, my dear child?'

"There are looks and tones which are never forgotten, and never shall I forget the utter despair in the eyes, lustrous and beautiful enough to look upon the glory of Heaven, and the anguish of the voice musical enough to sing the songs of everlasting bliss, as he said in tremulous tone, and broken sentences:

" 'I want to see a Catholic priest. I have paid several men to go for me. They have gone off and never returned. I have no more money with which to pay any one else.'

"In silence I listened and wept. At length I said:

" 'My dear young friend, can you not make confession to "our Father which art in Heaven," and ask Him for Christ's sake to absolve you from all the sins of which you may think yourself guilty? He will do it without the intervention of a priest, if you will only believe in Him and trust Him. Can you not do this?'

"The pencil of Raphael would fail to depict the anguish of his face; all hope left it, and, as he turned his despairng look upon the wall, tear drops glistened in his eyes and filled the sunken hollows beneath them. Again I took his passive hand in mine, and with the other hand upon his white forehead I told him he should see a priest—that I myself would go for one, and just as soon as he could be found I would return with him. Before leaving, however, I went to the ward where I had left Toby and the basket, and filling a little glass with wine I brought it to the sinking youth. He could not be induced to taste it. In vain I plead with him, and told him that it would strengthen him for the interview with the priest. 'I am going now, and will come back, too, as soon as I can,' I said to the dying youth, for to all intents and purposes he was dying then. Seeing the other patients watching my every movement with pathetic interest, I was reminded to give the rejected wine to the weakest looking one of them.

"Leaving Toby to either wait on, or to amuse the soldiers of the ward first entered (where I found him playing the latter role much to their delight), with hasty steps I went to the Catholic parsonage on Hunter Street. In response to my ring the door was opened by an Irish woman from whom I learned that the priest was not in, and would not be until he came to luncheon at 12 o'clock. It was then 11 o'clock, and I asked the privilege of waiting in the sitting room until he came. This being granted, I entered the room consecrated to celibacy, and perhaps to holy thoughts, judging from the pictures upon the walls, and the other ornaments. These things furnished food for reflection, and the waiting would not have seemed so long but for the thought of the poor suffering one who had given his young life for our cause."

Mary Gay waited in the Church of the Immaculate Conception, located across from City Hall and the Fulton County Court House. The man who "perhaps" had holy thoughts in this place of "celibacy" was the balding, thirty-three-year-old Reverend Thomas O'Reilly. The Irish-born priest had proven an indefatigable worker in the hospital, a familiar sight as he left the small wooden rectory in the morning, his Missal in one hand, food basket in the other.

"There goes Father O'Reilly," passers-by would remark.

Atlantans saw that he was making ecclesiastical history on other fronts—fraternization with the clergy of distinctly different faiths.

The day grew hotter. The flies buzzed their intrusive song of torpor on the parsonage ceiling. A smell of onions and grease drifted in from the kitchen. Finally:

"Intuitively I knew the sound of clerical footsteps as they entered the hall, and hastening to meet him I asked,

" 'Is this Father O'Reilly?'

"Receiving an affirmative answer, I told him of the youth at the Empire Hospital who refused to be comforted other than by a Catholic priest, and of my promise to bring one to him. Father O'Reilly said he had been out since early morning, visiting the sick, and would be obliged to refresh himself, both by food and repose, but that I could say to the young man that he would be there by 3 o'clock. 'O, sir, you don't realize the importance of haste. Please let me remain in your sitting room until you have eaten your luncheon, and then I know you will go with me. I too have been out ever since early morning, engaged in the same Christ-like labors as yourself, and I do not require either food or repose.'

"My earnestness prevailed, and in a short while we were at our destination. At my request, Father O'Reilly waited in the passageway leading to the ward until I went in to prepare the dying youth for his coming. I found him in that restless condition, neither awake nor asleep, which often precedes the deep sleep that knows no waking. Wetting my handkerchief with cold water, I bathed his face and hands, and spoke gently to him, and, when he seemed sufficiently aroused to understand me, I told him in cheerful tones that he could not guess who had come to see him. Catching his look of inquiry, I told him it was Father O'Reilly, and that I would bring him in. Opening the door, I motioned to Father O'Reilly to follow me. The dying youth and the Catholic priest needed no introduction by me. There was a mystic tie between them that I recognized as sacred, and I left them alone. Telling Father O'Reilly that I consigned my charge to him, and that I would come back to-morrow, I bade them good-bye and left.

"The contents of the basket had been gratefully received and devoured by those who deserved the best in the land, because they were the land's defenders."

The "emancipated spirit," by evening, took its "flight to heaven."

JULY 13

⚑ *Richmond Examiner*

"*Atlanta, Georgia*—Gov. Brown having official advices that persons within the military age, having Confederate details to remain at home in pursuit of their ordinary avocations, express a determination not to obey the recent order to report at Atlanta for the defense of their homes and state, has instructed the proper officers to arrest all such persons and send them under guard to Atlanta. If force is used against lawful authority, sufficient force will be sent to any point to overcome the resistance.

"He admonishes the men that have been detailed by the Confederacy for agricultural purpose that their crops will not be endangered by their absence for a short period."

⚑ *Southern Press Association*

"*Atlanta*—The enemy are massing on our right near Roswell. A portion of the Yankee army are on the south side of the Chattahoochee. Sherman's headquarters are near Vining's Station. Skirmishing across river continues near the bridge. Everything is quiet below."

Joe Semmes, the wholesale liquor dealer of Washington and Memphis, came into Atlanta where his army's commissary headquarters would be established—at least temporarily. No stranger to the Southern metropolis, he had numerous friends, including the Claytons and their letter-writing daughter, "Gussie."

He made himself comfortable in temporary lodgings and started a letter to his "beloved Eo." All was not well. The approaching envelopment of Atlanta was only one troublesome content of his Pandora's box.

He had to tell "Eo" that he found sickness in the Clayton household, that he had learned that his cousin, Raphael, had lost his raider *Alabama*:

"I arrived here on Sunday. The Army having crossed to this side of the Chattahoochee, where our lines now are, made it necessary that the supplies should be issued from here, being but about four and a half miles to the troops. The greatest consternation prevailed here when the movement became known, and thousands of idlers and speculators that crowded this den of thieves fled in dismay with what of their ill-gotten goods and money they could carry off. The troops laugh at the terrors of this class but feel great compassion for the unfortunates who must remain here should we evacuate the place.

"With some exceptions the people that remain are either those who are unable to leave or who will be pleased with the presence of the Army. Though every preparation has been made by the officers of the Government for the final evacuation of Atlanta, stores and manufacturers' machinery, etc. to be removed, I do not believe we shall give it up. The movements of the opposing armies may expose the city, like Petersburg, to the shells of the enemy, and to partial destruction, but I do not think the place will ever be abandoned now.

"The enemy yet hesitate on the opposite banks of the river, no considerable force having yet crossed. Our troops are eager to meet them, no matter at what odds, and we confidently expect some reinforcements from beyond the Mississippi, said to be already on the march on this side of that river. On the whole we are cheerful and confident, and there is no abatement in the spirits of the soldiers, and upon their reliance in the ability of the General, no matter what others may say.

"Genl. Bragg arrived here this morning, supposedly at the

request of Genl. Johnston, to consult with him. His appearance here will give great satisfaction to the troops.

"I found the Claytons in sad affliction when I arrived, Mary and Gussy, both very ill, and consequently their parents obliged to remain here, happen what may. Gussy has typhoid and pneumonia and Mary has a sort of nervous fever and is constantly under hallucination that she is about to die and will be lost. She is a mere shadow now, and was looking so fresh and handsome when I saw her before. Cousin Caroline and Mr. Clayton are worn out with watching at night and all day, and so is Pauline, Spencer's wife, who will not leave them until the Army should evacuate this point.

"John Dawson has returned to his regiment and is now in command, Colonel Magevney is acting Brigadier Genl.; commanding Vaughan's Brigade. Genl. V. having lost his foot lately, by a shell. Brad Lucket is quite well and dined here yesterday. I have not seen Warfield for some days, he is at work somewhere at the front.

"I suppose you have heard of the loss of the *Alabama*. Raphael is much condemned for fighting at all, and especially with his ship in bad condition after a long cruise around the world. The Yankee commander John A. Winslow played a regular Yankee trick. After he struck his colors, the sign of surrender, the *Alabama* came close up in the act of boarding when the Yankee fired into her which caused the loss of the vessel. Thank God, however, that cousin Raphael is safe, and I doubt not he will soon be afloat with another and finer ship.

"Sometimes of late in spite of all my occupation and the unceasing crowds of officers and men around me, I feel my peculiar longing for you my beloved and I become low in spirit and heartsick. I have been disappointed more than you dream of in not seeing you once more before this campaign, now it is impossible until winter, oh so long, perhaps not then. Your loving letters give me so much pleasure and comfort, that I want them always to be loving letters, sweet letters that make my heart rush into my mouth and my arms close upon—air. Bless you my precious Eo, for all those sweet words. I shall reply you with interest in all the way you love best."

Joe Semmes had joined many other Confederate officers and their staffs in Atlanta. Some, like himself, had tumbled in, post haste, in the last few days—or hours—while others had been in residence long enough to boast they were "settled." The best homes and servants had been commandeered already.

Pat Cleburne was comfortable at the Archibald Whitehead house on Marietta Road, near General Johnston. Major General Samuel G. French was at the Jennings' mansion on Turner's Ferry Road. Sam French, peppery, slight, and moustached, had been a classmate of General Grant's at "the Point." That hot Wednesday, he was more out of sorts than customary. He mopped his high, moist forehead as he confided to his notebook:

"The camp is filled with rumors.

"The enemy is reported to have crossed the river and then gone back. I rode to Stewart's headquarters and thence to Atlanta. I saw Capt. Maupin in the hospital. Poor fellow; he was shot at the Latimar house, through the breast. I went to see Gen. Johnston and found Gen. Braxton Bragg there. He comes from Richmond. What is his mission? Who knows? Is Sherman on this side of the river? Has Grant's failures in Virginia and Early's invasion of Pennsylvania affected movements down here? A few days will determine. O for brighter days for the Confederacy! I have been obliged to order the guards to fire on the cavalry when they go in the river to bathe with the Federal cavalry. Federals never venture in unless our men are bathing. Our men are not seeking fords; they are. This is what they are looking for."

But there remained many officers—and men—fighting a rearguard action south of the Chattahoochee. Lieutenant Andy Neal was among them. Ever nearing his own palatial birthplace on the corner of Washington and Mitchell streets in retreat, Andy paused long enough to write to his sister Emma:

"We were about the last command to cross to this side and fire the pontoons.

"We have a singular state of affairs in our front end, one I do not think altogether right. On one side our Battery is strongly posted supported by one of Cheatham's Brigade (Maury's). Just across the river are hundreds of blue coat Yankees of Fighting

Joe Hooker's Corps. We are not fifty yards apart and any of us would do anything to destroy the other. Yet we walk along the river banks talking as friendly and courteously as if to old acquaintances. The men laid aside their guns and are scattered up and down the river swapping canteens and hats and bartering one commodity for another. All day we lie in the shade of the banks and act very becomingly but at night the men commence cursing and taunting each other and carry on rich conversations. I was up all last night working our position and surprised them this morning as a frowning fort arose where yesterday there was but a red hill. They don't like it but as our boys tell them we will do them no harm if they keep out of range. If we get at loggerheads we will be much annoyed as the enemy is entrenched so near us. They are cautious about crossing this side and I scarcely think they will attempt it where Hardee's Corps is. They are feeling the Cavalry and I always tremble for the result when they have the fighting to do. I am convinced Sherman is sorely perplexed and wants to see what Grant is going to do before he pushes down farther. Johnston can save Atlanta by fighting for it but the preservation of the Army is infinitely of more importance than Atlanta. As long as our Army continues in the field Sherman can do little damage in Georgia and I cannot believe it is possible for him to remain in Georgia much longer. If we had a good General at the head of our army we would have the bulk of Sherman's army in twenty days. I don't believe Johnston ever did or ever will fight unless he gains some decided advantage and I look for nothing in that direction while so conservative a General as Sherman commands the Yankee Army.

"I had my box from Atlanta yesterday that Cousin Donie sent me. It was full of vegetables very nice and in tolerable good order. I sent to the Express office for Benny's and my box intending to send a man to him with as much as he wanted but Benny had sent and got his box the day before. He was to come up when they came but I suppose he cannot get off as Jackson's Cav. is busy watching the enemy on our left flank and I suppose Jackson wants all his couriers at present. I am glad the relief committee spared my bottles of vinegar and catsup as they come to hand very opportunely at present. I wrote a letter to Cousin Donie thanking her for the vegetables. I was not certain it came from her altogether.

"The box you sent us that was robbed by the Relief Committee was a most provoking circumstance but no worse than they have to do to set table for hosts of Quartermasters Commissaries stragglers and Dead Heads which congregate at the rear. The troops that build the works lie in the trenches and do the fighting do not get one twentieth of the vegetables and contributions that the ladies of the State have so generously stripped their gardens to furnish. I understand that thousands of crate-fulls came up on the cars. Since we left Dalton, vegetable tables have been issued to our Division twice. At Kennesaw while we were doing heavy work and hard fighting I drew rations for 94 men. They issued about a peck of potatoes, six or seven cabbage heads, two squashes and four or five beets. The other issue was as ridiculous, about as bad as when they issued ground peas at Dalton, three to the man.

"Our men get vegetable diet by cooking up polk, potato tops, May pop vines, kurlip weed, lambs quarter, thistle and a hundred kind of weed I always thought poison. I thought it trash at first but the boys call it 'long Forage' and it beats nothing. I am having good times now if the Yankees keep quiet and our General will let our pickets remain social. The commissary gives us bacon and corn bread enough and it is a sorry man that can't fight on that . . . the men that do the hard fighting and have all the hard living while the crowds at the rear get all that is intended at the front. But I have not nor never will complain of anything my country gives me."

That afternoon, General Bragg wired twice to President Davis in rapid succession:

"His Excellency, Jefferson Davis, Richmond:

"Have just arrived without detention. Our army all south of the Chattahoochee, and indications seem to favor an entire evacuation of this place. Shall see General Johnston immediately (1 P.M.). The enemy are reported by General Wheeler as having crossed two corps to this side of the river about nine miles above the railroad bridge. An official report has just reached General Wright that the enemy's cavalry, accompanied by artillery, crossed the Chattahoochee this evening nine miles from Newnan. Were at last accounts advancing on that place. Our army is sadly depleted and now reports 10,000 less than the return of 10th June. I find but little encouraging.

B. Bragg"

JULY 14

▰ *Nashville Union*

"The rebels, on Sunday, finding Sherman had effected a lodgment south of the river, burned the railroad and turnpike bridges, together with three pontoons.

"Their works were the strongest found on the whole line from Dalton, and were protected by abattis, so that a direct assault would have been an impossibility. The stream is at present shallow, and the bottom rocky, but no men could have forded it and charged up the embankment to their works.

"The entrenchments extended along the river bank for five miles, and were located in a position to sweep the surrounding country. Johnston had evidently been months in preparing them.

"After the flank movement commenced the rebel general offered no resistance, but fell back. We pursued to the fortifications around Atlanta, which were but eight miles distant. We know of no other point at which a stand can be made."

▰ *Cincinnati Commercial*

"Intelligence from the rear is frequently received, giving particulars of the operations of guerrillas who lurk about their homes during the daytime, with the oath of allegiance in their pockets, to disappear, mysteriously, at nightfall, nobody knows

where. . . . Better by far lay every house in ashes, send the helpless families north and support them until the close of the war
than permit these unprincipalled men to return home and perpetrate their villainy."

In Atlanta, little was published to satisfy the public's thirst
for news. Editor McCallahan of the *Appeal* dug tirelessly and
voraciously for any scrap of information that helped depict the
dreary and flaming scene that was yesterday. But he had little to
print these tid bits on, and his press itself was a rattling, partially mechanized junkpile.

The *Press Association* served the major newspapers of the
Confederacy, especially those in Richmond. But the dispatches
the correspondents filed from Atlanta generally did not find
their way back to Atlanta until weeks later when the city received out-of-town papers.

The brick *Intelligence* building at Alabama and Whitehall
streets was empty—hot, still, and reeking dankly of printers' ink
in the day, black, drafty, and looking utterly haunted at night.
Only the smell and the stray scraps of paper hinted that an important newspaper was once issued there daily.

Yet, if some voices were raised in desultory, futile complaint
of the lack of news, far more welled into a petulant chorus over
the dearth of mail. Soldiers growled that they had not received
letters in one, two, three weeks, and more. But the understaffed
postal clerks threw up their hands because the letters that did
arrive were, for the most part, too poorly addressed to readily
find their destination.

Somewhat the same situation existed at the Atlantic Office,
where telegrams piled up for General C. G. Dahlgren and
twenty-one others. Any one of them might be dead or alive. No
one seemed to know, or care.

Houses without occupants were on the increase. Many owners
closed the front door and fled, leaving the buildings empty,
silent, and forlorn. A few persons sought (against obvious odds)
new buyers.

John Peel was one of these. He had advertised his three-room
residence off and on throughout July: "with fireplace, kitchen

and garden." Today, he lowered his price. But who—other than General Sherman—desired Atlanta property?

Rumors continued thick as the July insects, rumors often calculated to bolster sagging morales. Colonel Taylor Beatty, Hardee's lawyer from Thibodaux, Louisiana, listened to an exceptionally imaginative rumor—"two steamers, with 500 frontier-type fighters were leaving Wilmington to steam to Point Lookout, Maryland, to liberate Confederate prisoners there." They would be armed, so ran the rumor, then hasten to join General Early's raiders, "now laying waste to Maryland."

Yet, since the debacle at Gettysburg, Beatty and other officers of his rank entertained fewer illusions of defeating Washington. They only hoped for a favorable, negotiated peace.

The men in the trenches, on the other hand, were more prone to dream. James R. Mathes, inching southward, ever southward with his outfit, between the Chattahoochee and Atlanta, wrote "Grandma" Smith, the well-known Confederate hospital matron:

"It has been almost impossible for me to get paper and envelopes. I beg you to forgive me for my neglect to one I hold ever dear . . . Our small brigade has lost heavily in this campaign, though it is in fine spirits, and is as determined as it was three years ago.

"I think that General Johnston is done falling back, and now it comes somebody else's turn to try it. Sherman has got tired of following Johnston as he did Polk in Mississippi, and I think or hope at least that before August he will retrace his steps . . . As they are skirmishing very heavy in front at this time I will come to a close."

Another communication was being sent from "near Atlanta" to General Braxton Bragg:

"Commanding Armies Confederate States, Richmond:

"Our present position is a very difficult one, and we should not, under any circumstances, allow the enemy to gain possession of Atlanta, and deem it excessively important, should we find the enemy intends establishing the Chattahoochee as their line, relying upon interrupting our communications and gain virtually dividing our country, that we should attack him even if we should have to recross the river to do so. I have, General, so often urged that we should force the enemy to give us battle as to almost be regarded reckless by the officers, high in rank, in this army, since their views have been so directly opposite. I regard it as a great misfortune to our country that we failed to give battle to the enemy many miles north of our present position. Please say to the President that I shall continue to do my duty cheerfully and faithfully and strive to do what I think is best for our country as my constant prayer is for our success.

> Respectfully,
> J. B. Hood
> Lt. Genl."

Late that evening, weary clerks at the Atlantic Office wrote down the tappings from distant Richmond, spelling out a message to General Johnston from Senator Benjamin H. Hill, of Georgia, who once opposed secession:

"You must do the work with your present force. For God's sake do it!"

JULY 15

■ *Nashville Times*

"At the last accounts, our forces were still strongly and securely entrenched at the Chattahoochee.

"There has been no pursuit of the rebels, and no advance from the banks of the Chattahoochee toward Atlanta.

"Passengers on the evening train today state that rumors prevail at Nashville that Gen. Sherman has captured 6,000 prisoners, but the time and locality are not stated . . . it is also stated that Gen. Sherman has ordered a correspondent of a New York paper out of his lines."

■ *The New York Times*

"From Sherman's army we have intelligence that while our forces have crossed the Chattahoochee, they had not, at the date of the last reports, advanced much beyond the southern bank of the river. No attempt had been made to pursue the rebels. For this there are doubtless ample reasons, without indulging even the faintest surmise that Sherman has given up the pursuit for good. The reports come that he had made large captures of prisoners."

In Atlanta, as in all of the South, money was impossibly inflated. Mrs. Hull spent five hundred dollars for a pair of buttoned shoes for Lucy, the first of their style seen in the city. Lucy recalled:

"I remember saying . . . that if I had a hundred dollars I would do—I forget what—and my father's pulling a $100 bill out of his pocket and handing it to me, saying, 'there, take it down the street and see if you can buy a stick of candy!' I stood rooted to the spot, and my mother took it away from me, saying 'George, how *can* you!'

"He answered bitterly that he had a wheelbarrow full, just like it."

General Bragg wired Jefferson Davis, in Richmond:

"I have made General Johnston two visits and been received courteously and kindly. He has not sought my advice and it was not volunteered. I cannot learn that he has any more plan for the future than he has had in the past. It is expected that he will await the enemy on a line some three miles from here, and the impression prevails that he is now more inclined to fight."

Johnston apologized for not paying the initial call upon Bragg, whom he had succeeded in December as commander of the Army and Department of Tennessee, "I have not visited you because absolutely afraid to leave my quarters."

That Friday, General Sherman, too, was reporting in a dispatch to Major General George H. Thomas, commanding the Army of the Cumberland:

"A scout in from Atlanta with dates to 3 P.M. 13th, says Bragg and staff had arrived and Kirby Smith with 20,000 was expected from Meridian. All bosh of course. All newspapers have quit Atlanta except the *Memphis Appeal*. That I suppose is tired of moving and wants to be left alone."

A local writer, Wallace P. Reed, evinced his objectivity and sense of humor with a sang-froid that maintained the undiminished envy, if not surprise, of his friends. The worse the times became, the more sublimely detached grew young Reed.

He noted that the late press manifested, "a degree of courage, cheerfulness, military knowledge and insight into the future more remarkable than can be found in the journalism of any country upon the face of the earth."

Even so, all—even those who criticized and ridiculed Atlanta's newspapers—were acutely aware of their absence now that the editors had fled. It was as though old friends had stepped, peremptorily, out of Atlanta.

Weeks', even months' old newspapers from other cities, torn, stained, and dog-eared from much perusal en route, were the fare of Atlanta readers. Yet, books were still available, and in S. P. Richards' store such as these were displayed prominently:

Les Miserables, Lady Audley's Secret, The Captain of The Vulture, No Name, Great Expectations, A Strange Story, The Aide-de-Camp, Clairmonde, and *Master William Mitten.*

There were also pamphlets, among them the many inspirational efforts of Dr. Charles Todd Quintard, pastor of the new, ill-starred St. Luke's Episcopal Church. The Connecticut-born Quintard, who was also a graduate physician, was in demand from all quarters for his multiple talents. Neither his Atlanta congregation, the 1st Tennessee Regiment who knew him as their chaplain, nor Dr. Stout's hospitals, could use him to satisfactory advantage.

Dr. Quintard sensed the end. It was coming, he knew, even though he could not predict the exact month. On the other hand, its very inevitability drove him to more frantic activity.

In Newnan, the shadow of defeat was already present. Nurse

Kate Cumming heard the Federals were advancing. Colonel Griffin, post commandant, had already recruited all hospitalized soldiers who could somehow limp or hobble along, given them rifles, and sent them out to hastily-dug trenches on the perimeter of the tiny village south of Atlanta. The colonel telegraphed to Johnston for help.

"We all went to work to prepare for the enemy's reception," Nurse Cumming recorded. "The first thing done was to send into the woods the Negroes, poultry, cattle, convalescents and all the nurses excepting those actually needed to take care of the sick.

"A wagon was loaded with all the valuables and sent to parts unknown. We had valises packed with a few clothes, and baskets filled with provisions, in case we should be compelled to take to the woods.

"We have been told that the enemy burn every hospital building, and we had no idea that they would show us any mercy. We packed our trunks and concluded to remain in the hospital, thinking it might be as safe a place as any.

"We had a large quantity of whiskey, which we were afraid to keep, for fear if the enemy should get it they would act worse than without it, so it was sent to the woods.

"All the surgeons left except Dr. Hughes, who remained at his post. The excitement in town was very great. I do not suppose there was an eye closed all night. On looking out we could see lights all over the place, the people moving everything that was movable.

"About 12 midnight Miss W. concluded to go down to her aunt's, living near West Point. The train was expected from Atlanta at 2 A.M. She got ready, and some of the men carried her baggage to the depot. I started with her; on our way down we met a gentleman, who informed us that the train would not be down, as the conductor was fearful of its being captured.

"We sat up all night long, and it was a night of dread. Every now and again some one came into town telling us that the enemy were but a few miles off. Every little noise we heard, we made sure they had come. A man came in and told us that they were on the outskirts of the town waiting for daylight."

JULY 16

Cincinnati Gazette

"Last night, Hardee's Corps, which was the last portion of the Rebel army on this side of the Chattahoochee, burned both the railroad bridge and the wagon road bridge over the river and retired to the other side. At the time I write this, therefore, there is no Rebel force on this side of the Chattahoochee, except guerrillas and straggling bodies of cavalry.

"The 23rd and another corps are across the river. The rest of the army is rapidly following. Sherman crosses tomorrow, and there is not much doubt that he will push straight on to Atlanta . . . don't consider it certain, however, that there will be no further fighting this side of Atlanta."

Richmond Examiner

"Rumors of another attempt by the enemy to cut the West Point Railroad are in circulation, but nothing certain of the movement is yet known.

"The following official report was sent by command of Gen. Johnston to headquarters last night:

" 'Since the failure of the enemy to cut the West Point Railroad near Newnan, both armies have been quiet and occupy their former position. Ours is much improved by rest and bathing, and all are in fine spirits.' "

On that Saturday, Joe Johnston telegraphed a former West Point schoolmate, Jefferson Davis:

"As the enemy has double our number, we must be on the defensive, my plan of operations must, therefore, depend upon that of the enemy. It is mainly to watch for an opportunity to fight to advantage. We are trying to put Atlanta in condition to be held for a day or two by the Georgia militia, that army movements may be freer and wider."

As Sherman's cannon boomed nearer the great Georgia city,

hysteria became more prevalent. Any taint of "Unionism" was ever-present tinder for a lynching. A soldier, just in from the bayous of Mississippi, chanced to find a copy of *Uncle Tom's Cabin* in a bookstore. Quickly, he clomped out to find companions who might help him tar and feather the luckless proprietor.

Fortunately, the overzealous soldiers were so noisy in their preparations that word preceded their return by minutes. No *Uncle Tom's Cabin* was to be found, even after the store was ransacked. When the soldiers, who reeked of bad whiskey, left they were muttering threats against their buddy whom they now believed was trying to make fools of them.

Drunken soldiers on overnight passes were only a part of the noxious rabble in Atlanta. Stragglers who might have been out of the trenches for days or weeks prowled the streets day and night like slovenly-uniformed vultures. The decent women of Atlanta, going to market or to the hospitals, were propositioned and otherwise insulted regularly.

To venture from home at night meant courting rape, if not death. Even houses were a doubtful sanctuary against drunken marauders.

There was another and often overlooked factor working against the ladies of Atlanta: the jaded belles of the evening who had wintered with the army in Dalton, then escaped ahead of the advancing Yankees, were now poised to fly again to safer perches. Frequenting the depot in hopes of a free ride south, they were, naturally enough, taking with them what the idle, brawling soldiers held so dear. Where, now, could the young men find release for their passions?

Just south of the station a far milder diversion continued its tawdry existence—Humbug Row. It remained the bane of one Atlanta physician-druggist, Dr. John Stainback Wilson, who wrote:

"Here is a kind of camping ground for lotterymen, patent medicine vendors, and all kinds of small shows. Here flourish the prize-package business, the educated hogs and uneducated men; monsters of all kinds, human and inhuman, corn doctors, root doctors, and all kinds of doctors except regular doctors.

Here are the microscope-men, the balloon-men, the telescope-men, the sham jewelry-men."

The militia drilled with an unmatched earnestness in City Hall Park. Heretofore exempt firemen, were now, by edict, a part of the local guard. Boys fifteen and men seventy had the greatest of difficulty in convincing the conscription officer that they were, respectively, too young or too old to serve.

A story was told of the father who took his fifteen-year-old boy to headquarters and offered to turn him over for the bounty offered as incentive to the under- and over-aged cases. The officer protested the boy looked old enough to be drafted without a bounty, but finally paid when the father insisted he was three months under the age limit. The father gave the boy a dollar, as his share, before he said goodbye to this latest recruit.

One disgruntled youth chopped off several finger tips with an ax, hoping to avoid service, then was sentenced to a regimental kitchen as punishment.

"We waited in vain for the enemy," wrote Nurse Kate Cumming in Newnan, following her sleepless vigil. "I thought I never had heard of cavalry taking so long to come a few miles. Our head cook did not leave, saying he was tired of running. We had about 60 badly wounded men, who had to have something to eat; so, having no cooks, we all went to work and got breakfast ready, fully expecting the Yankees to eat it instead of our men.

"After breakfast there were still no tidings of the foe. We went to work and prepared dinner; Miss W. peeling potatoes and shelling peas, etc. all the time wondering if the Yankees would like their dinner, as we knew that they would not be backward in helping themselves; but by dinner time the joyful tidings arrived that General Johnston had sent cavalry and driven them back. . . .

"We breathe free again, but only for a little while, as I do not see what is to prevent them coming in at any time. The men are coming back very much exhausted. The Negro women are nearly all sick, and vowing they will never run again. One old woman, who I am certain, the enemy could not be paid to take, is nearly dead. The women carried all their clothes with them, as they hear the Federals rob black as well as white. Many an amusing story is related about the hiding.

"It is a blessing we can laugh, for the great anxiety is enough to kill any one. I cannot help wishing that our *kind* northern friends who *love* us so dearly that they will have us unite with them, whether we will or no, only had a little of it."

A few miles to the northeast, in Decatur, Mary Gay the girl who had brought Father O'Reilly to the dying soldier's side, learned the unbelievable from Uncle Mack, the Negro blacksmith, on her way to the village post office:

" 'Did you know, Miss Mary, that the Yankees have crossed the river, and are now this side of the Chattahoochee?'

" 'Why no,' I said and added with as much calmness as I could affect, 'I do not know why I should be surprised—there is nothing to prevent them from coming into Decatur.'

"With an imprecation, more expressive than elegant, that evil should overtake them before getting here, he resumed hammering at the anvil, and I my walk to the post office. Nor was Uncle Mack the only one who volunteered the information that, 'The Yankees are coming—they are this side the river.'

"The time had come to devise means and methods of concealing the winter clothing and other accoutrements entrusted to my care by our dear soldiers. In order to save them, what should I do with them?—was a question which I found myself unable to answer. An attempt to retain and defend them would be futile indeed. And I have no right to jeopardize my mother's home by a rash effort to accomplish an impossibility. But what shall I do with these precious things, is the question. A happy thought struck me, and I pursued it only to find it delusive. The near approach of Sherman's army developed the astounding fact that Dr. A. Holmes, of Decatur, a Baptist minister of some prominence, claimed to be a Union man, in full sympathy with any means that would soonest quell the rebellion. This I had not heard, and in my dilemma I went to him to impart my plans and ask advice. He was morose and reticent, and I hesitated; but, driven by desperation, I finally said: 'Dr. Holmes, as a minister of the Gospel, are you not safe? All civilized nations respect clerical robes, do they not?'

" 'I think so,' he said, and continued by saying, 'I have other claims upon the Federal army which will secure me from molestation.'

"A look of surprise and inquiry being my only answer, he said, 'Amid the secession craze, I have never given up my allegiance to the United States.'

" 'Why Dr. Holmes!' I said, in unfeigned surprise.

" 'I repeat most emphatically that I have remained unshaken in my allegiance to the United States. I have no respect for a little contemptible Southern Confederacy whose flag will never be recognized on land or on sea.' "

Mary Gay was certain she had heard Dr. Holmes pray for the Southern cause and its success. Now convinced she was on enemy ground, she hurried home without discussing the matter of soldiers' clothing.

With the aid of her deaf maid, Telitha, Mary began to move the nine bulky boxes of winter uniforms sent by her brother Tom, from Dalton, which belonged to him and his two superiors, Brigadier General H. B. Granbury and Colonel Bob Young. Tom had warned, "should they be found in your possession by the enemy then our home might be demolished, and you perhaps imprisoned or killed upon the spot . . . are you willing to take the risk?"

Mary was, yet she went to work with a certain frenzy to hide the evidence. She locked roors, drew the blinds, and gave fast orders to Telitha in sign language, as well as a pantomime warning of how the Yankees would cut both their throats if the boxes weren't concealed. Telitha's eyes popped as she repeated the gestures.

Mary and her servant strained their shoulders against a wardrobe in one corner of the dining room, struggled and panted until the massive piece of furniture had been pushed into the middle of the room. Then, holding her skirts about her as she clambered to the top of her perch from the dining room table, she began working with a hammer and chisel.

A jagged hole appeared in the plaster and lath of the ceiling as her hammer beat a muffled tattoo and the plaster vanished in little limey, irritating clouds.

"Very slow work it was at first, as the licks had to be struck upward instead of downward, and the plastering was very thick. Finally the chisel went through and was withdrawn and removed to another place and by repeated efforts I secured an aperture large enough to insert my fingers, and a few well-directed licks round and about, so cracked and weakened the plastering that I was enabled to pull off some large pieces . . . more than once the wardrobe had to be moved that I might pull off the plastering, and then with the greatest care pry off the laths. At length the feat was accomplished and I laid the lids of the boxes, which had been reserved for this purpose, across the joists and made a floor upon which to lay the goods, more than once specified in these sketches. When the last article had been laid on this improvised shelf, I gazed upon them in silent anguish and wept. Telitha caught the melancholy inspiration, and also wept. Each lath was restored to its place and the perilous work was completed, and how I thanked the Lord for the steady nerve and level head that enabled me to do this service for those who were fighting the battles of my country.

"But the debris must be removed. While the doors were yet closed and fastened, we pounded and broke the plastering into very small pieces and filled every vessel and basket in the house. I then went out and walked very leisurely over the yard and lot, and lingered over every lowly flower that sweetened the atmosphere by its fragrance, and when I was fully persuaded that no spy was lurking nigh I re-entered the house and locked the door. Picking up the largest vessel, and motioning Telitha to follow suit, I led the way through a back door to a huge old ash-hopper, and emptied the pulverized plastering into it. In this way we soon had every trace of it removed from the floor. The dust that had settled upon everything was not so easily removed, but the frequent use of dusting brushes and flannel cloths, disposed of the most of it."

Mary wrote a note to her mother, "inviting her to come home," to be delivered by Telitha. She had taken the unusual precaution of packing off her mother and Toby to the depot, for fear that Toby might talk. She chose the depot, a popular "emporium of news" where mothers, sisters, and sweethearts congregated in the hopes of word either via railroad trainmen or the "Confederate scouts that were ever and anon dashing through Decatur, with cheerful messages and words of hope." Thus, Mary reasoned, neither her mother nor Toby would be suspicious.

Noticing the shadows were long, Mary started to prepare a "good luscious dinner." She thought of the soldiers who had paused to drink out of the big oaken bucket by the well and wondered if some of them would arrive for dinner. Just in case, she mixed an extra quantity of flour "for biscuits and tea cakes."

JULY 17

■■■ *The New York Herald*

"*Nashville*—The report from New York to the effect that Atlanta has been occupied is without foundation. There are all kinds of rumors regarding the evacuation of Atlanta by the enemy, but nothing is known positively of this.

"One of the reports say that during the delay of General Sherman at the river, the enemy has been enabled to get his valuables away; but in opposition to this it is well known that all had been sent away weeks since to Augusta. The evacuation of Atlanta really began several weeks ago.

"General Sherman yesterday moved out of his works on the south side of the Chattahoochee to attack Joe Johnston's forces, if found in front of them, or occupy the city in the event of his retreat. Nothing later than the information that he had moved has been received here; but I hope tomorrow to announce the occupation of Atlanta."

(Mr. W. F. G. Shanks, correspondent)

General Sam French had hoped the Yankees would not fire
at him that Sunday. In many ways he was finding it a different
conflict from the late Mexican War.

"The enemy commenced a more rapid and continued fire
from their batteries near the railroad bridge where I have
pickets" he wrote. "This as usual presages some movement. And
here it is:

" 'Hold your command ready for a movement!'

"It does seem strange that we cannot have one quiet Sabbath.
Sherman has no regard for the Fourth Commandment. I wish
a Bible society would send him a prayer book instead of shipping them all to the more remote heathens; but it would be
the same in either case. The one is wicked by nature; the other,
I fear, is becoming so from habit. Perhaps 'Tecumseh' has something to do with it. There is much in a name."

Kate Cumming left her hospital and saw her friend Miss W.
off at the Newnan railroad station.

"After she left," Kate wrote, "we were informed that there was
a raid near West Point and that Miss W. will reach there in
time to meet it. It is useless to think of going any place and
getting rid of the enemy, as they seem to have it in their power
to overrun the whole country. Miss W. and I have agreed that if
either should lose our clothes, the one spared would share with the
other. The enemy have a particular liking for ladies' wardrobes.
I presume they send them to their *lady-loves* in the North. I
wonder how they feel in their stolen finery!

"I do not suppose that the men would rob us as they do if
they were not incited by the importunities of their women.
Many letters, taken from dead Federals on the battlefields, contain petitions from the women to send them valuables from the
South. One says she wants a silk dress; another, a watch; and one
writer told her husband that now was the time to get a piano,
as they could not afford to buy one, 'O shame where is thy
blush?' . . .

"This afternoon we went to a funeral in the Methodist
Church. Dr. Adams officiated as the deceased was an Episco-
palian—young Colston of Louisville. He was the color-bearer of

a Kentucky regiment, and a gallant soldier. He was buried with the full honors of war. The day was very lovely."

Mary Gay awoke early in Decatur, from a night of "unbroken rest and sleep." As the sun poked over the magnolias and oaks in her back yard, she stared upward at the tinted cherubs on the bedroom ceiling. She wondered if "another day of surprises and toil" was ahead.

Before putting on her nightdress she had, together with her mother, emptied several trunks. Then the two women filled them with quilts, blankets, bedsheets, china, cut glass, relics, and family papers, all to be removed to Atlanta for shipment farther south.

Without waiting for breakfast, Mary ran to the house of a friend, Ezekiel Mason. She asked to hire his team, wagon, and driver to haul the heavy trunks to the depot. Soon, she, Toby, and baggage were aboard a freight train, erupting clouds of smoke and wood sparks as it pounded toward Atlanta. There were no other passengers, and the conductor warned that Federal cavalry could be expected momentarily.

But soon the wheels were clacking over the increasingly irregular and gouged tracks of the Atlanta yards, rolling past the low warehouses, factories and mills east of the city.

"There was unusual commotion and activity about the depot in Atlanta," she wrote, "and a superfical observer would have been impressed with the business-like appearance of the little city at that important locality. Men, women, and children, moved about as if they meant business. Trains came in rapidly; and received their complement of freight, either animate or inanimate, and screamed themselves hoarse and departed, giving place to others that went through with the same routine. Drays, and every manner of vehicles, blocked the streets, and endangered life, limb, and property, of all who could not vie with them in push, vim, and dare-deviltry. In vain did I appeal to scores of draymen, white and black, to carry my trunks to the home of Mr. McArthur, on Pryor street—money was offered with liberality, but to no avail. Despairing of aid, I bade Toby follow me, and went to Mr. McArthur's. He and his good wife were willing to receive the trunks and give them storage room, but could extend no aid in bringing them there. At length, as a last resort, it was decided that Toby should take their wheelbarrow and bring one trunk at a time. I returned with him to the depot, and had the most valuable trunk placed upon the wheelbarrow, and with my occasional aid, Toby got it to its destination. A second trip was made in like manner, and the third was not a failure, although I saw that Toby was very tired. Thanking my good friends for the favor they were extending, I hurried back to the depot, myself and Toby, to take the first train to Decatur. Imagine our consternation on learning that the Yankees had dashed in and torn up the Georgia Railroad track from Atlanta to Decatur, and were pursuing their destructive work towards Augusta. Neither for love nor money could a seat in any kind of vehicle going in that direction be obtained, nor were I and my attendant the only ones thus cut off from home; and I soon discovered that a spirit of independence pervaded the crowd. Many were the proud possessors of elegant spans of 'little white ponies' which they did not deem too good to propel them homeward. Seeking to infuse a little more life and animation into Toby, I said:

" 'Well, my boy, what do you think of bringing out your little black ponies and running a race with my white ones to Decatur? Do you think you can beat in the race?'

" 'I don't know'm,' he said, without his usual smile, when I assayed a little fun with him, and I evidently heard him sigh. But knowing there was no alternative, I started in a brisk walk towards Decatur, and said to him, 'Come on, or I'll get home before you do.' He rallied and kept very close to me, and we made pretty good time. The gloaming was upon us, the period of all others auspicious to thought, and to thought I abandoned myself. The strife between the sections of a once glorious country was a prolific theme, and I dwelt upon it in all its ramifications, and failed to find cause for blame in my peculiar people; and my step became prouder, and my willingness to endure all things for their sakes and mine, was more confirmed. In the midst of these inspiring reflections, Toby, who had somewhat lagged behind, came running up to me and said:

" 'Oh! Miss Mary, just look at the soldiers! And they are ours, too!'

"To my dying day I shall never forget the scene to which he called my attention. In the weird stillness it appeared as if the Lord had raised up of the stones a mighty host to fight our battles. Not a sound was heard, nor a word spoken, as those in the van passed opposite me, on and on, and on, in the direction of Decatur, in what seemed to me an interminable line of soldiery. Toby and I kept the track of the destroyed railroad, and were somewhere between Gen. Gartrell's residence and Mr. Pitt's, the midway station between Atlanta and Decatur, when the first of these soldiers passed us, and we were at Kirkwood when that spectre-like band had fully gone by. Once the moon revealed me so plainly that a cheer, somewhat repressed, but nevertheless hearty, resounded through the woods, and I asked:

" 'Whose command?'

" 'Wheeler's Cavalry,' was the simultaneous response of many who heard my inquiry.

" 'Don't you know me? I am the one you gave the best breakfast I ever ate that morning we dashed into Decatur before sun up.'

" 'And I'm the one, too.'

" 'O, don't mention it,' I said. 'You are giving your lives for me, and the little I can do for you is nothing in comparison. May God be with you and shield you from harm until this cruel war is over.'

"I missed Toby, and looking back, saw him sitting down. I hurried to him, saying, 'What is it, my boy?'

" 'O, Miss Mary, I am so sick. I can't go any farther. You can go on home, and let me stay here—when I feel better I'll go too.'

" 'No, my boy, I'll not leave you.' And sitting by him I told him to rest his head upon my lap, and maybe after awhile he would feel better, and then we would go on. In the course of a half hour he vomited copiously, and soon after told me he felt better, and would try to go on. More than once his steps were unsteady, and he looked dazed; but under my patient guidance and encouraging words he kept up, and we pursued our lonely walk until we reached Decatur.

THE NEW YORK HERALD.

WHOLE NO. 10,184.   NEW YORK, FRIDAY, AUGUST 5, 1864.   PRICE THREE CENTS.

SHERMAN.

THE CITY OF ATLANTA.

The Defensive Works of the Rebel Army at Atlanta and the Position of Sherman's Lines on July 27.

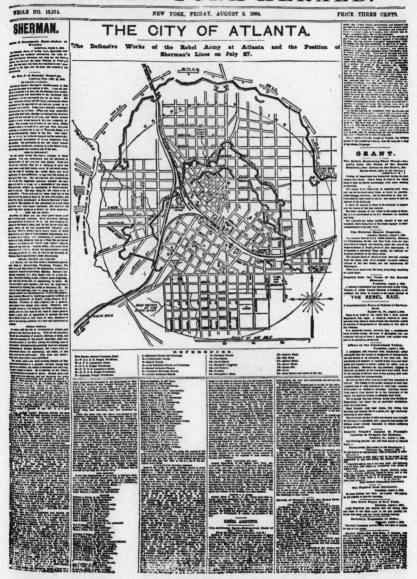

Map of Atlanta showing the Confederate defensive lines and the position of the Union forces. This map, reproduced in the *New York Herald* of August 5, 1864, was prepared by Sherman's Engineers.

City Hall Square, Atlanta, as it looked shortly after the war. The only major change in the skyline was the appearance of the square spires of the Church of the Immaculate Conception between the Second Baptist Church *(on the left)* and the Central Presbyterian Society *(on the right).* *(Courtesy Atlanta Historical Society)*

An artist's conception of City Hall Square.

City Hall Square with an encampment of the Second Massachusetts Infantry. (*Courtesy Atlanta Historical Society*)

Another artist's view of City Hall Square. The spires are those of the Second Baptist Church and the Central Presbyterian Church. *(Courtesy Atlanta Historical Society)*

Meeting room in the lower level of the Central Presbyterian Church. Left relatively undisturbed at the time a new brick structure was erected over it, this room is the only surviving portion of any church that was in existence at the time of the siege of Atlanta.

Father O'Reilly's Church of the Immaculate Conception. *(Courtesy Atlanta Historical Society)*

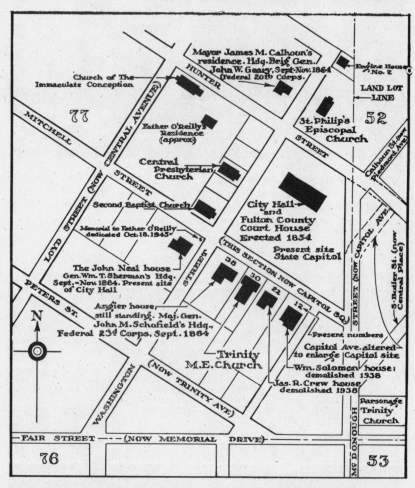

Street plan of Atlanta showing the vicinity of City Hall Square. *(Drawn by William Kurtz. Courtesy Atlanta Historical Society)*

Drawings of Atlanta by a staff artist of *Leslie's Illustrated Weekly*. These views depict the city on the eve of Sherman's evacuation.

House occupied by General Thomas who often sat with General Sherman on the broad porch to listen to band concerts. *(Courtesy Atlanta Historical Society)*

Scene at Loyd and Hunter Streets showing Federal soldiers preparing to remove citizens to Rough & Ready. *(Courtesy Atlanta Historical Society)*

"As soon as we entered the town, we perceived that we had overtaken Wheeler's Cavalry. They were lying on the ground, asleep, all over the place; and in most instances their horses were lying by them, sleeping too. And I noticed that the soldiers, even though asleep, never released their hold upon the bridles. At home, I found my mother almost frantic. She knew nothing of the causes detaining me, and supposed that some disaster had befallen me individually. A good supper, including a strong cup of tea prepared by her hands, awaited us, and I attested my appreciation of it by eating heartily."

Meanwhile, at his new quarters in Atlanta, Joe Semmes, now a Confederate supply officer, began answering what he thought was a "perfect harvest of letters." He wrote his wife, "Eo":

"The letter from Clara was to inform me of her expected departure with Myra on a trip to Europe, and was a farewell as only Clara can write. She expects to start for Wilmington in a few days, there to run the blockade to Nassau. They will go under charge of an old friend of Mr. Knox and direct to England, thence to France, and a winter in Italy. . . . With regard to the enclosed letter from Mrs. Titus I hardly know what to tell you to do. I am not willing as a mere pecuniary matter, that you should receive the miserable trash, which the Yankees call money, and I presume gold was not sent by Genl. Dix. He could have communicated at any time with you by Flag of Truce as thousands have done, and I don't fancy this mode of his in sending money by another party, as though he wished simply to perform a business duty. I therefore suggest that you pay no attention to Mrs. Titus' letter, or to Mr. Alden. When the war is over your annuities will be due in gold, and will do you more good than now. It is against the laws of our Country to use Yankee money, and it will ill become the wife of an officer in my position to be seen with Federal money.

"I am sure you will agree with me on reflection, but I would like to have your own views, for you sometimes see things clearer than I.

"Brad has just come in and gone, he was about writing to Jennie, but he was ordered to be ready to move; some move of the enemy is on foot, and our troops are ordered to be ready to meet it.

"Were you surprised at the Maryland news? Our Army was at Silver Spring, the Blairs' place, and on the 7th St. road, only 3 miles out. I fear since the failure of the object of the movement that Early will find it difficult to retreat without severe loss. You must know the real object was to unite with 18,000 prisoners of ours who were at Point Lookout, and who were to be first released by a separate expedition, and take Washington. The plan was revealed by a traitor.

I cannot write more at present. . .Yours,

J."

Late that Sunday evening, General Johnston received a stunning telegram from Samuel Cooper, Adjutant and Inspector General in Richmond:

"Lieutenant-General J. B. Hood has been commissioned to the temporary rank of general under the late law of Congress. I am directed by the Secretary of War to inform you that, as you have failed to arrest the advance of the enemy to the vicinity of Atlanta, and express no confidence that you can defeat or repel him, you are hereby relieved from the command of the Army and Department of the Tennessee, which you will immediately turn over to General Hood."

And, shortly, Johnston, in the Niles house on Marietta Road, within plain hearing of the sharpshooters and skirmishers, was drafting his reply. He resolved not to file it until the next day.

"Command of the Army and Department of Tennessee has been transferred to General Hood," he wrote. "As to the alleged cause of my removal, I assert that Sherman's army is much stronger, compared with that of Tennessee, than Grant's compared with that of Northern Virginia. Yet the enemy has been compelled to advance much more slowly to the vicinity of Atlanta than to that of Richmond and Petersburg, and penetrated much deeper into Virginia than Georgia. Confident language by a military commander is not usually regarded as evidence of competence."

JULY 18

✉ *Richmond Sentinel*

"*Nashville*—It is understood that Gen. Joseph E. Johnston has been relieved from his command of the Army of Tennessee, and Gen. Hood, who has been made a full General, ordered to take command of the army which is now in front of Atlanta.

"The *Augusta Chronicle* . . . says that a gentleman just from Atlanta reports that Gen. Johnston burned the Chattahoochee bridges on Saturday. Our baggage wagons, pontoon bridges, etc. have passed through Atlanta, and are now between that city and Decatur.

"The same paper says: 'We are informed on good authority that Hooker's corps crossed the Chattahoochee on Saturday, when they were met and driven back by Hardee, who captured 500 prisoners.' "

▤ *The New York Herald*

"On July 17, the army moved forward to within 5 miles of Atlanta, the left, under Gen. McPherson, occupying Decatur. The enemy appeared to be in force in the woods about the city. This movement resulted in occupying a line forming an arc of a circle to the northeast of Atlanta, that point being the center of the circle. This position did not appear to be entirely satisfactory to Gen. Sherman, and when our correspondent left Gen. McPherson's army was at Decatur.

"On the 18th, Gen. Hooker's corps, having moved out of the line, was going into position on the left of McPherson. Other troops were marching to extend the line still further southward.

"The army is in the most encouraging condition and it is believed that the most sanguine hopes of the capture of Atlanta will shortly be much more than realized."

(Mr. W. F. G. Shanks, correspondent)

General Hood received a very early dispatch from Secretary of War, James A. Seddon:

"You are charged with a great trust. You will, I know, rest to the utmost your capacities to discharge it. Be wary no less than bold. It may yet be practicable to cut the communications of the enemy or find or make an opportunity of equal encounter whether he moves east or west. God be with you."

Then General Hood was strapped to his horse and, with an aide, rode north to see General Johnston at the Niles house.

And to the northeast, on the road to Buckhead, General Sherman was moving into Sam House's place. It seemed to him a "good house."

S. P. Richards, book dealer and choir singer, delayed writing his Sunday entry until Monday morning, after the news of Johnston's replacement had arrived:

"We have been again permitted to meet at the sanctuary for the worship of God. The enemy draws nearer and nearer tho' to our city. All of a sudden Gen. Johnston has been relieved of the command of the Army and Gen. Hood or 'Old Pegleg' as the soldiers style him placed in command, so that there is thought to be a prospect for a fight before Atlanta is given up, as Hood is said to be a fighting man, if he *has* only one leg. The ordinance of baptism was administered in our church this morning to two candidates, a lady and a deaf-mute young man."

Richards, as all others in Atlanta, wrote his diary at peril of his life. Citizens remembered the recent lynching in Montgomery, Alabama, of Jacob Starr, for keeping a diary. The irrational mob believed him a spy, taking notes for the Federals.

Colonel Beatty was considering the day's news.

"No one knows the cause of Johnston's removal," he wrote in his diary. "I am afraid it may do harm at this moment—because the army still has confidence in Johnston and does not know Hood.

"Moved camp out to Peachtree Creek later in evening. Have been ready to move all day. It is now said that the Corps commanders, including Hood, have asked the President to return the command to Johnston."

In Decatur, the day commenced "clear, bright and beautiful." There was, to Mary Gay, the freshness of May in the "pure and delightful" air.

"Blossoms of every hue and fragrance decked the landscape, and Ceres and Pomona had been as lavish with their grains and fruits as Flora had been with flowers.

"And I, assisted by Toby and Telitha, had gathered from the best of these rich offerings, and prepared a feast for Wheeler's Cavalry. By the way, strive against it as I would, I was more than once disturbed by the mental inquiry: 'What has become of Wheeler's Cavalry? I saw it enter Decatur last night, and now there is not a soldier to be seen. It is true a large number of scouts came in this morning, and spoke comforting words to my mother, and reconnoitered around town fearlessly, but what has become of them?' Hope whispered: 'Some strategic movement that will culminate in the capture of the entire Yankee army, no doubt is engaging its attention.' Yielding to these delusive reflections, and the seductive influence of earth, air and sky, I became quite exhilarated and hummed little snatches of the songs I used to sing in the happy days of childhood, before a hope had been disappointed or a shadow cast over my pathway.

"These scenes and these songs were not in keeping with the impending disasters even then at our portals. Crepe draperies and funeral dirges would have been far more in keeping with the developments of the day.

"Distant roar of cannon and sharp report of musketry spoke in language unmistakable the approach of the enemy, and the rapidity of that approach was becoming fearfully alarming. Decatur offered many advantages as headquarters to an invading devastating foe, 'and three hundred thousand men' under the guidance of a merciless foe ought to have entered it long before they did—and would have done so if their bravery had been commensurate with their vandalism.

" 'Yank! Yank!' exclaimed our deaf negro girl, Telitha, as she stroked her face as if stroking a beard, and ran to get a blue garment to indicate the color of their apparel, and this was our first intimation of their appearance in Decatur. If all the evil spirits had been loosed from Hades, and Satan himself had been turned loose upon us, a more terrific, revolting scene could not have been enacted.

"Advance guards, composed of every species of criminals ever incarcerated in the prisons of the northern states of America, swooped down upon us, and every species of deviltry followed in their footsteps. My poor mother, frightened and trembling, and myself, having locked the doors of the house, took our stand with the servants in the yard, and witnessed the grand *entre* of the menagerie. One of the beasts got down upon his all-fours and pawed up the dust and bellowed like an infuriated bull. And another asked me if I did not expect to see them with hoofs and horns. I told him, 'No, I had expected to see some gentlemen among them, and was sorry I should be disappointed.'"

She watched others kill or make off with all the chickens and ducks from the coop in back, except for one setting hen. Soon, after further reconnoitering by Federal cavalry, the main body of the army came in "like an avalanche." Mary and her mother remained outside in bright sunshine and the clouds of dust kicked up by the unbelievably vast army. There was something of the echo and menace of thunder in the pound of endless wagons, the tread of heavy boots, the clop of horses' hoofs.

Eventually, the sight of commissioned officers nerved Mary and her mother to enter the house, accompanied by Telitha. Another servant, Emmeline, annoyed Mary by becoming friendly with the army's camp followers, the bummers, or foragers.

Men of the hard-bitten Major General Kenner Garrard's 2nd Cavalry Division were now encamped over the Gay's several acres, apparently using it as their headquarters.

"Soon what appeared to us to be an immense army train of wagons commenced rolling into it," Mary observed. "In less than two hours our barn was demolished and converted into tents, which were occupied by privates and non-commissioned officers; and to the balusters of our portico and other portions of the house, were tied a number of large ropes, which, the other ends being secured to trees and shrubbery, answered as a railing to which at short intervals apart a number of smaller ropes were tied, and to these were attached horses and mules, which were eating corn and oats out of troughs improvised for the occasion out of bureau, washstand and wardrobe drawers.

"Men in groups were playing cards, on tables of every size,

and shape; and whiskey and profanity held high carnival. Thus surrounded we could but be apprehensive of danger; and to assure ourselves of as much safety as possible we barricaded the doors and windows, and arranged to sit up all night, that is, my mother and myself.

"Toby complained of being very tired, and 'hurting all over,' as he expressed it. We assisted him in making the very best pallet that could be made of the material at our command, and he lay down completely prostrated. Telitha was wide awake, and whenever she could secure a listener chattered like a magpie in unintelligible language accompanied by unmistakable gestures—gestures which an accomplished elocutionist might adopt with effect—and the burden of her heart was for Emmeline. Emmeline having repudiated our protection, had sought shelter, the Lord only knows where. Alas, poor girl!

"As we sat on a lounge, every chair having been taken to the camps, we heard the sound of footsteps entering the piazza, and in a moment loud rapping, which meant business. Going to the window nearest the door, I removed the fastenings, raised the sash, and opened the blinds. Perceiving by the light of a brilliant moon that at least a half dozen men in uniforms were on the piazza, I asked:

" 'Who is there?'

" 'Gentlemen,' was the laconic reply.

" 'If so, you will not persist in your effort to come into the house. There is only a widow and one of her daughters, and two faithful servants in it,' I said.

" 'We have orders from headquarters to interview Miss Gay. Is she the daughter of whom you speak?'

" 'She is, and I am she.'

" 'Well, Miss Gay, we demand seeing you, without intervening barriers. Our orders are imperative,' said he who seemed to be the spokesman of the delegation.

" 'Then wait a moment,' I amiably responded."

Mary returned with her mother. One of the officers introduced himself as Major J. W. Campbell.

" 'We have been told that it is your proudest boast that you are a rebel, and that you are ever on duty to aid and abet in every possible way the would-be destroyers of the United States government. If this be so, we cannot permit you to remain within our lines. Until Atlanta surrenders, Decatur will be our headquarters, and every consideration of interest to our cause requires that no one inimical to it should remain within our boundaries established by conquest.'

"In reply to these charges, I said:

" 'Gentlemen, I have not been misrepresented, so far as the charges which you mention are concerned. If I were a man, I should be in the foremost ranks of those who are fighting for rights guaranteed by the Constitution of the United States. The Southern people have never broken that compact, nor infringed upon it in any way. They have never organized mobs to assassinate any portion of the people sharing the privileges granted by that compact. They have constructed no underground railroads to bring into our midst incendiaries and destroyers of the peace, and to carry off stolen property. They have never sought to array the subordinate element of the North in deadly hostility to the controlling element. No class of the women of the South have ever sought positions at the North which secured entrance into good households, and then betrayed the confidence reposed by corrupting the servants and alienating the relations between the master and the servant. No class of the women of the South have ever mounted the rostrum and proclaimed falsehoods against the women of the North—falsehoods which must have crimsoned with shame the very cheeks of Beelzebub.

"No class of the men of the South have ever tramped over the North with humbugs, extorting money either through sympathy or credulity, and engaged at the same time in the nefarious work of exciting the subordinate class to insurrection, arson, rapine and murder. If the South is in rebellion, a well-organized mob at the North has brought it about. Long years of patient endurance accomplished nothing. The party founded on falsehood and hate strengthened and grew to enormous proportions."

Mary continued. The abashed officer, when she concluded, praised her "spunk" and said he would recommend she not be sent away from Decatur. Then Major Campbell offered to check through the house to see if the soldiers had caused any damage. In the front room they found Toby, sick, lying down on a pallet. The Major summoned a doctor.

"We now resumed our inspection of the interior of the house," Mary continued. "The contents of every drawer were on the floor, every article of value having been abstracted. Crockery scattered all over the rooms suggested to the eye that it had been used to pelt the ghosts of the witches burned in Massachusetts a century or two ago. Outrages and indignities too revolting to mention met the eye at every turn. And the state of affairs in the parlor baffled description. Not an article had escaped the destroyer's touch but the piano, and circumstances which followed proved that that was regarded as a trophy and only waited removal.

" 'Vandals! Vandals!' Major Campbell sorrowfully exclaimed, and all his friends echoed the opinion, and said:

" 'If the parties who did this work could be identified we would hang them as high as Haiman.'

"But these parties were never identified. They were important adjuncts in the process of subjugation.

"After wishing that the worst was over with us, these gentlemen, who had come in no friendly mood, bade us good night and took their leave."

That afternoon, among the sick and wounded arrivals at Atlanta was Walter A. Clark, an orderly Sergeant with Company B of the famous "Oglethorpes" (the 9th Regiment Georgia State Troops). The Augusta youth, a lawyer in civilian life, unable to recover from a smoldering illness contracted while in position along the Chattahoochee, had requested further hospitalization.

"With me there went from the division hospital to Atlanta a boy soldier, who did not seem to be over 14 years of age, and I do not think he was as tall as his gun. If not the original of Dr. Ticknor's 'Little Giffen of Tennessee,' he was certainly his counterpart for he was 'utter Lazarus, heels to head.' Atlanta was only a distributing hospital. The sick were being shipped to points on the Atlanta and West Point Road. Reports from that section were anything but favorable. Sick and wounded were said to be 'dying like sheep.' Having no special desire to die in that way or any other way, if possible, to avoid it, I asked assignment to some hospital on the Georgia Railroad.

" 'All full,' said the surgeon, 'no room anywhere except on Atlanta and West Point Road. Train leaves at 7 o'clock in the morning. Report here at that hour.' "

Sergeant Clark walked off to hunt lodgings in Atlanta.

By afternoon word of Johnston's removal reached the Newnan Hospitals.

"I knew nothing of the relative merits of the two commanders," wrote a nurse, Mrs. Fannie A. Beers, from Richmond, "and had no means of judging but by the effect upon the soldiers by whom I was then surrounded. The whole post seemed as if stricken by some terrible calamity. Convalescents walked about with lagging steps and gloomy faces. In every ward lay men who wept bitterly or groaned aloud or, covering their faces, refused to speak or eat. From that hour the buoyant, hopeful spirit seemed to die out. I do not think anything was ever the same again. For, when after the awful sacrifice of human life which followed the inauguration of the new policy, the decimated army *still* were forced to retreat, the shadow of doom began to creep slowly upon the land. The anchor of *my* soul was my unbounded confidence in President Davis; while he was at the helm I felt secure of ultimate success, and bore present ills and disappointments patiently, *never doubting*.

"Meantime, disquieting rumors were flying about, railroad communication was cut off here and there, and with it mail facilities. Of course the Confederate leaders were apprised of the movements of the Federals, but at the hospital post we were constantly on the *qui vive*. Large numbers of convalescents were daily returning to the front, among them Lieutenant Cluverius, Mr. Vaudry, and Captain Weller."

General Hood now was noting, "the evening of the 18th of July found General Johnston comfortably quartered at Macon."

Yet, out on the Marietta Road, a company of soldiers swinging by the Niles house, cheered for "Old Joe!" . . . and were sure they saw him come to the door and wave to them. Heartened, they marched down the deeply rutted pike, chorusing:

The soul of Jackson stalks abroad
And guards the camp tonight!

JULY 19

■ *The New York Herald*

"*Washington*—The latest official information from General Sherman is that his army crossed the Chattahoochee in several different places north of the railroad bridge. The movement was made with such celerity as to take the enemy by surprise; and, therefore, the resistance to his advance was feeble on the part of the rebel cavalry.

"Our cavalry was at once sent to operate on the railroad east of Decatur, one of the objects being to cut off communication between Atlanta and Augusta, thus preventing the removal of stores to the latter place, and the reinforcement of Johnston.

"Our main army was within 10 or 12 miles of Atlanta. All the operations of our army were progressing in the highest degree favorably."

"*Nashville*—The reports of the capture of Atlanta, Georgia, by our forces are all premature, though . . . we expect to hear of its capture in a few days."

Sergeant Walter Clark awoke that morning, resolved to miss the hospital train for West Point. Feeling better, he wrote:

"As I had fully determined not to go on that road I reported at 8 o'clock instead of 7, and a few hours later I was pleasantly quartered in the hospital at Oxford, Georgia, where I had spent 2 years of college life. Four years before almost to a day I had left its classic halls little dreaming that I should return to its familiar scenes in sickness and in weariness, a victim of grim-visaged war. For many months the college exercises had been suspended and the chapel, recitation and literary society halls were being utilized as hospital wards. At the time of my arrival, ladies and older citizens who had not been absorbed by the war, felt some apprehensions of a raid into the village by Sherman's cavalry which was only 40 miles away.

"Among these ladies, however, there was one to whom the expectation of such an event brought no feeling of anxiety. Born and reared in the North, she felt assured that no Union soldier's vandal hand would molest any of her possessions. Asked by one of her neighbors what she proposed to do in the event of their coming, she replied, 'they'll never trouble me or mine. I am just going to sit down and see the salvation of the Lord.' "

Clark settled into his cot in the former college chapel which also served as dining hall. Scarcely fifteen minutes' horseback ride from him, to the south, at Covington, "Grandma" Smith was uneasy. Mrs. (S. E. D.) Smith of Memphis, had nursed soldiers since the beginning of the war. She followed the armies through the South in spite of the fact that she had been semi-crippled since birth. Her twenty-year-old son, Private I. N. Smith, had been fighting with Cheatham for some time. Warned by the doctors to prepare "for the worst," Grandma Smith had little choice of action.

"Of course I had nothing to do but stand with those to whom I had pledged my fidelity," she wrote in her diary, "so long as they offered up their lives upon the altar of their country, and I contemplated myself, or my position, as being one of them, and subject to whatever suffering or hardship that they were. I tried to prepare myself to receive them, if they did get there, as patient as possible. As it had never been my sad lot to meet them in any other manner, I must confess it required all the nerve I could possibly command to be able to submit to being made prisoner by the enemies of our country. I was determined, at all events, not to attempt to play off Union, or bother with Northern principles, as (to the disgrace of the whole South), so many hundreds did in order to save their property, etc. Yet, if taken captive by them, I expected to be treated badly in consequence of the business in which I was engaged, and was endeavoring to prepare myself for the worst."

In Decatur, Mary Gay was in a state of "suspense and painful apprehension of trouble." She had spent the previous night nursing Toby with the medicine furnished by the Union army doctor.

"Measles had developed, and we felt hopeful that it would prove to be a very slight attack; and such it might have been, could we have controlled him properly, but the excitement and ever-varying scenes in the yard, and as far as vision extended, were so new and strange to him that, when unobserved, he spent much of his time at a window commanding the best view of the scene, and, thus exposed to a current of air, the disease ceased to appear on the surface and a troublesome cough ensued.

"Having been without food since the preceding morning, our thoughts turned to the usual preparation for breakfast, but, alas, those preparations had to be dispensed of, as we had nothing to prepare. This state of affairs furnished food for at least serious reflection, and the inquiry, 'What are we going to do?' found audible expression. The inexorable demands of hunger could not be stifled, and we knew that the sick boy needed hot tea and the nourishment which food alone could give, and yet we had nothing for ourselves or for him—so complete had been the robbery of the 'advance guards' of the Grand Army of the Republic, that not a thing, animate or inanimate, remained with which to appease our hunger. 'What are we to do?' was iterated and re-iterated, and no solution of the question presented itself. Even then appetizing odors from the campfires were diffusing themselves upon the air and entering our house, but aliens were preparing the food and we had no part in it. We debated this question, and firmly resolved not to expose ourselves to the jeers and insults of the enemy by any act of ours that would seem to ask for food; but that we would go to other Southern citizens in the war-stricken and almost deserted town, and, if they were not completely robbed, ask them to share their supplies with us until we could procure aid from outside of the lines so arbitrarily drawn.

"In this dilemma an unexpected relief came to us, and con-

vinced us that there was good even in Nazareth. And a large
tray, evidently well-filled, and covered with a snow-white cloth,
was brought in by an Irishman, who handed a card to my
mother containing these words:

" 'To Mrs. Stokes and daughter, Miss Gay, with compliments
of (Major) Campbell.

" 'Please accept this small testimonial of regard and respectful
sympathy.'

"The latter part of the brief message was the sesame that secured acceptance of this offering, and my mother and myself
jointly acknowledged it with sincere thanks, and again we
thought of Elijah and the ravens. The contents of the tray—
coffee, sugar, and tea, sliced ham and a variety of canned rel-
ishes, butter, potatoes, and oat-meal and bread, were removed
and the tray returned. That tray, on its humane mission, having
found its way into our house more than once, opportunely reappeared. We enjoyed the repast thus furnished, although briny
tears were mingled with it.

"The day passed without any immediate adventure. Great
activity prevailed in army ranks. The coming and going of cavalry; the clatter of sabre and spur; the constant booming of cannon and report of musketry, all convinced us that the surrender
of Atlanta by the Confederates was but a question of time. A
few thousand men, however brave and gallant, could not cope
successfully with 'three hundred thousand' who ignored every
usage of civilized warfare, and fought only for conquest."

Rumors flew easily, aimlessly, like lint in an afternoon's
breeze. "Lee," they whispered, "in Richmond, had dispatched
General Bragg or General Beauregard, with a powerful army to
the relief of Atlanta. Maybe Lee was coming himself."

"The tide had turned before Petersburg, and General Grant
had fallen."

"Sherman was drawing back, his army demoralized."

Yet, wrong as her assessment was of the Union strength, Mary
Gay, for one, realized that wishing could not make it so. Rumors,
even on second evaluation, all proved not only as prevalent but
as transitory as lint in the air.

In General Sherman's camp there was no time for listening to

gossip, encouraging or otherwise. That afternoon, for example, small, cocky Captain Lewis M. Dayton, aide-de-camp, was transmitting Number 39 of the Commander's Special Field Orders: "Headquarters, Military Division of the Mississippi
In the Field near Decatur, Ga.

"If fired on from the forts or buildings of Atlanta, no consideration must be paid to the fact that they are occupied by families but the place must be cannonaded without the formality of a demand.

         By order of Major General W. T. Sherman."

General Hood moved into the L. Windsor Smith house on Whitehall Street near Hunter, by evening. It was known as the "finest wooden building in the city." His junior officers were not at all surprised that their young leader, now that he had successfully intrigued for power, would commandeer an ostentatious G.H.Q.

They only marveled that he had not dispossessed the Rawsons from their immeasurably lovely "Terraces."

Once settled, he began dictating a grapeshot volley of orders, having first solemnly assured Richmond as well as his staff of his "readiness to fulfill the grave orders devolving upon me."

At midnight, as the confident, wooden-legged general continued to boom memoranda and orders, a fire broke out in downtown Atlanta. The origin was uncertain although, as everyone knew, the blaze could not have been caused by shelling. Enemy artillery was not within range.

The sound of firebells awoke the residents of the city. Window curtains were drawn open, one by one. General Hood continued to dictate in the L. Windsor Smith house. Soon, it began to rain.

JULY 20

◆ *Southern Press Association*

"*Atlanta*—The enemy made strong demonstrations yesterday and this morning on our right near Decatur. Gen. Hood attacked their right at 4 o'clock this afternoon on Peach Tree Creek near the Chattahoochee. In a few minutes the enemy were driven into their works. The colors of the 83rd New Jersey and about 800 prisoners were captured from Hooker's corps. Our loss was not heavy; mostly slightly wounded. Brig. Gen. Stevens, of South Carolina, was wounded, it is feared mortal. Major Preston, formerly of Gen. Johnston's staff, was killed.

"There was some skirmishing on our right where the enemy attacked our entrenchments. After being repulsed, our cavalry, under Gen. Wheeler, drove them with repeated charges towards Decatur.

"Yesterday evening, Reynolds' (Arkansas) brigade, which crossed Peach Tree Creek, drove the enemy back, taking two stands of colors and 130 prisoners.

"Our troops are in fine spirits tonight."

It was a cloudy, sultry Wednesday. S. P. Richards was in his store early. He wanted to see if the fire which had destroyed McPherson's store and several other establishments across the street the night before, had in any way damaged his books, magazines, music sheets, and stationery.

A twenty-nine-year-old sergeant from Dover, Ohio, with Company A, 124th Regiment, Ohio Volunteers, Andrew K. Rose, was camped in a field "close to city," and today he "picked blueberries." He neglected to make the weather entry he had diaried day by day during the war.

To William Graham of the 53rd Illinois Volunteers, it was "cloudy at daylight." After coming into camp at 6:00 A.M. the sergeant was "near 8 on the march. Formed line of battle with the 16th Iowa in front. Marched through a piece of woods by

our right flank and finally found ourselves in front of the
enemy. Here we lay behind a fence which we made in temporary breastwork. We lay here probably half an hour, while a
battery shelled the woods opposite.

"Finally we were ordered forward and advanced through a
cornfield and into and through a piece of woods, then through
another open space of ground with a ditch and up a hill to a
fence which we crossed and formed a line of battle with the
16th Iowa on our left, the 32d Ohio on our right and the 90th
Iowa in the rear of the 32d."

Shortly before noon, Er Lawshe, of Atlanta, was crossing Ivy
and East Ellis streets, past the home of H. Muhlenbrink, owner
of the Saloon and Ten-Pin Alley, on Whitehall Street. Other
residences at this intersection, five blocks northeast of Five
Points, belonged to John Collier the attorney, Frank P. Rice
the lumber dealer, and to the Schenck Brothers, machinists at
Winship's Iron Works.

The day had become humid. Lawshe mopped his brow as he
hurried along, noticing as he did so a small girl and her parents
walking by Rice's place, on the northwest corner, directly opposite him. He did not recognize the trio and assumed them to
be refugees.

Suddenly, there was a rattle and whish of air just over his
head. In the next instant, he was deafened and stunned by an
explosion and enveloped in a choking cloud of dust. When he
could see again, the child was in the middle of the intersection,
lying on her face, in a welling puddle of blood. Her mother and
father, dazed, were struggling to their feet.

Lawshe gaped, finding it difficult to believe the first shell had
fallen on Atlanta, and that he had been but yards away from it.
When he reached the little girl's side, he could see she was
dead.

Other citizens were hastening towards the intersection of Ivy
and East Ellis, attracted by the blast and the brown cloud of
dust and smoke now slowly dissipating over the rooftops.

On the other side of Atlanta, Mollie Smith, a young lady,
heard the shell explode. One of her brothers said:

"What a big gun!" and another brother, who was present at the Battle of Manassas, said,

"That is a shell. They are going to bombard the city."

Andy Neal, now in Atlanta, wrote in a letter:

"I just sent a box by express to your address at Griffin containing the overcoat I got from home last winter. Army is again in motion and the prospects are fine for warm work soon. We have been digging dirt for twenty four hours and have good substantial works. The Yankees have crossed the river, frightened away the cavalry and are making a noise some eight hundred yards in front with our skirmishers. The general staff officers and couriers are dashing about furiously as if they expected the Yankees this evening but I have no idea they will make an attack. I hear they are already on a big flank by way of Decatur. I never felt that Atlanta would be given up without a fight until lately. If the enemy will press on now I fear our Army will fall back to East Point.

"I had a full history of the removal of Gen. Johnston this morning from one of Cheatham's Brigadiers who is an old friend and schoolmate at the University of Virginia and at the Lebanon Law School. President Davis has been wanting Johnston to give battle ever since he crossed the Etowah and thinks he could have offered it at Dallas and New Hope. Johnston would not divulge his plans to the President but told him he intended to fight at the first opportunity. As soon as Johnston crossed the Chattahoochee it was resolved to relieve him from command of the Army. Hood was placed at the head because Hardee had refused command at Dalton last winter and the President was incensed at it. The change was very unexpected in the army and deeply regretted but I cannot regard it as calamity. Johnston has never stood well with the Administration and he has obtained no favors in this campaign. With an Army of little over 50,000 of all arms he has had to confront a host of 150,000. Since the appointment of Hood I think the Administration will feel bound to sustain him and their own honor and capacity being involved will do everything to sustain him. Forrest will now go to the enemy's rear and if necessary Mississippi be given up. Dick Taylor will be ordered up and

all but most necessary communications be sacrificed till the
enemy be expelled. I heard that Bragg was dissatisfied with the
conduct of the campaign in Virginia and it is predicted he will
be relieved from duty. Lee has 5,000 men more than Grant
according to Gen. Bragg and ought not to have been acting on
the defensive but driven the enemy back. Polk's Corps captured
some 250 prisoners at dark yesterday without a fight."

Word was received that General Johnston had arrived in
Macon and joined his family at the home of Major General
Howell Cobb. He would not comment to a newspaper reporter
on future plans.

By afternoon, fighting erupted along the Peachtree stream on
the northern outskirts of Atlanta. One Confederate soldier,
W. P. Archer, believed the Southerners had surprised the Yankees at mealtime, as he wrote:

"The Battle of Peachtree Creek was on good and strong. At
first the Federals seemed demoralized and panic-stricken and
everything seemed to favor the Confederates, but this situation
did not last long, for just over beyond the creek lay thousands
of bluecoats, who came sweeping down like a thunderbolt upon
the thin lines of Hood's Confederates. For two hours and thirty
minutes the battle raged."

And Sergeant William Graham, after laying down his knapsack, joined in the "charge over an open field through a low
piece of woods bottom then up a hill upon the enemy, which
had two pieces of artillery which limbered up and left in a
hurry. There we established ourselves by throwing up rails and
hitting below the border of the hill. Upon the hill was a house
of hewn logs by the side of which our skirmishers took post and
were firing upon the enemy when General Gershon came up
and was wounded in the leg before he reached the house after
which he was taken off. We commenced making our works secure by throwing up dirt."

E. B. Fenton of the 20th Connecticut Volunteer Infantry
was in the core of the fighting:

"Four times during that afternoon the rebels tried to carry
our line but were as often sent reeling back. From 3 o'clock
until 8 we stood with no cover, and without assistance or relief,

and yet maintained our position and repulsed every assault of the enemy. In front of us were found the dead and wounded of the 23rd, 44th and 55th Mississippi Regiments who had been brought against our regiment, which itself sustained a loss of nearly half its officers and men.

"The first attempt of Gen. Hood to show the rebel army 'how to fight instead of how to retreat' resulted in a loss on his part of more than 6,000 men."

W. P. Archer was among the defenders who retreated into the main line of fortifications north of Atlanta, "leaving our dead and wounded, besides those who were missing, also leaving our rifle-pits in possession of the enemy."

Fenton was seriously wounded himself:

"The roar and crash of battle ceased; the sulphurous smoke had cleared away, but how strange the scenes about us! The plains and hillsides were strewn with corpses of men where they fell. The dead and dying were lying close together, where a few short hours before all was excitement—the excitement of many a brave comrade's last battle—now an oppressive silence prevails; there is the groaning and the crying of the wounded. In quiet tones we speak to each other. The question passes back and forth, 'where are you wounded?'

" 'Through the body.'

" 'And you?'

" 'An arm broken.'

" 'My knee smashed with a piece of shell,' or

" 'A minie bullet through the foot . . .'

". . . so the low replies pass around.

"Words of cheer are spoken. While over the faces of some the strange, pale look is coming that betokens the approach of death.

"One lies near who has always been jolly and full of fun in the ranks, but now jesting is forgotten. A few feet away lies an officer—lately promoted—the smile still on his face, so suddenly had the bullet cut the thread of life.

"The ambulance corps with their stretchers were kept busy. The hospital tent was full of the wounded."

Fenton thought this the end for "weary marches, sleepless

nights, battle, danger and death," but a beginning where "surgeons held court supreme."

Captain J. P. Austin, of the 9th Kentucky Cavalry, who had once served with Colonel John H. Morgan's raiders, galloped into Atlanta in the early evening. His horse was dirty and sweaty, but he was unhurt. He wrote home:

"Our army fell back to Atlanta under a heavy fire from the enemy's batteries, located to the left of the Peachtree road.

"We found the city in a wild state of excitement. Citizens were running in every direction. Terror-stricken women and children went screaming about the streets seeking some avenue of escape from hissing, bursting shells, as they sped on their mission of death and destruction. Perfect pandemonium reigned near the Union Depot. Trunks, bedclothing and wearing apparel were scattered in every direction. People were stirring in every conceivable way to get out of town with their effects."

Austin, who had been captured after Shiloh and imprisoned for several months, listened to stories he thought exaggerated. One man avowed that Sherman "had the plan of every bridge along the line and whenever our men would destroy any one of them he would have it duplicated without delay."

At 10:00 P.M. Andy Neal, of Atlanta, was postscripting his letter, started earlier, before mailing it:

"We have had some sharp fighting on the lines today resulting I fear in no good to us. I had heard of some successes but most places we failed to accomplish anything. Cheatham and Cleburne Divisions moved out and attacked the enemy in force. They succeeded in driving them handsomely for over half a mile till they came to the main lines strongly entrenched."

Into the night the city was alive with noise—men and women shouting and hurrying, and the rumble of wagons bearing the wounded. Many Federals were taken to the Atlanta Medical College, where Dr. D'Alvigny had operated continuously from mid-afternoon.

The merchants who remained redoubled their efforts to move families and stocks south, but no wagons were available. Some, such as W. B. Young and his two thousand sewing machines, had scant prospects of ever liquidating.

Sergeant Graham, of Illinois, worked "until nearly midnight and then lay down to rest, while our skirmishers kept up firing all night."

No one slept in Atlanta.

JULY 21

■ *The New York Herald*

"*Louisville, Kentucky*—On Monday morning, Decatur, Georgia was occupied by our forces, thus cutting off all rebel communication with South Carolina by way of Macon.

"Deserters and stragglers had been coming into our lines in great numbers since we crossed the Chattahoochee. They represent that all hope of saving Atlanta has disappeared."

■ *The Norfolk New Regime*

"*Fortress Montore, July 18, via Baltimore, July 19*—We have information from the front that a great battle has been fought in Georgia resulting in the complete overthrow of the Confederate force, the capture of Atlanta and 15,000 Rebel prisoners. Three cheers for Sherman."

■ *The National Republican* (Washington)

"The Government received dispatches from General Sherman this morning announcing that the enemy assaulted the Union lines three times yesterday, and was repulsed each time with little loss to us.

"Most of our men fought behind earth works, hence the small loss, but the enemy coming out of the defences of the city to offer battle, became more exposed and suffered greater loss."

■ *The New York Herald*

"*Nashville*—Reports have been received from General Sherman at the front and state that General Johnston yesterday

moved out from Atlanta and attacked the left wing of his army
at Decatur. The assault was made with great vigor and desperation and resulted in a most bloody repulse. Johnston's army,
therefore, retired again to its works. It is not known yet whether
the attack was made to cover a retreat by way of the Macon
roads or was intended as a rally with the hope of defeating us."
                    (Mr. W. F. G. Shanks, correspondent)

✕ *Southern Press Association*

"*Atlanta*—Reynolds' brigade attacked the enemy's line of skirmishers last evening at Peach Tree Creek, and took possession
of their entrenchments. He then charged the reserve pickets,
supported by Dilworth's corps, and captured one hundred and
fifty prisoners.

"The 85th Illinois regiment lost in killed and wounded alone
one hundred, while that of the 69th Ohio was severe."

For E. B. Fenton of the 20th Connecticut Volunteers, and the
other wounded of Peachtree Creek, a "long and weary night,"
was lightening into another hot day.

"In the early dawn," he wrote in his diary, "as we begin to
distinguish our comrades here and there, we speak to them.
Some of them answer with feebler voices than before, and some
are silent forever, having entered their last sleep in this night.

"The sun rises, and another day wears on, the living among
the dead, wounds are growing sorer and more painful, cries
begin to be heard from those whose wounds are in the body and
very serious. One poor fellow, an Irishman, lay near to me, so
badly wounded that the surgeon exclaimed, shaking his head,

" 'There is no hope whatever of saving this man, he cannot
possibly live.'

"An ugly wound in the head and a shattered hand told the
sad story."

But for Sergeant William Graham, of Illinois, Thursday was
a "bright morning," and after breakfast "whilst lying behind
our works I discovered some intimations of an intent upon our
part to make a charge upon the enemy works a half mile away.

"Presently we saw Leggett's division, the 3rd charging into
two lines. They went up in a gallant style and when near the

woods we were ordered over ours and forward on the double quick . . . our men were beginning to fall fast and were met by heavy fire of the small arms. Our color bearer was wounded in the thigh but they were again reused by our other bearer. We lost 60 killed and wounded and finally all had to retire in squads of 8 and 10 at a time and regain our works. There we lay for some time and finally relieved by another regiment and marched to the left of the lines. About 4 o'clock were sent on picket duty to the rear. A heavy shower took place at 5 or 6 o'clock. In the engagement today our sergeant Major Orrin Bull was killed, Captain Krause of the Co. I was mortally wounded. Also Lt. Gilmore Co. I was badly wounded. Private Granby of V. Co. was killed and Private Sanborn K Co. wounded and Sgt. J. J. Woods, color bearer of the regiment wounded in the thigh."

Action swirled around the Ponder House, off the Marietta Road, little more than a mile and a half from the center of the city. Another chapter was thereby written in the tragedy of the mansion Ephraim G. Ponder built for his beautiful bride, Ellen.

Its boxwood and fruit trees, landscaped gardens, and graveled paths once were equaled only by Rawson's "Terraces" on Pryor Street. The elegant two-story house was built of stone and surfaced with white plaster. Outbuildings, spread over one hundred acres, included an attached brick kitchen and quarters for sixty-five slaves, all of them trained mechanics and virtually free.

But Ephraim, broken hearted, left Atlanta in 1863, and filed for divorce. He charged the lovely Ellen with drunkenness and adultery. The slaves themselves recounted in confidence the "illegitimate pleasures" of their mistress, the high-pitched laughter ringing from the darkened mansion late at night, sometimes shadowy, half-naked figures moving past the opened windows on a hot summer's evening.

Ellen fled with her slaves to Macon in the spring. The house began to look cursed. The weeds grew in a tangle over the flower beds, and the evening breezes whined their lament through windows which young boys had broken with stones . . . but beyond this neglected, "haunted" estate began the infinity of gentle hills, the softer, sweeter country aromas replacing the muddy, dusty, brick-city smells.

Ponder's house was fortified just in time. The second floor bristled with snipers, as did the widow's walk. Spiked fortifications of wood, or *chevaux-de-frise*, rambled like ugly rows of porcupines over the lawns which once had nourished privet hedges. Intricate trenchwork, boarded and sand-bagged, roamed the length and breadth of the estate, all of which was now under assault by Major General John W. Geary.

Further slaughter, W. P. Archer, an Atlanta soldier, testified, was caused by the well on the estate:

"It was here at this terrible place that John Shropshire, brother of ex-Deputy Sheriff Andrew J. Shropshire, was killed while at the Ponder House well getting water, he making the 27th man that had been killed at this well. The roof and curbing around the top of this well was literally perforated with minie balls. John Shropshire was a prince of a fellow but he had his life shot out of him in an effort to obtain water for his comrades who were suffering in the ditches, as he had as many as a dozen canteens strapped on him when he was killed. It was risk your life or perish for water."

The house was blasted and blasted again as the day wore on. Jagged chunks of masonry were chewed out of the second-floor walls. The defenders perished within, and others took their place. Even thirty-pound Parrott shells were lobbed at the big target, leaving huge holes. Somehow, the mansion stood even after the wooden slave quarters were burned and riddled into gaunt skeletons.

The sharpshooters (many of whom were from Atlanta and remembered the gossip about Ellen Ponder) speculated, between lulls in the battle, on how many tons of shot and shell were accumulating within their uncertain fortress.

Three miles further west, off the Sandtown Road, near Willis' Mill and Dr. Wilson's place, Joseph Willis, with the help of neighbors, Laban Helm and William White, finished a project —an immense dugout in the rear of his farmhouse. He had reinforced the earth walls with timbers, and furnished the interior with a table, chairs, and mattresses. He provisioned it as best he could with non-perishables; the mill pond a few yards outside of the shelter entrance would provide water.

With Hood's army strongly entrenched on a ridge to the east, the Federal 14th Army Corps plainly in view on a parallel ridge to the west, and bullets and shells already whistling overhead, Willis decided it was time to crawl below.

He collected his wife and six children, White, his wife and two daughters, Helm, his wife and little boy, plus eleven others from the neighborhood who ran across the fields at the last minute—and all twenty-six of them filed into the dugout. Willis pushed timbers across the doorway as the sound of battle swelled in volume, petulantly.

In Atlanta, residents considered similar protection. Those with cellars felt safe. Others started to spade up small hollows in back yards which they called, simply, "gopher holes."

In Decatur, General Garrard was meeting with his staff officers in Mary Gay's parlor. She wrote in her notes:

"The teamsters and army followers were lounging about promiscuously, cursing and swearing and playing cards, and seeming not to notice the approaching artillery until their attention was called to it, and then they contended that it was their men firing off blank cartridges. I intuitively felt that a conflict was on hand. Ma and I held whispered conversations and went from one window to another, and finally rushed into the yard. Men in the camps observed our excitement and said, 'Don't be alarmed, it is only the men firing off their blank cartridges.'

"The irony of fate was never more signally illustrated than on this occasion. I would have laid down my life, yea, a thousand breathing, pulsing lives of my own, to have witnessed the overthrow of the Yankee army, and, yet, I may have been the means of saving a large portion of it on that occasion. Dreading, for my mother's sake and for the sake of the deaf girl and the sick boy, an attack upon the forces which covered our grounds, I ran to one of the parlor doors and knocked heavily and excitedly. An officer unlocked the door and opening it said:

" 'What is it?'

" 'Our men must be nearly here,' I replied.

" 'Impossible,' he said, and, yet, with a bound he was in the

yard, followed in quick succession by each member of the con-
clave.

"A signal, long, loud and shrill, awakened the drowsy, and
scattered to the four-winds of heaven cards, books and papers,
and in a few minutes horses and mules were hitched to wagons,
and the mules, wagons and men were fairly flying from the approach of the Confederates. Women and children came pouring
in from every direction and the house was soon filled. Before
Garrard's wagon train was three hundred yards away, our yard
was full of our men—our own dear 'Johnnie Rebs.' Oothcaloga
Valley boys, whom I had known from babyhood, kissed, in passing, the hand that waved the handkerchief. An officer, ah, how
grand he looked in gray uniform, came dashing up and said:

" 'Go in your cellar and lie down, the Federals are forming
a line of battle, and we, too, will form one that will reach across
these grounds, and your house will be between the two lines.
Go at once.'

"My mother ran and got Toby's shoes and put them on for
him, and told him to get up and come with her, and as he went
out of the house, tottering, I threw a blanket over him, and he
and Telitha went with ma to our near neighbor, Mrs. Williams,
her cellar being considered safer than ours. I remained in our
house for the two-fold purpose of taking care of it, if possible,
and of protecting, to the best of my ability, the precious women
and children who had fled to us for protection. Without thought
of myself I got them all into the room that I thought would be
safest, and urged them to lie down upon the floor and not to move
during the battle. Shot and shell flew in every direction, and
the shingles on the roof were following suit, and the leaves, and
the limbs, and the bark of the trees were descending in showers
so heavy as almost to obscure the view of the contending forces.
The roaring of cannon and the sound of musketry blended in
harmony so full and so grand and the scene was so absorbing that
I thought not of personal danger, and more than once found
myself outside of the portals ready to rush into the conflict—for
was I not a soldier, enlisted for the war?

"Nor was I the only restless, intrepid person in the house on
that occasion. An old lady in whose veins flowed the blood of

the Washingtons was there, and it was with the greatest difficulty that I restrained her from going out in the arena of warfare. The traditions of her ancestors were so interwoven with her life, that, at an age bordering on four-score years and ten, they could not relax their hold upon her; and she and I might have gone in opposite directions had we fled to the ranks of the contending armies.

"Mine was, no doubt, the only feminine eye that witnessed the complete rout of the Federals on that occasion. At first I could not realize what they were doing, and feared some strategic movement; but the 'rebel yell' and the flying blue coats brought me to a full realization of the situation, and I, too, joined in the loud acclaim of victory. And the women and children, until now panic-stricken and silent as death, joined in the rejoicing. All the discouragements of the past few weeks fled from me, and hope revived, and I was happy, oh, so happy!"

Sherman's intelligence reports that afternoon included one from Major General George H. Thomas, commanding the Army of the Cumberland, "prisoners say that our shells yesterday fell into Atlanta, producing great consternation."

At 7:00 P.M. Sergeant Andy Rose of Ohio, recorded "a little rain shower."

All evening Atlanta throbbed with a massive army operation pounding through its heart. Some of the soldiers said they were with Lieutenant General William J. Hardee whose entire corps was being hauled out of the Peachtree line for a mysterious night march to the east.

After the shower the evening became hot and still. Soldiers discarded blankets and coats as they trudged through the streets. Little children picked up the garments and ran off, squealing with delight. The vast activity was puzzling, as Wallace P. Reed the Atlanta writer, observed:

"The citizens were unable to fully understand the situation. The movements of troops had but little significance to them, because they knew nothing of what was transpiring beyond the breastworks. It was impossible for a civilian to obtain trustworthy information. That fierce fighter, Hood, was in command, and the non-combatant who dared to question him ran considerable risk of being hustled off to the trenches. The subordinate officers and soldiers had but one reply to make to all questions. They said that the policy of falling back had been abandoned. Sherman had been drawn far enough into the interior, and his men were to be slaughtered like sheep as they threw themselves upon the impregnable defences of the Gate City."

It was nearly midnight before the last of Hardee's corps vanished into the gloom past Oakland Cemetery and out the Decatur road. Only a faint hint of dust, the smell of sweaty men, and the acrid, ever-present stench of horses lingered to whisper of the evening's march.

JULY 22

✉ *Southern Press Association*

"*Atlanta*—About two o'clock this afternoon the enemy attacked our left, under Gen. Stewart, with great vigor. They were received with a galling fire from both artillery and infantry which caused them to falter, when the order was given to charge.

"Our troops left their breastworks and charged with great gallantry, driving the enemy from two lines of entrenchments and inflicting immense slaughter, capturing a large number of prisoners and twenty-two pieces of artillery.

"Among their killed is Gen. McPherson, who was shot through the heart, Brigadier Gen. Giles A. Smith and (the Yankee) Gen. Hood. Gen. Gresham lost a leg.

"Gen. Hardee having passed around the enemy's flank is now in their rear doing great execution.

"The fighting still continues. . . .

"Gen. Wheeler last evening attacked the enemy's left in neighborhood of Decatur and drove them back, capturing two hundred wagons, with supplies and a large number of prisoners. He is still pursuing."

■ *The New York Herald*

"Nashville—A lady who left Atlanta a week ago describes the stampede of the citizens from that city on the approach of General Sherman's army to the Chattahoochee River as ludicrous in the extreme. She says there was greater panic there than that which prevailed in Tennessee on the fall of Fort Donelson.

"4:00 P.M.—Despatches to private parties state that Atlanta was this morning occupied by General Sherman's forces, and that General Thomas' headquarters are in that city. This statement is credited in official circles and I think no doubt need be entertained in regard to it."

"Washington, 10:00 P.M.—Reports have been rife today that Atlanta has been captured by General Sherman. Up to this time such is not the case; but the Government are in receipt of information that Johnston has been superseded by General Hood, who had been bloodily repulsed in an attack upon Sherman's lines. The final capture of the city cannot be much longer delayed.

"The battle between the two armies was very severe and bloody and the defeat of the rebels most complete."

■ *The New York Tribune*

Office of the Associated Press, New York—The Western Union Telegraph Company are in communication with Atlanta, Georgia, today, messages from that place of this date having been transmitted over their wires.

"No official announcement of the capture of occupation of Atlanta has been received at this office up to this hour, 3:30 P.M."

S. P. Richards, stationer and diarist, had not slept. Although it was Friday, and not Sunday, he wrote in his diary:

"All last night our city was in a complete hub-bub with army wagons and soldiers and marauders as though the whole army

was passing through. A lot of cavalry robbers broke into the
stores and stole everything that they took a fancy to. They
stripped our store of paper and other stationery that we had
there, and about thirty dollars of money. Today our last newspaper departed, the *Appeal,* also the Postoffice, and every other
establishment and individual that intended to go, as the enemy
was confidently expected to take possession tonight."

Near the army's warehouses at East Point, Supply Officer
Joe Semmes, wrote to "Eo":

"Our communications have been cut as I foretold you and
this is a chance just offered to write you. Before day this morning we evacuated Atlanta but left the Army in line of battle
around the city and in fact *in it*—a terrible battle is raging at
and around Atlanta and our unfortunate relatives Mr. Clayton,
Cousin Caroline and the three sick girls, one ("Gussy") at the
point of death, and the smaller children are compelled to remain in the midst of it. God grant they may none be killed, but
the enemy have full range of the town and I dread the worst.
The girls were too ill to be moved and they all determined to
stand by them to the last. Such is one of the horrors of this
infernal war. The town is left full of women and children and
old men—many too of our wounded, too badly hurt to be removed.

"Day before yesterday we fought them and drove them to the
works. Dawson carried his regiment over the Yankee breastworks and within 75 yards of their main works, which he
could have carried, but was not supported on his line; he lost
45 men. Mr. Turley's son was wounded but is safe. Hardee
moved at two this morning to the rear of the enemy, and if
successful Atlanta is saved, if not the Lord knows what will become of this Army.

"My last was written on Sunday, enclosing a letter from Mrs.
Titus, saying that Alden told her to tell you, he had money
sent by Genl. Dix for you. I don't want you to send for it. I
am well considering I have been up nearly all three nights at
hard work. God Bless you, J.

"I write on my lap in the woods. Major Preston whose family
were so kind to Clara and Julia is killed."

Some blocks north of Semmes, at East Point, W. P. Archer broke camp with his outfit at daylight and marched to the Fair Ground for provisioning, "a small ration of hard tack and sow belly, and a water bucket full of bourbon whiskey, with a small tin dipper to dip it with on the side.

"About 8 o'clock we had orders to move hurriedly due north until the road leading out to the old Atlanta Rolling Mill was reached, and to form along the road.

"When we had reached this point our command formed on both sides of the road. While in this position, Claiborn's (Cleburne) division of Hardee's corps passed, and here I wish to say that in all my experience I never saw a more graceful rider astride a horse, or a grander looking man than Pat Claiborn. . . . when Claiborn's command had passed us we were ordered to fall in behind them. When the old rolling mill had been reached our command was ordered to deploy to the right. Claiborn's division kept straight on in the direction of where the Yanks were tearing up the Georgia Railroad, between Atlanta and Decatur. Our command went in rather a southeast direction. We had not gone a great way until the rattle of musketry told us that the fight was on. Our command soon came to an old pine field . . . here we had come in range of their guns. Minie balls were rattling like hail up among the pines, cutting off limbs and twigs everywhere. Occasionally a shell or solid shot would come screaming through the pines like so many wild animals.

"Here we were ordered to lie flat down on the ground, as every shell seemed to be hunting for us, as they came lower and lower . . . About one hundred yards from where we were in the old pine field was a piece of cleared land about one hundred yards wide, inclining towards the east. At the lower side of this strip of land was a good set of entrenchments, with no soldiers in them, and the plan was to fill up this vacancy with our command. On double-quicking through this open space into the works, we lost five men, killed outright, and several wounded, and about the same ratio throughout the regiment."

To their left was a battery of four or more cannons worked

by Captain Francis DeGress of Illinois, taking heavy toll of the Confederates. The 42nd Georgia Regiment planned to knock it out. The command was given, and the regiment stormed across the fields towards the rapid-firing cannons. Archer continued his account:

"When they had advanced to a certain point the Confederates raised the Rebel yell and charged bayonets right on to the battery. The fighting was terrific; hand to hand fighting, with butts of their guns, etc., was general around the battery. Finally the men who commanded the guns, routed and panic-stricken, fled and left their guns in the hands of the victorious Forty-second Georgia. But General Logan, who commanded a division of Western Federals, on hearing of the loss of their fine battery, addressed his men, telling them that it never would do to let Washington hear that the Rebels had their fine battery; to follow him, that he would retake it. Over behind a large clump of woods his division formed, and at the command charge, they came like a storm above the thunder of artillery and the rattle of musketry. You could hear the Yankee battle cry, 'Husa! Husa!' etc. Astride a fine dapple gray horse, with hat in hand he led his men.

"Time and time again the little band of Confederates stood their ground, repulsing the blue lines of Logan's Federals, only to see them rally again, and come with more men than ever. Finally after desperate hand to hand fighting, three or four to one, the Confederates had to give up and get away as best they could, leaving the guns again in the hands of the victorious Logan. How Gen. Logan escaped that day has always been a mystery to me. I guess his time had not come. During the fighting General McPherson, while out on his horse reconnoitering, came too close to a bunch of Confederates, who occupied a clump of bushes.

"General McPherson, on riding out into the open, not more than one hundred yards away, was discovered by the Confederates, who began to yell at the top of their voices, 'shoot the man on the horse!' "

Major General James B. McPherson, thirty-six-year-old commander of the Army of the Tennessee, wheeled too late. He fell, pierced through the heart.

A Confederate leader, Major General W. H. T. Walker, division head of General Hardee, was killed a few minutes later. He was on a rise of ground, studying the battlefield through a telescope. His men rallied for a bayonet charge as the Rebel yell blended with the Yankee "Husa! Husa!" It was a primitive, savage chorus.

The Union forces were in "great confusion," Colonel Taylor Beatty, of Louisiana, decided, and that "if we could have held our position it would have been an utter rout."

A "good many" shells were exploding around Beatty in the city and he marveled at the number of people remaining through the day's bombardment, especially the women.

"About 4 o'clock we heard heavy firing," S. P. Richards wrote, "and rapid discharges of musketry to the eastward, and, before dark, crowds of prisoners began to come in that our forces had taken in a successful flank movement by Gen. Hardee. It then began to appear likely that Gen. Hood intended to hold the city if he could."

Colonel Barnett, aide to Hood, conveyed orders all afternoon at informal headquarters which had been established in the hot glare of the July sun—next to a park near the general's house. Barnet noted in his diary:

"We dragged out tables and chairs and the General directed the battle by couriers who rode out Hunter Street. Colonel Hamilton brought the news Gen. William H. T. Walker was killed.

"I ascended the cupola of the City Hall and heard the bullets whizz by. A shell burst in the street and narrowly missed Major A. J. West. I soon saw we had lost the battle."

Several times Hood rode his horse as far as a hillock on the Lucius J. Gartrell estate, where he could see smoke puffs from the distant battleground—and, farther east, to Oakland Cemetery.

The rattle of small-arms fire crackled so distinctly throughout Atlanta that Wallace P. Reed, the young writer, believed "the forces were butchering each other on Whitehall Street." Cour-

iers dashed back and forth to Hood's street-table headquarters
with "a bright, exultant look," announcing:

"We've got em . . . whipping them like hell . . . we'll capture
Sherman's whole army!"

The onlookers cheered, and "a few score citizens lounged
about the place," Reed continued, "watching the iron face of
the general in the vain hope of reading his thoughts. Suddenly
the park was invaded by the hospital corps. Long tables were
stretched out, and a crowd of professional looking men in uniform took charge of them and commenced opening their cases
of instruments. They were surgeons. It was not long before
ambulances and wagons rolled into the park by the dozen, and
the wounded were hastily taken out and placed upon the tables.
After that it was cut and slash, for the work had to be done in
a hurry.

"The green grass took on a blood-red hue, and as the surgeon's saw crunched through the bones of the unfortunates,
hundreds of gory arms and legs were thrown into the baskets
prepared to receive them. This ghastly sight was too much for
the citizen lookers on. They had seen one phase of the horrors
of war, and they cared to see no more. One by one they disappeared, and soon the park was given up to the surgeons and
their patients, the grim general meanwhile awaiting the returns
a few yards away.

"When the engagement was over the people had a very confused idea of what had occurred. They knew that the city had
not been captured. They saw large squads of Federal prisoners
marched in. They were told that McPherson had been killed.
With these facts to guide them, it is little wonder that they
jumped to the conclusion that the Confederates had won a big
victory, and some of the most sanguine predicted that Sherman
would beat a retreat. Perhaps for the first time since Johnston's
removal, the non-combatants felt thoroughly satisfied with Hood.
They had found out that he would fight, and how could there
be any doubt as to the result when the men in gray were pitted
against the men in blue?

"The rattle of musketry had died away. The groaning
wounded had been carried to the hospitals, and the prisoners

had been disposed of. Once more the civil life of the city was astir."

Sergeant Graham, of Illinois, was on picket duty, and "very fatigued from yesterday's doings. . . . The enemy was seen in squads about a half mile away from our hospitals and they commenced moving the wounded back to the rear. About 6 o'clock afterwards we were attacked by the enemy and driven in. They attacked with heavy fire and we had a hard day's work. General McPherson was killed. I do not know our losses at present. Many of our regiment is missing. F. Coffeen killed Co. I— Sigler wounded Co. A. Our right was in the squad of 5 or 8 men and came in the best they could and at night but half the regiment was collected. We lay back in a temporary breastwork all night on a hill. The enemy was badly beaten, but we lost many good officers as well as men."

O. L. Braumuller, the eleven-year-old son of a music store proprietor, lived next to Hood's headquarters on Whitehall Street. He had been alone with his mother since his father was in Nashville, trying to sell Tennessee bonds (and drums he had been manufacturing for the army).

That Friday, he recalled, was "the hottest day I believe I ever saw. We could hear the firing around the city, and occasionally got a few tidings of the battle from soldiers passing."

The house had been struck once, and young Braumuller figured the Federals were aiming at Hood's headquarters. A dugout had been completed in the back yard and he and his mother planned to spend the nights in it.

Mollie Smith, a young Atlanta resident, watched a young lady of the neighborhood, who had died in the morning, being buried in her garden. There was no coffin. The family feared to journey to the cemetery because of the shelling. All through the burial, Mollie heard the firing and occasionally, she thought, a Rebel yell.

The Federals, meanwhile, were advancing on Covington. "Grandma" Smith, the nurse from Memphis, was told that Conyer's station, ten miles north, was already captured and aflame. She climbed the dome atop her hospital and saw the distant smoke spiraling up from the burning buildings at Conyer's.

Two hours later, a young girl helper ran excitedly to her, shouting that "blue coats" were entering Covington at full gallop.

"I looked a little to the left of where I stood and sure enough here come some half a dozen dashing up, as though they intended to sweep everything before them. In the meantime orders had been distributed throughout the hospital for every one to save themselves as best they could; and if ever I saw what is called pell-mell I saw it there and then. Every one who could walk broke for the pine thicket.

"Some did not stop under five miles, and some went fifteen. Dinner was being issued to the wards just as they first appeared, and before I was half done, there were not hands sufficient to carry the waiters to the rooms. Some were at the table eating; and you believe me, they did not stop to finish their dinner. Some were crying out, 'good bye, grandma; you must do the best you can! We hate to leave you in the hands of those fellows; but if we remain here, we will be taken prisoners by them, and then we can do no one any good.' I told them to run with all their speed, and escape if possible. And, sure, they took me at my word, and made good their escape.

"I hastened to the wards of the sick and wounded to see how the poor helpless boys were standing the excitement. It was indeed a pitiful sight to look on, one that would melt the most callous heart to sympathy, to see them unable to help themselves, and of course were at the mercy of those who were not expected to show mercy to any. Nearly the first question, almost simultaneously asked by all, was, if I was going to leave them."

She assured them that she would not. It heartened them although the druggist, ward master, and other nurses fled past as they spoke. Just outside the hospital doors many were caught by the Federal cavalry and taken away as prisoners. Grandma Smith believed that the Yankees had promised them they would not be molested if they were attached to the hospital.

"Yet it is a known fact that as the African cannot change his color or the leopard his spots, neither can the real Yankee change his principles. . . .

"Poor fellows, we did so much hate to see them dragged off to prison, especially as they were so much needed in the hospital. We were then left with no assistance, as all of the assistants were taken off but one young man (who was smart enough to play off as a patient) and those who had gone so far as to escape capture. A kind negro woman was also left, who said that principle made her stay with old miss to help take care of the poor soldiers. She didn't see what made all de fool niggers an' wimmin run for, no how; de Yanks didn't want dem. She wan't 'fraid ob dem; she was gwine to stay right dar, and stand her ground, so she was. And she made good her word, but not failing at intervals to rail out against 'dem fool nigga's an' wimmin;' saying, that if she was old miss, 'dat dey shouldn't put dar foots back here, after leaving her and de poor helpless boys to take care ob demselves.'

"Well, as soon as I could leave my business, I went to the office to see how our surgeons had stood by their helpless charges; and to my unspeakable surprise and alarm, I found Drs. Robertson and Doyle surrounded by some half a dozen Yanks. Dr. Robertson was addressing them with much eloquence, as he was fully competent to do; saying. 'You have come and taken me prisoner while performing my duty as surgeon. The men whom you have disabled while contending for their just rights on the battle field, are under my charge. You have gone contrary to military rules in molesting me. I shall, therefore, appeal to General Girard for redress. I could have made my escape, but before I would have forsaken these, my wounded comrades, I would suffer myself to be shot down here in this yard.'

"He then called the attention of the captain, saying, 'Let me introduce to you my chief matron. She is in hopes you will not suffer her to be molested. She wishes to be allowed to remain with these, her patients. She is the only one out of five ladies who were willing to run the risk of being captured for their sake; and I ask you to see that she is respected.' I was surprised, as well as satisfied, to receive a polite assurance that

I should receive all the respect due one engaged in such a charitable work; and should any of his men attempt to molest me, just report to General Girard."

Grandma Smith was left alone that long afternoon. Not one in fifty of her patients, she calculated, was able to give another so much as a drink of water, and many were in dying condition. Almost all were on the critical list. She was shocked later when several shouting and threatening Yankees came into the wards.

"One patient asked: 'You are not going to molest us, are you?'

" 'Oh, no,' said they, 'we will only parole you now, and when you are able to be moved, we will send you to prison.' 'Well, you will not trouble grandma, will you? She stays with us.' 'Well, I suppose we will have to banish her to the North, or make her take the oath.' 'Nary time will you do either,' said I. 'One who ranks a little higher than you requested me to report to General Girard if one of you dared to molest me, and I will do so.' They soon sneaked out.

"It was but a short time until the doctor was released, and back at his post. How relieved I was of a heavy burden. I was in great dread that they might take him off, and one so faithful deserved better treatment. Besides, some of his patients could not live without the very best of medical attention, and his assistants had just all they could do in their own wards.

"But after the excitement of a few hours, all was well again, with the exception of nurses and cooks. What a time I had, no one could give the most faint idea. Yet it is an old and true saying, that 'where there is a will, there is a way' to surmount the most difficult tasks; and I found it true in that instance, to my own experience and profit. I, with the faithful one negress, who still kept abusing 'dem dar fool niggers an' wimmin,' prepared the supper for all hands, dished it up between us, and our own true soldiers and friends, with another who came in unexpectedly, ate our supper as usual.

"We cleaned up and prepared the cooking room and fixtures for breakfast; then we took our rounds through all the wards, dressing wounds and preparing them for as pleasant a night's

sleep as circumstances would admit of. We endeavored to leave
nothing undone that would add in the very least to their comfort. Poor, dear fellows; how lonely they seemed without their
nurses, and how hard it was that they should be deprived of
their services in the manner in which they were, for they were
worthy nurses.

"After we were through with our patients, and I had watched
by the bedside of one whose life was fast ebbing out, until my
strength was almost gone, I retired to my room, but not to
sleep, for at that time, as on many other occasions, sleep appeared to have deserted me. I could not sleep when I knew one
of our brave fellows was breathing his last, far away from those
who would have watched over him unceasingly, and smoothed
his dying pillow, and shed tears over his departing spirit. Besides, I did not know at what time some Yankee might make
his appearance and frighten us. I was sitting near my window,
which gave me full view of the ward in which lay the dying
soldier.

"Every groan he made reached my ears, and went to my heart
—as if my own dear son was in his stead, which made the gloom
much more awful to me under the very unpleasant circumstances, and tried my soul to its utmost capacity. While in this
condition and wondering if my husband and son were safe,
or were they among the slain or wounded of that awful day's
struggle before Atlanta, until I becamce unconscious of the
lapse of time, and I had forgotten the fact that I was a prisoner,
cut off from them by the destruction of the railroads, and
thereby all communication cut off by which I could hear from
them. My situation became to me almost intolerable."

On her bedside table lay a letter from Freddy W. Brinkman,
a former patient. During a short lull in the fighting he scribbled:

"Grandma, I must close my letter now for the truce is out,
and we are ordered in the ditches, in case the enemy should
make another attack. I wish you would let my lady acquaintances read the papers when you get through with them, and
whenever I have an opportunity to procure more, I will send

them to you. Jimmie and Johnnie join me in sending their best respects to you. No more at present, but remain, as ever,

Your faithful and devoted friend."

Captain Joseph Vale was with the cavalry which had seized Covington.

". . . near this place," he reported, "we ran into a train of refugees from Kentucky and Tennessee who stated that they had been running away from the 'Yankees' for over two years because they were led to believe that certain death awaited them if caught or overtaken. They being but harmless citizens, though strong secessionists, were brought in, and men, women and children fed, kindly treated, and eventually sent to their distant homes at the expense of the Government; the only thing they lost was all their serviceable horses."

And two miles to the north, at Oxford, Walter Clark was eating midday meal in the college chapel when the alarm was sounded, followed at once by the clatter of horse's hoofs.

"There was some commotion outside and the men hurriedly left the table to investigate its cause . . . a few feet from the door on a horse covered with foam sat a red-headed Yankee in blue uniform and with full equipment. The expected raid had materialized and Garrard's division of Federal cavalry had possession of the town. Most of the convalescents returned hastily to their quarters without finishing their dinner.

"The writer, not knowing when or where his next meal would be taken returned to the table and replenished his commissary department to its fullest capacity. The raiders scattered through the village, pillaging to some extent private residences, destroying government cotton and in this way burning the home of Mr. Irvine, an old citizen of the place. In due time they reached the premises of the lady, to whom reference has already been made.

"Her husband was not at home. He was an honored minister of the Methodist church and was considered the champion snorer of the conference to which he belonged. It was said that his family had become so accustomed to the sonorous exercise of his talent in this line that during his absence from home at night, they were forced to substitute the grinding of a coffee mill to secure sleep. I am not prepared, however, to vouch for the absolute accuracy of this statement. Whether on this occasion he had received intimation of the enemy's approach, and emulating the example of other male citizens of the village, had made himself conveniently absent, I do not now recall.

"His wife, possibly relying on the fact that she was Northern born, or on providential interposition, for exemption from any war indemnity that her blue-coated guests might be disposed to exact, received them courteously and as long as their levy was confined to chickens from the barnyard or hams from the smoke house she managed to maintain her equilibrium. But when, in addition to these minor depredations, they bridled her pet family horse and led him forth to 'jine the cavalry,' patience ceased to be a virtue.

"This crowning indignity furnished the straw that fractured the spinal column of the proverbial camel. She rose in her righteous wrath and in plain and vigorous English she gave them her opinion of the Yankee army general, and of her unwelcome guests in particular. Her indignant protest was unavailing. The stable was thenceforth tenantless, and as Tennyson might have said, she mourned for the tramp of a vanished horse and the sound of a neigh that was still.

"At 3 P.M. the convalescents were formed into line with orders to report to the provost marshall. We had marched but a little way, when a Federal colonel ordered us to disband until 5 P.M. I had borrowed the novel *Macaria* from a Miss Harrison in the village and decided to spend the interval in completing its perusal. I retired to my cot in the college chapel, but somehow the book did not interest me. Visions of a Federal prison peered at me from every page and I gave it up. Having made an engagement to take tea with Mr. Harrison's family that evening, I concluded, if allowed to leave the building, to return the book. Going down to reconnoiter I saw one of our men walk up the street without being halted, and with as indifferent air as I could assume, I followed suit.

"Reaching Mr. Harrison's house I found the family anxious and excited. Mr. H., to avoid capture, had concealed himself in the garden. I expressed my regrets to Mrs. H. that I was unable to keep my engagement, as I had another, which was a little more pressing. She insisted that I remain with them until the hour for leaving and I sat down to meditate on the fate that the future had in store for me. When a boy I had often sung the old hymn containing the words:

" 'Sweet prospects, sweet birds and sweet flowers,' but the prospect that loomed up before me that summer afternoon had no flavor of sugar or honey and, as I now recall it, not even a trace of sorghum molasses to shade its bitterness. As I sat there on the piazza, a Federal brigade passed in a short distance of the house followed by a crowd of contrabands. One of the soldiers came in and took a ham from the pantry without taking the trouble to ask for it. Others passed through the yard on other errands.

"Nothing was said to me and I made no special effort to attract their attention. I was saying nothing, but I was doing some pretty tall thinking. The idea had occurred to me, either, as Judge Longstreet has said, by 'internal suggestion or the bias of jurisprudence,' that if I remained quietly where I was, I might be overlooked and I decided to make the experiment."

During the afternoon, Clark heard of the shooting of Mr. Jones of Covington, an avowed Union hater. Mr. Jones was waiting with his squirrel rifle by the court house when the cavalry rode in.

" 'Don't shoot,' the first Union soldier shouted to him, but his purpose was not to be changed and his victim dropped from the saddle. Reloading his rifle and changing his position to another street a second squad of prisoners came by and again his rifle brought down its game. Reloading the third time he intercepted a platoon of cavalry and fired into it, wounding two of them. They captured him, shot him to death and then beat out his brains with the butts of their rifles. He doubtless anticipated such a fate and went coolly to certain death with no hope of fame and with only the satisfaction of getting two for one.

"Geo. Daniel, a Confederate quartermaster, chanced to be at home on furlough in Covington . . . He had been out bird hunting that morning and on his return was captured by the

Yankees, who enraged by the killing of two of their men by
Jones, determined to shoot Daniel simply because he was found
with a gun in his hand. His protest that he was out for no
hostile purpose availed him nothing. He was ordered to face
his executioners and an effort was made to bind a handkerchief
over his eyes. He drew it away and said. 'No, a Confederate
soldier can face death without being blindfolded.' The rifles
rang out and he fell, another victim to the humane influence of
Northern civilization."

As the shadows of afternoon lengthened, Clark watched the
convalescents being marched out of Oxford by the Union
cavalry. His heart "grew lighter" as the line trudged off into
the distance and finally vanished. Closing his book, *Macaria,*
which he believed had saved him from capture, he walked back
to the hospital, and his cot.

Another patient, Colonel H. D. Capers, of the 12th Georgia
Battalion, was somewhere in the countryside, having leaped
through a rear window earlier in the day. The cavalry, over-
taking the Colonel's Negro servant at a road fork, demanded the
direction followed by the Colonel. The Negro blandly pointed
out the wrong one, and watched the horsemen gallop off.

Oxford and Covington, scorched by the cavalry, were left
alone that night.

In Atlanta, the firing dwindled to the sporadic crack-crack
of small arms, stabbing the perimeters of the city, on which
burned the campfires of both Yankees and Confederates.

JULY 23

◤ *Southern Press Association*

"*Atlanta, July 21—*Gen. Wheeler last evening attacked the
enemy's left, in the neighborhood of Decatur, and drove them

back, capturing 500 wagons with supplies, and a large number
of prisoners. He is still pursuing.

"There was very little fighting after dark yesterday.

"Two thousand prisoners, including 75 command officers, 25
pieces of artillery and seven stands of colors have been brought
in.

"The losses on either side are not yet known. Ours were
severe in officers.

"Comparative quiet reigns this morning. There is some little
skirmishing on our left."

■ *The National Republican* (Washington)

"The Government is in receipt of a dispatch today from the
telegraph operator at Chattanooga, via Louisville in the following words,

" 'Atlanta is not ours yet. Our forces find strong opposition.
It seems that we are in possession of a part of the city but the
enemy hold the rest.' "

■ *Harper's Weekly*

"The Rebel army was chiefly massed against our right. The
struggle ended with Hood's defeat, with a loss on our side of
about 2500 and on that of the rebels of about 6000. Genl.
McPherson was shot while reconnoitring. He became separated
from his staff for a moment and a rebel sharpshooter shot him
from ambush. On Saturday there was an arrangement for the
burial of the dead and the care of the wounded; this could not
have been a truce, as Sherman in the meanwhile kept his heavy
artillery playing upon the city.

"Hood's design in making the assaults on Wednesday and
Friday was to destroy our forces on the right after which the
army would be strong enough to confront if not defeat the
remainder of our army. The plan promised a good degree of
success. Sherman's line was 14 miles long, and weak in the
centre. But the day was gained by Sherman, through the daunt-
less courage which the separate divisions resisted the furious
charge of Hood's army.

"The loss of the mills at Roswell, which were destroyed by

Sherman's army in its movement on Atlanta, was a severe blow to the Confederates. In addition to extensive flouring mills, there were large cloth manufactories, producing monthly 30,000 yards of cotton and 15,000 of woolen goods—principally for the army."

Hood dictated a dispatch to Secretary of War, James A. Seddon, in Richmond:

"In the engagement yesterday we captured 18 stands of colors, instead of five, and 13 guns, instead of 22, as previously reported.

"Brig. Gen. Mercer was *not* wounded.

"All quiet today except for a little picket firing and occasional shells thrown into the city."

Under cloudy skies, Sergeant Graham moved out from his post of the previous night "by the main road to a position on our left and commenced breastworks. Afterwards tore them down and built others further back. A flag of truce was sent in by the enemy to bury the dead and to take off wounded to last until 8 A.M. We now lay east of the town of Atlanta with immense breastwork in every possible direction and with other works and it will be hard for them, the enemy, to harm us much within them. Lay on arms all night up in the line at 8 o'clock."

Every tree not yet cut down was being felled within a mile of Atlanta's inner defense line to give the gunners a clear field. Any Negro who could be found was put to work on the immense project. The sounds of axes, saws, and oaths, the sights and smells of black, glistening bodies, filled Atlanta.

A few refugees fled down the two remaining thoroughfares to Macon and West Point. There was an unanticipated business flurry on this Saturday.

"People crowded the stores," wrote Wallace Reed, the Atlanta writer, "and the roar of battle gave place to the hum of traffic. The prudent housekeepers who had been laying in supplies of provisions in anticipation of a siege, continued their shopping . . . coffee at $20 a pound, sugar at $15; flour at $300 a barrel—these were still for sale, and there were many other things at proportionate prices. No butter, however, no chickens,

no vegetables, and, in fact, nothing that would tempt an epi-
cure. At a restaurant a guest would get a plate of ham and eggs
and a cup of coffee for $25. On this very day a young man
stepped into a clothing store and bought a felt hat for $150, a
pair of shoes for $100, and a sack coat, of good durable cloth,
for $200. These prices seemed reasonable enough to him, be-
cause at the same place six months before he had paid $600 for
a shawl."

Everyone wanted to know how the war was going and the few
remaining newspapermen were besieged with questions. In a
restaurant, one veteran journalist was asked about yesterday's
"Battle of Atlanta."

" 'I cannot promise you full details . . . my paper is conveyed
by spies to Sherman's headquarters, and I have to be very
cautious.'

" 'But, major,' said an anxious listener, 'is it all right?' The
major frowned and glared at his interrogator.

" 'Why, d—n it, sir, of course it is all right! What do you mean
by such a question, sir?' 'I didn't know,' was the hesitating response. 'Well, confound it, sir, if you didn't know it was your
duty to trust those who do know.' 'But,' continued the journalist, softening a little, 'I know you are anxious, and I don't
mind telling you that we have got Sherman just where we want
him.' 'Good!' interrupted several. 'Yes, he is now so far from
his base of supplies that it will be an easy matter to cut him off,
and then you will see whether his starving troops will fight or
not. My prediction is that they will desert to us, surrender,
scatter—anything but fight. Mark that down!'

"The listeners turned away with new confidence, and they
whispered to each other that the major had just seen General
Hood, and knew what he was talking about. One young man
was not convinced, and besides it made no difference to him
whether the major was right or not. He was a Unionist, working
in one of the government shops, and he had been notified that
day that his services were no longer needed, and that he would
be conscripted. Just after dusk this fellow slunk out of town
through the woods on the right of the Georgia railroad. He had
gone only a mile or two when he heard the sound of approach-

ing feet. He darted into the bushes, but the threat to fire upon him brought him out, and he found himself a prisoner in the hands of the Confederates. He told a plausible story, but it was no use. The next day he was on picket in a suit of Confederate gray.

" 'At first I fired blank cartridges,' he said afterwards, 'thinking that the Federal pickets would understand me. But they didn't, durn 'em, and I got so blind mad to think of their firing at a good Union man that I fired balls after that, and I shot to kill. When a fellow hears musket balls whizzing about his ears it is no time to stand there like a sentimental fool wasting blank cartridges!' "

"The enemy," S. P. Richards affirmed, "have thrown a great many shells into the city and scared the women and children and *some* of the *men* pretty badly. One shell fell in the street just below our house and threw gravel in our windows . . . this seems to me to be a very barbarous mode of carrying on war, throwing shells among women and children. The city authorities required me to do police duty, and I had to stand on guard on McDonough St. from 8 to 10 and 2 till 4 this night, and carried a musket for the first time in my life! My wife and children (two boys and two girls) had to put their beds on the floor behind the chimney to be secure from shells which were thrown into the city all night long. No more fell near our house however, and but little damage was done anywhere."

Semmes penciled in a letter to "Eo":

"I wrote you yesterday and sent my letter by private hand (to be mailed somewhere south of here) from East Point. You will have learned of our partial victory. It would have been a complete victory but for the cowardice of the *Georgia Brigade,* whose bad conduct not only deprived us of complete success, but cost in the lines of many valuable men. I cannot learn that Brad is hurt and therefore feel sure he is safe. The hospitals all have to send to me and his name is not among the number of wounded and he is not reported killed. You may imagine my grief when I heard of poor Dawson's being badly hurt. I have seen him. He cannot speak . . . his lower jaw is terribly shattered, his teeth on both sides driven out and a portion of his tongue cut off. He may recover, but if so is disfigured and maimed for life. I can write no more about him until I see him again tonight. Cluskey is mortally wounded, I saw him, too, you remember he was from Washington.

"Our loss is severe. Many of the old Regiment are wounded, but they did as they always do, most splendidly. As soon as I can I will call to see the Claytons, and see how they fared during the battle.

"God bless you and mine,

J.

"We took 28 guns and about 3000 or 4000 of the wretches."

John Henry Marsh, friend of Dr. Charles T. Quintard, wrote the Army chaplain—St. Luke's minister, from the trenches:

"We carried several lines of the enemy's entrenchments, killing numbers of the enemy, capturing many prisoners, and several pieces of artillery. I grieved to say that our loss was very heavy in men and officers, especially in officers. Many of the noblest and most gallant spirits in the Army of the Tenn. have been sent off. They have truly sacrificed life; for our glorious cause and country. In walking through the hospitals on the morning after the fight, I could not restrain my tears; Gordon, Weems, Cluskey, Dawson, Walker, Murray, Martin, and many other noble spirits were down. Some of the warmest and most intimate friends I had in the Army were shot and torn to pieces. The Great God in his infinite goodness and mercy saw fit to spare my worthless life again. Oh, Dr.! how deeply thankful I felt at being permitted to go through the battle with life when so many nobler and better spirits were being cut down at every step around me . . . Dr., I never prayed on the battle field before; but this time I prayed to the Great God to spare me . . . even while I write minnie balls whistle over and around, the ring of the rifle never ceases. The announcement of Gen. Johnston having been relieved of comd causes the greatest gloom."

Mollie Smith, the young Atlanta lady, visited the wounded, accompanying a group of older women who were taking refreshments to the tent hospitals.

"On arriving there," she wrote, "we found our men had been

sent off. We gave the provisions to some Federals who had been wounded and captured the day before. We could not help feeling sorry for them, although they were trying to destroy our homes and ruin our country. We spoke kindly to them and they seemed grateful and said they were sorry they ever entered the army and would be glad when the war was over.

"On my way home I expected every moment to be struck by a shell, as they were flying in all directions, but I reached home in safety."

"I am now in position about a hundred yards from the nursery we visited when I came from Pensacola," Andy Neal of Atlanta wrote his mother. "I had the misfortune yesterday to have my horse killed in the action by a shell. I was holding him by the bridle when the shell exploded between us doing me no hurt except stunning me considerably. My horse received a wound in the fight of the 20th as I was riding at the head of the battery which came over disabling him. I intend in future to ride a Battery horse in Battle for it is more trouble to get good horses than ever. Mine was worth $2000 but I do not know that the Government will pay me that much for him. I intend to take a good horse from the Battery for the present and instead of asking the Government to pay for the horse killed ask that I be allowed to keep one, a proposition I think will be assented to.

"I have had due inquiries and searches made for the box Cousin Martha sent me but can hear nothing of it. I suppose it was sent to the Griffin R. Committee and as usual taken by them to feed a lot of straggling soldiers who had deserted their posts at the front and were plundering and pillaging all over Atlanta. I am getting to think these relief committees are the greatest humbug about the Army. Their attentions are universally directed at those least deserving. I had rather see one dirty ragged soldier return to the Army to stand by us in the trenches than all the Committees about here.

"I rode over Atlanta yesterday and it really makes me sad to witness the ruin and desertion of the place. The soldiers have broken open many stores and scattered things over the streets promiscuously. There is the same noise and bustle on Whitehall

but instead of thrift and industry and prosperity it is a hurried
scramble to get away fleeing from the wrath to come. If Sodom
deserved the fate that befell it Atlanta will not be unjustly punished for since this war commenced it has grown to be the great
capital place of corruption in official and private circles. While
I regret the loss of Atlanta on account of its great value to the
Country as a military base and its incalculable value on account
of its Arsenals, foundries, manufacturies of railroad connections
I can scarcely regret that the nest of the speculators, thieves, etc.
is broken up. The constant and glorious patriotism and self-
sacrificing devotion to our Cause displayed by the women of
Atlanta is the only redeeming virtue of the place . . .
"P. S. The Q. Master has not paid us off in four months."

Colonel Taylor Beatty, Hardee's military lawyer, had heard
another rumor: that Lieutenant General S. D. Lee was on his
way with 10,000 fresh troops.

"Where he is to get them I don't see, especially if Smith is in
Mississippi and has not been whipped that we know of . . . considerable firing all day on the town; I believe, though, that no
damage has been done."

Meanwhile, the surgeons continued their work in the park.
Local soldier W. P. Archer, wrote: "you could not put your finger down on any part of a man's person that you could not find
some soldier hit by a minie ball or piece of shell.

"Reports on both sides agree that the loss was about eight to
ten thousand on each side, probably more on the Federal side,
from the fact that they were mostly aggressors. This battle gave
the Federals another big advantage, as they after the battle obtained a position east of the city where they could fire their
shells and solid shot into the heart of the city with ease, which
they did.

"Out on the railroad . . . non-combatants, women and children, who were unable to refugee and get out of the way, tun-
neled under the banks of the railroad cuts, and lived there, to
keep from being killed by Sherman's shells. These shells being
fired high up over our lines of fortifications, in a kind of rainbow fashion, would come screaming and drop over the city,
bursting and sending their missiles in every direction."

In Oxford, Miss Fair, a beautiful refugee from Charleston, crawled out of hiding in the attic of a neighbor's house (the Rivers). Miss Fair had bobbed and dyed her wavy, brown hair and applied burned cork to face and hands. Wearing a "cracker" bonnet and home-spun dress, and carrying a basket of parched, ground peas, disguised as a Negro market woman around Federal encampments south of Marietta, she was, in reality a Confederate spy.

Her latest letter, to Governor Brown, outlining the information she had obtained about Sherman's plans, was in the Oxford post office when Garrard's cavalry stormed into the town. The mail was seized.

Miss Fair's father—guiltless but terrified—had clambered up out of the well in his friend's back yard, where he had shared a clammy night's dwelling with snakes and frogs.

One letter, from A. F. Samuels of "near Atlanta" was addressed to Grandma Smith in Covington: "I have been very busy dressing the wounded, and have not had time to answer before now; and as it is almost dark, I cannot promise to write you a long letter this time.

"Our regiment was badly cut up, a great many of the boys were killed and wounded. Gus Flotron and Freddy Brinkman were seriously wounded, and I greatly fear that Gus will die. They were wounded in the charge made yesterday. I suppose that you have heard that I am now staying at the Division Hospital, where I can do a great deal more good than in charging Yankee breastworks. I could not stand the hardships of the campaign, and my health is completely prostrated. I expect to be ordered on duty in some of the hospitals shortly and I should be only too happy to come to you, and remain with you until the termination of this unholy war. I feel that my proper sphere is not to inflict, but to relieve human suffering, and I long to be in a position where I can exercise my vocation to good purpose. It is getting too dark to write any more, and I will now close, by bidding you God speed.

Your devoted friend."

Joe F. Harper, Company H, 9th Tennessee Regiment also wrote to his former nurse:

"Mrs. S. E. D. Smith:

"Though youth and beauty are blighted, and though old age is creeping over thy honored brow, yet there is a strong attraction of filial affection for thy parental love and care impressed on my heart that time and change cannot efface.

Joe F. Harper."

Captain J. C. Van Duzer, cipher operator, United States Military Telegraph Service, tapped to Major T. T. Eckert, in Washington, at midnight:

"As I write, our heavy artillery is at work and large fires are burning in Atlanta, supposed to be the enemy destroying stores preparatory to evacuating."

Young O. L. Braumuller sat in front of his mother's new dugout in the back yard, next to Hood's headquarters, and watched the shells. "They made a beautiful fireworks display."

JULY 24

■ *The New York Times*

"*Washington, Sunday, 10:00 P.M.*—Official dispatches of another battle before Atlanta fought on Friday were received by the authorities last night. At the time of sending the dispatch the contest was still going on, but the results, as far as developed, were favorable. A position had been gained from which Sherman was able to bring his siege guns to bear on the city. Extensive fires were raging within its limits as though the enemy were burning stores, etc.

"During this engagement, Gen. McPherson was killed. This sad report it was at first hoped would prove unfounded but it has been fully confirmed."

"*Baltimore, Sunday, July 23*—A private dispatch received by a relative of Gen. McPherson in this city last night, dated near

Atlanta July 23, announced that that gallant officer was killed in battle the day previous, and his remains would be sent home in charge of members of his staff."

>< *Mobile News*

"I can give you no idea of the excitement in Atlanta. Everybody seems to be hurrying off, and especially the women. Wagons loaded with household furniture and everything else that can be packed upon them crowd every street, and women, old and young, children innumerable, are hurrying to and fro, leading pet lambs, deer and other little household objects of affection, as though they intended to save all they could.

"Every train of cars is loaded to its utmost capacity and there is no grumbling about seats for even the fair ones are glad to get even a standing place in a box car. The excitement beats anything I ever saw, and I hope I may never witness such again. But in the midst of all this the soldiers are cool and cheerful, and sanguine."

>< *Nashville Watchman and Reflector*

"I have seen the children of once wealthy slaveholders clad in the coarse negro cloth which formerly was only used by slaves."

All was "quiet," according to General Hood's morning report to Secretary Seddon, "except a little picket firing and occasional shells thrown into the city."

Sherman, ever nearer to his opposing general, replied, "Certainly not!" to the request of the Christian Commission to send delegates to the front: "oats and gunpowder are more important now than any kind of moral or Christian agents. Each regiment at the front now has a chaplain."

At the same time he advised Major General H. W. Halleck, Chief of Staff, in Washington: "On making up reports and examining the field, I find the result of Hood's attack on our left more disastrous to the enemy than I reported. Our loss will not foot up 2,000 killed and wounded, whereas we have found over 1,000 rebels dead, which will make, with the usual proportion of wounded, a loss to the enemy of full 7,000. General Garrard

has also returned, perfectly successful, having completely destroyed the two large bridges near Covington, 40 miles toward
Augusta, brought in 200 prisoners and some good horses, and
destroyed the public stores at Covington and Conyers, including
2,000 bales of cotton, a locomotive and a train of cars. Our
communications are yet all safe, and the army in good condition
in all respects. As soon as my cavalry rests I propose to swing the
Army of the Tennessee round by the right rapidly and interpose
between Atlanta and Macon, the only line open to the enemy."

General Kenner Garrard informed Sherman from headquarters of the 2d Cavalry Division that ". . . one train (platform) was
burnt at Covington and a small train (baggage) at station near
the Ulcofauhachee captured and burnt. The engine to the last
train was detached across the river. Citizens report a passenger
train and a construction train, both with engines, cut off between Stone Mountain and Yellow River. Over 2,000 bales of
cotton were burnt. A large new hospital at Covington for the
accommodation of 10,000 patients from this army and the Army
of Virginia, composed of over 30 buildings, besides the offices,
just finished, were burnt, together with a very large lot of fine
carpenters' tools . . . in the town of Oxford 2 miles north of
Covington, and in Covington was over 1,000 sick and wounded
in buildings used for hospitals. The convalescents able to walk
scattered through the woods while the firing was going on in
town and I did not have time to hunt them up . . . those in hospitals together with their surgeons were not disturbed."

There was no choir-singing on that lazy, cooler Sunday for
the English-born stationer, S. P. Richards, since "the foe is still
outside and continues to pop shells at us. No church in the city
open. Father came in this morning but left in such a double
quick that I did not see him. Jabe also came in, for the first time
since he left last Wednesday night. He has moved the stock and
negroes to Mr. Stanley's . . . miles from Atlanta without loss or
accident. Father is still at the farm with Old Dinah."

Yet church bells pealed at least once. A shell resounded
against the bell of the first church built in Atlanta, Wesley
Chapel, at Pryor and Houston streets. However, the belfry was

not seriously damaged, and the Reverend Lorenzo D. Houston was out of the church at the time.

Picket firing was heard continuously along the crescent formed by Sherman's army, extending an estimated two-thirds of the way around Atlanta. The siege guns were spotted at intervals dotting this same crescent. The citizens could do nothing but strengthen their bombproofs and prepare for the worst.

"The men moved about the streets as usual," Wallace Reed, Atlanta's writer-historian, found, "discussing the topics of the day, and dodging an occasional shell. The ladies busied themselves with their household matters, with their ears on the alert for the well-known sounds of danger. Many times during the day a busy housewife would unceremoniously drop her sewing and gathering her little ones together, would make a wild and precipitate plunge for the back yard, where the family would quickly disappear into the bowels of the earth, there to remain until there was a lull in the storm of lead and iron.

"Most of the shells had percussion caps, and, as fully three-fourths of them had struck on the wrong end, they failed to explode."

The clearing of trees and strengthening of forts and breastworks were directed by the military engineer, Colonel L. P. Grant, of Atlanta.

"The last letter that I wrote home was to Sarah and dated July 9th," started Private Alonzo Miller of Company A, 12th Wisconsin Infantry, to "Dear Father and the Rest."

"Since then I, or the Regiment, has moved several times. It moved to Marietta and on to the Chattahoochee River, crossed it on to Decatur, passed through the village. Our men had gotten there before our Corps did, destroyed the railroad track. Decatur is six miles from Atlanta. We marched on two miles, then Co. A 12 went out on skirmishing that night, built pits in the morning, was ordered to charge on the Rebs, which we did, and drove their skirmishers back to their breastworks and took a part of the work, but the Rebs were too strong; our forces could not hold them. Fell back a little but not without fighting like sixty. Our Company had 5 or 6 killed and 15 or more wounded. We held our ground the best we could. Made pits at night, we made good works. The Regiment lost 150 or more, 21 killed I know of. The bullets missed me, but quite a number fell by my side. In the morning the Rebs fell back. Now we occupy their works and about noon the Rebs charged on our rear, captured some of our wagons and then made a charge of our whole lines. I tell you it was which and t'other, fighting on three sides, but we held them and were reinforced by a Corps coming in. Recaptured some of our wagons, took two Regiments of Reb prisoners. I tell you I lay close to the ground if ever I did one time. The Reds had one end of our fort on one side, our men the other, fighting like sixty. In the morning the Rebs fell back . . . the Rebs lay piled up, dozens or more killed and wounded. The Rebs got it killed without number. I could stand up on the breastworks and count 50 dead Rebs, some dressed in fine clothes as if they came out to fight for the day, with new guns. Our loss was large, but nothing compared to theirs. We have worked days and nights. I have worked building works that will hold them back. We are within two or three miles of the city. I was out last night helping dig a pit for our picket post works until 12 o'clock and then went out on the picket. Stood one hour, then back to the pit. Was relieved by 4 o'clock A.M. I went back to our Camp, got my breakfast, then I took a nap. Today I have a chance to rest. While we were marching I had plenty of blackberries. One day I ate two quarts. There have been any amount of them. Green apples I have when the Rebs will let me get them, but here we got to stay close to our works . . . Our Army is doing something today at other places . . . This is my last sheet of paper."

Alonzo, twenty-three years old, from Prescott, Wisconsin, was a member of Major General Frank P. Blair's 17th Army Corps.

Salvaged from the battlefield was a scrap of unsigned letter: "Saturday night I had a note from Grif (Griffin) Killian; Mrs. C.'s brother lost leg July 21st, and died that night at Solomon home . . . Great many wounded are coming down every day, probably one or two hundred on an average. I am anxious to see that dear old face and curls up here."

A neighbor's family came to young Mollie Smith's house, "seeking shelter, saying their home had been struck by a shell and that much damage had been done. Because our house was built of brick, people thought we were proof against the shells. . . . We moved some bedding into the basement and slept there. . . . Other friends came in during the day and wanted to stay with us, feeling we were secure."

O. L. Braumuller, just a boy, felt constrained by the restrictions of war. He wrote:

"I couldn't run around town and mix with the soldiers, for I had the full responsibility of taking care of mother."

Grandma Smith welcomed back most of the soldiers who had fled into the woods surrounding Covington, and thereby escaped "northern prisons, where they would have been treated as if they were brutes, in violation of all principles of humanity, religion or civil modes of warfare."

Since the road to Covington was cut: "We felt like we were confined in a temporary prison. Yet, when our boys, who had deserted from necessity for a time, returned, we felt like ourselves again; and with glad hearts we greeted them, as though we had not seen them for months. All were joyful.

"Many were the laughable stories each one had to relate concerning their flying trip in the country. One of them, Frank Hodge, of the Fifth Arkansas Regiment, was minus a leg, and outran others who did not have to go on crutches. They collected in squads near houses, and the family damsels supplied them with plenty of good provision—not forgetting to stand picket ready to give the alarm, should the enemy appear. Some made promises that they would never desert old grandma again; that it was too bad that she should be left all alone. Little did they know how soon their fidelity would be put to the test by another Yankee dash, when they were just becoming quiet from the effects of the former. We had hoped that General Hood would keep them too closely engaged in front for them to have any time for working in the rear of his army, and giving us another scare. Yet we kept a careful lookout; so, if possible, not to be surprised. The patients who could be moved, were sent in wagons to Social Circle, and from there by cars to Greensboro and Augusta. Therefore, we were gradually guarding against another fright, which to some of us who had remained, was somewhat unexpected. Owing to supplies being cut off, evacuation was necessary; but it was being done gradually, as there was some of the patients not in a condition to be moved."

A. F. Samuels, one and a half miles from Atlanta, wrote another letter to "Grandma."

"Dear Friend," he began, "I resume my pen this morning if for no other reason than to avoid sending you a blank sheet. I always dislike receiving a blank sheet, it looks to me unfriendly. Freddy Brinkman and Gus Flotron were both dying when I saw them last. This makes two more brave and noble spirits that our company have to mourn. We left Dalton with thirty-six; thirteen of those have been wounded, and eight killed —twenty-one in all. But I hope they have taken their flight to a better world, 'where the wicked cease from troubling, and the weary are at rest.' I am fearful that the sad scenes which I have passed through in this war will leave a cloud upon my spirits for the rest of my life; but I hope that it has been the means of bringing me into the ark of safety. It has taught me to place my trust in God alone, and to read and love His Holy Word. Who then can say that it has not been a real blessing to me? You have doubtless heard of poor Conner's death. I was with him when he breathed his last. We conversed earnestly for a long time, and I cannot help remarking one expression that fell from his lips a short time before he died. Taking hold of my hand, he uttered in a very peculiar and solemn tone, 'Doc, this is the last campaign.' God grant his words may prove true.

"The roar of cannon and rattle of musketry are dinning in my ears as I write, and from my very heart I utter a fervent prayer to God to spare the few friends that I have left. Alas, how few in number! I almost feel desolate.

Your earnest friend."

The smell of woodsmoke, instead of gunpowder, hung over Decatur, where Sherman's men were once more ripping up the railroad tracks and twisting them over roaring bonfires, kindled from the ties. The piney fumes were thick in Mary Gay's house as she read the Bible to Toby, pausing finally to ask if he thought he would die.

" 'Yes'm, I think I am.'

"I bowed my head close to him and wept, oh, how bitterly.

" 'Miss Mary, don't you think I'll go to heaven?' he anxiously asked.

" 'Toby, my boy, there is one thing I want to tell you; can you listen to me?'

" 'Yes'm.'

" 'I have not always been just to you. I have often accused you of doing things that I afterwards found you did not do, and then I was not good enough to acknowledge that I had done wrong. And when you did wrong, I was not forgiving enough; and more than once I have punished you for little sins, when I, with all the lights before me, was committing greater ones every day, and going unpunished, save by a guilty conscience. And now, my boy, I ask you to forgive me. Can you do it?'

" 'Oh, yes'm!' "

At Toby's request she went to the Floyd spring to obtain a pitcher of cool water. It took her almost half an hour to return with the clear, pure water. The boy drank thirstily of it and Mary thought he was better. But by evening his temperature soared, his breathing became labored, momentarily eased again. Then, with unbelievable suddenness—he was dead.

Mary ran for her mother. "We stood and gazed upon him as he lay in death in that desolated house, and thought of his fidelity and loving interest in our cause and its defenders, and of his faithful service in our efforts to save something from vandal hands, and the fountain of tears was broken up and we wept with a peculiar grief over that lifeless form.

"My mother was the first to become calm, and she came very near to me and said, as if afraid to trust her voice:

" 'Wouldn't it be well to ask Eliza Williams and others to come and lay him out?'

"Before acting on this suggestion I went into another room and waked Telitha and took her into the chamber of death. A dim and glimmering light prevented her from taking in the full import of the scene at first; but I took her near the couch, and, pointing to him, I said:

" 'Dead!—Dead!'

"She repeated interrogatively, and when she fully realized that such was the case, her cries were pitiable, oh, so pitiable.

"I sank down upon the floor and waited for the paroxysm of grief to subside, and then went to her and made her understand that I was going out and that she must stay with her mistress until I returned. An hour later, under the skillful manipulation of good 'Eliza Williams'—known throughout Decatur as Mrs. Ammi Williams' faithful servant—and one or two others whom she brought with her, Toby was robed in a nice white suit of clothes prepared for the occasion by the faithful hands of his 'Miss Polly,' whom he had loved well and who had cared for him in his orphanage."

Meanwhile, sputtering fuse shells arced into Atlanta, presenting—to a few citizens—"a beautiful appearance, resembling so many rockets."

Soon the large warehouse on Hunter Street, between Whitehall Street and Mrs. Durham's home, was on fire, spreading to the rear of Davis' modern brick building on Whitehall. Water pressure dropped, imperiling that entire side of the street.

The shelling increased as though Sherman's gunners, like fireflies, were attracted by the mounting flames. Shells streaked out of the night skies, resembling long-tailed, angry comets.

JULY 25

✉ *Southern Press Association*

"*Atlanta*—The enemy made an attempt last night to break our lines but were repulsed by Cheatham after a conflict of one hour.

"During the day quiet prevailed around the city, the only demonstration being occasional picket firing. At midday today the Yankees opened with shell again upon the city, shelling it one hour, with some vigor. No notice of his intention to shell the city was given to enable the women and children to be removed to places of safety. His barbarous violation of the usages of civilized warfare only enabled him to murder a few non-combatants. Most of the shells came from twenty pounder Parrott guns in position on the line of the Western & Atlantic Railroad, with occasional missiles from another gun east of the city.

"The gallant operations of Wednesday and Friday seem to have impressed the Yankees with a wholesome desire to strengthen their flanks, which they are doing. Their display of rocket signals has been brilliant, indicating some movement on their part."

▨ Richmond Sentinel

"There has been continuous skirmishing for the past two days. Many shells from the enemy's batteries have entered the city, and a few houses have been struck, but no material damage has been done.

"The enemy's extreme right endeavored to gain possession of a commanding eminence between their and our lines, but were repulsed by the 11th Texas Regiment."

▤ The New York Times

"*Nashville, Wednesday*—Information received from an officer at the front says in two battles in front of Atlanta, Ga., we have destroyed the better portion of the enemy's best two corps.

"All the prisoners captured on the 22d and 23d unite in saying that the rebel Gen. Hood was killed on the 23rd."

Shortly after midnight, two soldiers knocked on the door of Mollie Smith's house, requesting permission to bring over a sick lady who lived in a wooden building across the street.

"It was pouring down rain," wrote Mollie, "and of course we could not refuse to give shelter. We did not know who she was, but we ministered to her wants until daylight. The men came for her, took her away, and the house she left was almost destroyed by shells.

"Just as the family seated themselves at the breakfast table, a thirty-two-pound shell struck the house. It hit the room above the dining room, and the brick wall amounted to nothing in the way of protection. The shell made an opening of some three feet in the wall, tearing into atoms the door leading into the hall. It passed into the opposite room and exploded near the piano, wrenching off one leg and carrying it to the opposite side of the room, where it turned it upside down.

"One end of the sofa was torn to pieces, every pane of glass broken in the windows and the blinds smashed. Pieces of shell penetrated to a closet in an adjoining room and tore some clothing. Other pieces went through the floor, and the bedclothes caught on fire. The house was so filled with smoke that we thought it was blazing. Some soldiers who were camped near us rushed in and took part of our things out into the street, where they stayed all day. The shelling was so great that my father could not have them put back until night.

"The family and friends ran off, not knowing where to go or what to do, and, of course, the soldiers enjoyed our breakfast."

The Union troops watched shells dropping into the stricken city and heard their distant blasts, concluding that the siege would not "last much longer." They were confident that the last railroad artery into Atlanta would be cut before the week was out.

Smoke from the warehouse blaze of the previous night mingled with that from burning railroad ties to hang like a shroud over the city. People coughed and rubbed at their stinging eyes.

At daybreak, Mary Gay woke Senator Robert Jones, a family friend, to inquire about a coffin for Toby. There seemed little time in which to bury him before the Union troops reoccupied Decatur. She asked Uncle Mack, the blacksmith, and his associate, Henry, to dig a grave and prepare for the burial.

"After consultation with my mother, it was agreed that that should take place as soon as all things were in readiness. Mr. Jones made a pretty, well-shaped coffin out of good heart pine, and the two faithful negro men already mentioned prepared with care the grave. When all was in readiness, the dead boy was placed in the coffin and borne to the grave by very gentle hands.

"Next to the pall-bearers my mother and myself and Telitha fell in line, and then followed the few negroes yet remaining in the town, and that funeral cortege was complete.

"At the grave an unexpected and most welcome stranger appeared. Uncle Mack told me he was a minister, and would perform the funeral service—and grandly did he do it. The very soul of prayer seemed embodied in this negro preacher's invocation; nor did he forget Toby's 'nurses,' and every consolation and blessing was besought for them. And thus our Toby received a Christian burial."

Since shells "seemed to be flying in every direction," Mollie Smith's family left their house and sought the railroad tracks for safety.

Mollie's mother had remembered to pack a bandbox containing her best bonnet, "one of her treasures which had been a gift from my brother just before he left for the army." Two stray dogs bounded down the tracks, yelping and fighting. They ran headlong into the bandbox, dumping the hat onto the dusty ties.

"Her indignation was so great and she was so much concerned over her hat that she failed to see that I was also in danger until someone said: 'Mrs. S. thinks more of her bonnet than she does of her daughter.' It undoubtedly seemed true at that time, for nice bonnets were scarce. . . . The dogs ran against me and knocked me over, but no damage was done either to me or to the bonnets. The incident created no little stir for a while. . . .

"My father found us and told us a friend on Alabama Street said for us to come to her house, that she had not been troubled with shells. We gladly accepted the invitation and while resting, our thoughtful cook prepared us something to eat.

"We had not tasted food that day. Our cook, however, on leaving home, had snatched up the coffee bin, a chunk of ham and a batch of dough. She soon had the meal ready and we had just seated ourselves at the table when, bang, came a shell and buried itself in the ground near the gate. We knew the next one would strike the house, so we did not stop to eat but jumped into a government wagon, placed at our disposal, and went out

Peters Street a mile or two, and stopped on a high hill over-looking the city.

"We spread our dinner, picnic fashion, and had commenced eating when a man rode up and said: 'For mercy's sake, get away from here, the Yanks will see this wagon and mule, think you are some soldiers camped here, and shell you. This place was Hood's headquarters and he was shelled out only two days ago. You must leave.'

"We decided to risk the shelling and finished our meal un-molested. We could see the shells flying over the city, and when one exploded in the air, there was a white smoke. We could also hear the crash when the houses were struck. We remained on that hill for hours watching the shells and wondering when we could go back to our homes.

"As we were going out of the city we met the militia, several hundred strong, coming in, and we had to stop until they had passed. It seemed a long time to us, especially as the shells were flying over our heads.

"In the wagon were old and young ladies, children and serv-ants. When the shells came whirling by the old ladies would exclaim: 'Lord, have mercy on us,' but the young ones would laugh. We thought it was fun to be running away from home and riding around in a covered wagon. It was certainly very exciting, but too soon we saw the serious side.

"About sunset father found us and took us to a friend's home, where we gladly spent the night."

From "Camp 154th Senior Reg't Tenn. Vols., in line of battle near Atlanta," a soldier she knew only as "Johnny," wrote to Grandma Smith.

"Through the mercy of God I have been spared through two dreadful conflicts, where the leaden messengers of death came thick and fast around me, and where death was stared in the face by thousands of those gallant souls of Hardee's Corps. It is with a heart beating with thanks to His holy name that I at-tempt to write you a few lines this morning in answer to yours of the 20th, which was handed to me by Mr. Midlebrook, who arrived last evening. Oh, dear grandma, would I were with you, where I could express myself as I wish; but it is impossible, so I shall content myself with writing you a few lines.

"You have, perhaps, 'ere this heard of the last battle we have had, but I fear have not heard the worst that is to come—that is the loss (I fear) of my two companions, Gus and Freddy, and the wounding of Jimmie and Willie. Thus you see I am left alone with but one with whom I love to associate, Tett Perkins. Willie was wounded on the 20th, when we so recklessly charged the enemy's works. He was taking a wounded man from the field when he was wounded in two places, shoulder and leg. Gus, Freddy and Jimmie on the 22d, where we gained such a victory. We had driven the enemy from his first works, and were firing from them ourselves, when Gus came running by me, calling me to come on, saying 'there they go.' I called him to me, and made him stay, as he was rushing heedlessly on to death. My attention was called away for a moment, when one of the boys called me, and there lay Gus weltering in his own blood, shot through the head, the ball entering the right eye, coming out in front of the ear, and tearing away half of it. Oh! you cannot imagine my feelings to see my old messmate the second time thus struck down by the enemy. I never left him until I got him started back to the division hospital, which I was a long time in doing, as I could get no litter to carry him from the field to the brigade hospital. I got some of the boys to help me, and with two or three blankets I got him off. Almost his first words were, 'Wesley, write to mother Smith and Mrs. Neal.' Jimmie Thirl assisted me in getting him off the field, and then went back to the command, and in a short time came back slightly wounded.

"I was going for some water, when some one called me; I looked, and saw little Freddy sitting up, leaning against a tree, and oh! what a different person from what he formerly was. I did all I could for all the boys, and then went back to the command. I went over the portion of the field we had fought over, and I am glad to know that Gus and Freddy are revenged. I have not heard from the boys to-day. Yesterday evening Midlebrook told me Freddy was dying; Gus had been sent off. I have strong hopes that Gus will recover. Freddy I did not think from the first would get over it; the ball entered just below the nipple of the right breast, coming out below the ribs on the same side. I believe he is resigned to the will of God, and if he should die, I earnestly hope he may go to a better land. I conversed with him sometime after he was wounded, but he had taken so much opium he was almost asleep. Oh, have I not cause to be thankful to God for thus sparing me, while there were many, perhaps better than I, called 'to that bourne from whence no traveller returns?'

"Grandma, I must bring my letter to a close. I wish I had time, I would write all the evening. I am going to hunt for Jimmie, and give him the tobacco pouch. I have some trophies of the battle I want to send down by uncle Jim, if I can see him. You see what fine paper and envelopes I have, besides a fine gold pen and pencil, with a pocket inkstand. I will write again as soon as I find where you are. There is no mail to the army now, therefore it will be sometime before you get this. I wrote to Mrs. Neal, and told her to let you know the contents of her letter, provided you were in Covington. No more. May God bless and ultimately save us in Heaven, is the prayer of

Your affectionate friend,

Johnny."

Joe Semmes wrote to "Eo" of the "great affliction of the Clayton family . . . the death of poor Gussy and Dawson's being again badly wounded. The enemy continue their wanton shelling of the city—one battery of 20-pound Parrott guns in particular fires regularly every 3 minutes day and night into the very heart of the city never replying to our batteries or firing upon our lines—of course some of the unfortunate people get killed and wounded, though a great many have left, and others have and are constructing caves in which to hide. A shell struck in Mrs. Clayton's back building and exploded under a bed in which were two children without harming them but burnt up the building. For 30 hours they shelled my Depot where our stores were being issued: without intermission the shells struck all over, around and everywhere—but one teamster was killed and one wounded. On my representing the condition of Depot and that the enemy had the exact range, Genl. Hood ordered us with the trains of cars a little out of the range and now I am writing in a car on the R. Road whilst the shells are flying over me and about 200 yards to my left right straight into the center of the city.

"In spite of the danger and the horrors around me cannot help being amused sometimes at the ludicrous incidents which occur and it is really fascinating to watch at night the flying shells which look like great shooting stars coursing through the air and explodng with a bright red glare. But enough of the terrible scenes of this all important city—a city destined to become celebrated for either our glorious success or defeat. It is to be held at all hazards and Sherman will try to take it at all and any cost. . . .

"I am well during all these troubles, and am chiefly troubled because I no longer hear from you. . . . God bless you and pray for me.

Your devoted husband."

The shelling produced a new category of persons . . . the "siege liars." These individuals compounded the difficulties and discomforts of the situation with their peculiar genius for prevarication.

" 'Do you know that Sherman is going to open fire with three hundred cannon all at once' " was a typical opener for a siege liar, according to Wallace Reed, the writer.

" 'Great heavens! Is it possible? How do you know?'

" 'I don't know,' replied the other, 'but it seems to be well understood that it is a fact. Sherman has demanded the surrender of the city by a certain hour to-day, and if we refuse he is going to wipe us up with his big guns.'

" 'But can it be true?'

" 'Yes, I think so. Some of the fellows around headquarters heard all about it. I'm going home and move my family down into the bomb-proof.'

"Each day some such rumor was started. Nobody had time to investigate. The only thing to be done under the circumstances was to have everything ready for a hasty run to cover."

More credible still were the atrocity reports. On this Monday, for example, it was learned that a seventeen-year-old girl was raped and murdered by Federal soldiers twelve miles north of

Atlanta. The mother and father were first ejected from their farmhouse.

Nor were the armies immune from such misinformation. "About 11 ordered to be ready with our troops for something but don't know what," Sergeant William Graham, of Illinois, recorded. "False alarm. Rumor of reinforcements arriving for us."

General Hood, an admirer wrote, "is about 6 feet 2 inches high, with full broad chest, light hair and beard, blue eyes and is gifted by nature with a voice that can be heard above the roar of battle." Nevertheless, on this day he employed a field order rather than his vocal chords to exhort the Army of Tennessee:

"Soldiers: Experience has proved to you that safety in time of battle consists in getting into close quarters with the enemy—guns and colors are the only unerring indication of victory. The valor of troops is easily estimated, too, by the number of those received. If your enemy be allowed to continue the operation of flanking you out of position, our course is in peril. Your recent brilliant success prove your ability to prevent it. You have but to will it and God will grant us the victory which your commander and your country so confidently expect.

J. B. Hood, General"

In Newnan, nurse Kate Cumming learned that "Drs. Henderson, Devine and Reese are on their way there. Dr. H. has spent the week at the Gamble Hospital with Dr. Wildman. Dr. W. is an Englishman. Last Monday our surgeons made up their minds that Dr. Henderson had been sent here by Dr. Foard to 'spy out the nakedness of the land.' It was in vain I protested that I believed such was not the case. In going into the wards I found the nurses all busy getting ready for the great inspector, as they called him. I did not try to undeceive them, as I knew the wards could not be injured by a little extra cleanliness. . . .

"The nurses were sadly disappointed, as no inspector had been round to see how nicely they had put on their comforts and set their little bottles in military array."

Outside of Atlanta, late that night, Sergeant Graham admired the display of rockets thrown up, "by us."

O. L. Braumuller, the boy who lived next door to General

Hood, was again sitting in front of his dugout watching the night's bombardment when "a few shells exploded nearby." Then, he "sort of lost interest in the affair."

JULY 26

■ *The New York Times*

"*Nashville, Monday, July 25*—The remains of General McPherson reached here at 9 A.M. today and were escorted through to the Louisville depot by the 13th Regulars. Capt. Lamont, of the Tenth Tennessee Infantry, Col. Scully of the Regular Artillery, Generals McElroy and Gillom, and Gov. Johnson and Staff were in the procession, which comprised all the officers of the different departments in the city.

"The remains leave by special train at 12 o'clock noon accompanied by a guard of the 13th Regulars, of two officers and 50 men to Sandusky, Ohio. . . .

"Our army is in good condition and the situation is favorable.

"Official news is in from in front of Atlanta. It is meagre but no reverses are reported. Gen. Sherman still maintains his position and is vigorously advancing."

▧ *The Richmond Gazette*

"All that we really know is that the fighting has been very heavy, that the losses have been severe on both sides, and that Gen. Sherman up to Saturday last, did not occupy Atlanta.

"In losing Gen. McPherson, Gen. Sherman has lost his best officer and it is doubtful whether there now remains in the Army of Tennessee a commander who is capable of adequately filling his place."

✄ *The Richmond Inquirer*

"The news of the victory at Atlanta . . . delighted the public as much as any that has been received during the war. It caused a general joy throughout the city and will carry the same to all quarters of the country. Gen. Hood has signalled his acceptance of command of the Army of Tennessee with a brilliant victory, and justified his selection by success. . . .

"Light breaks from the only dark point in our lines. Atlanta is now felt to be safe, and Georgia will soon be free from the foe. The central army of the Confederacy has recovered its prestige and defeated the exultant foe."

The *Macon Telegraph* printed a letter to "Dear Clisby." It read:

"Last night I slept undisturbed for the first night in three in consequence of the shelling of the city. Since Friday a 20-pound Parrott shell has been thrown into the city every 10 minutes until 4 o'clock yesterday afternoon. The picket firing ceased about the same time, and all has been perfectly quiet till this hour, when only a musket or two has been heard. What this sudden cessation means I am unable to tell. Some think it means a fight today, some think a notification to non-combatants of a general shelling of the city, others think a new movement of the two armies. Great many houses have been pierced by shell. A shell exploded in Mr. John Lovejoy's dining room, another on the corner of Judge Ezzard's house, and I could mention at least 200 more, and wonderful to say only one or two persons have been hurt. Mrs. Weaver was wounded, the same shell killing her child in her arms.

"A dozen shells have struck Wesley Chapel and the parsonage. Two batteries have the range of the Car Shed and the Wesley Chapel, and they peg away night and day, making line shots in the direction of the State Railroad bridge. The women and children fly to the cellars and the men walk about carelessly watching where the shells strike. Everyone is sanguine of success. I refrain from alluding to the army. Suffice it to say all right.

"The Executive Aid Committee is well represented in Mr.

McLin, who distributed 5,400 rations yesterday to the unfortunate women and children of Atlanta. This was a contribution
from the brave men of Stevenson's Division. May they live long
to bless the country.

"Parties who have arrived at Macon from Atlanta report the
Yankee loss in the recent engagement at 18,000 and our loss at
7,000. The Yankees lost five general officers, names not given,
and we one, Gen. Walker. Nearly all the Yankee dead and
wounded fell into our hands."

On that cloudy Tuesday, the Office of the Quartermaster
General officially announced its evacuation to Macon, "where it
will remain for a short time" before continuing on to the state
capital, Milledgeville.

Sergeant Graham, from Illinois, found picket firing "sharp,"
and once during the morning his outfit was ordered to man the
breastworks in anticipation of another assault by Hood.

In Newnan, Fannie Beers, a Richmond nurse, had been "dis-
quieted" for several days over rumors that one of Sherman's
tough cavalry leaders, Major General Edward McCook, was
planning a raid on the village. Newnan, already full of the sick,
wounded, and refugeed, was the destination of additional hundreds daily. All became apprehensive at the prospect of fighting
in so congested an area. Mrs. Beers had her little boy with her;
her husband was fighting outside of Atlanta.

Kate Cumming, a fellow nurse in Newnan, received, "a lot
of badly wounded; some of them . . . shot near the spine which
paralyzes them so that they can neither use hands or feet. There
is one very large man, named Brown, who is as helpless as an
infant. Another, Captain Curran, is almost as bad. A fine-looking young man from Kentucky has lost a leg and arm; there
is but little hope of his recovery. Mr. Pullet, a Georgian, is
wounded through the lungs; the least movement causes the
blood to run in streams from his wound; the doctors have little
hope of saving him. Mr. Thomas is wounded through the head;
his brain is oozing out, and at times he is delirious. Mr. Orr is
injured in the spine, and is perfectly helpless. Mr. Summers of
Mississippi is wounded in the right hand and can not feed himself. Mr. Harper is badly wounded, and can scarcely eat any-

thing. Mr. Latta, his friend, had his leg amputated. I have written to the chaplain of their regiments, the Twelfth and Forty-seventh Tennessee, informing him of their condition. Mr. Henderson from Tennessee is severely wounded. We have so many poor, helpless fellows, that it is heart-breaking to look at them. I went down to the train when they arrived and they were a sad sight to behold. A handsome Texan died as soon as he was brought up to the hospital. A particular friend and one of his officers were with him. There were about 50 brought to our hospital. A number were sent to the Gamble.

"The first thing we did was to get them something to eat. We had buttermilk which they relished.

"Mrs. Captain Nutt, a lady from Louisiana, brought us some nice rags, an article which we were entirely out of; and she also gave us her aid. Mr. Moore also assisted. At a time like this the nurses are all kept busy attending to the wants of the surgeons. We washed the men's hands and faces, and fed them.

"Among these martyrs is a young man who, the surgeons are certain, shot himself intentionally. We have a case of that now and then. Some time ago, a man, rather than be returned to duty, cut three of his fingers off with an ax, and a bad job he made of it.

"As Miss W. is gone, Mrs. W. takes her place; so we have many more duties now than we had. Many of the men are unable to feed themselves. I go over at mealtime and assist the nurses.

"Mr. Rabbit, a member of Garrety's battery, is here badly wounded. He has suffered awfully from having gangrene in his wound. Dr. Wellford, his surgeon, thought at one time he would lose his leg.

"There is an old lady here taking care of her sick son; she lives across the river about 15 miles distant. She says she has the *felicity* of having the Federal cavalry surrounding her place. They go into houses and what they do not carry away they destroy. They have a dreadful antipathy to crockery, and break all the poor peoples' dishes.

"I met a Mr. Miller visiting Mr. Dougherty's who told me that these vandals had called on him, and after robbing him of

every thing worth taking, took some dressed leather that he
prized very highly; and before his eyes cut it into pieces. It
seems to me that they are bent on creating a market for their
own wares."

By evening, in Atlanta, Sergeant William Graham received
orders to be ready to march. In the chilly dark "at 2 A.M. in the
morning we left our works quietly."

JULY 27

■ *The New York Times*

*"Washington—*Official information from Atlanta states that
there were no operations yesterday, but there was hard work
in the trenches. There had been no fighting."

*"Two Miles from Atlanta—*Hood is covering the removal of
the army and government property; and if he remains much
longer in our front must be captured by our army, which is
closing in around that doomed city.

"Gate City is already being evacuated. Men, women and children, human and inhuman chattels are being hurried south,
and the *Atlanta Appeal* alone seems to stand at the post of
danger."

✉ *Richmond Sentinel*

"There had been no dispatch received from Georgia up to
6 o'clock last evening.

"We learn from the Georgia papers that Sherman's raiding
parties are operating on the Montgomery and West Point and
Georgia State roads, with the design of cutting off supplies from
Atlanta."

Much of the enveloping Union army marched until 4:00 A.M.
At daybreak, detachments stacked their rifles west of the rail-

road between Atlanta and Marietta and ate breakfast. The food
was cold—and wet.

Atlanta, on that damp Wednesday, began its second week of
shelling. The casualties were surprisingly few. Many buildings
were hit and, as Wallace Reed noted in his personal journals:

"An exploding bomb would tear up several rooms in a
house, or when it fell in the street a deep hole would be left,
big enough to swallow an army wagon with its mules. The
people, however, were so watchful that they managed for a time
to escape injury. It was no uncommon thing for a lady to walk
some distance to see a neighbor. Sometimes she would be
caught on the way in a pattering shower of shells, and then she
would run merrily into the nearest yard and huddle down in
a bomb-proof, perhaps with perfect strangers. But that made no
difference. A common danger made everybody well acquainted,
kind and hospitable.

"People living in the vicinity of tall steeples and the smoke
stacks of mills and factories had a hard time. The enemy's guns
were trained upon these prominent objects, and sometimes
their fire was too hot for anything. Then, too, the outgoing
trains made a rumble that could be distinctly heard by the outside gunners, and random shots were constantly fired as feelers."

The previous night, the members of a family in the southern
section of Atlanta had sat on their piazza, fanning themselves.

"Occasionally," Wallace Reed reported, "a fuse shell ascended
with a whish into the mid-heavens, and burst with a deafening
explosion. The watchers were not much afraid of these missiles,
as they could see their approach a long way off.

"Suddenly there was a thunder clap in the next yard. Several
panels of the fence were knocked down, and a few stray fragments of shell knocked off two or three of the banisters of the
piazza. In less than ten seconds the family had found its way
into the reliable bomb-proof.

" 'Pshaw! I am not going to stay down here this hot night,'
said the only man in the party. 'I'll go up to my room and finish
reading the *Life of Napoleon*, and if there is any real danger
I will come down to you.'

"There were tears and protests, but the colonel, as he was

called, was stubborn. So he went upstairs in the wing of the
building nearest to the bomb-proof and seated himself by a
window, where he had the advantage of a light, and could also
look out upon the city. The shelling was terrific, but the inmates of the dug-out, every time they took a peep, could see
the colonel turning over the pages of his Napoleon, apparently
forgetful of the stirring occurrences around him.

"Had a volcano broken loose? The ground trembled under
the shock of the explosion, and after the lurid glare had died
away, the dense fumes of sulphur filled the air, and made the
atmosphere so thick that nothing could be seen. Before the
terrified people in the bomb-proof had pulled themselves together, something very much like a singed cat, only much
bigger, rolled down into their midst, and then sat up with a
sneeze.

"It was the colonel! There were frantic inquiries, and a close
inspection of the victim, but it was soon discovered that he had
escaped without any more serious damage than a few bruises,
and the blackening of his face with gunpowder.

" 'How did it happen?' asked everybody in a chorus.

" 'Don't ask me,' replied the colonel irritably. 'You know as
well as I do. It must have been a twenty-four pounder. I know
I can't hear, and I can hardly see and I'm all choked up with
sulphur and rubbish.'

"Just then his wife, who had looked out gave a cry, 'Where is
the left wing of the house?' she asked.

" 'Don't know. Don't ask me. I couldn't bring it with me,
you know. It was all I could do to get here myself.'

"When morning dawned the extent of the wreck could be
seen at a glance. The shell had completely demolished the
wing in which the colonel had been sitting in an upper room,
and his escape appeared miraculous."

The shelling slackened in Atlanta, but the rain started. Taylor Beatty, for one, thought it a "good shower," and hoped for
more.

Before Sergeant Graham had paused in his early morning's
march, Grandma Smith was packing a number of her patients
off farther south. It was yet dark, and quiet in Covington.

She had breakfast ready for her wards by dawn. As the trays started down the long rows of cots, she recorded, the ward master called out:

" '. . . the Yankees are in town again!'

" 'Oh,' says I, 'surely you are mistaken.'

" 'No, I am not. Just look up the street, yonder, and you will see them yourself.'

"I did look; and sure enough there they came in full tilt close at us. The boys all began saying, 'Grandma, what shall we do?'

" 'Stay just where you are; run in the cellar and hide; or jump in bed and play off sick, like Chris, and I'll see that they do not get you.' All who had time, did so; but some were not fast enough. In about two minutes some four or five dirty, drunken scamps dashed up, almost in the door, saying 'Oh, you d— Rebels, come out of there, and march on the square, where General Stoneman is. We will show you how to fight against the Union.'

"The boys gave me an enquiring look. Says I, 'Go with them, boys, like gentlemen and soldiers; they won't keep you long.'

"In the meantime, Dr. Robertson came and requested me to see that none escaped, for Dr. Nichol, the post surgeon, had surrendered the hospital and all the inmates. I then felt indeed like I was a prisoner; but I knew that our surgeon would not suffer us to be imposed upon, and I continued serving up breakfast, with the assistance of the still faithful negro woman, who did not have quite the same grounds for abusing 'dem dar niggers,' for one man stood his ground, saying 'he see 'nuff ob dem Yanks toder time, and he wan't 'fraid ob dem dat he knowed.'

"While I stood gazing at the two boys who they were taking off, three or four who had remained in the yard pretending to be sentinels, rode up to the kitchen window, and demanded, 'hand us out them biscuit there, and that chicken; we are hungry.'

"The cook gave them a quizzical glance. I ordered him to give it to them, for I saw they were drunk, and I was afraid of their doing mischief. There they set on their horses until they devoured the last mouthful that was on hand, and swore because there was no more. By way of quieting them, I said, 'Gentlemen, I hope you will not so far forget the dignity of gentlemen, and that your mothers were women, as to impose on a lone woman because she is in your power.'

"One of them began to reel, and spit, and mouthe out, 'Oh, no, madam, we will not forget our mother; she was a nice and mighty good woman.' I felt greatly relieved when they were called off. Our poor boys had to fast until more was cooked for their breakfast.

"Our head surgeon was again marched off to headquarters by a motley set, but was soon relieved by the intercession of a Federal surgeon of the same name—Wm. H. Robertson. He showed every mark of a gentleman in his treatment of the faculty, for which they were under many obligations to him.

"The sick boys kept their beds during the most of the day. Those who had taken refuge in the cellar, remained there closely hid, while I picketed and supplied them with food. If ever a set of Yanks were cheated out of a trophy, it was Stoneman's set of vagabond depredators that day. Our two boys that were carried off, returned in a short time. Oh, did not my heart leap with joy when I saw them returning.

" 'What did you tell us, grandma?—you said we would not stay long.' 'How did you get off so soon?' I asked. 'Well, just as we presented ourselves to his honor General Stoneman, a courier dashed up, and I gave him a paper. On looking at it, he said to us, "you can go to h—l, for all I care, I have no use for you now." '

" 'I know why, says I; 'I guess General Wheeler and his men are too close on his heels for his good health. . . .'

"As soon as I had completed the morning repast, I walked up to one of our wards on the square, to see how they were doing after they had been surrounded all morning by their tormenters. I hardly noticed the band of thieves who had been first among us; but I was compelled to notice these, as they made themselves more conspicuous than the first. I thought, as I had to be among, and annoyed by the detestable hords, I would look at them as they were passing. I stood in the door and viewed them to my heart's disgust as they defiled. Here they came dashing through the town pell-mell, while their stars and stripes still floated to the breeze on the square; and if ever the once revered banner of a country was trailed in the dust, it truly was at that time, to the disgrace of those bearing it. The sight which met my eyes there, as displayed by the defenders of this once noble flag, was surely disgusting in the extreme, and one calculated to inspire in the hearts of all honest Southern people the most bitter hatred towards the invaders of their homes under the plea of defending the honor of the stars and stripes. Chickens, eggs, turkeys, ham, and in fact every available article they could possibly find to steal, they had on their horses. From the manner they hastened off, it was very evident that something was in the rear that did not appear very attractive to them.

"They had quite a number of stolen horses and mules, on which they had mounted about as many sable riders, social companions, for their forward move. The unfortunate negroes had been gulled off by their equality friends. Some of them could be heard bidding their friends good bye, saying they were free, and were going to fight 'de white trash.' Poor, deluded creatures. . . .

"While we were standing in the door gazing at the vast crowd of flying foes, our attention was attracted to a very dirty Yankee, who came dashing up and peeped in, and at the same time hurriedly enquired, 'How many patients have you here?'

"I answered three.

" 'You have been sending them off, ha?' " 'Yes; every one we could,' I replied. " 'Are there any of the Ninth Texas here?' " 'No; none in your reach.' "

Householders in Covington were told by the cavalrymen that they were en route to liberate Andersonville. A few soldiers threatened to return for "vengeance" if they found their countrymen to be receiving the cruel treatment in prison as was rumored.

By evening, Major General George Stoneman's cavalry was galloping out of town, with the advance pickets of Joe Wheeler's horsemen already riding hard after them. Grandma Smith, appreciative of her "deliverance," heard the firing between the opposing cavalrymen.

"Quiet had begun to prevail again," she wrote, "dinner was given to the patients, and the general duties of the evening were in progress, when suddenly another fright, more fearful than that of the morning, though it proved a hoax, that ten thousand Yankee infantry were near town, and would soon be there, and would sweep everything before them. But this all soon blew over, and all was cheerful.

"Now the hidden boys came out in the fresh air, and all right. The sick left their beds, delighted at their speedy recovery. All were ready to join in the changing events of the day, and many were the merry laughs at the Yankees being so completely humbugged out of a number of Rebel prisoners. That night many of them came to the conclusion that escape was the better part of valor. Having run the risk of being captured more than once within the last few weeks, they adopted the old adage, that 'a burnt child dreads the fire.' Therefore, several left."

Union forces were moving position for the night. The rain began again, and many of the troops lay in the soggy fields.

Others crawled near campfires to reread the letters received "from home."

Railroad passengers from Macon and Griffin had not yet arrived in Atlanta by midnight. According to rumor, the locomotive, *Sunshine,* blew up at Lovejoy's Station, killing the engineer, James Hiskeith.

JULY 28

◤ *Southern Press Association*

"*Macon*—Latest advices from Atlanta by train and telegraph are to yesterday evening.

"We learn by the train which left at nightfall that the enemy attacked our left, extending from the city towards the Chattahoochee, yesterday and were repulsed and driven about a mile. Late last evening orders were received by telegraph to send cars and bring the wounded to the rear.

"A telegram from a high officer to Gen. Johnston, dated Atlanta, yesterday, has been received here stating that fighting is now going on, and we have driven them. Details not known. Generals Stewart, Walthall and Loring are reported wounded.

"Private telegrams from Griffin report General Wheeler was wounded. A cavalry force of the enemy, strength unknown, struck the Macon and Western Railroad below Jonesboro, this morning, and are reported to be tearing up the road in this direction. Another cavalry force of the enemy is today reported near Clinton, advancing towards this place.

"Gov. Brown today issued a proclamation ordering all aliens in the State who refuse to volunteer to defend the State which affords them protection, to leave the State within 10 days; also that the orders of Confederate officers attempting to protect from active service their favorites in civil pursuits, when the State needs all who are able to bear arms in front of the enemy, cannot be respected by the State officers. While it is not his purpose to cripple the Confederate Government in providing all necessary support for the army, he will execute the laws of the State, compelling all detailed persons attending to ordinary business to aid in repelling the enemy.

"He denies the Confederate Government's right to divest the State of its jurisdiction over the whole militia by mustering into service and detailing them to remain at home engaged in the common avocations of life. All persons claiming to be employed by the Confederate Government must be exempted by certificates of the State authorities, on evidence that they are constantly employed and are indispensably necessary."

At daylight, Sergeant William Graham moved past William Coursey's place and the Poor House to a position near the Lick Skillet Road and Ezra Chapel, a meeting hall on the west side of Atlanta. "We pulled our rail pens for breastwork. Continued firing at the lines. Killed a calf and had some meat.

"About 8 ordered forward and after forming two or three times we finally stopped one and are now putting breastworks. Firing all along the line. This is a movement on the enemy left to advance the line. After getting our works the enemy commenced an attack on the 15th Corps, upon our train and right but were repulsed after five distinct charges. Very heavy musket firing; the attacks extended to the right of the 17th Corps."

That Thursday morning fight became one of the most sanguinary the Atlanta soldier, W. P. Archer, had experienced. He watched his friends being carried off the field through the woods to division hospitals.

"Their litters, being noted, were as bloody as if hogs had been stuck on them; their flagstaffs were shot to pieces; their colors were shot into ribbons, and not more than one-half of that fine brigade that left that morning returned."

At 9:45 A.M. Brigadier General F. A. Shoup, Hood's Chief of Staff, hurried a dispatch to Surgeon A. J. Foard, Medical Director, Army of Tennessee—"The commanding general desires you to thank the proper authorities of the several relief associations for the valuable assistance they have rendered the sick and wounded of this army. He highly appreciates their efforts and is glad to assure them they are rendering vast service."

Captain Evan P. Howell, across the city from Ezra Church, wrote his wife, Julia, in Augusta. A few weeks before he had evacuated Julia and one-year-old Clark from their home on the Chattahoochee. Frightened by the nearing cannon fire, Julia had filled her apron with biscuits, tied the cow behind their wagon as a supplier of fresh milk for the boy, and plodded from the danger area at a pace dictated by the cow.

Their home was in ashes. Evan had not heard from Julia since then, "owing to the fact I *presume* of the breaking up of the usual mail route from Atlanta to Augusta by the Yankees. Your last letter was dated the 18th and I am now exceedingly anxious to hear from you again. But I am not at all certain that you will get this nor am I certain that I will receive one from you in some time.

"We are still standing quiet since our big fight on last Friday. We occupy the ditches around town, and the enemy just in front of us; sharp-shooting and cannonading now and then. The enemy shell the city once in a while, doing no other damage than kill a few women and children. A lady was nursing her child in town the other day and a shell burst in the house, killing the child, and the splinters from the house wounded the lady frightfully in the face.

"Dean and Charlie are well. Jerry wishes to be remembered to his family. I have one of Grandpa Howell's boys 'Tom' staying with me now, he is a fine negro and waits on me very well. He ran off and left his wife for fear the Yankees would get him, and came to me. He is a very likely boy. I wish so much I could be with you to eat your nice okra soup and your corn, etc. I do hope that the next summer will permit us to enjoy ourselves under our own vine and fig tree. And then our earthly happiness will begin. Or has it already commenced and will then only mature . . .

"You asked me in your last letter if I would like to have a needle case. I would like very much to have a very small one fitted out with thread and buttons."

Joe Semmes, in his warehouse at East Point, had not heard from his wife, Eo, since July 10. "I have told you how precious your letters are to me and you little know how keenly I feel the loss of them. I trust before many days the mails will reach me again.

"Since my last, after a good deal of trouble, the Claytons succeeded in getting away with nearly everything. I gave them three good cars which had contained meal and into two they put all their household goods and the other made a comfortable chamber for the sick girls and Cousin Caroline herself. They did not get off a minute too soon for today we hear that the only Railroad left to us, the one by which they left, has been cut by the enemy.

"The Batteries which played upon the city proper have ceased their fire, from what cause I cannot learn, but as we placed in position some superior guns I suppose they may be knocked out. Only such shells and shot as overshoot the works now fall in the city, and but three have come close to us in the last twenty-four hours.

"Yesterday about 12 o'clock, immediately in front of me, the enemy assaulted our lines furiously but were quickly and easily repulsed, with what loss I cannot say, only Genl. Ector lost a leg. The enemy were making another flank move yesterday and we look for another fight in a day or two. Hood is determined to fight them whenever he can get a fair chance. Warfield's command was in the battle of the 22nd and lost 22 men and a Major wounded, none killed outright, he was unhurt. Billy Walker who used to be with Speed in Memphis was killed, he was related to the family by the mother's side and was a very fine young man and a good soldier. Genl. S. D. Lee is in command of Hood's old corps.

"This is all the news I can tell you of myself. I can only say that I am tolerably well, and love you as much as you could wish, and much more than I know how to put on paper.

"What shall I do about the money for Julia's board? I can raise it but how can I send it? You have never told me about the receipt of the 10 pounds of sperm candles I sent you last spring. They cannot now be had, and I am determined you shall have them if they were left in Montgomery. I send a heartfull of love to all my little ones and my relations. God bless you."

Julia, Semmes' oldest daughter, was in a convent in Charleston; little Eo, Malcolm, and Eustis were with their mother.

At 4:40 P.M. General Shoup again transmitted an order to Dr. Foard—"You will please cause the wounded to be shipped to the rear as rapidly as possible tonight. As soon as you ascertain what can be accomplished, report the facts."

In Newnan, scouts announced before evening that the Federals were crossing the river in large numbers. Nurse Kate Cumming looked out of her hospital window. She saw the sky glaring in the direction of Palmetto, a small town on the railroad.

"We knew then what we had to expect, and got ready as

usual; whiskey, and every thing of any consequence, was sent off; the men who were able taking to the woods.

"Some of the Negro women refused to go this time, as they had such a hard time of it before; but off they went, 'truck' and all. The old woman who suffered so much before we could not prevail upon to remain behind the others."

And, "as dark came" around Ezra Church, Sergeant Graham relaxed in a strange quiet though "some shells exploded in our camp at dusk, doing no damage. The loss on our part was light, that of the enemy heavy."

Trains rolled south from Atlanta, evacuating the Gate City's hospitals, in accordance with Hood's orders. Taking advantage of the confusion, drunken Confederate cavalrymen looted stores in Atlanta. "The greatest outrage our soldiers have ever committed," as one irate citizen declared.

Sherman flashed Thomas: "Let two of your Napoleons or 20-pounder Parrott batteries keep up fire on Atlanta all night, each battery throwing a shot every 15 minutes, partly for effect and partly as signal to our cavalry."

JULY 29

■ *Frank Leslie's Illustrated Weekly* (New York)

"Gen. Logan's 15th Corps has again added to the imperishable honors won on many a bloody field. It has met the enemy again and routed them. The battle of the 28th was more brilliant than any of its predecessors, from the fact that the whole rebel army was massed against a single corps, with a view, if possible, of breaking it, and getting at our communications in the vicinity of the Chattahoochee. . . .

"The skirmishing commenced early in the morning . . . the assailants, after driving in our pickets, moved up steadily and with a steady step, opening out when within 400 yards of our fortification. Gen. Hood superintended the movement, and was seen riding up and down the lines encouraging his men, and pointed out the early victory he anticipated, while his subordinates were equally busy in urging the lines forward. Along our lines they observed a general and his staff moving slowly and halting as if to confer with every regimental commander . . . the commander was Gen. Logan. There was a storm of bullets flying around him; he wavered not but continued his movements down the lines. 'Keep your men here,' was his order to each regimental commander, 'till the rebels are within easy range, then let no shot be thrown away.' Meeting no force, the assailants took courage, and when within 200 yards raised a tremendous yell, and started on the double quick but at that instant the signal was given and every battery double-shotted with canister was let loose, and the apparently deserted fortifications being lined with heads, and at every foot a shining musket was aimed at the assailants. I have frequently heard of the murderous fire poured forth from the heights of Bunker Hill and from behind the cotton bales of New Orleans, but how feeble those when compared with the destroying volley which swept in a single instant hundreds of men into eternity and laid thousands upon the earth maimed, many of them for life, on the plains before Atlanta.

"The human tide which flowed on with apparently irresistible force now ebbed and rolled back in terror and dismay."

■ *The New York Times*

"The battle of the 28th inst. was an assault in force on the Fifteenth Corps and appears to have resulted in as complete a defeat of the rebels as that of the 22d. Six hundred and forty-two dead rebels were buried by our forces after that battle."

✕ *Atlanta Appeal*

"The progress which the enemy has made toward the heart of the Confederacy, and the enterprise he has manifested by his raids upon our railroads and undefended points, ought to convince our people that there is no security from danger but

in active, energetic, self-defence. The people of the Gulf States
have so long lived remote from the actual theater of the war,
that they have flattered themselves with the belief that their
homes would never be visited by the relentless invader. The
events of the last few weeks will serve to disabuse them of this
fond delusion, and teach them that if they would continue to
live as freemen, they must arm and rally to the front in their
own defence.

"The guns of the tyrant foe are now thundering at their
very doors, and supineness and inaction now are criminal; yea,
suicidal. No one will for a moment deny but there are able-
bodied men enough in the State of Georgia, and Alabama either
to annihilate Sherman and his army or to drive them howling
back to the Ohio River. Will they not, at a crisis like this,
come promptly to the rescue and aid our veteran soldiers in
the good and holy cause? If those living south of us would
defend their homes, their property, their liberty and the rights
they have inherited from a heroic ancestry, now is the time
and Atlanta the place to make that defence. . . .

"Arms are now plentiful and what is now needed is men and
boys to load and shoot them."

Friday dawned humid and foggy. There was an oppressive
silence as two armies waited, almost face to face, in Atlanta's
wasteland of jagged wooden parapets.

At breakfast time, a few shells whined into the Union camp,
"but done no injury," as one soldier wrote in his notebook.
After breakfast, sometimes wriggling forward on their stomachs,
opposing pickets changed the watch.

"Poor Gladden," Colonel Taylor Beatty observed, "was dead
when I got there—had just died—he was shot through both
legs. Made preparations to bury him." General Hardee's lawyer
was shocked to learn that all officers but one of the First Louisiana had been wounded at Ezra Church.

The Union forces were back in Decatur. On Mary Gay's
front yard the tents of the Army of the Ohio were spread. Ever
since Toby's funeral she had heard the "thunder tones" of
artillery echoing from hill to hill.

That day, Mary resolved to smuggle Northern newspapers to Atlanta. She hoped their contents would be "valuable to my people."

There was an "insolent" quality to the enemy soldiers, which made her doubly desirous for a quick end to the war. However, one exception threaded his way through the Blue encampment rolling away from her doorstep—a "tall, lank, honest-faced Yankee."

Gaining the porch, he removed his cap and mopped his brow with a stained handkerchief. The morning had turned hot, almost breathless, and even the flies clung with languor to the paint-peelings of the front columns.

" 'Is Miss Gay in?' he asked.

"I responded that I was she, and he handed me a letter addressed to myself. I hastily tore it open and read the contents. It was written by a reverend gentleman whose wife was a distant relative of my mother, and told that she was very ill. 'Indeed,' wrote he, 'I have but little hope of ever seeing her any better, and I beg you to come to see her, and spend several days.'

"I showed the letter to my mother, who was sitting near by, and, like myself, engaged in studying the situation. She strenuously objected to my going, and advanced many good reasons for my not doing so; but my reasons for going counteracted them all in my estimation, and I determined to go.

"Taking Telitha with me, I carried the letter to the Provost Marshall and asked him to read it and grant me the privilege of going. After reading the letter, he asked me how I obtained it, and received my statement. He then asked me if I could refer him to the party who brought it to me. Leaving the letter with him, I ran home and soon returned with the desired individual who had fortunately lingered in the yard in anticipation of usefulness. Convinced that the invitation was genuine, and for a humane purpose, this usually morose marshall granted me a 'permit' to visit those poor old sick people, for the husband was almost as feeble as his wife. I told the obliging marshall that there was another favor I should like to ask of him, if he would not think me too presumptuous.

" 'Name it,' he said.

"I replied, 'Will you detail one or more of the soldiers to act as an escort for me? I am afraid to go with only this girl.'

To this he also assented, and said it was a wise precaution. He asked me when I wished to come home.

" 'Day after tomorrow afternoon,' I told him, and received assurance that an escort would be in waiting for me at that time.

"It now became necessary to make some important preparations for the trip. A great deal was involved, and if my plans were successful, important events might accrue. A nice white petticoat was called into requisition and, when I got done with it, it was literally lined with Northern newspapers: The 'Cincinnati Enquirer' and 'The New York Daily Times,' 'The Cincinnati Commercial Gazette' and 'The Philadelphia Evening Ledger' under the manipulation of my fingers, took their places on the inner sides and rear of the skirt, and served as a very stylish 'bustle,' an article much in vogue in those days. This preparatory work having been accomplished, it required but a few moments to complete my toilet and, under the auspices of a clear conscience and a mother's blessing, doubtless, I started on a perilous trip. The ever-faithful Telitha was by my side, and the military escort a few feet in advance.

"After a walk of a mile and a half, I reached my destination for that day. I found the old lady in question much better than I had expected. Nervous and sick himself, her husband had greatly exaggerated her afflictions. By degree, and under protest, I communicated to these aged people my intention of carrying information to Hood's headquarters that might be of use to our army. Both were troubled about the possible result if I should be detected; but my plans were laid, and nothing could deter me from pursuing them."

Meanwhile, scouts arrived at Kate Cumming's hospital and reported that the Union troops had gone "in the direction of Jonesboro, on the Macon Road. We had respite again."

At 3:25 P.M. General Shoup transmitted an urgent order to Hood's three corps commanders, Hardee, Lee, and Cheatham: "The supply of ammunition is very small. General Hood appeals to you to use every means to reduce its expenditure.

Skirmishers even must not fire except in cases of necessity. This is important."

A bitter joke swept the trenches around Atlanta following the slaughter at Ezra Church.

"Well, Johnny, how many of you are left?" a Union picket supposedly called out.

"Oh, about enough for another killing," was the grim answer from the Confederate picket.

Colonel Beatty succeeded in obtaining a "good" coffin to bury his friend, Gladden. Services were held at 6:30 P.M., close by the officers' tents. Beatty prepared to change his post in the morning—"hd. qutrs. have already moved."

Life in Atlanta went on. Dr. Logan, exhausted from caring for the wounded and shipping them south, left Atlanta to try to reach his family, already sent away. He believed they were cut off by Sherman's army.

A son was born late in the afternoon to Dan Pittman.

Richard Peters, traveling through Georgia and Alabama in connection with railroad and defense work, was at home where he hoped to remain for two weeks.

There was an evening lull in the shelling.

JULY 30

■ *The New York Times*

"*Washington, Friday, July 29*—the latest official dispatches from Gen. Sherman's army state that he is steadily drawing his lines closer around Atlanta.

"He has as yet received no tidings of the cavalry force sent out to cut the Macon and Columbus Railroad which is the only means of escape to the rebel army from Atlanta.

"Washington, Friday, July 29—A dispatch received here claims that Gen. Hood has made efforts to renew the assault upon Gen. Sherman's lines, since the Battle on Friday last. They were, however, feeble efforts, and easily and promptly repelled, with an aggregate loss to Sherman of only about a hundred men."

Richmond Sentinel

"Nashville—No one would grieve for the loss of the city of Atlanta more than we, and few, perhaps, apprehend its loss. We learn, from both public and private sources, that new troops in large numbers are daily joining Hood's army. We hear that there are many more on their way to join it; and expect daily to hear that all Sherman's lines of communication with the base of operations are cut. We hear of no fresh troops on their way to join him. Kentucky is full of 'rebel guerrillas.' A general rebellion against the Federal Government is daily apprehended. More Federal troops are needed there, and are earnestly called for; but the United States Government can spare none to send. . . .

"If he cannot take Atlanta today, he will be still less able to capture it tomorrow, and the next day and the next.

"But suppose he were to take it? Would this better his situation? No, but make it far worse. He would lose a third or a fourth of his army in the battle by which he won it, be in no condition for a forward movement, and less able than ever to retrace his steps to Chattanooga, and thence to Nashville. Victory or defeat will be equally fatal to him. Cut off from reinforcements, he is situated just as Pyrrhus was in Italy, when looking over the field of battle after a splendid victory, that great warrior exclaimed,

" 'One more such victory and I am undone.'

"Let Sherman gain two great victories over us, and he and his army are ours. But we will have them on cheaper and better terms. He will gain no victory. His lines of communication will be cut off. He will be compelled to attack Hood behind his intrenchments—will be defeated; and, seeing no hope of escape, he and his army will surrender at discretion. This is the most probable result and at all events, sooner or later, and whether he captures Atlanta or not, he and his army will be captured or cut to pieces in the attempt to retreat."

Cots whitened the Court House lawn in Newnan. Kate Cumming was with her patients when a courier rode into town. He announced to a crowd of the curious, who quickly congregated around him, that the Yankees were but six miles away.

A locomotive at the depot, at the foot of the hill from the hospitals, pouring woodsmoke into the hot, dusty air, emitted "a most unearthly whistle," followed immediately by musketry firing. All the men who had been idling about the Court House, townspeople and ambulatory patients, took to their heels.

"I never saw men run as all did," was the observation of Kate Cumming who hereupon followed their example: She thought she should gather up the trinkets and money given her by the wounded soldiers for safe keeping. She had put the little cache down on one of the surgical dressing tables. As the little Scottish nurse rushed across the hard-packed clay street, bullets "whizzed past" her head.

Fannie Beers, on duty before dawn, was about to serve breakfast in one of the hospitals down the street from the Court House. She was thinking what a "bright and lovely" day it was when she heard the crack-crack of rifle fire followed by shouting and a general commotion in the streets below her windows.

Curiosity consumed Mrs. Beers and she clattered down the worn wooden hospital stairs and outside. At the same time, Kate, clutching the trinkets and money, raced past the hospital and up the nearest hill.

Both nurses became part of a moment-by-moment swelling crowd, more anxious to gain the nearest rise and watch the fighting as spectators than they were to flee.

Word was passed that Brigadier General Philip D. Roddey arrived from West Point by train with six hundred cavalrymen, some dismounted, the previous night. En route to Atlanta, they hastily grabbed their arms when they learned of the impending Federal raid—their first warning being the engineer's whistle. The engineer himself had been asked to surrender by an advance Union cavalryman who could not know the identity of the train's passengers.

Mrs. Beers heard the cries of "The Yankees! The Yankees!" all about her. She later recorded:

"The firing continued for a few moments, then ceased. When the smoke cleared away, our own troops could be seen drawn up on the railroad and on the depot platform. The hill on the opposite side seemed to swarm with Yankees. Evidently they had expected to surprise the town, but, finding themselves opposed by a force whose numbers they were unable to estimate, they hastily retreated up the hill. By that time a crowd of impetuous boys had armed themselves and were running down the hill on our side to join the Confederates. Few men followed (of the citizens), for those who were able had already joined the army. Those who remained were fully occupied in attending to the women and children.

"It was evident that the fight was only delayed. An attack might be expected at any moment. An exodus from the town at once began.

"Already refugees from all parts of the adjacent country had begun to pour into and pass through, in endless procession and every conceivable and inconceivable style of conveyance, drawn by horses, mules, oxen, and even by a single steer or *cow*. Most of these were women and boys, though the faces of young children appeared here and there,—as it were, 'thrown in' among the 'plunder,'—looking pitifully weary and frightened, yet not so heart-broken as the anxious women who knew not where their journey was to end. Nor had they 'where to lay their heads,' some of them having left behind only the smoking ruins of a home, which, though 'ever so lowly,' was 'the sweetest spot on earth' to them. McCook, by his unparalleled cruelty, had made his name a horror.

"The citizens simply stampeded, 'nor stood upon the order of their going.' There was no time for deliberation. They could not move goods or chattels, only a few articles of clothing; no room for trunks and boxes. Every carriage, wagon, and cart was loaded down with human freight; every saddle horse was in demand."

Kate Cumming recognized General Roddey, who had mounted his horse without taking time to saddle the animal or don his uniform coat. "A lady and myself tried to procure him a saddle, but were unsuccessful; the lady got him a blanket.

"It was rumored that the enemy had surrounded the town and would likely fire upon it. We all suffered much from suspense, as we had many wounded and if there was a battle in town, they would fare worse than any others. How I did hate to think about all the poor fellows lying so helpless, momentarily expecting a shell to be thrown in their midst.

"We had them all moved into the strongest buildings; the Court House was crowded, although every one said a cannon ball could easily penetrate its walls.

"Roddey's men were drawn up in line of battle on one side of our hospital. The citizens sent baskets of provisions to the soldiers who were in battle array, and we sent them what we could."

Mrs. Beers supervised the moving of the Negroes attached to the hospital out of the town to places of temporary safety. They joined other slaves belonging to residents of Newnan.

"These poor creatures were as much frightened as anybody and as glad to get away. Droves of cattle and sheep were driven out on the run, lowing and bleating their indignant remonstrance.

"While the citizens were thus occupied, the surgeons in charge of hospitals were not less busy, though far more collected and methodical. Dr. McAllister, of the 'Buckner,' and Dr. S. M. Bemiss, of the 'Bragg,' were both brave, cool, *executive* men. Their self-possession, their firm, steady grasp of the reins of authority simplified matters greatly. Only those unable to bear arms were left in the wards. Convalescents would have resented and probably disobeyed an order to remain. Not only were they actuated by the brave spirit of Southern soldiers, but they preferred anything to remaining to be captured—better far death than the horrors of a Northern prison. So all quietly presented themselves, and, with assistant-surgeons, druggists, and hospital attendants, were armed, officered, and marched off to recruit the regiment before mentioned.

"The ladies, wives of officers, attendants, etc., were more difficult to manage, for dread of the 'Yankees,' combined with the pain of parting with their husbands or friends, who would soon go into battle, distracted them. Fabulous prices were offered for means of conveyance. As fast as one was procured it was filled and crowded. At last, all were sent off except one two-horse buggy, which Dr. McAllister had held for his wife and myself, and which was driven by his own negro boy, Sam. Meantime, I had visited all the wards, for some of the patients were very near death, and all were in a state of great and injurious excitement. I did not for a moment pretend to withstand their entreaties that I would remain with them, having already decided to do so. Their helplessness appealed so strongly to my sympathies that I found it impossible to resist. Besides, I had an idea and a hope that even in the event of the town being taken I might prevail with the enemy to ameliorate their condition as prisoners. So I promised, and quietly passed from ward to ward announcing my determination, trying to speak cheerfully."

Kate Cumming, Fannie Beers, all the men and women in Newnan—hospital staffs, patients and townspeople—awaited the battle. On one hill the Union troops could be seen planting a cannon aimed at the heart of the village.

During this time, Mary Gay was continuing her journey from Decatur to Atlanta, which she had started the day before.

"The rising sun of another day saw Telitha and me starting on our way to run the gauntlet, so to speak, of Federal bayonets. These good old people had given me much valuable information regarding the way to Atlanta—information which enabled me to get there without conflict with either Confederate or Federal pickets. Knowing the topography of the country, I took a circuitous route to an old mill, Cobb's I believe, and from there I sought the McDonough road. I didn't venture to keep that highway to the city, but I kept within sight of it, and under cover of breast-works and other obstructions, managed to evade videttes and pickets of both armies. After walking fourteen or

fifteen miles, I entered Atlanta at the beautiful home of Mrs.
L. P. Grant, at the southern boundary of the city. That estimable lady never lost an opportunity to doing good. On this occasion, as upon every other offering an opportunity, she remembered to do good. She ordered an appetizing lunch, including
a cup of sure-enough coffee, which refreshed and strengthened
me after my long walk. Her butler having become a familiar
personage on the streets of Atlanta, she sent him as a guide to
important places. We entered the city unchallenged and moved
about at will. The force of habit, probably, led me to Mrs.
McArthur's and to Mrs. Craig's on Pryor Street. The head of
neither of these families was willing to accompany me to Confederate headquarters, and without a guide, I started to hunt
them for myself. What had seemed an easy task now seemed
insurmountable. I knew not in what direction to go, and the
few whom I asked seemed as ignorant as myself. Starting from
Mrs. Craig's, I went towards the depot. I had not proceeded
very far before I met Major John Y. Rankin. I could scarcely
restrain tears of joy. He was a member of the very same command to which my brother belonged. From Major Rankin I
learned that my brother, utterly prostrated, had been sent to
a hospital, either in Augusta or Madison.

"Preferring not to stand upon the street, I asked Major
Rankin to return with me to Mrs. Craig's, which he did, and
spent an hour in pleasant conversation. Mrs. Craig was a delightful conversationalist, and while she was entertaining the
major with that fine art, I retired to a private apartment, and
with the aid of a pair of scissors ripped off the papers from my
underskirt and smoothed and folded them nicely, and after re-
arranging my toilet, took them into the parlor as a trophy of
skill in outwitting the Yankee. Telitha, too, had a trophy to
which she had clung ever since we left home with the tenacity
of an eel, and which doubtless she supposed to be an offering
to 'Marse Tom' and was evidently anxious that he should receive it. Having dismissed Mrs. Grant's butler as no longer
necessary to my convenience, Major Rankin, myself and Telitha
went directly to the headquarters of his command. The papers
seemed to be most acceptable, but I noticed that the gleanings

from conversation seemed far more so. The hopefulness and enthusiasm of our soldiers were inspiring. But alas! how little
they knew of the situation, and how determined not to be
enlightened. Even then they believed that they would hold
Atlanta against Herculean odds, and scorned the idea of surrender. At length the opening of Telitha's package devolved
on me. Shirts, socks and soap, towels, gloves, etc. formed a compact bundle that my mother had sent to our soldiers.

"I now turned my thoughts to our negroes, who were hired
in different parts of the city. Rachel, the mother of King, hired
herself and rented a room from Mr. John Silvey. In order that
I might have an interview with Rachel without disturbing Mr.
Silvey's family, I went to the side gate and called her. She
answered and came immediately. I asked her if she realized the
great danger to which she was continually exposed. Even then
'shot and shell' were falling in every direction, and the roaring
of cannon was an unceasing sound. She replied that she knew
the danger, and thought I was doing wrong to be in Atlanta
when I had a home to be at. I insisted that she had the same
home, and a good vacant house was ready to receive her. But
she was impervious to every argument, and preferred to await
the coming of Sherman in her present quarters. Seeing that I
had no influence over her, I bade her goodbye and left.

"Telitha and I had not gone farther than the First Presbyterian Church, not a square away from the gate upon which I
had leaned during this interview with Rachel, before a bomb-
shell fell by that gate and burst into a thousand fragments,
literally tearing the gate into pieces. After this fearfully im-
pressive adventure, unfortified by any 'permit', I struck a bee
line to Mrs. Grant's. An old negro man belonging to Mrs. Williams, who had 'come out' on a previous occasion, was there,
and wanted to return under my protection to his home within
the enemy's lines. Very earnest assurances from Mrs. Grant to
that effect convinced me that I had nothing to fear from be-
trayal by him, and I consented that he should be a member of
my company homeward bound. Two large packages were ready
for the old man to take care of, about which Mrs. Grant gave
him directions, *sotto voce*. Putting one of them on the end of

a walking cane, he threw it over his right shoulder, and with his left hand picked up the other bundle. Telitha and I were unencumbered. We had not progressed very far before we encountered our pickets. No argument was weighty enough to secure for me the privilege of passing the lines without an official permit. Baffled in this effort, I approved the action of the pickets, and we turned and retraced our steps in the direction of Atlanta, until entirely out of sight of them, and then we turned southward and then eastward, verging a little northward. Constant vigilance enabled me to evade the Yankee pickets, and constant walking brought me safely to the home of my aged and afflicted friends, from which I had started early in the morning of that day. These friends were conservative in every act and word and, it may be, leaned a little out of the perpendicular towards that 'flaunting lie,' the United States flag; therefore they were favorites among the so-called defenders of the Union, and were kept supplied with many palatable articles of food that were entirely out of the reach of rebels who were avowed and 'dyed in the wool.' "

In Newnan there had been several hours of suspense, and sporadic firing. Unexpectedly, in early afternoon, cheers rang above the firing, and Kate Cumming heard that General Wheeler's cavalry was pounding down the highway to relieve the beleaguered defenders, boys, old men, and Roddey's meager cavalry.

"O, how joyfully we hailed them! They came galloping in by two different roads; the enemy in the meantime hearing of their approach, were retreating. They were hotly pursued and when, four miles from town our men came up with them, they made a stand and had quite a battle.

"We heard the booming of cannon, it seemed to me, about two hours. We eagerly listened to hear if it came nearer, as then we would know whether we were successful or not; but it did not seem to move from one spot. We had no idea in what force the enemy were, so did not know what to expect.

"About 4:00 P.M. word was brought that we had killed and captured the whole command. Then the wounded from both sides were brought in. I do not know how many there were in all, but not over nine or ten were brought to our hospital.

"Hundreds of well prisoners marched in a different manner from what they had expected.

"Captain ——, a patient in one of the hospitals, went to the battle as a spectator. He took charge of a prisoner, promising to bring him to town. Instead of doing so, he took him into the woods and shot him. A gentleman who was with him did not see the deed, but heard the shot.

"A friend has told me that when our soldiers were informed of the circumstance, they were very indignant, and vowed, if they could lay hands on the captain, they would hang him.

"Such men ought not to be permitted to bring dishonor on a brave people, and deserve punishment. I have never been an advocate of the black flag, but I think it would be mercy to an act of this kind. For then the enemy would know what they had to expect and would fight valiantly before giving themselves up. This unfortunate man had surrendered in the faith that he would be treated as a prisoner of war.

"There might be some excuse for a man in the heat of battle refusing to take prisoners, when he saw his comrades slain around him, but this captain had no such excuse. He has been guilty of murder, and of the most cowardly kind. . . .

"When this captain was asked by a friend why he had committed the deed, he gave as justification the barbarous treatment of his mother and sister by Federal soldiers. . . .

"Dr. Hughes and other surgeons were for hours on the battlefield, attending to the wounded. Dr. H. says he never worked harder in his life. Four-fifths of the wounded were Federals who appeared very grateful for what he did for them.

"At the commencement of the battle, Dr. H. and others had sent word around to the citizens, telling them to prepare food for our soldiers by the time they would return.

"Mrs. W. and myself were kept busy all the afternoon receiving the food. All—rich and poor—sent something. One crowd of very poor-looking women brought some cornbread and beans, which I am certain they could ill afford. They said they would gladly do without themselves, so our brave defenders had them.

"When the men came in, some of the nurses helped us to serve out the food, as we found it impossible to do so by ourselves. We were very busy till about 10 o'clock when an officer proposed that some of the commissary officer should take the things and divide them.

"The men had remained in the yard while we handed them the food. They put me in mind of a lot of hungry wolves. Poor fellows! Many of them had not eaten any thing in a long time. They were mainly Wheeler's men; Roddey's men had been fed by the citizens.

"I heard many complaints against General Wheeler; the men say, if he had acted differently, not one of the raiders would have escaped. As it is, many hundreds have escaped, and their general, McCook, with them.

"It seems that General Roddey had his men all ready to make a charge and General Wheeler would not give the word of command . . . our men speak very highly of the manner in which the people of Newnan have treated them."

Meanwhile, Mrs. Beers walked outside of the town, holding aloft a wood torch, to greet Wheeler's incoming cavalry. So confused had been the day, she was not even certain it would be Confederate cavalry. If not, she hoped to "intercede for my sick, perhaps to prevent intrusion into the wards."

"The men had ridden far and fast," she wrote. "They now came to a halt in front of the hospital, but had not time to dismount, hungry and thirsty though they were. The regimental servants, however, came in search of water with dozens of canteens hung around them, rattling in such a manner as to show that they were quite empty. For the next half-hour, I believe, I had almost the strength of Samson. Rushing to the bakery, I loaded baskets with bread and handed them up to the soldier-boys to be passed along until emptied. I then poured all the milk I had into a large bucket, added a dipper, and, threading in and out among the horses, ladled out dipperfulls until it was all gone. I then distributed about four buckets of water in the same way. My excitement was so great that not a sensation of fear or of fatigue assailed me. Horses to the right of me, horses to the left of me, horses in front of me, snorted and pawed; but God gave strength and courage: I was not afraid.

"A comparatively small number had been supplied, when a courier from Roddey's command rode up to hasten the reinforcements. At once the whole column was put in motion. As the last rider disappeared, and the tramping of the horses died away in the distance, a sense of weariness and exhaustion so overpowered me that I could have slept where I stood. So thorough was my confidence in the brave men who were sure to repel the invaders that all sense of danger passed away.

"My own sleeping-room was in a house situated at the foot of the hill. I could have gone there and slept securely, but dared not leave my charges. Sinking upon the rough lounge in my office, intending only to rest, I fell fast asleep."

While Fannie Beers slept Union squads near Atlanta, on a "graves party," counted 2,400 Southerners they had buried by late evening.

A rhythmic chant filled Sherman's army—"tobacco and Atlanta, tobacco and Atlanta!" A shortage of smoking tobacco had grown acute.

JULY 31

✉ *Southern Press Association*

"*Macon*—A force of cavalry appeared in Jones county day before yesterday. Night before last they cut the Central railroad in two places, at Gordon and near Walnut Creek bridge, two miles from here. At the same time, they made a demonstration on Macon, and were repulsed yesterday after some severe skirmishing.

"During the fight, several shells were thrown into the suburbs. One fell in the city. It is not known what damage has been done to the railroad. The Yankees are reported to be falling back near Clinton. Their strength is not known. Our loss is 40 killed and wounded.

"*Griffin, Georgia*—Passengers by the train from Atlanta report that a Yankee raiding force entered Newnan yesterday—Roddey's cavalry happened to be on hand and pitched into the raiders and defeated them with great loss, killing a large number and capturing from 700 to 1,000 prisoners. A gentleman who was there says he counted 96 dead Yankees in one place. Col. Brownlow is reported killed.

"We captured all their artillery.

"This is supposed to be the same party that tore up the road at Lovejoy's. We captured a large portion of the wagons taken from us at Fayetteville."

■ *The New York Times*

"*Washington*—Information from Gen. Sherman's army represents affairs to be in the highest degree satisfactory. Our movements for the past day or so have met with no opposition from the enemy, but they crouch behind their fortifications, thus evidently showing they are afraid of the artillery of Gen. Sherman.

"The weather here has been intensely warm for the past two days, thermometer 95° in the shade.

"Gen. Sherman is again in motion in front of Atlanta. The army began moving yesterday on the last line of communication with the rest of the Confederacy left to Hood. An early engagement is anticipated, as the armies are so near to each other that the slightest movement may stir up a fight.

"Most of the people in this vicinity who have remained have provided themselves with bombproof habitations in the ground and during the tremendous cannonading of Wednesday clung to them like woodchucks."

"Nothing unusual happened yesterday," it appeared to General Sam French. "Today is Sunday, and it dawned as though peace had spread her white wings over the land, for not a gun has yet been heard, and so it continued most of the day. Divine service was held in the brigades, and in the pond in front of my quarters a baptism took place."

Several hundred yards west of French's outposts, on the next hilltop, the main "hot shell" battery of Sherman's artillery was operating. Massive siege guns had arrived from Chattanooga It was frustrating to Sam French to watch the Federals heat cannon balls over a wood fire, then load their guns and lob them overhead into Atlanta. The battery was so strongly defended that French could not attempt to carry it by assault.

Colonel Taylor Beatty of Louisiana, rode into the city early to send a telegram "to Tew's wife (shot through the entrails)." The telegraph line was not operating and the streets were filled with officers and gossip.

"The railroad is cut between here and Macon and it is said a good many of our wagons were sent to the rear and burned . . . we have captured and destroyed one of the raiding parties but it seems that there was another which got as far down as Macon where they were fighting the militia this morning or last night. The trains, it is said, will go through this evening."

Citizens suggested that Hood rescind a standing order about blowing train whistles. Engineers had been instructed to sound whistles loudly all the way into Atlanta—in the hopes of fooling Sherman's gunners into thinking troop-laden trains were arriving in ever-increasing numbers. So far, the result had been to make the passenger depot the obvious target.

Meanwhile, a militiaman was pecking away at a dud shell with a rock. It had fallen near his post shortly after dawn, and he grew covetous of its powder.

He had been hammering for nearly four hours when the shell suddenly detonated. He was shockingly mutilated before the eyes of passers-by who had watched him from a safer distance.

Mrs. Beers was awakened by another nurse who said there was a dying patient in a ward across the square of Newnan.

"As we passed out into the street," she later recorded, "another beautiful morning was dawning. Upon entering Ward

No. 9, we found most of the patients asleep. But in one corner, between two windows which let in the fast-increasing light, lay an elderly man, calmly breathing his life away. The morning breeze stirred the thin gray hair upon his hollow temples, rustling the leaves of the Bible which lay upon his pillow. Stooping over him to feel the fluttering pulse, and to wipe the clammy sweat from brow and hands, I saw that he was indeed dying, a victim of that dreadful scourge that decimated the ranks of the Confederate armies more surely than many battles —dysentery—which, if not cured in the earlier stages, resulted too surely, as now, in consumption of the bowels.

"He was a Kentuckian, cut off from home and friends, and dying among strangers. An almost imperceptible glance indicated that he wished me to take up his Bible. The fast-stiffening lips whispered, 'Read.'

"I read to him the Fourteenth Chapter of St. John, stopping frequently to note if the faint breathing yet continued. Each time he would move the cold fingers in a way that evidently meant 'go on.' After I had finished the reading, he whispered, so faintly that I could just catch the words, 'Rock of Ages,' and I softly sang the beautiful hymn.

"Two years before I could not have done this so calmly. At first, every death among my patients seemed to me like a personal bereavement. Trying to read or to sing by the bedsides of the dying, uncontrollable tears and sobs would choke my voice. As I looked my last upon dead faces, I would turn away shuddering and sobbing, for a time unfit for duty. Now, my voice did not once fail or falter. Calmly I watched the dying patient, and saw (as I had seen a hundred times before) the gray shadow of death steal over the shrunken face, to be replaced at the last by a light so beautiful that I could well believe it came shining through 'the gates ajar.'

"It was sunrise when I again emerged from Ward No. 9. Hastening to my room, I quickly bathed and redressed, returning to my office in half an hour, refreshed and ready for duty.

"The necessity for breakfast sufficient to feed the hungry patients recalled to me the improvidence of my action in giving away so much bread the night before. It had gone a very little way toward supplying the needs of so large a body of soldiers, and now my own needed it.

"There was no quartermaster, no one to issue fresh rations. Again I had the cows milked, gathered up all the corn-bread that was left, with some hard-tack, and with the aid of the few decrepit nurses before mentioned made a fire, and warmed up the soup and soup-meat which had been prepared for the convalescent table the day before, but was not consumed. My patients, comprehending the situation, made the best of it. But the distribution was a tedious business, as many of the patients had to be fed by myself.

"I had hardly begun when some of the men declared they 'heard guns.' I could not then detect the sound, but soon it grew louder and more sustained, and then we *knew* a battle was in progress. For hours the fight went on. We awaited the result in painful suspense. At last the ambulances came in, bringing some of the surgeons and some wounded men, returning immediately for others. At the same time the hospital steward with his attendants and several of our nurses arrived, also the linen-master, the chief cook, and the baker. With them came orders to prepare wards for a large number of wounded, both Confederate *and Federal*. Presently a cloud of dust appeared up the road, and a detail of Confederate cavalry rode into town, bringing eight hundred Federal prisoners, who were consigned to a large cotton warehouse, situated almost midway between the hospital and the railroad depot.

"My terrible anxiety, suspense, and heavy responsibility was now at an end, but days and nights of nursing lay before all who were connected with either the Buckner or Bragg Hospitals. Additional buildings were at once seized and converted into wards for the reception of the wounded of both armies. The hospital attendants, though weary, hungry, and some of them terribly dirty from the combined effect of perspiration, dust, and gunpowder, at once resumed their duties. The quartermaster reopened his office, requisitions were made and filled, and the work of the different departments was once more put in regular operation.

"I was busy in one of the wards, when a messenger drove up, and a note was handed me from Dr. McAllister—'Some of our men too badly wounded to be moved right away. Come out at once. Bring cordials and brandy—soup, if you have it—also fill the enclosed requisition at the drugstore. Lose no time.'

"The battle-field was not three miles away. I was soon tearing along the road at breakneck speed. At an improvised field-hospital I met the doctor, who vainly tried to prepare me for the horrid spectacle I was about to witness.

"From the hospital-tent distressing groans and screams came forth. The surgeons, both Confederate and Federal, were busy, with coats off, sleeves rolled up, shirtfronts and hands bloody. But *our* work lay not here.

"Dr. McAllister silently handed me two canteens of water, which I threw over my shoulder, receiving also a bottle of peach brandy. We then turned into a ploughed field, thickly strewn with men and horses, many stone dead, some struggling in the agonies of death. The plaintive cries and awful struggles of the horses first impressed me. They were shot in every conceivable manner, showing shattered heads, broken and bleeding limbs, and protruding entrails. They would not yield quietly to death, but continually raised their heads or struggled half-way to their feet, uttering cries of pain, while their distorted eyes seemed to reveal their suffering and implore relief. I saw a soldier shoot one of these poor animals, and felt truly glad to know that his agony was at an end.

"The dead lay around us on every side, singly and in groups and *piles;* men and horses, in some cases, apparently inextricably mingled. Some lay as if peacefully sleeping; others, with open eyes, seemed to glare at any who bent above them. Two men lay as they had died, the 'Blue' and the 'Gray,' clasped in a fierce embrace. What had passed between them could never be known; but one was shot in the head, the throat of the other was partly torn away. It was awful to feel the conviction that unquenched hatred had embittered the last moments of each. They seemed mere youths, and I thought sadly of the mothers, whose hearts would throb with equal anguish in a Northern and a Southern home. In a corner of the field, sup-

ported by a pile of broken fence rails, a soldier sat apparently
beckoning to us. On approaching him we discovered that he was
quite dead, although he sat upright, with open eyes and extended arm.

"Several badly wounded men had been laid under the shade
of some bushes a little farther on; our mission lay here. The
portion of the field we crossed to reach this spot was in many
places slippery with blood. The edge of my dress was red, my
feet were wet with it. As we drew near the suffering men,
piteous glances met our own. 'Water! water!' was the cry.

"Dr. McAllister had previously discovered in one of these the
son of an old friend, and although he was apparently wounded
unto death, he hoped, when the ambulances returned with the
stretchers sent for, to move him into town to the hospital. He
now proceeded with the aid of the instruments, bandages, lint,
etc., I had brought to prepare him for removal. Meantime, taking from my pocket a small feeding-cup, which I always carried
for use in the wards, I mixed some brandy and water, and,
kneeling by one of the poor fellows who seemed worse than the
others, tried to raise his head. But he was already dying. As soon
as he was moved the blood ran in a little stream from his mouth.
Wiping it off, I put the cup to his lips, but he could not swallow,
and reluctantly I left him to die. He wore the blue uniform and
stripes of a Federal sergeant of cavalry, and had a German face.
The next seemed anxious for water, and drank eagerly. This
one, a man of middle age, was later transferred to our wards,
but died from blood-poisoning. He was badly wounded in the
side. A third could only talk with his large, sad eyes, but made
me clearly understand his desire for water. As I passed my arm
under his head the red blood saturated my sleeve and spread in
a moment over a part of my dress. So we went on, giving
water, brandy, or soup; sometimes successful in reviving the
patient, sometimes able only to whisper a few words of comfort
to the dying. There were many more left, and Dr. McAllister
never for a moment intermitted his efforts to save them. Later
came more help, surgeons, and attendants with stretchers, etc.
Soon all were moved who could bear it.

"Duty now recalled me to my patients at the hospital.

"My hands and dress and feet were bloody, and I felt sick with horror.

"As I was recrossing the battle-field accompanied by Dr. Welford, of Virginia, the same terrible scenes were presented to the view. The ground was littered with the accoutrements of soldiers—carbines, pistols, canteens, haversacks, etc. Two cannon lay overturned, near one of which lay a dead Federal soldier still grasping the rammer. Beneath the still struggling horses lay human forms just as they had fallen. Probably they had been dead 'ere they reached the the ground, but I felt a shuddering dread lest perhaps some lingering spark of life had been crushed out by the rolling animals.

"We had nearly reached the road when our attention was arrested by stifled cries and groans proceeding from a little log cabin which had been nearly demolished during the fight. Entering, we found it empty, but still the piteous cries continued. Soon the doctor discovered a pair of human legs hanging down the chimney, but with all his pulling could not dislodge the man, who was fast wedged and only cried out the louder.

" 'Stop your infernal noise,' said the doctor, 'and try to help yourself while I pull.' By this time others had entered the cabin, and their united effort at length succeeded in dislodging from the chimney—not a negro, but a white man, whose blue eyes, glassy with terror, shone through the soot which had begrimed his face. He had climbed up the chimney to escape the storm of shot, and had so wedged himself in that to release himself unaided was impossible. Irrepressible laughter greeted his appearance, and I—I am bitterly ashamed to say—fell into a fit of most violent hysterical laughter and weeping. Dr. Welford hurried me into the buggy, which was near at hand, and drove rapidly to town, refusing to stop at the hospital, landing me at my room, where some ladies who came from I know not where kindly helped me to bed."

Fannie Beers was soon asleep, under heavy sedation.

Kate Cumming, meanwhile, had found Newnan a scene of "military display."

"Nearly all of the cavalry are here. I have seen many handsome flags—trophies. I went and asked for a piece of one, which was given me.

"The wounded prisoners have been taken to the Buckner Hospital. The cannon that we expected would shell Newnan is here. The firing we heard did not do any damage. It is said that there was so much consternation among the enemy that they did not know where they were firing.

"Some of the negro men from the Gamble Hospital have been telling us that there was quite an exciting scene there yesterday morning when the raiders came in. All were at breakfast and knew nothing of the enemy's approach till they commenced firing. They fired right into the hospital at the same time shouting and yelling at a terrific rate. The negro men got out of their way as quickly as they could. A number of the citizens were shot at, and some captured. All are now released.

"One of our patients, Mr. Black, a Kentuckian, who was stopping at a farm-house was roused from his bed and made a prisoner. He was with them when they heard Wheeler and Roddey were after them, and says he never saw men so badly frightened. They treated him well, as they knew the tables would soon be turned.

"Many of them told him, and indeed I have heard it from others, that when they came here they felt confident that they would be captured. Their time would be out in a week; they would then be of no service to the United States Government. By sending them on this raid they would draw cavalry from our army.

"My wonder is that the enemy fight as they do, when they are treated with such inhumanity by their own people.

"Dr. Henderson has come back from the army and has started for Mobile. I expect he will have a hard time in getting there, as the road between Opelika and Montgomery is reported to be torn up by the late raiders."

In Covington, Grandma Smith was helping evacuate the hospital. After breakfast she supervised the carting of trunks and boxes of medical equipment and bedding to the depot. She tried to have them stacked as close to the track as possible in case of a rush for the train.

"There was a vast crowd already collected," she wrote, "and the ground was completely strewn with every description of plunder that could be thought of. All were anxious to leave the land of Dixey. Each one seemed to have an eye single to their own individual interest in relation to making good their escape in case a train should arrive, and one was momentarily expected. But hope, which often sheds its rays of promise, withered. The portals of the anxious heart are lighted up by it only to be darkened by a driving cloud of disappointment. As in all our terrestial undertakings, so in this, we were doomed to disappointment."

In Atlanta people sought shelter from an early afternoon shower.

On Fairlee Street, near Walton, a block from St. Luke's Church, Maxwell Berry, a contractor, came home for Sunday dinner. A new notebook was in his pocket. Berry, who wore a Lincolnesque sort of beard, had given thought, then selected brown-eyed nine-year-old Carrie from among his four daughters and one son.

The war and, indeed, the shelling had gone on long enough, he told Carrie, without some member of the family maintaining a day-by-day diary. Carrie he considered the most serious-minded of his children, and could be depended on to keep a faithful chronicle, even as she had been to knit socks and care for her one-year-old sister, Zulette ("Zuie") or four-year-old Fannie.

Soldiers often camped in the back yard of their one-story frame house, amongst the magnolia, and flower beds, and, when they did, Mrs. Berry baked endless pans of cornbread for them. They were so grateful that they sometimes wrote letters of appreciation.

That afternoon, little Carrie, placing a piece of gum in her mouth from a sweetgum tree, her candy, walked in her usual quick way along the graveled paths in the yard, passing between the soldiers' tents, pausing to pat the pony one of the men had given her, then sat down between the vegetable patch and the chicken pen. She made her first entry.

"Gen. Johnston fell back across the river on July 19th, 1864, and up to this time we have had but few quiet days. We can hear the *canons* and muskets very *plane,* but the shells we dread. One has busted under the dining room which frightened us very much. One passed through the smokehouse and a piece hit the top of the house and fell through but we were at Auntie Markham's, so none of us were hurt. We stay very close in the cellar when they are shelling."

It was hot again after the rain, and when Carrie had finished she put her pencil down and listened to the lazy locust hum of almost August which not even the siege could stop. She wondered if, before supper, she would have time for her favorite game—blind man's buff—providing the shells did not fall.

At dusk it rained again. Near midnight picket fire was exchanged. The shots cracked over the tree-stumped earth ringing Atlanta, stabbing the night with spasmodic, angry blue-red flames.

August, 1864

Southern Press Association

"*Macon*—The raiders have made no demonstration against this place since Saturday. They have withdrawn from the line of the Central railroad, and are now between Clinton and Monticello.

"When our cavalry were operating against them they apparently made Clinton the center from which they sent out parties to operate against Macon, Griswoldville, Gordon and the line of railroad at this place and Griswoldville. They were repulsed at the latter place, but succeeded in burning 27 cars. At Gordon they burnt about 30 cars, and the freight depot, and Oconee bridge and the track.

"The telegraph line is only partially destroyed."

The New York Times

"It may be regarded certain that a large rebel force exists in Atlanta. It has been developed at the skirmish line beyond a doubt, where their pickets are as numerous as our own.

"Just now there is a lull. Sherman is studying the board. His adversary has a slight advantage. Sherman is the skillfullest player, and it is his next move. He'll checkmate Hood, sure."

"The month of August," wrote Sherman, "opened hot and sultry, but our position before Atlanta was healthy, with ample supply of wood, water and provisions. The troops had become habituated to the slow, steady progress of the siege; the skirmish-lines were held close up to the enemy, were covered by rifle-trenches or logs, and kept up a continuous clatter of musketry. The main lines were held farther back, adapted to the shape of the ground, with muskets loaded and stacked for instant use. The field-batteries were in select positions, covered by handsome parapets, and occasional shots from them gave life and animation to the scene. The men loitered about the trenches carelessly, or busied themselves in constructing ingenious huts out of the abundant timber, and seemed as snug, comfortable and happy as though they were at home."

Gen. Sam French, among those opposing Sherman, awoke in a less satisfied frame of mind, as "the enemy commenced artillery fire on the redoubt in front of my house. One shell killed a mule in the yard, another broke my wagon tongue, while a third knocked the pipe from Hedrick's (my orderly) mouth, etc.

"My application to be relieved from duty was returned disapproved, and I was informed that I would not be relieved."

Soon the rain resumed.

"Nothing of much importance has transpired during the week that we are aware of," S. P. Richards, the bookseller, noted. "We have had *shelling* semi-occasionally but this far none of the deadly missiles have reached our house and we could look upon them at a safe distance with composure. For fear that they should ever reach us I have done several hard days' work preparing a 'pit' in our cellar, to retreat to for shelter. One pierced the top cornice of our store and went into Beach & Root's building opposite.

"I have had to stand on guard every other night the past week and drill a little with the militia, but the duties have not been arduous and I will not complain so long as we have no other duty to perform. If they go on making us do *active service* at 'the ditches' or 'the front' I shall try to get off from it. Our garden is helping us out a great deal these hard times. We have not suffered much from thieves and have given away such 'truck' as we did not need. Corn, tomatoes and butter-beans are now in full feather. The enemy have made two raids below us, one upon the Macon R.R. which they *cut* near Jonesboro, but not badly; another upon the Central R. R. near Macon, and doubtless astonished the Maconites by throwing several shells across the river into their quiet city! From what we hear, however, it seems that both these parties have 'come to grief' by being overhauled by our forces.

"Our city is very quiet now except when the shelling is in

progress. Yesterday, the Lord's Day, not a Protestant Church was open; all the ministers have forsaken their posts except the Catholic; they had service I noticed. The Episcopal minister I think is here but the Church is under repairs. I had to drill at the City Hall instead of singing at the Sanctuary. On Sat. night, though, our choir met at our house and sang. We have seen it stated in a Griffin paper that Col. Lamar and Lt. Col. Van Valkenburgh of the 61st Georgia Regt. were killed at the Battle of Monocacy, and I fear it is true. It is a dreadful blow to James' wife, if so, for she seems to be devoted to him, and has been hoping and fearing for so long a time. It really seems as though sooner or later the sword claims all as its victims, however long it may spare. Sherman's host still surrounds us, no, not exactly surround, but still besiege us on the North and North-west trying to come in. Our General is trying to out-general and hoodwink them, but it appears doubtful which will gain the point. It is to be hoped the contest will not be prolonged indefinitely for there is nothing much to be had to eat in Atlanta though if we keep the R.R. we will not quite starve, I trust."

Nine-year-old Carrie Berry noted the rain. "And we thought we would not have any shelling today so I nurst Sister while Mama would do a little work."

"You may fire from ten to fifteen shots from every gun you have in position into Atlanta that will reach any of its houses," Sherman ordered General Schofield at 1:30 P.M. "Fire slowly and with deliberation between 4:00 P.M. and dark. I have inquired into our reserve supply and the occasion will warrant the expenditure. Thomas and Howard will do the same."

On Marietta Street, sandbag ramparts were reinforced to protect both buildings and pedestrians.

Soldiers, weary, dirty and hungry, doggedly defended the small patches of Atlanta earth to which they had fallen back after Peachtree Creek. One, Hosea Garrett, Jr., color-bearer of Hardee's 10th Texas, had been lying in "the ditches near the city" for a week.

"The enemy," he wrote his uncle, the Reverend Hosea Garrett, of Chappell Hill, Texas, and whom he knew as 'Elder H. Garrett,' "has almost quit shelling this portion of our line. It is said they are concentrating their forces on our center; for what purpose, I cannot say. I hardly think they will charge our works. I have heard repeatedly that the Yankee Gents can't get their men to charge rebels' works, and I believe it from what I have seen. I have heard them blow their forward calls but could not get their men to advance. . . .

"I suppose you have heard, or will before this reaches you, that Gen. Hood is in command of this Army. For what reason Johnston was released it is more than any of us know. The army had the utmost confidence in Genl. Johnston and I will say that I have not heard a man say anything about it but what regretted his being released. All that I hear say anything about Genl. Hood say that he is too fond of charging the enemy's works. We had rather not charge them, but would rather be charged by them, until our number equal their. We are all quite tired of this war but will stay as long as life lasts or see the end of this cruel war. . . .

"Father (John Garrett) is in the enemy's line. How they have treated him I cannot say, as I have not heard from him in more than a month. I suppose that they have taken all that he had, for I understand that they take even the ladies' wearing apparel, also that of helpless children.

"I can't believe that God will let such a people go unpunished. I believe that the day for their overthrow is not far distant. I have heard that they cut the throat of every wounded man that they came across in Miss. They drove Forrest back the first day 5 miles, and this is the treatment that our brave soldiers, wounded at that, received at their hands. And I heard that some of our men found some of their wives tied to stakes and dead from the cruel treatment that they received from their foul hands. If such as this will not make men desperate, what will? We are not what we should be in a religious point of view, but I am certain that we have no soldier that would commit such outrageous acts on helpless women and children as theirs has been guilty of. I would to God that our entire Army were true Christians. I have been spared this far, for which I thank God, for both by day and night, I desire and entrust in the prayers of all relatives and friends in Texas. . . .

"J. L. Clark fell, pierced through the head with a minie ball on the 27th May. John Gary fell on the same day, shot through the body, but was carried to the Field hospital and died in a day or two. . . .

"Tom Barton of our Co. is dead. His brother William wounded in some hospital. George Hill that lived with Kevanaugh is also killed. I could mention numbers of others, but not of your acquaintance. H. D. Malone of our Co. was also killed, not far from Marietta. . . . Col. Wilkes son killed not far from the same place. All the bravest men in our Co. have been killed. . . . There are thousands of families that were in fine circumstances that have been broken up by the enemy, and I do not see anything but starvation for such unfortunates. . . .

"I have been thinking for some time that I would like for you to preach my funeral at Old Providence Church if I should fall in our struggle for liberty. . . . I have selected the 2d chapter of Paul to the Ephesians, 8th verse. It reads, 'For by grace are ye saved through faith and that not of yourselves: it is the gift of God.' . . .

"There is considerable roar of cannon on our left. It may be that the enemy is shelling the city."

Thomas Jefferson Newberry, of Yalobusha County, Mississippi, had fought through more than two years of war without being hurt or becoming sick. He worried that he had gained weight, but was resigned to remain in the army "as long as the war lasts."

He wrote, from Atlanta, to his father, M. C. Newberry, in Coffeyville:

"I must drop you a few lines this evening to let you know that I have come through the late battle safe. It was fought on the 28th of July a few days ago. I have bin in four battles since I left home. I have bin in eight battles besides several skirmishes. Our last battle we lost our Capt. Reynolds. He was Comdding our Company, he was mortally wounded. I expect he is dead by this time, he is from Oxford, Miss. William Brown was killed, poor fellow, he was a good Soldier and a brave one. He was shot through the head above the right eye with a minnie ball. He fell dead. I don't think he hardly knowed he was struck.

You can tell Mr. Brown that he was killed and that he lost a brave Son and a noble Soldier. I thought I would write him a letter.

"Well Father We are constantly mooving. Sometimes we move from one end of the line to the other several times a day. Pen and ink wont begin to tell you of our movements, so I cant tell you of nothing only of the fights and not able to tell you anything about them only when they occurred. Tell Mr. Mitchell John says he come through safe. He would rite but says he has no paper. I have not herd from you in a month or more I am looking for a letter from you every day. I write to you every few days. I had to throw away my knapsack in our last fight. If you ever get Layton send him here I want him to toat my clothes. Tell Mr. Boyle John says he is well and come through the fight safe. John Mitchell will send a note in this to his farther. Tell Johny howdy and Mary Susan and Addie and tell them to write. Goodbye and howdy. Write soon and often.

Your Son, T. J. Newberry."

Civilians in Atlanta all but forgot the aroma of coffee. A mixture of roasted cereals and (it was said) sawdust with a hint of coffee beans was black-marketed at soaring prices. The hospitals fared little better. Fannie Beers found only one sack of "precious *real* coffee" remaining at her hospital in Newnan. It was, thus, an experience to be awakened by an attendant holding a cup of fresh, genuine coffee. Mrs. Beers drank it, indulged in a further luxury—a warm bath—and was at work in the wards by 6:00 A.M. Today, her problem was a new one, involving conscience and her hatred for the North. She was compelled to nurse Federal soldiers.

"Pray for strength," Dr. Gore had told her, "to cast out evil spirits from your heart. Forget that the suffering men, thrown upon our kindness and forebearance, are *Yankees*. Remember only that they are God's creatures and helpless prisoners."

Mrs. Beers admitted to herself it would be the hardest battle of her life, determined as she was to "do right." Her will to help, however, was stiffened by an unexpected realization, as she observed attendants carrying bloody legs and arms away from the Federal wards for burial behind the hospital. Now she knew, "some of their surgeons were far rougher and less merciful than ours; and I do not believe they ever gave the poor, shattered fellows the benefit of a doubt. It was easier to amputate than to attend a tedious, troublesome recover. So, off went legs and arms by the wholesale."

To Fannie Beers it was an exhilarating, spiritual revelation when in "five minutes" she felt "all animosity" vanish and "my woman's heart melted within me."

They were strangers, she recognized, and unwelcome strangers, "but far from home and friends, suffering, dying. The surgeons said to me, 'Madam, one-half the attention you give to your own men will save life here.'

"The patients were badly—many fatally—wounded. They were silent, repellent, and evidently expectant of insult and abuse, but after a while received food and drink from my hands pleasantly, and I tried to be faithful in my ministrations.

"I believe that most of the soldiers in this ward were from Iowa and Indiana. One . . . a captain of cavalry, who was shot through the throat and had to receive nourishment by means of a rubber tube inserted for the purpose. A young man in a blue and yellow uniform—an aide or orderly—remained at his side day and night until he died. His eyes spoke to me eloquently of his gratitude, and once he wrote on a scrap of paper, 'God bless you,' and handed it to me. He lived about five days.

"The mortality was very considerable in this ward. I grew to feel a deep interest in the poor fellows, and treasured last words or little mementoes as faithfully for their distant loved ones as I had always done for Confederates.

"Among the personal belongings taken from me by raiders at Macon, Georgia, was a large chest, full of articles of this kind, which I intended to return to the friends of the owners whenever the opportunity offered.

"In another ward were several renegade Kentuckians, who constantly excited my ire by noting and ridiculing deficiencies, calling my own dear boys 'Old Jeff's ragamuffins,' etc." Fannie told them that Dr. Gore was a Kentuckian, and one of the wounded Federal soldiers replied, "Well, I'm a Kentuckian, too, what have you got to say about *me*?"

Mrs. Beers replied icily: "I think you hold about the same relation to the true sons of Kentucky that Judas Iscariot bore to the beloved disciple who lay upon the bosom of our Saviour." She stalked out of the ward, though confessing to herself the whole repartee had been "spiteful."

Grandma Smith, meanwhile, had progressed a scant ten miles from Covington to the tiny flatlands village, Social Circle, surrounded with the hospital staff, a few patients and an uneven mountain range of crates and personal luggage. The noise, the unending chatter, the confusion, had not abated. The day's swelling humid heat, while compounding the torment of the wounded and sick, was ripening the odors from the gangrenous cases which hung fetid in the pine-sweet summer air.

"All eyes," Grandma wrote, "were fixed in the direction that should bring to our hearts great joy, waiting for the cars to come that would soon take us from danger to the land of liberty, for we felt that we were perfectly surrounded, and as if the walls of a prison encompassed us; and, to add to our already unhappy state of mind, it was rumored through the crowd that we need not be surprised if, instead of the expected train of relieving cars, the Yankees dashed in upon us, as they were near by. But we were at their mercy at any moment, and we had no way of helping ourselves. So, there we sat, still hoping that the train would venture that far. Soon some one came dashing up, saying, 'save yourselves if you can. The Yanks are within two miles of the place!'

"If you ever saw a flock of sheep frightened, in a close pen, and no way by which to get out—or anything else of the same nature, you can imagine something of the excitement which prevailed at that time among us; and then imagine a flock of wild deer, badly frightened, running first one way, then another, no two going the same way, and you have a faint idea of what took place in that crowd. Their movements seemed perfectly aimless, except that the general desire was to get away from the Yankees; and what become of the most of them I am unable to say, as I never saw them afterwards.

"The depot was minus men, women, children, and negroes, in the shortest possible time, as if there had never been one on the ground. The young man who was conducting us out, Johnnie Davis, of the 154th Tennessee regiment, and one of the Misses Conner, had gone a short distance, to see an old friend of her's, where they were when the startling intelligence reached them. I do not suppose that they hardly knew how they made their way to the depot, as they were almost unable to speak from excitement and running. Almost as quick as thought the boxes and trunks were thrown into the wagon, and up the hill we ran, and, without ceremony, took refuge in a side room of the post office, expecting every moment to see a brigade of Yankees dash in upon us.

"Every few moments some one of us would act as scout, or outside sentinel. In the course of an hour, or perhaps more, the joyful tidings that it was all a hoax were sent flying through town; that a few of Stoneman's men had been seen trying to make their escape to parts unknown, General Wheeler having proved the winner of the day in an engagement with him, some few miles from Covington, capturing the raiding general and most of his men, and leaving the stragglers to the mercy of the wide woods; and many of them were seen skulking in the outskirts of the neighborhood; and it was reported that some were found not far off, in a starving condition."

Grandma Smith, nonetheless, spent the afternoon in the post office. At dusk, a "stalwart looking man" poked his head in the door.

" 'Lord God!,' he exclaimed as if frightened.

"One of the young ladies was sitting in the door. He inquired of her, 'who are those persons in there?'

"She replied, 'Ladies from Covington.'

" 'Have you seen any Yanks pass here this evening?'

" 'No.'

" 'Are there any Rebs here?'

" 'Yes, plenty of them.'

"He immediately turned on his heels and was off in so short a time that the young men who were in the room never got a sight of him. On turning the corner of the house he met the negro man who had charge of the wagon, and made particular inquiry who our party were; where we were going; and whether any Yanks had passed that day, etc. I think it was one of the enemy's stragglers. It put us on our guard, fearing he might repeat his visit; but we saw no more of him."

The little group settled down to sleep there the night.

Before dark, in Atlanta, Carrie Berry and her family "had to run to the cellar." On the opposing side, however, the shelling which sent citizens scurrying for refuge appeared "sublimely grand and terrific." This was the opinion of Captain David P. Conyngham, youthful Irish-born officer and correspondent for *The New York Herald*.

"The din of artillery rang on the night air," he wrote. "In front of General Geary's headquarters was a prominent hill, from which we had a splendid view of the tragedy enacting before us. I sat there with the general and staff, and several other officers, while a group of men sat near us enjoying the scene, and speculating on the effects of the shells. It was a lovely, still night, with the stars twinkling in the sky. The lights from the campfires along the hills and valleys, and from amidst the trees, glimmered like the gas-lights of a city in the distance. We could see the dark forms reclining around them, and mark the solemn tread of the sentinel on his beat. A rattle of musketry rang from some point along the line. It was a false alarm. The men for a moment listened, and then renewed their song and revelry, which was for a while interrupted. The song, and music, and laughter floated to our ears from the city of camps, that dotted the country all around.

"Sherman had lately ordered from Chattanooga a battery of four and a half inch rifles, and these were trying their metal on the city.

"Several batteries, forts, and bastions joined in the fierce chorus. Shells flew from the batteries, up through the air, whizzing and shrieking, until down they went, hurling the fragments, and leaving in their train a balloon-shaped cloud of smoke. From right, and left, and centre flew these dread missiles, all converging towards the city. From our commanding position we could see the flash from the guns, then the shells with their burning fuses, hurtling through the air like flying meteors."

AUGUST 2

>< *Richmond Sentinel*

"We are without later intelligence from Atlanta. United States papers of the 30th say that Sherman is gradually drawing nearer to the city. The report that Atlanta has fallen is not true. We have every reason to believe that the next news from Georgia will be of a cheering character."

■ *The New York Herald*

"Our skirmishers are actually throwing rifle bullets into Atlanta. A few more assaults and Hood's army will be played out. So close are we to Atlanta that I might say we have invested it . . . the fall of Atlanta is only a question of a few days."

"*Washington*—The situation at Atlanta is considered by the government and by General Sherman as very favorable.

"It is reported semi-officially that since Gen. Hood took command of the rebel army he has lost 25,000 men in killed, wounded and prisoners. Nothing better could be wished than that he should continue to dash his army to pieces against Sherman's lines.

"The end in Atlanta is not far distant, and the final victory there will have an important influence upon the campaign in Virginia."

To General Sam French, the shells seemed to whine overhead like lazy cicadas. His anger boiled as he thought of Richmond. He addressed another letter to the lair of the Confederacy, and

then made his own memorandum—"I wrote to the Adjutant General to be relieved from command in or serving with this army!"

Matthew Andrew Dunn, bivouacked not many yards from French's headquarters, started a note to his wife, "Stumpy." The thirty-one-year-old farmer from Amite County, Mississippi, was a member of Company K, 33rd Regiment, Mississippi Volunteers. He found little time in the past month to continue organizing Baptist Bible classes among his regiment. When not fighting, he had conducted a fruitless half year's campaign to collect $390 he figured his company and the Confederate Government owed him.

Now, during a lull, he sat down behind the breastworks. He pulled his hat half over his forehead, and committed his loneliness to paper.

"Dear Stumpy: I avail myself of the present opportunity to write you a few lines—knowing that you are uneasy about me. I think I will have an opportunity of sending this a portion of the way by hand. I am happy to say to you that my life is yet spared and my health is good. I sent word to you in Clem's letter a few days ago that Tad was wounded on the 22d but it was a mistake. But since then on the 27th he was in another battle and was shot through the leg below the knee which caused his leg to be amputated above the knee. His Brigade went in the fight before ours, and as we went in I met him lying on the road side. I stopped with him a few minutes and he told me that he did not think the bone was broken. But I suppose after the doctors examined it they thought it best to take it off. I know it will nearly kill Ma to hear of it but it is a portion of the horror of this Cruel War. The fight he was in on the 22d was a very hard one but a complete thing on our part. He captured three horses and Jimmy Perkins one. Their brigade captured 14 pieces of artillery and many prisoners. They charged the Yankee works and the Yankees being very stubborn they remained behind their breastworks until our men scaled them, then they had a hand to hand fight. . . .

"Our Division met with a serious misfortune on the 20th of July—we charged the Yankees and our brigade being on the extreme right of the Division we were badly cut to pieces by a Brigade on our right not coming up to support our flanks. Over half our Regiment that was engaged was killed and wounded. . . . We lost our Col. He charged waving his sword until he fell. . . . John H. Turnipseed was killed a few days ago while on picket. We are losing some of our near and dear friends but I hope God will soon stop it. We are enduring many hardships but I try to submit to it cheerfully, feeling assured that we will come out all right.

"I suppose Porter and Betty are married at last. It must have been a sudden thing as you never spoke of it in your letter of the 24th. That is the last letter I have had from you. I am very anxious to hear from home. Oh my love if I could only see you and our dear little ones again what a pleasure it would be. But God only knows whether I will have that privilege or not. I want you to try to raise them up right. Train them while they are young—and if I am not spared to see you I hope we will meet in a happier world. I want you to be fully reconciled for it. If I am wounded I will be home as soon as I can and if I am killed I hope that I am prepared to go. . . . Try and send me a letter every chance you have as the Yankees cut our Rail Roads occasionally which stops communication. Tell Julia that Clem will not write as Paper is scarce but he is all right and Hemp and Prior also, and Jimmy. Tell Ma that Tad will be sent home as soon as he is able. . . . I can't write all the news for want of paper and this is badly done as I am writing on a plate . . . kiss the children, and tell them to be good children. I hope God will bless us. Good bye my dear. Your husband.

M. A. Dunn

"Andrew has just come in with a nice bucket of rice and squash and a very fancy shirt for me. He keeps me in good clothes."

A neighbor sat down to write Mrs. William Barnes a congratulatory note. The elderly Atlanta lady was refugeeing south. Her caretaker this morning, seeing a large cannonball in the back yard and a hole in the wall of the house, went inside. The heavy shot, he found, had plunged through the roof, a small feather bed in the attic as well as Mrs. Barnes' own larger bed, a thick bolster atop it, and then on outside. The rooms, reported the caretaker, were filled with "more feathers than a chicken coop after a possum fight."

A guest, believed to be a slightly injured soldier, who had just checked out of the Trout House, was equally lucky. A shell exploded in his room, leaving torn lathe and scorched wallpaper, but miraculously did not damage adjacent rooms.

Before noon it turned "quite hot" in Atlanta. A vidette pit, at almost the northern extremity of Peachtree Street, was now one of the principal targets of "firing along the picket lines." So heavy had been losses in this one strongpoint that soldiers referred to it as the "dead hole." In front of Columbus Pitt's home, it was but seven feet long, four feet wide and four feet deep, banked with red clay in front, planked on the bottom.

Facing it, no more than one thousand yards distant, was a similar pit of Federal sharpshooters, all believed equipped with rifles mounting telescopic sights. Before the defenders grew more wary, seventeen of their number were killed. There was strange, grim testimony to Union marksmanship: each Confederate who lost his life was shot cleanly through the head. Not one man was wounded in this pit; he survived or was slain instantly as he poked his head above the red clay bank to peer across the No Man's Land which, until a few weeks ago, had been one of Atlanta's busy thoroughfares.

In the same area, on ground reddened by the slaughter of July 20, Major Stephen Pierson, of Morristown, New Jersey, was noting other happenings. Back of his position was a long, open slope. Down it, spent round shot or unexploded shells of the Confederate cannons would roll. "They seemed to go very slowly, but I once saw a soldier put out his foot to stop one; the momentum broke his leg."

The dueling of the heavy artillery was "very nice practice," in Pierson's estimation. "Secure behind our bombproofs as we lay in full sight of the city, we used to watch the Rebel shells as they came over; we could see the flash, and sometimes the shells themselves, before they reached us, giving us plenty of time to get to cover. Sometimes the men were a little careless,

General Hood's headquarters after being taken over by Colonel Barnum. *(Courtesy Atlanta Historical Society)*

Decatur Street, from a photograph taken during Sherman's occupation. The Masonic Hall, large building with peaked roof, is nearest the camera; behind it is the Trout House. *(Courtesy Atlanta Historical Society)*

The back yard of Carrie Berry's house, from a photograph taken a few years after the war. The yard, with its shrubs, flowers, graveled paths, and hedges, appeared much the same that summer of 1864 when soldiers camped on the grass and shared living space with a pony, a dog, and numerous chickens. *(Courtesy Mrs. Zulette Franklin)*

E. E. Rawson's home, "The Terraces," which was later occupied by General Geary. *(Courtesy Atlanta Historical Society)*

Looking north along Whitehall Street before the Federal troops marched out. *(Courtesy Atlanta Historical Society)*

Front page of the *Daily Intelligencer,* July 5, 1864. Optimism was the keynote of the Atlanta newspapers up until the day they left the city. This issue of the *Intelligencer* finds, among other things, that Sherman's army is "much dispirited." *(Intelligencer Collection, Courtesy Western Reserve Historical Society)*

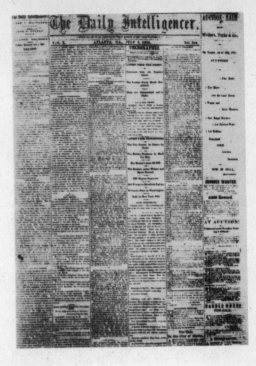

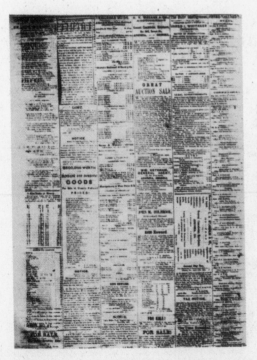

Poetry, timetables, auction sales, lost article and runaway slave notices, tax and legal announcements, were among the profusion of wordage that filled the Atlanta newspapers even during the feverish days of siege. *(Intelligencer Collection, Courtesy Western Reserve Historical Society)*

General William T. Sherman. *(United States Army Photograph)*

General John B. Hood, C.S.A. *(National Archives)*

General Sherman and his staff at Federal Fort No. 7 after the fall of Atlanta. *(Library of Congress)*

Looking west, about a mile from downtown Atlanta, this is the exact site where Sherman and his aides posed on that late autumn day in 1864.

Bishop Henry C. Lay. *(Courtesy University of North Carolina Library)*

The Rev. Charles Todd Quintard. *(Courtesy the Quintard family)*

Father Thomas O'Reilly. *(Courtesy Van Buren Colley)*

Benedict J. Semmes. *(Courtesy Mrs. Amy Semmes)*

Carrie Berry, as she appeared in her early teens. *(Courtesy Mrs. Zulette Franklin)*

Two Federal officers, identified only as "Hoffman and Wharton." The original caption on this photograph indicates that it was taken in front of a house on Peachtree Street "after breakfast." *(Courtesy Atlanta Historical Society)*

Mary Rawson. *(Courtesy Mrs. R. L. Foreman)*

Lizzie Perkerson. *(Courtesy Mrs. Angus Perkerson)*

S. P. Richards. *(Courtesy Mrs. Robert Sterrett)*

or the lookout failed to give notice and then there was apt to
be trouble. On one occasion I remember seeing two soldiers,
sitting on each side of a stump, upon which was their can of hot
coffee. Along came a shell and exploded; one of the pieces
passed between the two without touching either, but sent the
coffee flying. Their surprise and astonishment over, they began
to curse the Rebs for spoiling their breakfast."

In Newnan, once more "comparatively safe," Fannie Beers
grew increasingly anxious to see her husband at Atlanta. As a
nurse, she was also concerned for all the soldiers in the city's
trenches "lying day after day, always under fire . . . suffering
from insufficient food, exposed to the scorching sun or equally
pitiless rain, sometimes actually knee-deep in water for days."

Patients fresh from the wasting Atlanta struggle had told the
same story: the bombardment, "heavy and incessant," was interrupted sometimes at sunset "when carts were hastily loaded
with musty meat and poor corn-bread, driven out to the
trenches, and the rations *dumped* there."

It seemed to Fannie Beers that many factors besides "shot
and shell" were conspiring to kill her husband and her friends
crouching in the foxholes of Atlanta.

"I could not bear it," she decided. "The desire to see my
husband once more, and to carry some relief in the shape of
provisions to himself and his comrades could not be quelled.
Many things stood in the way of its accomplishment, for, upon
giving a hint of my project to my friends at Newnan, a storm
of protest broke upon my devoted head. Not one bade me God-
speed, *everybody* declared I was crazy. 'A *woman* to go to Atlanta under such circumstances; how utterly absurd, how mad.'
So I was obliged to resort to deception and subterfuge. My
first step was to request leave of absence, that I might forage
for provisions to be sent to the front by the first opportunity.

"Dr. McAllister very kindly accorded me his permission, placing at my disposal an ambulance and a driver, advising me,
however, not to follow the main road or the beaten track which
had already been drained by foragers, but to go deep into the
piny woods. Said he, 'Only one of our foragers has ever been
through that region, and his reports were not very encouraging.

The people want to keep all they have got for home-consumption, and greatly distrust "hospital people," but if success is possible, you will succeed.' In anticipation, this ride into deep, odorous pine woods seemed delightful."

Kate Cumming attended a funeral late in the afternoon: the eldest son of one of Newnan's leading families—the Taylors. Captured by the Union forces during the fighting in Virginia, he contracted tuberculosis in prison. His parents appealed directly to Secretary of War Stanton, and the young man was sent home to die "amid the endearments of home."

Among the recent arrivals at the Newnan hospitals was Private John Will Dyer, of Kentucky. Half-crippled with lumbago, he had been brought from Atlanta atop a box car, through alternate sunshine and rain showers, using a "plank for my pillow." Since his pains and stiffness had been eased by mustard plasters and hot liniments, he had been given duties at the wards. He was horrified at what he had to witness.

"We had no anaesthetic dressing," he wrote, "and all wounds were treated with the cold water treatment which was to thickly bandage the wound and keep continually wet with cold water, till all signs of inflammation disappeared and the flesh began to show granulations. Then the water was discontinued and dry bandages substituted. Sometimes gangrene would develop and unless quickly removed was sure death to the patient. Our method of removing gangrene was to burn it out with nitric acid—aqua fortis. This was very severe and trying on the nerves of the nurse as well as the patient.

"When pouring the acid on the 'proud' flesh you would see smoke rise, the flesh sizzle and crisp up, and all this time the patient's screaming in agony, it took a stout heart and steady nerve to apply it. I hope never to have to do it again."

In Social Circle, Grandma Smith still awaited a train. She had slept fitfully in her stuffy post office refuge. She felt her full 47 years. She read letters from soldier friends in the midst of the "carnage" of Atlanta, and answered them. "We have the precious boon to know that we were considered worthy of their dying remembrance, amid the rain of shot and shell . . .

untold suffering as martyrs on the battlefield . . . worn out by sickness and hard service."

During the morning, the little town cheered the news that General Stoneman had been captured and "carried through Macon." Mrs. Smith also learned that the head surgeon from Covington, who happened to be in Macon, recognized Dr. Robertson among the captured Federals "who had so kindly pleaded for him in Covington." The Confederate doctor, "a perfect gentleman," expressed his own gratitude by securing the release of Dr. Robertson.

It deeply impressed Grandma Smith that there should be such evidence of humanity and chivalry "in the very midst of one of the bloodiest wars ever known."

Later in the day, she moved to the home of a "kind lady" where she had "quite a pleasant time." She learned how the ladies of Social Circle had been taking care of the sick and wounded as the trains shipped them through the hamlet. Her hostess also informed her "how energetic Dr. Lee had been in providing them with comfortable quarters on the cars, although he was not the surgeon on detail to transfer them. When he saw that the proper surgeon was not there, he assumed the place for the good of the suffering; and, like a true gentleman, went forward and saw them safe on the train. All honor is due to the noble and valiant soldier—such as he; and long will his name be dear in the hearts of many soldiers whom he found suffering for the want of that humane attention which was due them, and which so many failed to receive. The man who would wantonly neglect such objects of charity, and suffering humanity, is not a true soldier, or the soldiers' friend."

As evening settled over the pine woods to the west, Grandma Smith once more offered to stand her share of the night's watches. On the outskirts of Social Circle, sentries listened— but heard nothing, other than the muted summer-night sounds of Georgia. There were no echoes of skirmishing and— disturbingly—no sounds of an approaching train.

West of Atlanta there was "brisk firing on the picket line." William Graham had just donned fresh clothing, issued in late afternoon. Somehow it made him feel better.

Carrie Berry had spent a quiet Tuesday. "We have not been shelled much today, but the muskets have been going all day. I have done but little today but nurse Sister. She has not been well today."

And over the soldiers in Atlanta hung a strange melancholy. No longer rang the confident, noisy songs from the places where fighting men congregated, places now close to the very trenches where they might die.

Songs like this familiar, sad one rang like a dirge:

> When this cruel war is over,
> Then we'll all come home again,
> Yes, we'll all come home again.

AUGUST 3

■ *The New York Times*

"*Nashville, Wednesday*—Gen. Stoneman's raid along the Macon Railroad met with a great success in cutting the rebel line of communications, and thus completely isolating Atlanta. But I regret the necessity to add that one division of cavalry, while returning, met with a serious disaster. The Macon Railroad was torn up for 18 miles, the rails twisted, the ties, tanks, bridges and depots burned, and the road rendered useless for months to come.

"Returning by way of Newnan, captured a large wagon train, filled with much valuable private property belonging to rebel officers, and among other property was Gen. Wood's papers and a quantity of whiskey, which fell into the hands of the General and his forces.

"About this time the rebels, under Gen. Ransom, attacked Gen. McCook, and a fight ensued, in which McCook's command was routed, and the greater part of his command captured. About 500 of the troops have reported at Marietta, and gave fearful stories of losses. The command, at starting, numbered about 3200. Gen. McCook is reported killed."

"*Louisville, Wednesday*—The Nashville Union of today says, 'Apparently well authenticated but unofficial information has been received. Gen. Stoneman has not only cut the Macon Railroad, but defeated the rebel Wheeler at Proctor's Creek, that the latter lost from 500 to 1,000 men, and that his dead and wounded fell into our hands.'"

◪ *Southern Press Association*

"*Atlanta*—Affairs are very quiet this morning. There was some picket firing during the night, but nothing of importance occurred.

"Fifty prisoners were captured near Newnan, and were sent South from West Point yesterday. About one thousand in all were captured."

That day began bright and warm. Sergeant Graham of Illinois, saw the sun glint off Atlanta's Steeples, as well as brighten the gaunt chimneys—"Sherman's Sentinels"—which dotted the surrounding countryside, all that remained of many homes. Action had so dwindled that he could count the early morning exchange of shots—two.

"We have a fort on the right of us in the same line of works. About 9 commenced advancing our line on the right and at 10 some 20 prisoners brought in. Our batteries are playing up the enemy's line. At 12 some more prisoners are brought in.

"At 12 it rained very hard for a half hour and immediately after a battle commenced and is raging."

The problem of funerals increased in Atlanta. The mourners were in a hurry. The procession raced as fast as possible to the cemetery and could hardly control its collective impatience to have the burial done with and rush home.

This morning, a hearse, carrying the dead son of one of Atlanta's oldest citizens, had started down Decatur Street on the lonesome, dreary, and dangerous ride to Oakland Cemetery. Suddenly, a rattle overhead, a flash, a roar—and a huge hole was torn in the road just behind the hearse. The driver leaped from his seat, swearing he would not continue a foot further, then ran off. Finally, a Negro mule-teamster, who happened along, offered his assistance and the procession moved on.

Late the previous night there had been similar trouble. Hoping for a respite in the shelling, grave-detail officers had set midnight as the time for burying four soldiers newly killed in the defense of the city. A wagon carrying their bodies was halfway across Atlanta when a shell materialized seemingly out of nowhere and exploded 50 feet above the driver's head.

The army teamster was thrown to the ground, the mules, panicking, lunged ahead. The bodies, unprotected by coffins, bounced out of the careening wagon one by one. By the time the bruised driver overtook the wild team, all four corpses had been scattered at intervals across Atlanta.

As the day began, Fannie Beers commenced "foraging" for her journey from Newnan to Atlanta. The ambulance arrived, drawn by a mule which had been captured from the Union cavalry raiders.

"I gaily climbed into it and, waving merry adieux to half-disapproving friends (among them Dr. Hughes, with his distressed face, and Diogenes, who looked daggers at me), set off in high glee. The ride along the pleasant road was lovely; early birds sung sweetly; the dew, yet undisturbed, glistened everywhere, the morning breeze blew freshly in my face. As the sun began to assert his power, I became eager to penetrate into the shady woods, and at last, spying a grand aisle in 'Nature's temple,' bade the driver enter it. For a while the result was most enjoyable. The spicy aroma of the pines, the brilliant vines climbing everywhere, the multitude of woodland blossoms blooming in such quantities and variety as I had never imagined, charmed my senses, and elevated my spirit. Among these peaceful shades one might almost forget the horror and carnage which desolated the land.

"The driver was versed in wood-craft, and called my attention to many beauties which would have otherwise escaped me. But soon his whole attention was required to guide the restive mule through a labyrinth of stumps and ruts and horrible muddy holes, which he called 'hog wallows'; my own endeavors were addressed to 'holding on,' and devising means to ease the horrible joltings which racked me from head to foot. After riding about two miles we came to a small clearing, and were informed that the road for ten miles was 'tolerbal clar' and pretty thickly settled.

"So after partaking of an early country dinner, also obtaining a small amount of eggs, chickens, etc., at exorbitant prices, we resumed our ride. . . . Oh, the sullen, sour-looking women that I sweetly smiled upon, and flattered into good humor praising their homes, the cloth upon the loom, the truck-patch (often a mass of weeds), the tow-headed babies (whom I caressed and admired), never hinting at my object until the innocent victims offered of their own accord to 'show me round.' At the spring-house I praised the new country butter, which 'looked so very good that I must have a pound or two,' and then skilfully leading the conversation to the subject of chickens and eggs, carelessly displaying a few crisp Confederate bills, I at least became the happy possessor of a few dozens of eggs and a chicken or two, at a price which only their destination reconciled me to.

"At one house, approached by a road so torturous and full of stumps that we were some time before reaching it, I distinctly heard a dreadful squawking among the fowls, but when we arrived at the gate, not one was to be seen, and the mistress declared she hadn't a 'one: hadn't saw a chicken for a coon's age.' Pleading excessive fatigue, I begged the privilege of resting within the cabin. An apparently unwilling assent was given. In I walked, and, occupying one of those split chairs which so irresistibly invite one to commit a breach of good manners by 'tipping back,' I sat in the door-way, comfortably swaying backward and forward. Every once in a while the faces of children, either black or white, would peer at me round the corner of the house, then the sound of scampering bare feet would betray their sudden flight. Suddenly I caught sight of a pair of bare, black feet protruding from under the bed. Presently an unmistakable squawk arose, instantly smothered, but followed by a fluttering of wings and a *chorus* of squawks. So upset was the lady of the house that she involuntarily called out, 'You Isrul!' 'Ma'am,' came in a frightened voice from under the bed, then in whining tones, 'I dun try to mek 'em hush up, but 'pears like Mass Debbel be on dey side, anyhow.'

"Further concealment being impossible, I said, 'Come, you have the chickens ready caught, I'll give you your own price for them.' She hesitated—and was lost, for producing from my pocket a small package of snuff, to which temptation she at once succumbed, I obtained in exchange six fine, fat chickens. As I was leaving she said, in an apologetic tone, 'Well, I declah, I never knowed you was going to light, or I wouldn't have done sich a fool-trick.'

"Stopping at every house, meeting with varied success, we at last, just at night, arrived at a farm-house more orderly than any we had passed, where I was glad to discover the familiar face of an old lady who had sometimes brought buttermilk and eggs to the sick. At once recognizing me, she appeared delighted, and insisted upon my 'lighting' and having my team put up until morning. This I was glad to do, for it was quite out of the question to start on my homeward journey that night. Greatly I enjoyed the hospitality so ungrudgingly given, the appetizing supper, the state bed in the best room, with its 'sunrise' quilt of patchwork. Here was a Confederate household. The son was a soldier. His wife and his little children were living 'with ma' at the old homestead. The evening was spent in talking of the late battle. Here these women were, living in the depths of the woods, consumed with anxiety, seldom hearing any news, yet quietly performing the monotonous round of duty with a patience which would have added lustre to the crown of a saint.

"I talked until (wonderful to relate) my tongue was tired: my audience being the old, white-haired father, the mother, the wife, and the eager children, who were shy at first, but by degrees nestled closer, with bright eyes from which sleep seemed banished forever."

The train, meanwhile, was yet to arrive in Social Circle. Nor was there any prospect of one materializing down the creaky, rusty rails, as another nurse was equally concerned with travel.

"Of course," Grandma Smith realized, "we could not remain where we were. Some plan must be devised and adopted to enable us to get away. . . . I proposed that the wagon should be loaded with our plunder, and I would take two of the crippled soldiers, and the Negro man, and go to Rutledge, a station several miles below. We could make two trips that day, and one the next morning; and we thought that by the next evening we would get a train.

"All agreed to the plan and we were soon mounted upon the boxes and moving off for Rutledge."

She herself found the spectacle amusing: "An old rebel woman and boys with crutches in hand, perched upon goods boxes, winding their way to they knew not where? Surely the venture seemed almost incredible. Several persons stopped us on the roadside, and would invariably inquire, 'My good madam, where are you going to?'

"On informing them, they would say, 'Why, you need not go there; the Yanks were there yesterday, and tore up things generally. Have you seen any Yanks on your way?'

" 'No sir'; or madam, as the case might be.

" 'Why, I wonder you have not. Don't you hear those guns?'

" 'Yes.'

" 'Well, it is them fighting. I wonder they do not get you. You had better turn back.' But nary time did we turn back until we reached the place for which we had started.

"One lady, a Mrs. Hardins . . . seemed to marvel greatly at our rashness, and called our attention to the report of guns just in the rear of her field. She said they had been fighting all morning; and that the negroes had left the field, and come to the house for safety. The old lady put up quite a pitiful story, saying the Yanks had taken some of her mules; and our doctors had taken some half-dozen bundles of oats, and spread on the floor of their wagon for their wives to rest upon, and went off and did not pay her one cent for them. I asked her if that was all she had lost since the beginning of the war.

"She replied, 'Why, yes; and that's enough. I did not have that to spare.'

" 'Well,' said I, 'if that is the whole amount of your losses in this great struggle for independence, you have been extremely fortunate indeed. Many in your own State have lost everything, and are now penniless; and yet they do not complain, because they know it is the fate of war; and more especially one waged against a people who are merely contending for their own legitimate rights.'

" 'Well, I don't want to lose anything by any of them. I think the doctor ought to pay me for my oats.'

"We bade her good by, saying, 'We wish you may lose nothing else.'

"We soon reached the depot; and on arriving there who should we see but two of our boys, Bud Carrington and Lieutenant Bean, both belonging to the Virginia army, who had started for that point early the previous morning, before our plan was gotten up. On recognizing us they seemed very much astonished, and called out,

" 'Where in the world are you going, grandma?'

" 'Why, right here,' I said.

" 'What is your notion for making this disastrous move?'

" 'In order to get a train.'

" 'That you cannot get. There will be no train here to-day. It is too uncertain, as well as dangerous, for them to venture here. Do go back. The Yanks are all around us. Do go back if you can. For I am afraid you will be caught.'

"With that, the railroad agent came out, and said, 'Oh, my dear madam, please don't put your things off here. The Federals were here yesterday, and burned and destroyed eight thousand dollars worth for me; and if they should come and find this hospital property here they would not leave anything. I know they are stragglers from Stoneman's command; but they are the more to be feared than the main army. I beseech you to return. The train cannot come up no how; and we would all be in great danger were you to remain.'

"As nothing else would satisfy the contending parties, and my confidence in those two Virginia soldiers admonished me that to take their advice would be the better part of discretion, and with a heart too full of sad disappointment for utterance, we turned our course back to Social Circle, where we knew the rest of our party were in anxious waiting for the empty wagon. Our journey back was of a more interesting character than the former. We were halted at almost every turn, and something related that was calculated to put, or, in other words, keep us on our guard. I did not fear for myself, but the two wounded soldiers I knew would be captured if the enemy came upon us; but the boys sang, whistled and seemed merry, chatting away as though there was no danger whatever from Yanks.

"The poor negro was more uneasy than any of us, fearing, if they came upon us, they would take his team, and make him join them, leaving the rest of us in the road to finish our journey as best we could.

"Fortunately for us, while also mysterious, not the glimpse of a Yank did we get in all our route. One man came running to us, perfectly excited, saying, 'Arn't you afraid to travel this road?'

" 'No; what's up,' said I.

" 'Why, didn't you see the two Rebel officers dashing through the woods just now?'

" 'Yes; and what of that?'

" 'Why, they asked the woman at that house yonder if there were any Yanks in the neighborhood.'

" 'Why, yes,' she replied, 'plenty of them right over yonder. My husband is over there, with them. He piloted them, and carried them to where some Rebs were. Listen, don't you hear them shooting?'

"A mistaken woman that time. She thought she was giving information to Yankees, and her information caused the capture of the good Union husband, and the clan he had piloted, so we were informed, for, as a natural consequence, the two Rebs made good use of the opportunity offered them, and the Union woman's directions."

In Macon, the printing presses of *The Daily Intelligencer* resumed their familiar clacking-shuffling, in a building at Third and Cherry streets.

"Our hopes are not too sanguine," asserted the refugee editors, "for the prospect to us has never been without the beautiful sunlight of prospective victory lighting our hearts through the gloom and the dark shade of defeat through which we have travelled these many weary months past. Our confidence in the prowess of General Hood and his invincible army of veterans is unabating and with such firm belief we wish to imbue the spirit of the people and the army. So long as the feeling that all will end well enthuses us, we are unconquerable, and we will be successful."

A party was planned for 5:00 P.M. the next day for Brigadier General Alfred C. Iverson to celebrate his repulse of the Stoneman raiders. Citizens were asked to bring coffee, milk, and "other supplies" to the grove behind the Wesleyan Female College, in Macon.

Iverson had become a Macon saviour with his hasty assemblage of an army—soldiers on leave, some well, some sick, civilians with their old flintlocks, even postmen and firemen—which defeated, then captured Stoneman. General Johnston himself had been a spectator of the strangely-manned conflict.

"Today," wrote Private Alonzo Miller, the Wisconsin farmer, camped ever closer to the heart of Atlanta, "finds me well excepting a sore jaw. Yesterday I had two of my double teeth drawn. They brook up and all the roots are not out yet so today its some sore and hurts me to eat. Yesterday I went and washed my shirt and socks and only have one shirt so I have to dry it quick to put on. I have one pair of those socks that mother knit winter before last and have worn them all the time too."

Rufus Mead, twenty-eight-year-old commissary sergeant with the 5th Regiment, Connecticut Volunteers, was feeling better, after being "kinder under the weather" yesterday. Now less than three miles from Five Points, Mead, a county surveyor wrote to his "Dear folks at home," in Redding, Connecticut (near Danbury):

"We are here in the same position yet and everything in front of us seems very quiet, not hardly a cannon fired yesterday and none so far today.

"I don't pretend to know anything about our future movements, so have to trust they will be as the past, i.e., successful seeing they are in skilful hands. I am sorry Hooker has left us

but he is not the only General we had confidence in; in fact we
have all good ones here now.

"Unfortunately our cavalry expedition has proved a failure.
It is not fully ascertained how much our loss is, but it is reported now from 2,000 to 2,500 cavalry with all their equip-
ments and 600 mules they had captured. Genl. McCook is
thought to be a prisoner along with the 2,000. Lt. Col. Brownlow cut his way back with his command and says they destroyed
a great deal of property—cut railroads &c &c had several brushes
with Wheeler's cavalry—whipped him every time till on their return they found themselves surrounded by such a force it was
impossible to get out.

"We can hardly spare 2,000 cavalry just now especially as the
enemy will have so much more to bother us and cut our communications in the rear. It is the worst accident we have had so
far on this campaign.

"We see in the papers that the Rebs are in Tenn. again but
can't find out how large a force. I hope Grant wont need to send
any of his troops to stop them.

"The progress is slow, but on the whole I think encouraging.

"You must have got through haying early this year. I presume
the drought facilitated matters somewhat. I hope it has rained
ere this. We have just showers enough so it is not dusty at all,
we could not ask for more favorable weather.

"I guess after all you had better get the boots made and sent
by mail if it does cost letter postage. I guess it would be over 3
dollars, and boots here are worth from 12 to 15 dollars—not as
good as Ben would make either.

"I see by the Danbury paper that Redding has raised 16 out
of 34 men. How does she get them, by hiring some out of the
state or does she get some to volunteer from the town? If so
who are they?

"I received a letter from Martin, also from Linns yesterday,
and from Elbert and Hen Holley the day before. The 12th
Conn. are now at Bermuda Hundred it seems and Hen in the
Co doing duty.

"He says he likes that change of climate and water, but don't
have quite as easy times in the Co as he did in New Orleans.

I hope he will stand it six months longer then he will be out of it, so make room for the 500,000 to come.

"I hope Capt. Crofut & his partners will get home safely. It must seem a long time to them away from home.

"I think our Regt.'s old men must surely be home before this. It seems to be a hard matter for our Officers to get away yet Some try awful hard but they remain still.

"Lt. Titus left yesterday, as his resignation was accompanied by certificate of being wounded & unfit for service. He will send some money to you (that he owes me), when he gets to Nashville or home. I have other letters to write and cant think anything more to interest you so Good Bye. Your Son & Brother."

There was one factor still galling to Rufus: the way the Confederates stripped the countryside. All he could retrieve were "a few apples and berries." As further ignominy he had to witness his own horses and mules being served the choice green corn. The teamsters passed out what was left to the troops.

Late in the afternoon, newly-taken Southern prisoners spread rumors in Union lines of the arrival of ten thousand fresh Georgia State militia in Atlanta.

A number of Federal prisoners were placed in freight cars on a siding at East Point in the evening and started south.

It was Carrie Berry's birthday and she wrote in her diary: "I was ten years old, but I did not have a cake. Times were too hard so I celebrated with ironing. I hope by my next birthday we will have peace in our land so that I can have a nice dinner."

John Peel, an Atlantan, was beginning to feel that he had been singled out for more than his share of the shelling. A projectile smashed into his house on Spring Street, exploding inside. It was the fifth to strike his residence. Others had torn up shade trees in the yard, the fencing, the well, and the smoke house. His house, which had been for sale, was now withdrawn from the market.

A piece of shrapnel ripped through the window of an inbound train from Macon, killing a lady passenger. She was taken to the morgue, pending identification.

AUGUST 4

Richmond Sentinel

"All was quiet at Atlanta yesterday. A private dispatch received yesterday from a distinguished gentleman at the seat of war in Georgia gives a very hopeful account of affairs at Atlanta."

The New York Herald

"Generals Sherman, Thomas, Howard, Hooker, Stanley and others were enjoying themselves yesterday in front of General Wood's quarters when some of those noisy visitors came whizzing around. They did not flurry them in the least or interrupt their council though there was a small arsenal of the 'darned things' flying around them."

The Atlanta Register

August 3—On the 3rd a lady, a gentleman and his little daughter were killed in Atlanta by fragments of Yankee shells, and about 11 o'clock at night Mr. Warner, the superintendent of the gas works, and his little daughter lying in the same bed were killed by a round shot. The child was severed in two, dying instantly, the father had both thighs cut off close to the body and lived about two hours.

"We call these murders, though the murderer will be treated with the utmost courtesy when he falls into our hands. He knows that all this fire upon a position in the rear of our army will not drive them from their lines and it is only to gratify his own diabolical propensities that he keeps up the bombardment upon unarmed people. What a retribution is in store for the people who are carrying on this hellish work! The whole world will mock at their calamity and laugh when their fear cometh."

At the corner of Elliott and Rhodes streets, passers-by paused to stare at a shell-blasted structure, then hurried on. It was the little frame house in which Mr. Warner and his six-year-old daughter died, together.

In Macon, workmen tore down the streamers, then folded the chairs and tables which had been placed in the grove behind the Wesleyan Female College for Gen. Iverson's party this afternoon. He had been ordered back to the front.

A resident of Atlanta who signed himself "P." decided that there was good prospect of another, "general" engagement. He didn't want to miss it.

"I suppose," he wrote the *Intelligencer,* "the telegraph has apprised you ere this of the fighting which took place on our right center about five o'clock yesterday evening. The militia man our works on the right, running to the center; the Yankees attempted to charge our pickets in front of our works on this portion of our line and were repulsed with heavy slaughter. Early yesterday morning a similar attempt was made on our left and met with a similar result. While the fighting was going on, I could hear a Yankee band playing 'Yankee Doodle' away to our left.

"I thought at that time a general engagement had commenced, but after the severe repulse which the Yankees met with it dwindled down to mere sharp-shooting and skirmishing again.

"The enemy threw about thirty shells into the heart of the city yesterday evening, without doing much damage.

"From Tuesday at 12 M. until Wednesday at 1 o'clock no shells were thrown into the city. An occasional shell came over into our midst during last night.

"A person who visited here before the army fell back on this place, after an absence of two weeks from the city, is astonished at the great change that has been effected but it is not near so great as one might suppose from the big yarns he hears at a distance. I notice women and children walking about the streets as though there was no army within a hundred miles of the city. I notice too, in perambulating the town that about two thirds of the residences of the city are occupied by families and several of them the oldest inhabitants of the place.

"I also notice that some of our most substantial and influential citizens are still in the city; among them I see J. K. Williams, Dr. J. S. Denny, Markham, Muhlinbrink, A. S. Myres, David

Mayer, W. Herring, A. Austell, the three Lynches, John, James and Peter and many others.

"The Yankee wounded which are in our hands at this place are in the Medical College and I understand the Yankees hit it occasionally.

"Atlanta will never be taken by the Yankees in my opinion.

"P.S. Nearly all the Newnan raiders who tore up the M. & W. R. R. have been captured. The prospects are brightening."

And in the same column "Pueri" deplored the straggler situation,

"Being 'in for the war' in soul and body I am as little disposed to complain at outrages committed by our soldiers as any man and would rather concede to them the right to take, by force, from those having an abundance and refuse to sell upon reasonable terms when they are in actual need, than otherwise. But, sir, there is reason in all things and should as well be a stopping place. I will give you an instance or two of recent outrages committed by them which you will please publish for the benefit of all concerned. I only refer to roving stragglers, however, who, as the sequel will show, are doing us but little service and much injury.

"The proximity of the enemy and the unknown events of the next few months rendered it necessary, in the judgment of my father, for him to remove his family farther down the country for safety. His residence is near the Macon and Western Railroad, a few miles above Jonesboro. In removing, he left a beautiful young crop on his plantation under good fences, and amply provided with attendants to resist any ordinary incursion. But, sir, those brave (?) fellows have overpowered every resistance, and have completely destroyed not only his crop but have wantonly and unnecessarily destroyed almost everything else. Gardens are plundered, bee hives are robbed, young hogs butchered, corn fields are gone into, and after having filled their sacks with roasting ears and fed their horses, they march out without putting the fence up, thus leaving all the rest of the corn at the mercy of cattle, horses, hogs & c.

"If this state of affairs is not speedily and effectively stopped by the proper authorities, what are farmers' families and stock to subsist upon; and how are they to feed the powerful armies now in the field defending our homes from the brutal enemy? While the army is in the field bleeding for its homes, many stragglers are in its rear, plundering the fathers and families of those who do the fighting.

"Another incident came under my own observation, worthy of note. A carload of private property was stopped at a Station on the Macon and Western Railroad and publicly robbed, or 'charged' as they call it in spite of the defending owner. I do not believe that, that great and good man, Gen. Hood, knows of all this, or effectual means would be adopted to put a stop to it.

"I am just out of Atlanta, and am sure you would hardly know the place. In addition to the many damages done to public and private buildings by a few stragglers some days ago, to which the efficient Provost Marshal General put a stop by rigid and commendable measures, are holes in and corners knocked off of houses and the ground torn up generally. It is a dry, hot place, and not a female can be seen. Pretty heavy firing is now going on some 3 miles southwest of Atlanta and some 2 miles west of the Macon and Western Railroad. I can give you no results. I am pleased to see that the Militia are so highly appreciated. They are no longer called the New Ish."

Thursday dawned cool and cloudy with prospects of rain. Picket firing continued its muted spitefulness. At noon, the Federal soldiers, who had been idling at cards, whittling, letter writing, and sleeping were called to reinforce the pickets.

When shells whined over the Berry home, Maxwell decided the family better spend the day in the cellar. Carrie, who took Zuie down in her arms, had come supplied with sweet gum and yarn. She wondered if the family would ever be in a position to go on the buggy rides she loved.

In Atlanta, Lieutenant Andy Neal of the Marion Light Artillery debated whether to write any more letters, since the mails had been so disrupted.

"The raiders," he finally penned his sister Ella, "have frightened the Army Post Office out of all propriety and we have had no mail for 13 days but have hopes of getting one this evening as we had a man to go to Macon for it. I very unexpectedly found a box at Mrs. Pittmans for me last Monday evening. I was riding down town on business and happened to call to see if Mr. Pittman was at home when I heard of the box. I believe everything was in good order and I have to thank all of you for it but I came near committing an awkward mistake as I was all day of opinion that Cousin Martha Bailey had sent me the box and was preparing to thank her for her favor when I found a piece of 'Cotton States' and at once recognized the things as having come from home. I hope Cousin Martha did not get her box off in time for it is annoying to have them lost. I will send Benny some coffee and sugar by some of his company who are coming for Gen. Walthall on whose line we are at present.

"I have been getting along very quietly ever since we have been on this line till yesterday. At the position where we have been there has been a little firing as our pickets were 1000 yards in our front. Yesterday I was placed with my section in a fort about 100 yards from the Ponder Home on the State Road. The Yankees have their line of battle and several Batteries a short distance in our front and on our right have approached so near our works by digging that we can keep out no pickets. Almost all the shells they throw into the City come screaming just above our heads. Generally they commence on this fort and throw around it shells and then elevate their guns and send the balance into the city. For awhile we exchanged shots with them but where Batteries are as well protected as our and the Yankee Batteries before us about as much is made of Artillery duels as the sledge hammer makes out of the anvil. Atlanta is considerably marked by the enemy's shots. In some parts of town every house has been struck a dozen times. The houses about the foot of Alabama Street are much battered. I see two balls have gone into our house, one in Bud James' room and one in the parlor.

"Very few people think the enemy will get any nearer Atlanta but they have ruined its value to us in a great measure. Our Army has been strengthened by the Militia and reinforcements from Forrest have come in. Besides these, all the bands, cook details, extra artillery, men drivers and dead heads have been brought to the front and given muskets. Thus we will be enabled to hold our long lines and have force enough to operate on the flanks. We are constantly stirred up with reports of reinforcements from Virginia and the Mississippi but no troops have been ordered here yet.

"Gen. Hood watches his flanks closely and has twice whipped the flanking columns out. We had heavy fighting between the skirmishers yesterday on our right and left. Just in front of us there was no attack. We repulsed the charges at both places but I have heard no particulars.

Your affectionate brother A. J. Neal."

The cloudy skies fulfilled their portent. By early afternoon the rain was cold, insistent. Captain Evan P. Howell, who had recently evacuated his wife Julia and one-year-old son Clark to Augusta from their home along the Chattahoochee, fretted over the weather. Thinking back with a certain nostalgia on the day Julia filled her apron with freshly baked biscuits, hitched the family cow behind their wagon, and fled from the advancing Federals, Captain Howell wrote:

"This is a rainy, disagreeable morning and I will try to make it an agreeable one by writing to you. We have not moved from our position on the west of Atlanta yet. We had pretty heavy firing on our right and left yesterday but they did not shoot a shot at us. The day before they fired a few over my Battery. The enemy are evidently trying to turn our left and strike the Macon Road below or about West Point. No other news about here. . . .

"My health is now better than it has been since I was taken sick twelve months ago. And I think now that I will get well entirely and get fat again. Then I want the war to end and our housekeeping to begin, and such a happy time we will have will be too good to tell. . . .

"To think of it, we have been married going on *four years*. Don't time fly? Why it seems as if it was only last year that I was courting you, and yet how many scenes have crowded past since then. How very different is the grand panorama of human life looked at through the vista of the past that it is viewed as it slowly changes its scenes dragged on by the weary present. . . .

"I want you to get a good recipe for making hard soap, nice

soap. It is impossible to buy it now. I hope the boy keeps well. Kiss the little fellow for me."

Thirty women were shopping in the large Market House, pawing over meager groceries and vegetables which scarcely covered the white tables. Meats were entirely absent. There was a sudden flash, a roar, and bits of timber flew through the dusty air. Some of the women fell to the ground.

A shell had hit the rear of the structure and exploded. James Parker and Robert McMaster, attending their stalls, were knocked down. When they were on their feet again and looked about, they realized that no injury had been sustained by themselves or the women marketers "except the fright they received."

In the air the smell of burned powder grew more acrid before it subsided. The ladies dusted off their dresses, picked up their baskets, and continued, perforce, their marketing.

In early afternoon Carrie paused in her knitting to scribble, slowly, under the cellar's candlelight. "The shells have been flying all day and we have stayed in the cellar. Mama put me on some stockings this morning and I will try to finish them before school commences." The rain accentuated the dank dreariness of the cellar and soon Zuie began to cough.

Captain Joe Vale, Pennsylvania cavalryman, now taking part in the siege of Atlanta, wrote:

"About one hundred and fifty yards to the right of the bivouac of the brigade was a hill on which, in a strong fort, a battery of heavy siege guns was mounted, and on an opposite hill one of the strongest of rebel forts of defense was constructed, also armed with heavy (sixty-four-pounder) siege guns. Our bivouac, located in the angle, was directly in the line of fire from this rebel fort, and almost daily the big shells from Atlanta, passing over the fort on our right, dropped down among us, sometimes exploding, but generally harmlessly burying themselves in the sand. Our acquaintance with, and experience of, these visitors began on the night of the 3d, when the rebels opened a converging line of fire on the battery to our right from five heavy batteries, located within easy range. The shells dropped into our camp at a lively rate, half a dozen coming at a time, and as all the boys not on duty at the line of breastworks were sleeping in their little shelters at the time, they got 'waked up' rudely enough! Shelters were knocked down, cook-tents demolished, camp-kettles scattered and destroyed with a good deal of din, and the boys promptly seeking cover in the trenches, without much regard to the completeness of their uniform, presented somewhat the appearance of Falstaff's regiment of ragamuffins. The occasion was commemorated as the 'shirt-tail dress-parade.'

"Attached to the brigade headquarters was a colored man named George, who from time to time when not exactly satisfied with the situation as cook and hostler, was wont to declare his purpose of enlisting, and entering on the work of the immediate overthrowing of the rebellion . . . up to this time, however, George had managed to avoid being under fire, though often complaining bitterly of the hard fate that kept him among the pack mules and camp kettles, when a fight was going on.

"When the shelling began, George was sleeping in the cook shelter, and only waked up when a sixty-four pounder shell burst in the vicinity, scattering the cookhouse, with its pans and kettles, over and around him! His longing to be in a fight, or at least under fire, was gratified at last! But George was not looking for it in that form and found the realization of his hopes and longings slightly different from his anticipations, and not wishing to 'get hurt,' popped into a 'gopher hole' as the old rebel rifle pits in our camping ground were called."

The next morning when Vale asked George where he was when it came time for food, the cook frankly admitted he was holed up, observing it was "a tempestuous night."

In Social Circle, a mid-morning flurry answered a train whistle's unmistakable toot in the distance. Grandma Smith was nearly trampled by townspeople, patients, and assorted transients in a rush for the depot. Chickens ran squawking for cover in dust swirls billowing up from the flying feet. But none of the townsfolk was allowed aboard the train when it finally ground to a halt. It was packed with refugees from Atlanta and elsewhere, some even astride the roof, with their bundles of clothes and possessions.

"It was everyone for himself," Grandma Smith realized, although amazed at the "incredible short space of time" it took to load the hospital goods. A contingent of soldiers was aboard the train to protect it from "scattered bands of Federals who were reported to be near the road." Mrs. Smith noted that others beside herself were jubilant:

"The persons composing the party gave full vent to their feelings, manifesting the greatest joy and gratitude for being taken away from so unpleasant a place and situation. Each one had his or her joke on the other. All enjoyed it fully. Some little burdens which they could scarcely have moved at any ordinary time were disposed of in various ways, and we were soon whirling away from Yankeedom as fast as the locomotive could possibly carry us, while our hearts, which had been before so cast down and desponding, were as cheerful for the time being as though the few days of sadness had never been.

"While we were enjoying our unexpected exit from Yankeedom, we did not forget poor Frank Hodges, who had gone out in search of wagons. We knew it would be a surprise to him on his return; and we imagined his disappointment and chagrin at finding himself deserted. Transportation was provided for him to follow on the next day, with the promise from our kind young lady friend, Miss Clark, that he should have a home with them that night."

Finally, Fannie Beers was ready to leave Newnan for the thirty-eight-mile journey to Atlanta.

"The next morning," she wrote, "when, after a substantial breakfast, I was once more ready to start, every member of the family made some addition to my stores, notably, a few pounds of really good country butter. This was always highly prized by the soldiers. As a general thing, when the cows were fed upon cotton-seed the butter was white and 'waxy,' this was yellow and firm. The oldest girl brought me a pair of socks she had herself knitted; one of the little boys, six eggs laid by his own 'dominiker,' which he pointed out to me as she stalked about the yard proud of her mottled feathers and rosy comb.

"Even the baby came toddling to the door saying, 'Heah, heah,' and holding out a snowy little kitten. The old gentleman, mounting his horse, offered to 'ride a piece' with us. Thanks to his representations to the neighbors, I was able in a short time to turn my face homewards, having gathered an excellent supply of chickens, eggs, hams, home-made cordials, peach and apple brandy, and a few pairs of socks. The old farmer also showed us a way by which we could avoid a repetition of the tortures of yesterday, and rode beside the ambulance to the main road.

"I remember well how he looked, as he sat upon his old white mule, waiting to see the last of us. His hat, pushed back, showed a few locks of silvery hair; his coarse clothes and heavy, home-made boots were worn in a manner that betrayed the Southern gentleman. The parting smile, still lingering upon his kindly face, could not conceal the 'furrows of care,' which had deepened with every year of the war. But, alas! I cannot recall his name, although I then thought I could never forget it.

"Upon arriving at Newnan, I lost no time in preparing my boxes for the front. Everything was cooked; even the eggs were hard-boiled. There was sufficient to fill two large boxes. Having packed and shipped to the depot my treasures, I prepared for the final step without hesitation, although not without some doubt as to success in eluding the vigilance of my friends.

"Announcing my determination to see the boxes off, I—accompanied by my maid—walked down to the depot just before train-time. There was only one rickety old passenger-car attached to the train. This, as well as a long succession of box- and cattle-cars, were crowded with troops,—reinforcements to Atlanta. Taking advantage of the crowd, I, with Tempe, quietly stepped on board, escaping discovery until just as the train was leaving, when in rushed Dr. McAllister, who peremptorily ordered me off; but, being compelled to jump off himself, failed to arrest my departure.

"I was in high spirits. On the train were many soldiers whom I had nursed, and who cared for my comfort in every way possible under the circumstances. I was the only lady on the train, so they were thoughtful enough to stow themselves in the crowded boxes behind, that I might not be embarrassed by a large number in the passenger-car.

"At last, as we approached Atlanta, I heard the continuous and terrific noise of the bombardment. The whistle of the engine was a signal to the enemy, who at once began to shell the depot. I did not realize the danger yet, but just as the train 'slowed up' heard a shrieking sound, and saw the soldiers begin to dodge. Before I could think twice, an awful explosion followed; the windows were all shivered, and the earth seemed to me to be thrown in cart-loads into the car. Tempe screamed loudly, and then began to pray. I was paralyzed with extreme terror, and *could* not scream. Before I could speak, another shell exploded overhead, tearing off the corner of a brick store, causing again a deafening racket. As we glided into the station, I felt safer; but soon found out that every one around me had business to attend to, and that I must rely upon myself.

"The shells still shrieked and exploded; the more treacherous and dangerous solid shot continually demolished objects within our sight. For a few hours I was so utterly demoralized that my only thought was how to escape. It seemed to me *impossible* that any body of soldiers could voluntarily expose themselves to such horrible danger. I thought if *I* had been a soldier I must have deserted from my first battle-field. But at last I grew calmer; my courage returned, and, urged by the necessity of finding shelter, I ventured out. Not a place could I find. The houses were closed and deserted, in many cases partly demolished by shot or shell, or, having taken fire, charred, smoking, and burnt to the ground.

"All day, frightened women and children cowered and trembled and hungered and thirsted in their underground places of refuge while the earth above them shook with constant explosions. After a while I grew quite bold, and decided to stow myself and my boxes in the lower part of a house not far from the depot. The upper story had been torn off by shells. I could look through large holes in the ceiling up to the blue sky. The next move was to find means of notifying my husband and his friends of my arrival. I crept along the streets back to the depot, Tempe creeping by my side, holding fast to my dress. Then I found an officer just going out to the trenches, and sent by him a pencilled note to Lieutenant Cluverius, thinking an officer would be likely to receive a communication, when a private might not.

"Soon after sunset, my husband joined me, and soon after

many friends. They were all ragged, mud-stained, and altogether unlovely, but seemed to me most desirable and welcome visitors.

"One of my boxes being opened, I proceeded to do the honors. My guests having eaten very heartily, filled their haversacks, and, putting 'a sup' in their canteens, returned to camp to send out a *fresh* squad. The next that came brought in extra haversacks and canteens 'for some of the boys who couldn't get off,' and these also were provided for.

"With the last squad my husband was compelled to go back to camp, as just then military rules were severe, and very strictly enforced. I passed the night in an old, broken armchair, Tempe lying at my feet, and slept so soundly that I heard not a sound of shot or shell."

Shells held little respect for the sanctity of the church. One burst inside of St. Luke's, another against the African Church on Collins street, while a solid ball drilled cleanly through the First Presbyterian Church.

Wesley Chapel continued to take more than its share of pummeling. It had been struck at least five times. After each hit the Sexton came timidily into the nightmare of rubble, dust, and torn prayer books and hymnals and swept up the best he could. He could do nothing about the jagged holes in the roof and walls.

The next morning, he would arrive to find the plaster-smelling litter confronting him again. The missiles entered Wesley Chapel from all directions. One solid shell had bounced through ten pews like some erratic bowling ball before finally coming to rest against the altar. The parsonage itself was badly torn up.

The Reverend J. S. Wilson's residence on Walton Street was also damaged slightly, in the minister's absence.

AUGUST 5

⊠ *Richmond Sentinel*

"The telegraph brings us some news from Georgia. There was considerable skirmishing, with musketry and artillery firing, on Wednesday. The enemy shelled Atlanta furiously, killing a lady."

▤ *The New York Herald*

"Nashville—The latest news from General McCook's cavalry expedition is highly encouraging and lessens the extent of the disaster. Gen. McCook has himself reached Marietta with 1200 men. A squad of 300 reached the same point a short time previous. The missing will not exceed 800.

"All prisoners previously taken by McCook were abandoned. About 500 mules were shot by him before Ransom captured them.

"Our loss in killed is slight, 4/5 absentees being prisoners.

"General Sherman alludes to the raid as successful.

"Everything is quiet at the front."

(Mr. W. F. G. Shanks, correspondent)

⊠ *Richmond Dispatch*

"We get some interesting intelligence from the Georgia papers. Everything seems to have changed in that state from the deepest despondency. Gen. Hood seems to have brought the people to the liveliest exultation. This is a very decisive point gained, and we presume that the repulse of the enemy on the 27th . . . and the capture of a great flanking raider—Stoneman—will hardly detract from the general joy of the people."

Grandma Smith arrived in Augusta at 5:00 A.M., safely, with a suspicion that the war, for her, was over.

"Poor Frank," she wrote, "said he never was so mad in his life as when he returned to Social Circle, and found us all gone; but he reflected on the tedious journey we had escaped, and was then glad we had been so fortunate. The wagons which were to have been at our disposal the following morning were not wanting, as we were safe and snug in Augusta, strolling around the streets of that strange and beautiful city, and wondering where the spot could be found where Mary got so badly frightened at the man with the moustache, when her husband, Major Joseph Jones, was strolling around town with her to see the sights. Ha, ha! we neither found the watermelon cart, or the man with his beard all on his upper lip who frightened Mary so, but thought we found his picture in one of the city galleries; it corresponded pretty accurately with the description the major gave of the man, at least."

"At last," Joe Semmes wrote to "Eo," "I have been gladdened by the sight of your dear hand again by the receipt of your letters of the 17 and 21st of July, and now I have the certainty of your receiving this as it is to be taken to you by Ben himself. When he first told me he was going to Gainesville I was nearly overcome for I have had lately the most intense longing for home and a little rest that I ever yet felt. In truth my precious wife I feel worn down mentally and bodily, and I sigh for a short respite of quiet and freedom from care which only can be obtained at your side. I could not be driven from this army unless it was to go to you and spend the time with you. Ben is very fortunate and though I envy him his trip I feel sure of the pleasure he anticipates, because he will see you too. I did hope that the next chance I had of sending home I could get to you the stationery you need; now it is not here and I can only send you what I can spare, neither can I send anything to the boys; the pistol is in the rear with my surplus baggage and I have nothing here for them, unless it is fragments of the Yankee shells, which are thrown promiscuously in and about town.

"I cannot write now and could not talk to Ben for you, although you will be disappointed I know. He will, however, tell you what I want. You never yet told me of the candles and I have requested him to ask about them in Montgomery to see, too, whether Clara and Myra have gone. I have never heard a word since the first letter on the subject, after that the road was cut. Tom was to leave for Louisiana about the 1st of August and I presume Ben will not see him. All my ideas are driven out by the din around me about bacon, beef, etc. I am positively ashamed to send my darling such a letter, it can't be helped as the train goes in a few minutes. Ben will tell you how I require the Brandy and please don't fail to make him bring it. If Alphonso went to Montgomery, he left I hope the Brandy with the Knoxes . . . Goodbye . . . God bless you."

On Fairlee Street, Carrie Berry spent Friday morning knitting in the back yard under clear, pleasant skies. The pony grazed nearby and the chickens ruffled their feathers in the warm, dusty earth. The soldiers had gone.

A few hundred yards northeast of the vidette pit on Peachtree Street, within Federal lines, engineers completed a platform atop the highest tree that could be found. Second Lieutenant Samuel Edge, signal corps veteran of Vicksburg, climbed up to it and tapped out that he could not only see the enemy's camps and houses of Atlanta but the "Macon Railroad on the other side."

He was in view of Confederate sharpshooters, but just out of their range. The Minie balls dropped short of his high perch, like spent pebbles. Lieutenant Edge rested his telescope on the wooden rail of the little platform and settled down for what he figured could be a long roost.

"My dear little nephew," wrote a Southern soldier, J. J. Miles, from somewhere in the camps under surveillance by Lieutenant Edge, "it is threw the will of the Lord that I am permitted to write you a short letter this morning. I am well and harty and I do sincerely hope when this reached you that you may be surrounded with the same health.

"Guston, I will send this by Mr. Armstrong of the 12th Mississippi Cavalry. The enemy ar shelling the city more or less every day. They was heavy skirmishing late last evening also during the night and ar still. Guston, I will give you the price of forage up here in this section of the country. Flour is $1.25 per pound and bacon is 500 dollars per lb. lard the same. Salt $100 per lb. molasses 20 dolls. per gal. By some flower bread sometimes baked up in biscuits. I pay from 2½ to 3 dolls per dosen or . . . 25 cts. a peace. I eaten a harty bate of stock pies yesterday for diner. They ar worth 100 dollars per quart. Guston I would like to now why you all don't write to me. I aught to get a letter from some of you every week but I don't get one once every month. I want you all to write oftener than you do or not a tall one or the too Paper is selling from 5 to ten dollars per quire. Broth L. H. came out to the regt. last week and stayed A bout 12 hours with me. His health does not improve any at all. Well, Guston, I think we will have a fine old Battle here in a few days. We gained a glorious victory . . . on the 2d Inst capture 24 stands of colors no casualties . . . well I will now quit by requesting you to eat a Bate of watermelons for me. Give my love to all, I remain your affectionate uncle as ever J. J. Miles."

Charles H. Smith, balding, one-time resident of Centreville, Virginia, arrived at the Atlanta depot with his large family. They had most recently refugeed from Rome, Georgia, via a circuitous route. Smith had a pseudonym for himself—"Bill Arp"—and he prided himself on a sense of humor. He had amused his traveling companions on his recent journeys by explaining, "I'm a good Union man, so-called, but I'll bet on Dixie as long as I've got a dollar."

In the station there appeared "all sorts of people . . . moving in all sorts of ways, with an accelerated motion. They gained ground on their shadows as they leaned forward on the run, and their legs grew longer at every step. With me, it was the second ringing of the first bell. I had sorter got used to the thing, and set myself down to take observations."

He inquired directions but no one replied, "for their legs were as long as light, and every bursting shell was an old witch on the road.

"Cars was the all in all. Depots were the centre of space, converging lines from every point of the compass made tracks to the offices of railroad superintendents. These functionnaires very prudently vamosed the ranch to avoid their too numerous friends, leaving positive orders to their subordinates.

"The passenger depot was thronged with anxious seekers of transportation.

" 'Won't you let these boxes go as baggage?'

" 'No, madam, it is impossible!'

"Just then somebody's trunk as big as a nitre bureau was shoved in and the poor woman got desperate.

" 'All I've got ain't as heavy as that,' said she. 'I am a poor widow and my husband was killed in the army. I've got five children and three of them cutting teeth, and my things have got to go!'

"We took up her boxes and shoved them in. Another good woman asked very anxiously for the Macon train.

" 'There it is, madam,' said I. She shook her head mournfully and remarked.

" 'You are mistaken, sir. Don't you see the engine is headed right up the State road, towards the Yankees? I shan't take any train with the engine at that end of it. No sir, that ain't the Macon train.'

"Everywhere was hurrying to and fro at a lively time.

" 'What's today . . . ?' said a female darkey, with a hoop skirt on her arm, and she was answered by an older man of her race.

" 'T'ain't no day, honey dat I eber seed . . . I reckon today is Runday from de way de white folks is movin' about . . . ain't afraid of Yankees but dem sizzlin bumbshells . . . gwine to git away from here, I is!'

"I went into a doctor's shop and found my friend packing up his vials and poison and copaiva and such like. Various excited individuals came in, looked at a big map on the wall and pointed out the roads to McDonough and Eatonton and Jasper and soon their proposed lines of travel were easily and greasily visible from the impression of their perspiring fingers. An old skeleton with but one leg, was swinging from the ceiling looking like a mournful emblem of the fate of the troubled city.

" 'You are going to leave him to stand guard, doctor?' said I.

" 'I suppose I will,' said he, 'got no transportation for him.'

" 'Take the screw out of his skull,' said I, 'and give him a crutch, maybe he will travel; all flesh is moving and I think the bones will catch the contagion soon.'

"A few doors further and a venerable auctioneer was sur-
veying the rushing, running crowd, and every now and then
he would raise his arm with a seesaw motion and exclaim,
'going—going—gone! Who's the bidder?'

" 'Old Daddy Time,' said I, 'he'll get them all before long.' "

Bill Arp, or Smith, walked into a friend's house. Several
men were seated around a bottle. One of the drinkers swore
he would unpack, "dinged if I'm afraid of a blue-tailed fly!"

And at that moment a "sizzing, singing, crazy shell sung a
short-metre hymn right over the house. 'Jake, has the dray
come?' he said, bouncing to his feet. 'Confound that dray—
blame my skin if I'd ever get a dray to move these things—
boys, let's take another drink!' "

Smith continued to listen to the group clinking glasses as
they chorused:

> The boy stood burning on the deck,
> When all had fled but him!

"By and by the shells fell as thick as Governor Brown's proc-
lamations, causing a more speedy locomotion in the excited
throng who hurried by the door, but my friends inside had
passed the Rubicon—vacant rooms and long corridors echoed
with their snores."

Mrs. Beers survived a morning which began when she was
awakened by "a terrible explosion near us." She was informed
that a house nearby had been hit squarely. A man and his three
children, asleep in an upper room, had been killed.

"This made me very uneasy," she wrote, "and increased
Tempe's terror to such an extent that she became almost un-
manageable." Fannie Beers spent most of the day in her room.

All afternoon, Bill Arp watched the trains come and go,
the "iron horses snorting to the echoing breeze. Train after
train of goods and chattels moved down the road, leaving
hundreds of anxious faces waiting their return. There was no
method in this madness. All kinds of plunder was tumbled in
promiscuously. A huge parlor mirror, some 6 feet by 8, all
bound in elegant gold, with a brass buzzard spreading his wings
on the top, was set up at the end of the car and reflected a beau-

tiful assortment of parlor furniture to match, such as pots, kettles, baskets, bags, barrels, kegs, bacon and bedsteads piled up together. Government officials had the preference and government officials all have friends. Any clever man with a charming wife or a pretty sister could secure a corner in more cars than one."

As the sun went down, Arp and his family were on board one of the trains, "without any idea where we would stop.

" 'Ticket, sir?' said the conductor.

" 'Nary ticket,' said I.

" 'How far are you going?" said he.

"Putting on an air of sublime indifference, I remarked that 'I was not very particular—that he knew the road and could suit himself.'

"He cut his eye along the line of my numerous offspring and observed that I had better scatter them as provisions were scarce.

"I paid him our fare to Covington and so got rid of his impertinence."

That evening Carrie Berry and her family moved to her Aunt Martha's large cellar on nearby Alabama Street, facing the railroad tracks. "We did not feel safe in our cellar," Carrie wrote in her diary, "They fell so thick and fast."

J. M. P. Calvo, a painter living on Mitchell Street, was sitting on his front porch talking with his family and smoking a cigar. The table was prepared for a late dinner. Suddenly there came a rush of air, a crashing above the people's heads. The family threw themselves flat onto the porch boards.

When Calvo cautiously arose to investigate he found a solid shot had passed into the house and through the table. It was the end of the plates and the other settings for dinner. Even so, the destructive instrument was not spent. It rolled out through the back wall and bumped to grudging rest in the rose garden.

AUGUST 6

Southern Press Association

"*Atlanta*—The enemy have been unusually active during the past 16 hours. About 4 o'clock yesterday afternoon a heavy assault was made upon the works held by our skirmishers upon the extreme left. After some stubborn fighting they succeeded in gaining possession of the position there, but subsequently were driven from it and our lines were reestablished.

"About 10 o'clock last night an assault was also made on our skirmish lines, extending from the centre to the extreme left, but the movement having been anticipated, resulted in a complete failure.

"Brisk skirmishing continued throughout the night up to the present time. Our loss in both affairs is insignificant.

"There was comparative quiet in the city last night, and but few shells were thrown, resulting in no damage."

The New York Herald

"*Louisville*—A letter dated one mile from Atlanta on the 31st of July from a prominent officer there to another here says, 'fires are now burning in Atlanta. They indicate that Gen. Hood is destroying a large amount of property, but whether with a view of evacuating the place is not known.'

"*Washington*—It is stated in official quarters here that the rebel report of Gen. Stoneman's capture in Georgia is incorrect, and that he succeeded in getting through all right, personally. . . .

"From several points along our lines we can plainly see Atlanta. We can see the burning houses and the smoke of the bursting shells floating over the doomed city."

Boston Daily Evening Transcript

"Maj. Gen. Hooker . . . arrived in Washington Thursday. In response to repeated calls for a speech he said,

" 'I did not come here to make a speech, nor shall you expect one. If this rebellion was to have been put down by speeches, enough have been made since its commencement to put down 40 rebellions.' "

Atop the Howard House, between Atlanta and Decatur, near which General McPherson was killed, Signal Officer A. F. Berry telegraphed to Captain C. R. Case:

"All quiet on this flank. Can see but few of the enemy in their works. Cannot see as many pieces of artillery as I did yesterday. Shells from the Twentieth Corps burst near the center of the city."

Samuel Mahon, twenty-four-year-old First Lieutenant with the Iowa Infantry, had a look at Atlanta. "We can see the city, its spires and cupolas glittering in the sun and seeming to defy the Yankee invader outside. May its pride fall the way Babylon fell."

Sergeant William Graham looked up at daybreak. It was overcast. He expected rain. "Part of the regiment went on duty at daylight," he noted in his soggy diary, "and were relieved in two hours by an Indian regiment, the 53rd (?). Still noisy. At 9 our relief went on to work in front and at half past 10 I was sent into camp to order the next relief with their arms. An attack expected.

"No rain yet but cloudy and warm."

Kate Cumming watched prisoners still filing into Newnan, "a deplorable sight . . . barefooted and bareheaded." After providing them with what old hats and shoes which could be found, hospital attendants served two gallons of soup, and bread. Many of Miss Cumming's patients offered to give their day's rations to the prisoners.

"One look at these poor creatures, I thought what a pity it was that the men in Washington could not be made to take their place; if this was done, I think we should have peace."

In making her Saturday rounds, she discovered that a majority of the prisoners were from Kentucky, Tennessee, North Alabama, and North Mississippi. She admitted to more respect for a "real Yankee." It was incomprehensible to her how any man "born on Southern soil can have any affinity with the enemy."

There was a two-year-old boy at the hospital "whom the men tried to get to speak to them, but he would not go near them. One of them said he thought it strange. I told him I did not, as instinct had taught the child who its worst enemies were. He said, 'why, we never hurt children!'

"I answered that burning their homes and destroying their food was not hurting them!

"Many of them answered, 'We never do these things, and would shoot a man as soon as you would, who would do so.'

"I asked them if any one had been shot for setting fire to Palmetto? They answered me; they could not find out who had done it. I told them that I expected they never would.

"They told us a good deal about how well the women of Georgia had treated them; they said they had given them food, and been very kind in every way. At this they need not feel at all flattered, as doubtless news had reached these ladies of the inhumanity with which many had been treated in North Georgia, and they thought it best wisdom, when in the lion's jaw, to extricate themselves as easily as possible.

"I know of many in this place who, as soon as they heard of the enemy coming, went to work to cook for them. We all know that this was not for love.

"There was a Captain Shortz of Iowa who had one of his hands cut off, and the other badly wounded. He was a pitiful sight. I told him I had more sympathy for him than I had for our own men. He asked me why. I answered, his conscience could not be at rest like theirs. He said that was a difference of opinion. All the men there told us the same old story—they were fighting for the Union.

"In another ward one of them, from New York, but a native of Cornwall, England, was nursing. I told him I was perfectly astonished to see one of his nation aiding the oppressor. He answered that he was ashamed of his native country for sympathizing with us as it had done. He was an abolitionist, and the first I had met.

"He said the main thing he disliked in being a prisoner was

that his time had expired and had he been free he would have been home. I asked him if all went home when their time was up. He said yes; there was nothing for them to do, as they had three reserves and they had only been fighting the first.

"We have certainly a bright prospect ahead of us, if we have the other two reserves yet to fight!

"I think the Federal government very inhuman. Why do they not send all the reserves to fight us at once, and not have their men killed by piecemeal, as they are now doing? The prisoners, one and all, told us that they could not be better treated.

"Some of our wounded have died lately. Mr. Hull, a fine-looking lad, was one. I think he was a member of Ross' Texas Cavalry. His brother was with him. A lieutenant, whose name I have forgotten, told me that Captain Haily is really killed. This gentleman was a particular friend of Captain H.; they had been school-boys together. He says a nobler or better man never lived."

The scarcity of knives, forks and spoons disturbed Kate Cumming, since patients and prisoners were compelled to eat with their fingers. Plates, cups, bowls, and pitchers of brown earthenware, were baked in a nearby factory.

In Macon, a twelve-pounder Parrott shell was placed on the editor's desk, at the *Intelligencer* and used as a candle-holder. The rifled missile was carried to Macon by Isaac Pilgrim, a printer with the newspaper. It was the only one, he believed, which struck the car-shed, and "not very inviting."

A long-time resident of Atlanta, Pilgrim had spent several days in the city. He returned to his job, carrying not only the shell, a number of Minie balls, shrapnel, and other souvenirs, but a detailed report on the bombardment.

"On corner of Hunter and Floyd Streets," Pilgrim commenced, "Goldburg's house, struck about 8 feet from the ground, passed into the cellar and exploded amidst the family wounding Dr. Gates' wife and child.

"On Pryor Street a shell passed through Mr. Hackett's house.

"Sherwood and Demerist's carpenter shop was struck, doing considerable damage.

"Mr. Kilby's house was struck, but did not do any damage only tearing a hole in the building.

"On Peachtree Street, Thomas Kile's building had a shell to explode in a room, which entered from the roof, but doing little damage. The building next to Kile's, had a shell to strike the roof and pass out at the gable end.

"All the Cherokee block, every building on it was struck in several places doing considerable damage.

"Judge Ezzard's residence has one end near the roof battered to pieces.

"The State Commissary building on Peachtree Street was struck with one shell. The damage very slight.

"The building used by Fields and Smith as a negro mart was struck, but the shell did not penetrate.

"A shell bursted at the window of Joseph Winship's residence, breaking the glass and otherwise damaging the house.

"A shell passed into the house occupied by Mr. J. F. Trout, tearing a wash-stand to pieces and exploding without material damage.

"A shell went into Dr. J. C. Powell's house, passed through two rooms and lodged in a box without exploding.

"A shell passed through the roof of Mr. Hariloin's house without much damage.

"A shell passed through an unoccupied house on the junction of Ivy and Peachtree Streets tearing it up considerably.

"About every third house on Peachtree has been struck and damaged more or less.

"Three shells struck the Female College, only one doing any material damage. It struck the belfry, tearing about half of it away.

"The house owned by Mr. Trout, on the street leading from the Trout House, was struck by two shells, but I could not learn the extent of the damage.

"Two shells struck the house of L. B. Davis, one in the garret, the other in the cellar. Damage slight.

"Five or six shells struck the residence of Mr. John H. Seals, doing a great deal of damage.

"One shot passed through the Coffin Shop of Mr. Chas. Bohnefield, on Luckie Street. Not much damage.

"Mr. McLendon's house, on Bridge Street, was struck in the roof, but not much damage.

"On Ivy Street, in the neighborhood where Col. Wallace and Mr. John Glenn resided, several houses were struck, I did not learn the names of the owners or the amount of the damage.

"The house of Dr. and Mrs. B. M. Smith on Peachtree had one corner torn off and the kitchen is riddled. The damage is heavy. . . .

"Tallulah Engine House was struck by a shell which passed through it.

"Some 20 shots have struck the W. & A. R.R. round house, and doing considerable damage.

"Three or four shots struck the State Depot.

"One shell struck the fine edifice of Mr. John Neal (Andy Neal's father) on the corner of Mitchell and Calhoun Streets near the roof but did not do much damage. . . .

"I do not think there is a house in the city but what has had a shell or shot to fall or pass very near it. . . .

"I hear of a great many persons being killed, though I cannot trace them to any person who actually knows it to be a fact. On my arrival I learned that a lady had been killed by a shell. I called on the lady's sister, who is an acquaintance of mine, and she informed me that it was news to her, as her sister was in the city of Macon.

"Rawson's house, on the corner of Whitehall and Hunter Streets was truck, knocking out a window and bursting in a room.

"Mrs. Valentino's store was hit on the roof, scattering the shingles in every direction. . . .

"A lady was killed on Peachtree Street Wednesday evening by a shell while she was ironing out some clothing. The lady's name is Smith. She was a refugee from Rome. The shell struck her in the breast, tearing her and mutilating her person very badly. A gentleman informed me of this who was trying to make arrangements for her burial. . . .

"A shell struck the house of Mr. Warren on Pryor Street,

next door to Hunter, on Thursday evening, on the end, scattering the splinters in every direction, wounding one lady very severely on the right arm. . . .

"All the houses in the rear of Winship's foundry have been injured by the shell and shot more or less. On Wednesday evening, between four and five o'clock the shell poured into that end of town like hail. A great many persons in the city have pits dug in their yards and bomb proofs made where they stay during the severest of shelling."

Fannie Beers became more accustomed "to the noise and danger" and, "with a heart for any fate," passed the day. The nurse had the "satisfaction of seeing and supplying some Alabama, South Carolina, and Tennessee soldiers."

By evening, the shelling was stepped up until she found it "terrific." Anxiety for her husband, somewhere in the trenches, "combined with her shuddering terror, made sleep impossible."

Carrie Berry wrote, "we have been in the cellar all day. Cousin Henry Beatty came this evening and brought some Yankee coffee for me to grind for him, some he had captured yesterday in a skirmish."

Sergeant William Graham removed breastworks he had helped construct earlier. "At dark and while moving to our new position in front 3 or 4 batteries opened on the enemy works and we had a lively time for an hour or so. Finally it died away with an occasional shot and we then enjoyed a nice rain until 11 o'clock at night when it cleared. Pickets firing all night and sometimes quite heavy but no attack made upon us. On the alarm guard tonite."

General Sherman prepared a late communication for General Howard: "I have no idea that the enemy will leave Atlanta unless compelled to do so."

AUGUST 7

✉ *Southern Press Association*

"Atlanta, August 6—Brisk skirmishing continued throughout yesterday and last night, on our left. A lively artillery duel took place last evening, between our batteries on Peach Tree Creek and the enemy—comparative quiet reigned in the city last night. The enemy continued to concentrate their forces on our left, Palmer's corps occupying the extreme right, with his head-quarters on the Sand Town road, and Stally's on the left, with his pickets extending to the Georgia Railroad.

"About 75 prisoners, including a captain and lieutenant, were brought in yesterday and last night.

"Gen. Wheeler has issued a congratulatory order to the cavalry on the defeat and rout of the enemy's raiding party.

"All quiet save some sharpshooting this morning."

▃▃ *The New York Times*

"Near Atlanta, August 1 (delayed)—Atlanta is not yet in Yankee possession. On Friday, the 22d of July, as I have before written you, an order was promulgated announcing the fall of Georgia's stronghold, and the whole army was deceived, as well as the correspondents, who—those connected with the Western papers —immediately repaired to Nashville to acquaint by telegraph their journals of the (supposed) fact. We who contented our-selves with the idea of visiting the city before describing it, rather have the joke on those clever fellows who 'saw the Star-Spangled Banner floating to the breeze from the public build-ings of Atlanta, and who heard the heavy tread of our victori-ous soldiers through the sombre streets.' My eagle-eyed friend of the 'Cincinnati Journal'—he who from the suburbs of the city witnessed the glorious entree of the Federal army—is much cut up about his vision extraordinary. He returned here yesterday and is still about a mile and a half from these suburbs. The enthusiastic Bohemian, he of capacious ears and telescopic eyes,

who heard the victorious tread of the Union army as it marched through the desolate thoroughfares of the Gate City, and who experienced an ecstatic gush as he beheld the National ensign climb the staff heretofore devoted to treason's rag, is expected to return as soon as he shall have fully recovered from his patriotic prostration. . . .

"To tell the truth, we are somewhat puzzled at the stubborn front presented by the enemy. Hood has been dreadfully worried since our encroachments commenced, and has experienced three disastrous defeats in which, according to the rebel newspapers, he has sustained a loss of 26,000 men. Yet he keeps up a bold front and audaciously stands his ground to the great dissatisfaction of our skirmish line. . . .

"We cannot with the least chance of success attempt to carry the enemy's fortifications by assault. . . .

"The cannonading has commenced all along the line, and as I write a lively shelling is going on in which both parties are participants. It is very quiet, however, along the skirmish line . . . 'Chickamauga.' "

When Sherman looked at the distant roofs and spires that bright, Sunday morning he raged that Atlanta still confronted him. He dispatched to Thomas:

"Telegraph to Chattanooga and have two 30-Pounder Parrotts sent down on the cars, with 1,000 shells and ammunition. Put them into your best position and knock down the buildings of the town. Slow progress here."

It was "wet under foot" as William Graham listened to the "constant noise in front." There was no movement, and "our right" had been pulled back; its weary members now "lay in camp," along the besieging lines.

The Reverend S. M. Cherry had been conducting services at the front since dawn when 'at 9:00 A.M. I reached the Missouri brigade of Gen. French's division, and found the soldiers gathering for prayer-meeting.

"At 11 o'clock brother Bounds was to preach the funeral sermon of Rev. Mr. Manning, a pious young minister of the Cumberland Presbyterian Church, recently appointed chaplain

of a Missouri regiment, but before he received his commission
he was killed in battle while in the discharge of his duties as an
officer of the line. As I approached Sears' Mississippi brigade, I
saw a group of soldiers, with uncovered heads, bowing beside a
row of new made graves, two of which contained the forms of
comrades now being consigned to the cold clay. Chaplain Latti-
more was engaged in prayer. I joined in the solemn burial
services of the soldiers slain in the strife on Saturday."

The Reverend Cherry arrived at the brigades of General M.
D. Ector, Evander McNair, and Samuel J. Gholson. He continued his narrative:

"I looked around for a suitable place for preaching. A central
point to the three commands was selected, but not a single tree
or shrub was to be found to screen us from the intense heat of
an August sun. Soon the singing collected a large congregation
of attentive soldiers. A caisson served for a pulpit, while the cannon, open-mouthed, stood in front of the foe. We were in full
range and in open view of the enemy, but not a single shell
or minie ball was heard hissing or hurtling near during the
hour's service. The soldiers sat on the ground, beneath the
burning sun, listening seriously to the words of life. At the
close of the sermon they crowded up to get Testaments and
papers. I regretted much that I could only furnish five of the
former to a regiment.

"On Friday an intellectual young officer came forward and
joined the Church. The day following he was killed in a skirmish with the enemy. During the service in Sears' brigade
there was a sharp skirmish in the front of that command, and
the pickets were so closely pressed that the officer in command
of the brigade sent a reinforcement to their support immediately after he returned from church. A continuous cannonade to
the left did not interrupt the service. Strange to see soldiers in
the line of trenches, with a sharp fire in their front, and a rapid
roar of artillery on their flank, and a shower over head, yet
quietly sitting or patiently standing to hear the preaching of
the gospel!"

A wounded soldier called to him.

" 'I am all right, sir; I thank God for it. For two years I have not seen a dark day. I *cannot doubt now.* I will meet my old mother in heaven. I am mortally wounded.'

"One ball had broken his arm and passed through his lungs. Another had passed through his thigh. He did not groan.

"In one division this Sunday eight sermons were preached in full sight of the Federal lines, and even within range of small arms."

"They are not afraid of death," added Chaplain A. D. McVoy, "and are ready to die when God calls them. . . . I witnessed the passing away of a Louisianian of Gibson's brigade, 4th La. the other day. Seldom have I seen a stronger Christian faith, a firmer reliance on God, and a clearer assurance of salvation in a dying hour. He was cruelly lacerated by a piece of shell that had ploughed deeply across his right side, and his sufferings were intense and unremitted. Still his mind was fixed upon God.

" 'Chaplain,' he said to me, 'I am dying. I have done my duty. . . . I have no fears; all is clear. Jesus died for me; I know he will save me.' "

Carrie Berry was thankful for a "quiet day—it all most seems like Sunday of old." She left her knitting, Mama, Zuie, and the rest of the family, then "Papa and I went to Trinity Church. Mr. Haygood preached. It is the first time I have been to church in a month."

S. P. Richards attended the same service, the first time *he* had been inside a church in three weeks.

"Rev. Atticus Haygood preached to us in the Methodist Church. Our cruel foe has the grace to cease from shelling us on the Sabbath, at least he has not done so yet. Last Wednesday night the horrid missiles of destruction whizzed past our house and discomposed us considerably. Heretofore they had all fallen short, but now we cannot tell at what moment they may strike us. A gentleman and his little girl, 10 years of age were both killed in bed by the same shell last week, and several others have lost their lives. Today we received letters at last from the world without, one from Harriet says that Mr. Taylor has at last had to go soldiering, and she confirms James' death. Upon entering our store today I was puzzled at finding the stove tumbled down and moved forward six feet, but the rubbish around and the side of the flue in the wall told that a shell had 'dropped in' but where it had made its entrance I could not discover until I went upstairs and then the mystery was explained. The shell had entered the roof and passing through five partitions of wood and plaster had pierced the side wall into the flue, and its force being expended it *dropped* in the flue to the store below and there exploded, doing the mischief before spoken of. I found the butt end of the shell the diameter of which is four inches and weights $3\frac{1}{4}$ pounds. The length was probably ten or twelve inches and the entire weight 16 or 20 pounds. I hope no more such visitors will enter our premises."

Joe Semmes attended Mass at the Church of the Immaculate Conception, where Father O'Reilly continued in attendance. The sacrament had an exhilarating effect on Semmes, who had been feeling ill for several days. The wet weather had started his old wounds throbbing.

"Before this reaches you," he wrote to "Eo," "Ben, who left two days ago for home, will have arrived and told you all about me. I wrote a few lines by him which were very unsatisfactory to me, if not to you.

"I have been quite unwell and was very feeble but today feel much stronger and better every way, especially since I have been to Mass for the first time since we left Dalton. During Mass I was nearly overcome by my emotions produced by the sacred presence of God bringing as it were my beloved wife and children close around me as it used to be before the war. I have hardly felt so profoundly your presence in spirit as I did today. Your prayers I felt were mingled with mine and though I could not see you in the flesh I felt you were by my side. It was consoling to me at this time especially for I am living in danger hourly and daily. Yesterday the enemy shelled us again heavily and rapidly, and many of the shot passed close over and around my quarters.

"Today they are quiet but hard at work for tomorrow when we look for a very hot fire.

"As long as it is necessary in the discharge of my duty to expose my life I do not feel any anxiety, but on the contrary a firm trust that God will protect me, but I have been uselessly and foolishly exposed and may be again. Do not, my beloved wife, give way to your fears about me, but trust in God and pray for me. The dangers to which I am exposed are as nothing compared with what our brave soldiers are undergoing every day.

"Not knowing whether Clara and Myra have started or not, I wrote yesterday to Cora for them as well as herself. I condemned their visit abroad, and urged that Clara should go to live with you and Ben at my expense, should she not have started. Tom was to go to Louisiana about Aug. 1st and promised to call to see you on his way. I advised him not to go, I think it is hazardous.

"The enemy are massing their troops on our extreme left, with a view to cut us off from our only railroad in running order now from Chattanooga, to within 2½ miles of Atlanta, and we can hear the whistle of the engine when they arrive at their lines, blowing furiously in defiance to us.

"I regretted very much that I could send nothing to the boys by Ben, but everything I had was away in the rear, and I could get nothing here suitable. I hope they will be satisfied with the will for the deed.

"I have seen another letter from John Dawson, he is doing tolerably well, but has lost some of his tongue and fears he will lose all his lower jaw teeth; he lives on milk, coffee and eggnogs and requires constant attention. As soon as he gets able I expect he will go to Gainesville, and remain until he recovers. This I understand is your wish and so informed him.

"Do not be frightened by the news from Mobile. The Yankee warships cannot get up to the city, and they cannot take it except by a heavy land force, which I don't believe they have; they are trying to force us to send troops from here, which will not be done. Mobile can and ought to be defended successfully by the troops now there aided by the militia of the state. The Navy part of the affair turned out just as I expected, and it would have been better to have kept our vessels inside the bar to operate against the smaller craft of the enemy fleet.

"Well, I must now close my rambling letter, darling, with the prayer that it may be the will of God, that we meet again this coming winter in health and in peace. Keep up your spirits for all will go well I am confident. Your devoted husband.

"Your enclosed letter was taken from the saddle bags of one of the captured raiders among a number of others, by one of my men, whom they had previously captured. The writer was a governess in a Mr. Winans family. Mrs. W. was Kate deKay and married the son of the great engineer of Baltimore, who made an immense fortune in Russia. I am staying at Mr. deKays you will see."

Fannie Beers' husband obtained a pass to visit her again, but "the day was darkened by the agony of parting." Nearly "impossible" to leave him in the midst of battle, it "required more courage than to face the shot and shell. But I could easily see that anxiety for me interfered with his duty as a soldier, so—we must part."

She started back for Newnan.

Mollie Smith and her family, who had quit their damaged house on Luckie Street, were living with a doctor friend. Two caves had been dug in his garden for shelter. "We were sitting on the front porch when a shell buried itself in the yard. As we expected the next to hit the house, we all started for the bomb-proof. . . .

"He (the doctor) was not very well . . . and was lying down asleep when his wife called to him to get out of the house immediately. He had hardly left when a shell exploded on the bed where he had lain. Feathers, cotton and shucks were scattered about promiscuously. We counted thirty holes in the bedspread."

Shells, however, had "ceased to disturb" Mollie at night. A louder report than usual "would arouse me, then I would look out of the window and, if the shells did not pass over the house I would go to sleep again." She found the bombardment "incessant day and night."

Another doctor, Ezekiel N. Calhoun, nearly seventy, was also sick. Dr. Calhoun, brother of Mayor James M., operated a drug store as a lucrative adjunct to his practice. In the war he had served as an army surgeon, and his present illness had arisen from drinking impure water while with Colonel Stiles' regiment on Skidaway Island.

Dr. Calhoun's large family included seven daughters, named for Southern States. One, Carolina Williams, widowed, lived with her father and mother, Lucy, together with a five-year-old son, Noble. Missouri resided nearby. One son had become a doctor, only to die before he attained thirty. Another, Pickens, had been killed while fighting in the Confederate army.

Many shells had already fallen in his yard, scattering the fine flocks of ducks, geese, and chickens the elderly doctor had patiently raised. One hit the smokehouse. His daughter, Louisiana, was rebandaging the wounds of a soldier in an ambulance which had paused in front of Dr. Calhoun's gate when a shell exploded overhead.

Since that occurrence, his daughters spent most of their time indoors or in the "gopher hole" behind the house. It had an entrance in the shape of a letter "L," was ten feet deep and covered with boards, ample in size to take care of the family.

One of the Negro women watched a shell hit in the garden this afternoon, then dug it out, although it was imbedded two feet deep. She brought it into the house, but Dr. Calhoun recognized it as a percussion-cap type, and unexploded. His daughters who were not already in the bombproof fled out of the house and towards the refuge at the sight of the long missile.

"Take it out!" Dr. Calhoun ordered, "and place it at the end of the yard, beside the garden path, under the grape arbor." The slave, now fearful of the shell, ran in her splay-footed gait down the path.

The grandson, meanwhile, was on his way to the drug store —his afternoon custom—for twenty-five cents worth of butterscotch candy. There a "broken-down gentleman," attesting to the personnel shortage in Atlanta, would hobble behind the counter and effect what seemed to young Noble a miserly weighing on the little scales.

The child had made a game of traveling the few blocks to grandfather's store. Every time a cannon boomed in the distance he would drop behind "some friendly fence or stone wall, then rise and go forward until startled by another report, and in this manner reach the store."

Once in a while his playing soldier assumed reality as a shell crashed on the street yards away and erupted with a doomsday roar. Like other older residents of Atlanta, he had learned to fear the shells which struck paving stones and ricocheted in an unpredictable direction.

General Sherman telegraphed to Washington:

"I do not deem it prudent to extend any more to the right, but will push forward daily by parallels, and make the inside of Atlanta too hot to be endured. I have sent back to Chattanooga for two thirty-pound Parrotts, with which we can pick out almost any house in town. I am too impatient for a siege, and don't know but this is as good a place to fight it out on, as farther inland. One thing is certain, whether we get inside of Atlanta or not, it will be a used-up community when we are done with it."

By dusk, Fannie Beers was once more in Newnan. Her hospital associates were "so overjoyed at my safe return that they forbore to upraid."

After dark, Sergeant William Graham helped conduct "about 20 prisoners . . . into the picket line who reported themselves as part of a corps from Charleston. They gave themselves up and said we would be attacked tomorrow."

By 9:00 A.M. he was helping to man the works "under heavy fire . . . but finally died away and we retired." Some 400 more prisoners were taken. Before turning in, the Union soldier made a last entry, "starlight tonight."

AUGUST 8

■ *The New York Herald*

"*Washington*—The military authorities here are satisfied that the rebel reports of the capture of Gen. Stoneman are substantially correct. The report of his escape probably arose from the return of General E. McCook, who was supposed to have been killed or captured."

▤ *The Daily Intelligencer* (Atlanta)

"On Saturday evening, the enemy attacked in heavy force Armstrong's cavalry and Bates' skirmishers on our extreme left and succeeded in driving the cavalry across the South branch of Utoy Creek, but in front of Bates they were repulsed with considerable loss, leaving their dead and wounded, about 100 prisoners the colors of the 8th (Federal) Tennessee and 104th Ohio in our hands.

"A night attack was expected and preparations made accordingly, but the night wore away without an alarm.

"About 10 o'clock yesterday morning another attack was made upon the same line by the enemy's skirmishers, supported by one line of battle, but were again repulsed with great loss. The attack was renewed the third time last night with three lines of battle. The enemy were again repulsed with heavier loss than before.

"One Corps has passed around to reinforce Palmer but matters today are unusually quiet.

"No shells were thrown in the city yesterday or today.

"Yesterday, services were held in several of the churches.

"The whole number of raiders captured thus far is 2800."

Sergeant Graham opened his eyes again to see the stars were gone. It was day, and "somewhat cloudy." But no attack had materialized although picket firing "has been constant." It seemed to him that the restless, harsh ripple of shooting had flowed on without interruption.

"The night of August 7," wrote S. A. McNeil, of the Army of the Cumberland, "was a trying ordeal . . . to me there was terror in the sound of a .54 cal. rifle ball fired from a point two or three hundred feet away, as it passed my head, but it was fierce to hear one as it struck the quivering flesh of a comrade.

"When morning came we were partly protected by earthwork, but we lost about 20 men killed and wounded. . . . Billy Williams was standing in the trench . . . when a ball struck his head. Billy was the leading tenor of our quartet. I helped to carry his body to a knoll in the rear of the main line, where we found a number of newly made graves. We prepared the grave, wrapped the body in his own blanket and laid him away to rest. There was no time for ceremony . . . no farewell salute by a squad of soldiers. The sound of Confederate shells as they came over the enemy was the only requiem sung at Billy's funeral.

"Sgt. H. N. Simmons of Co. F. with his penknife carved the name, company and regiment on a board taken from a cracker box. This board was placed at the grave."

Lieutenant N. Scott, of the 1st Regiment, Georgia militia, found a letter in the No Man's Land surrounding Atlanta. He did not know whether the Union soldier who had received it was dead or taken prisoner.

"Dear Son," wrote Henry Zimmerman, of Norristown, Pennsylvania, "it appears there are still rebel soldiers about; it would appear if all the reports are true of so many being killed at every battle and so many prisoners taken, and so many deserting that there can be but very few left.

"I thought they would a been exausted long before this time, if there is any truth in reports the war will be brought to a close this summer. This report of the Confederates sending to Washington is all garmon, they are making all the preparations they can for the spring Campaign and according to the papers they begin to feel strong again.

"Them Alabama Girls must be a spunkey set, are they good looking? It appears the inhabitants have to depend on your bounty from the army, how is it have they no provisions of their own, or has it all been taken from them or is it a country that don't Give much provision? It must be pretty tuff times for a community to live on crackers and bacon if they have been use to better fair.

"I wish the war was at its end, we will lose all our Young men if it continues much longer, and then we will not no what to do with the girls; make a Regt. of them? They got so habituated in visiting Camp Wm. Pome at chelton hill, that is a negro Camp or a regt. of unbleached men, the females got to visiting by hundred, some time as many as 500 a day. Col. Wagner issued orders forbidding any visitors without a pass from the proper officers. I saw Col. Wagner, he tended Court. One of his unbleached men shot a wite man, and he was tried at Montgomery County Court and convicted of voluntary manslaughter.

"Last Tuesday was a great day in our little borough. The 51st Regiment which had been out for about two and a half years, has reenlisted and came home last Tuesday on a furlough for 30 days. They were received in style. Arches and greens strung across the streets. All the fire companies were out with their machines. The Union League. Several bands of music. The 51st were paraded around town, and then taken to Reiff's Market House, where a bountiful dinner was provided for them, and they were then dismissed, and went to their respective homes. About 200 out of the regiment have reenlisted, leaving about 50 who would not reenlist. The town was full of people on that day. It seems the Regiment did not appreciate the reception very highly on account of some of the Copperheads who got mixed in amongst the rest.

"While the Regiment was still at Harrisburg Col. Hartranft telegraphed to know how the 51st was to be received. The answer was, 'With Arches and Greens.' He retorted that they had better make it greenbacks as they would be appreciated."

Carrie Berry was dressed "early . . . and cleaned up the house for Mama." When she was through it was time to nurse Zuie "while Mama got dinner." Cousin Eddie Stow was coming to eat with the Berrys. At noon, a shower drenched the city. It turned into an interrupted afternoon for Carrie. After Eddie Stow ate dinner and left, she "went up to Auntie's for the afternoon." She was relieved that "we have not had many shells today."

Major Charles W. Hubner's telegraph message center had been working around the clock in the American Hotel, on the corner of Alabama and Pryor streets. Hubner, ex-newspaperman, realized Federal gunners had the range of the nearby railroad depot, since shells had already dropped beside his hotel. Tonight one gun had been zeroed in.

"A shell entered the front door of the building and went through the basement where the telegraphers and myself were sleeping upon a row of cots. The shell passed under the cots, severing their supports and tumbling us on the floor.

"Hairbreadth escapes and casualties became hourly occurrences. However, it was somewhat disconcerting to me when a fragment of shell which had burst in front of the building came through the window where I was recording messages, and ripped off the page opposite to the one upon which I was writing."

Glowing shells streaked over the city, illuminating the sky with their fiery trails, and the residents, who had now watched them many nights, looked on with hypnotic fascination.

Fresh conflagrations were set—in Holland's cotton warehouse on Alabama Street, near the railroad, in other business structures on Marietta and Loyd streets—and three large residences were burned in the eastern part of the city. The flames sent an eerie red-yellow light over Atlanta and the sparks wafted down in smoldering cascades.

The five hundred men remaining in the volunteer fire companies fought the holocausts at peril of their lives. Union gunners, from the surrounding heights, trained on the fires and stepped up tempo in the direction of the blazes "with great rapidity." The firefighters, hampered by meager equipment and dwindling water supply, had to duck a banging rain of shells. They swore they would be safer in the foremost trenches.

Sparks flew in a thousand directions in Fourth of July showers of red, green, and blue whenever a ball smashed into the flames. Atlanta was lit up for blocks around. Guests in the hotels, if they had been asleep, drew on their clothes and watched at open windows or walked out into the streets. Many, ostrich-like, preferred to keep under cover during shelling, feeling more secure with even a thin roof overhead.

Not until after midnight did Federal batteries slacken fire. Atlanta slowly grew dark again as the angry red haze faded. Only blackened walls and smoldering embers remained of the warehouse on Alabama Street, the structures on Marietta and Loyd streets, and the three large residences.

Graham, who had slogged along the picket line all evening through noise and drizzle, noted that at midnight "it finally died down."

It was "all still" until a gray, moist dawn began its leaden hint in eastern skies.

AUGUST 9

■ *Boston Daily Evening Transcript*

"The *World's* Washington dispatch says the rebel movement on the upper Potomac is a feint to cover the sending of reinforcements to Hood—supposed to be not less than 30,000 veterans—from Lee's army. Much apprehension is felt in the matter."

■ *Southern Press Association*

"*Atlanta*—Last night and this morning passed without any demonstration on the part of the enemy. Some few shells are still thrown into the city without doing any damage. The enemy evince a disposition to extend their right further, which rests near the Campbellton road. A captain and lieutenant from Mc-Cook's raiders, who deserted from our army last winter, were captured yesterday."

■ *The New York Times*

"*One Mile from Atlanta, August 3 (delayed)*—The dispatches lately extensively circulated throughout the loyal States relative to the capture of Atlanta are false, so far as they assert that we are in the city. The siege—for our operations may now receive that term—is still progressing, having resulted thus far in the establishment of a strong series of fortifications within half a mile of the suburbs of the town, into which we have penetrated only in imagination as we daily survey with our eyes the distant houses and streets. The truth is glorious enough without indulging in extravagances. . . .

"Our engineers have determined the enemy's line so that

almost every part of it is well comprehended. Atlanta, as laid out on the city map, covers an area comprised in a circle of two miles diameter. Our opponents have fortified themselves very nearly on the corporation line. The main fort—a formidable work on the highest hill discernible—is exactly on the city boundary at the northern extremity of Peachtree Street. This fort, with several others, are plainly to be seen from almost any part of our fortifications. A continual succession of rifle-pits and forts surround the city, which on three sides, north, east and west, is inclosed by high ground. Gen. Sherman has drawn his lines, equally strong, so closely about the rebel works, that there is hardly half a mile intervening, in which to place the skirmishers, who are continually firing at each other."

(Special correspondent)

The rain ceased at 8:00 A.M., but clouds hung low and sultry. That day "was made memorable," General Hood believed, "by the most furious cannonading which the city sustained during the siege. Women and children fled into cellars, and were forced to seek shelter a greater length of time that at any period of the bombardment. . . .

"It was painful, yet strange, to mark how expert grew the old men, women and children in building their little underground forts, in which to fly for safety during the storm of shell and shot. Often 'mid the darkness of night were they constrained to seek refuge in these dungeons beneath the earth; albeit, I cannot recall one word from their lips expressive of dissatisfaction or willingness to surrender."

Wallace Reed, the young writer of Atlanta, thought of it as "that red day in August, when all the fires of hell, and all the thunders of the universe seemed to be blazing and roaring over Atlanta . . . everything had been comparatively quiet for a few days when . . . about breakfast time, a big siege gun belched forth a sheet of flame with a sullen boom from a Federal battery on the north side of the city. The Confederates had an immense gun on Peachtree Street, one so large and heavy that it had taken three days to drag it to its position. This monster engine of destruction lost no time in replying to its noisy challenger, and then the duel opened all along the lines on the east, north and west.

"Ten Confederate and eleven Federal batteries took part in the engagement. On Peachtree . . . the big gun of the Confederates put in its best work, but only to draw a hot fire from the enemy. Shot and shell rained in every direction. Great volumes of sulphurous smoke rolled over the town, trailing down to the ground, and through this stifling gloom the sun glared down like a great red eye peering through a bronze colored cloud. It was on this day of horrors that the destruction of human life was greatest among the citizens. . . . A lady who was ironing some clothes in a house on North Pryor, between the Methodist Church and Wheat Street, was struck by a shell and killed. Sol Luckie, a well-known barber, was standing on the corner, on Whitehall and Alabama, when a shell struck a lamp-post, ricocheted, and exploded. A fragment struck Luckie and knocked him down.

"Mr. Tom Crusselle and one or two other citizens picked up the unfortunate man and carried him into a store. He was then taken to the Atlanta Medical College, where Dr. D'Alvigny amputated his leg. The poor fellow was put under the influence of morphine, but he never rallied from the shock, and died in a few hours.

"A young lady who was on her way to the car shed was struck in the back and fatally wounded. On Forsyth Street a Confederate officer was standing in the front yard, taking leave of the lady of the house, when a bursting shell mortally wounded him and the lady's little boy. The two victims were laid side by side on the grass under the trees, and in a few minutes they both bled to death. The sun was sinking behind the western hills when the great artillery duel ended, and the exhausted gunners threw themselves on the ground. From a military standpoint there were no results worthy of mention. Nothing was gained by either side."

Captain E. C. Murphy, commanding the 1st Volunteer Fire Department, was on Whitehall Street at Alabama when the shell hit.

"All of a sudden," he wrote, "there came a moaning overhead

and a shell hit crack in the middle of Alabama Street. It ricocheted off the street and came straight to me. It hit a lamp post,
blip! and down I fell flat on my stomach. Right behind me was
an old negro man (Luckie) and the shell pieces, went right over
my head with a sucking noise and. . . . to him. When I got up
he was lying there covered with blood. Johnny Magee and I
wrapped him up in a horse blanket and took him to a little
hospital shack. . . .

"Half a dozen people were standing there at the time . . . I've
seen women knocked over in the street by shells and men killed
around me; but that was the narrowest escape I ever had."

There were many reports of deaths which could not be confirmed. In one backyard bombproof a family of six, together
with friends of the neighborhood, were supposed to have been
the target of a direct hit, which crashed through the roofing
of dirt and timber. But no one was able to identify them.

"We have had to stay in the cellar all day," Carrie Berry
wrote, "the shells have been falling so thick around the house.
Two have fallen in the garden, but none of us were hurt.
Cousin Henry Beatty came in and wanted us to move, he
thought that we were in danger, but we will try it a little
longer."

Another onlooker thought of the day as "an inferno of noise
swollen at frequent intervals by the roar of a falling building.
The very air was loathsome with the odor of burned powder,
while a pall of dust and smoke overhung the city."

Little Noble Williams, five-year-old son of Carolina Williams, enjoyed the display. He perched atop the grape arbor,
watching most of the afternoon, in spite of his mother's entreaties for him to come down into their garden shelter. His
grandfather, Dr. Calhoun was still sick in bed.

In the distance he watched stone and brick houses "which
seemed to have been made as special targets for practice," crum-
ble under the barrage.

A variety of structures were hit: the Trout House; the John
Neal mansion, the unoccupied *Appeal* office, a building near
the Macon and Western engine house formerly used as a
button factory, the railroad bridge on Market Street (struck

twice), several churches and innumerable stores, including Wood's jewelry on Whitehall Street which had its front smashed in. Most of these had been battered previously.

Colonel Taylor Beatty, while himself under fire in Atlanta, was more disturbed about the war in the Gulf, especially by the "news that Fort Gaines in Mobile Bay has been basely surrendered without resistance. Its commander was Col. Anderson of 21st Ala. He used to be on Genl. Gladden's staff. If we can ever get hold of him he ought to be flayed. It seems he communicated with Yankees by flag of truce. Went aboard their vessels and made the bargain (assumed against orders of Genl. Page, sneaky)."

Andy Rose, of Dover, Ohio, had awakened with a day-old headache still pounding at his temples. The shelling toward Atlanta from his guns had been as blows upon his head. Someone told him, at supper, that "100 guns had fired fifty shells each at Atlanta."

AUGUST 10

◼ *Boston Daily Evening Transcript*

"*New York*—The *Herald*'s correspondent, writing from near Atlanta, 1st inst., says the operations around the city have settled down to a regular siege. We are pounding away on every side. The city is doomed to be reduced . . . the rebels cannot continue long in Atlanta."

▧ *The Daily Intelligencer* (Atlanta)

"The heavy cannonading yesterday ceased at 5:00 P.M. . . . in the city one citizen was killed and a child wounded.

"The fire upon the city was the heaviest yet experienced, many buildings being struck.

"During the night and up to noon . . . all became quiet.

"A body of Federal cavalry pushed in the direction of Decatur last evening, but returned to their lines again.

"Rumors prevail that our cavalry have seized Marietta and destroyed the Yankee forces there, but no official information of the fact has been received.

"Rumor says that Sherman is being reinforced, but it is not credited.

"Eighty-seven prisoners were brought in yesterday."

Sherman sent an early-morning message to Thomas: "I don't hear the 4½-inch guns. Tell General Brannan to keep them going. Time is too valuable to be wasted. I have a report of the lay of the ground south of Utoy from General Schofield, about which I have asked him some questions, which I will telegraph you substance."

It was a cloudy, wet Wednesday. Sergeant William Graham relieved the guard at daylight, "cleared up and at 10 minutes to 10 the Major, Capt. Armstrong and a private were struck with fragments of shell but not seriously wounded.

"We had to seek shelter of our works as we were in a bad place of line."

Across the No Man's Land separating Graham from the defenders of Atlanta, one of the city's own sons fell—Lieutenant Andrew Jackson Neal.

General French had heard nothing from Richmond. Faced with the possibility that he might have to remain in his present position—a possibility which plagued him like the torment of a continuing nightmare—he resolved to make his physical surroundings as comfortable as possible. He started with the videttes, his advance sentries, who were mostly afoot now since there was a scarcity of horses.

"I rode out to our hospital this morning," he wrote. "The enemy seems disposed to get possession of my vidette line, which I have maintained up to this time. When the siege began I sent for my principal officers and told them all that I did not intend my camp should be rendered unpleasant from rifle balls, that the vidette line away in front must be held; that the picket line 500 yards in front should be strong and on it the fighting should be to the last extremity. The result of this course has been that my men are entirely free from annoyance, except from some artillery fire, and that is foolishly directed at our redoubts. I use artillery on their infantry camps and lines so as to destroy their rest both day and night. See the difference! While we sleep in safety, in some parts of the lines around the city no one can move without drawing the fire of the Yankees on themselves, so near are the lines together."

Fenwick Hedley, an Adjutant with the 32nd Illinois Infantry, Army of the Tennessee, confided vague misgivings of a stalemate to his diary: "Enemy's artillery much more active than in the early days of the campaign. We endured four hours' shelling today. The enemy, having heavier guns than ours, has it pretty much all his own way."

Sherman again telegraphed Gen. Thomas:

"I hear Brannan's guns at Geary's battery, and hear the shells burst in Atlanta. Send word to the battery to work all night and not limit themselves to 5-minute guns but to fire slowly and steadily each gun as it is ready; also order the gun on Williams' front to be got ready and put to work with similar orders tonight. Howard will get his 20's near the same point, which he pronounces much better than that at Geary's . . . Williams' right and Howard's left are on Proctor's Creek, from which you look up the valley to what seems the heart of Atlanta, the ridge on which are the railroad and White Hall being plainly visible, as also that by which the Marietta road enters the town, the intervening able being cleared ground giving a fine field of fire. I think the 4½-inch gun on Williams' right can demolish the big engine-house."

The Reverend Quintard, in addition to his duties as chaplain and pastor of St. Luke's and as a physician, had recently been helping a parish in Macon whose rector was ill. Friends in Atlanta watched the comings and goings of this wiry, busy figure, made all the more distinguished by his close-cropped goatee and Sherman-like hunger for black cigars. Children avoided being fondled by him, he reeked so strongly of tobacco.

Though aware that the shelling had made the "locality very unhealthy," he had an important mission at General Hood's. It was still raining at sunset, when he entered the big wooden house on Whitehall Street.

"On the tenth of August at headquarters I presented a class to Bishop Lay for confirmation. It included General Hood and some officers of his staff. In speaking to me the night before his confirmation, the General said, 'Doctor, I have two objects in life that engage my supreme regard. One is to do all I can for my country. The other is to be ready and prepared for death whenever God shall call me.'

"Learning that St. Luke's Church had been injured in the bombardment of the city, Bishop Lay and I made a visit to it. We looked in wonder at the sight that met our eyes upon our entering the sacred edifice. One of the largest shells had torn through the side of the building and struck the prayer desk on which the large Bible happened to be lying. The prayer desk was broken and the Bible fell under it and upon the shell so as apparently to smother it and prevent its exploding. I lifted up the Bible and moved the shell and gathered up all the prayer books I could find for the soldiers in the camps.

"Before leaving the church I sat in one of the seats for a few moments and thought of the dear friends who had assisted in the building of the church, and who had offered up the sacrifice of praise and thanksgiving in that place; of the Bishop who had but a short time before consecrated it; of the Bishop General over whom I had said the burial service there; of the now scattered flock and the utter desolation of God's house.

"As I rose to go, I picked up a handkerchief that had been dropped there at the child's funeral, which was the last service held there. I wrote a little story subsequently about 'Nellie Peters' Pocket Handkerchief and What It Saw.'"

Bishop Lay, the rites still lingering in his memory, wrote to a friend in Charleston: "In Strahl's brigade I preached and confirmed nine persons. Last night we had a very solemn service in Gen. Hood's room, some 40 persons, chiefly Generals and Staff Officers, being present. I confirmed Gen. Hood and one of his Aids, Capt. Gordon of Savannah, and a young Lieutenant from Arkansas. The service was animated, the praying good. Shells exploded near by all the time.

"Gen. Hood, unable to kneel, supported himself on his crutch and staff, and with bowed head received the benediction. Next Sunday I am to administer the communion at headquarters. Tonight ten or twelve are to be confirmed in Clayton's division. The enemy there are within two hundred and fifty yards of our line, and the firing is very constant. I fear it may be hard to get the men together. I wish that you could have been present last night and have seen that company down, all upon bended knee. The reverence was so marked that one could not fail to thank God that he has put such a spirit into the hearts of our leaders."

Sherman sent a final dispatch to Thomas:

"I hear the guns and the shells also. The enemy's battery of 32-pounders rifled are firing on us here from the White Hall fort to draw off or divert our fire. Keep up a steady, persistent fire on Atlanta with the 4½-inch guns and 20-pounder Parrotts, and order them to pay attention to the side firing by which the enemy may attempt to divert their attention. I think those guns will make Atlanta of less value to them as a large machine-shop and depot of supplies. The inhabitants have, of course, got out."

Carrie Berry was thankful—"we have had but few shells today. It has been raining nearly all day and we had to stay in the house very close."

And then young Lucy Harvie Hull wrote, from her home on Peachtree Street:

"We heard cannon all day and the soldiers passed back and forth, and we swung on the gate and watched them pass, so weary, barefooted, wounded and dirty, and we saw the neighbors moving out—taking everything they could away with them. Inside the house Mother was packing, cooking and nursing; for our servants all ran away except 'Uncle Dick' and Mammy."

A shell had knocked the chimney off their house. In a few weeks' time the pattern of life which Lucy had known had altered radically. No longer did the cracker wagons roll down Peachtree Street, no longer did mother make "beat biscuits by the wheelbarrow full," or Lucy help her roll bandages—for, now, all but the most critically ill and wounded soldiers had been transported south from Atlanta. Dr. d'Alvigny, at the Medical College Hospital, was one of the few well-known surgeons who remained in the city. And a Federal battery, firing almost literally in the back yard, rattled the remaining windows of the college, day and night.

Sergeant Graham thought his lines to be the "nearest of the town." The "enemy shelling" increased in violence as the evening wore on, "some shells bursting near our works . . . constant firing on the picket lines in front." Always the picket firing, the skirmishing.

"The picket firing never ceased, day or night," wrote Major W. H. Chamberlain, of the 81st Ohio Volunteer Infantry. "Sometimes it was lazy, scattered and weak, and again swelling into volleys like the beginning of a battle, and now and then being followed by the roar of artillery. Every day brought its list of casualties into the hospitals . . . a corporal of the 81st Ohio, Daniel Harpster, single-handed, crept out to a picket-post, where four Confederate soldiers were intrenched. Boldly pretending that he was strongly supported, he captured the squad and actually marched them into our lines. . . .

"It was a matter of common occurrence for intrenched skirmishers to get such deadly range of the enemy's batteries that the guns were practically silenced . . . a single sharpshooter in the night intrenched himself in a cornfield on the Chattahoochee River and silenced a gun on the opposite shore the next morning."

AUGUST 11

>< *The Daily Intelligencer* (Atlanta)

"The 'Savannah Republican' of the 7th inst. says, 'It is said that President Davis has telegraphed to high authority that if Gen. Hood will only hold his own a few days longer, he will be abundantly supported in both front and rear. That Gen. Hood will hold his own—that is, hold Atlanta—a few days longer, we have not a doubt. It may be though at the sacrifice of many of his gallant men, but yet, we believe, he will hold that city. It is cheering then to be assured that the President has at last determined to "abundantly" support him "in both front and rear." The sooner this is done, the sooner Sherman will be flying before the army of Tennessee routed, "horse, foot and dragoons," Georgia saved and Tennessee redeemed. . . .'

"The following facts were communicated to us by a gentleman whose veracity is unimpeachable and which illustrates the despicable character of Stoneman, the Raider, now a prisoner in this city: When at the head of a portion of his command in Jones County, but a few miles distant from this city, he entered the house of a highly respectable citizen, who was absent to avoid capture, and ordered his wife, an accomplished lady, to cook breakfast for him and his attendants. This she did, providing for them the best she could and which we doubt not was far superior in quantity and quality to what the brute and his men had ever been accustomed to. Having gorged himself with the good things set before him, this *Federal General* proceeded next to take a survey of the house in which he had been so hospitably, forced though it was, entertained. His first amusement was to draw his sword and cut to pieces several of the lady's dresses that were hanging against the wall of one of the chambers and having thus vented his diabolical malice, he next exhibited his licentious and beastly nature by making dishonorable propositions to the lady of the house herself.

Lucky it was for the lustful beast that the husband was not near to hear the insult . . . would that we had the power to deal with men of his sort when they fall into our hands! . . . no rule of civilized warfare would save them from the rope and the scaffold!"

The New York Times

"General Sherman is making gradual approaches and is very near the enemy's works, with works nearly as strong as theirs. It is thought that Hood has received reinforcements."

Thomas J. Key, General Cleburne's thirty-three-year-old Battery Captain, saw his commander in chief.

"Generals Hood and Cleburne," wrote the young publisher from Tuscumbia, Alabama, "rode along our front this morning and I was surprised to find the former so sociable and affable to all persons. He had none of the disgusting stiffness which so frequently attaches to men when they reach high positions. He saluted the humblest private in the road, conversed freely upon the condition of the army, and appeared in hopeful anticipation of ultimate victory. I called his attention to the reports of General Thomas, the Federal, on the fights of the 22d and 28th of July. He pleasantly remarked that Thomas had killed more rebels in his report than we had in the battle, or words to that effect."

By noon the weather was warm. The Confederate batteries began "throwing the shells" towards Sergeant Graham's regiment "and some of them came uncomfortably near us."

Private Alonzo Miller of Prescott, Wisconsin, recovering from a tooth extraction, wrote:

"As Captain has given me a check of $10 I will start it home, and as quick as possible. He keeps back $5 for his trouble. He thought that he ought to have something for his trouble of enlisting. This money is that premium money that he gets for enlisting us and gives to us. I gave up all hopes of getting it and if I had been killed I could not have gottin it or any one else. . . . The Rebs shell us quite freely. Yesterday they killed two horses and last night another just about two rods from where we are camped and today they killed one of our Company. The Rebs were a shelling, we all get close to the works. This man had some beans cooking and he went to see them. A shell struck in front of our works, a piece flew and struck him just above the mouth. Cut off both jaws and killed him instantly. He was one of the veterans. His name is Benjamin Humphry and he was a good soldier. He was buried the best of any soldier I have seen. Our chaplain spoke a few words in reference to how he was hurt, then read a chapter in the testament, and made a prayer. Some 20 of our Co. witnessed his burial.

"We make but little progress toward Atlanta, and it may be some time before we take the place. Our men have cut all the railroads that lead into Atlanta and if we lay and siege the place it will take some time, for we are two miles from the city . . . I go to sleep by hearing shell and bullets and wake up in the morning the same, and it is keeping up all day. I am getting so used to the noise I think no more of it than I would of flies buzzing. When they keep at a distance the Rebs have better guns than we, they can shoot farther, they pick our men at a distance."

Pushing through the scorched countryside west of Atlanta that afternoon, Major General Cox guided his horse off of the Willis Mill Road, toward fortifications recently abandoned by the Confederates. Recognizing the earth mound and entrance timbers that marked a bombproof, the Ohioan moved over to it—and saw the twenty-six adults and children who had scurried below ground on July 21.

"The inhabitants within our lines about Atlanta," he wrote, "had a hard time of it in spite of all efforts to mitigate their suffering. Their unwillingness to abandon their homes was very great, and it was very natural for all they had was there, and to leave it, was to be beggared.

"They sometimes, when within range of the artillery, built bombproofs near their houses, and took refuge in them, much as people of the western plains seek similar protection from tornadoes. In closing in on the west side of the town near the head of Utoy Creek we took in a humble homestead where the family tried to stay . . . just within my lines and not ten paces from the breastworks stands a log house owned by an old man named Wilson. A little before the army advanced to its present position, several relatives of his, with their families came to him from homes regarded as in more imminent danger, and they united their forces to build, or dig, rather, a place of safety. They excavated a sort of cellar just in the rear of the house, on the hillside, digging it deep enough to make a room some fifteen feet square by six feet high. This they covered over with a roof of timbers and over that they piled earth several feet thick, covering the whole with pine boughs to keep the earth from washing. In this bombproof four families are now living, and I never felt more pity than when . . . I looked down into the pit and saw there, in the gloom made visible by a candle burning while it was broad day above, women sitting on the floor of loose boards, resting against each other, haggard and wan, trying to sleep away the days of terror, while innocent-looking children, four or five years old, clustered around the air-hole, looking up with pale faces and great staring eyes as they heard the singing of the bullets that were flying thick above their sheltering place. One of the women had been bed-ridden for several years before she was carried down there. One of the men was a cripple, the others old and gray. The men ventured up and took a little fresh air behind the breastworks; but for the women there is no change unless they come out at night. Still they cling to home because they have nowhere else to go, and they hope we may soon pass on and leave them in comparative peace again."

For the families there was, however, an intermission before dusk. Joseph Willis asked for food, and the Federal troops rigged up rough tables under the walnut trees. One-by-one, adults and children, they crawled out, blinking their eyes at the heat and brightness. They devoured hard-tack and bully beef rations and swallowed cupfuls of coffee like famished people; then—when it appeared that the lull in fighting was over— all twenty-six went, uncomplaining, below again.

"A few days ago," Kate Cumming reported from her hospital in Newnan, "we received orders to pack up for a move.

We were told to send the worst wounded to the Coweta House. As we have learned to do everything with dispatch, all was ready for removal in a very short time. The cars were waiting for us, and the wounded who could be moved were put aboard. They disliked being left so much, that many pretended they were better than they really were. After everything was in readiness, about dark, I went to the Coweta House to bid the patients good bye. The men had been sent from the Bragg, Gamble and our hospitals. The galleries, halls and rooms were full, and there were no nurses, no lights, and nothing to eat or drink, not even water. I met Dr. Sellford, who had gone over for the same purpose as myself. Never were two persons more joyfully received than we were.

"One poor boy was crying like a child. Dr. W. came back home with me and we procured some of the nurses and, taking some of the rations which we had cooked and making a quantity of toddy, we carried all over. The men did not eat much, but the toddy seemed to revive them. We had also taken candles with us. I remained as long as I could be of any service. I believe Dr. W. was there till 12 o'clock that night.

"The next morning I went to see them, and found they had no breakfast, and there was little prospect of their getting any. No one seemed to have them in charge. I was told that Dr. Smith, one of the surgeons of the place, was to take care of them, but he was not there then.

"I heard no little grumbling, which was not much wonder. Many said they did not care how soon the enemy had them; that they could not use them worse than our own people had done.

"I looked around and discovered that there were no dishes, and no utensils in which to cook, even if we had anything to cook. There were no changes of clothing for the men, and no rags for their wounds. I told Mrs. W. the plight the men were in, and she said she would remain with them and run the risk of being captured. We sent for Dr. Hughes and he gave his consent for her to stay. I then asked him to send at least a change of clothing for the men who had left our hospital. He said he could not without orders. He left us, and after awhile some clothes were sent, and a lot of eggs and butter. . . .

"Sallie (a little girl who was in the hospital with us) and I got on one of the box-cars along with the ladies of the Gamble Hospital, Miss Rigby and Mrs. Dr. Wildman. We were just about starting when we were informed that our hospital would not leave before next morning. Sallie and I got off and remained all that night at Mrs. Dougherty's, who, as usual, was very kind.

"Mrs. W. stayed at the Coweta House, and by daylight next morning she came to me in great distress, saying she had not slept any all night, she had been kept awake by the groans of the men. And on trying to get something for them for breakfast and finding nothing, had become sick at heart, and sick in reality. I sent over a large can filled with edibles, and Mrs. D. sent a nice breakfast for about six. I then went to the hospital and between us we managed to get enough food for all. The men from the Gamble Hospital had been provided for; but there were not more than six or seven of them, so their things did not add much to the stock on hand.

"I resolved not to leave Mrs. W. as she was quite sick. I told the post surgeon I would like to remain. He informed me that I could not please him better than by so doing; that he had been disappointed in procuring the assistance of some of the ladies of the place. He expected Dr. Smith would have taken charge of the patients before that time, and see that they were properly cared for. . . .

"Dr. Gore, who remained a little while after the hospitals left, gave us a large box full of things which had been sent to him as donation for the wounded. There were some nice wines and many other useful articles in it. Dr. Gore did his best to induce the citizens to lend us their assistance."

Mrs. Cumming and those hospital attendants who could be spared spent the remainder of the day asking citizens to donate cooked provisions and anything else they could spare. By evening, Negroes arrived with a strange assortment on their backs including a wash-boiler, a wash-tub, and a small tub for bathing wounds. A Negro washwoman came along.

"I am completely worn out," Kate continued, "as the day has been very warm. We do not know the moment the enemy may be on us, but we will have to make the best of it if they come. Our clothes have all gone with the hospitals, so we have nothing but ourselves to care for now.

"Mr. Moore remained to help take care of the wounded, and he has done his part in procuring food; he has got a friend to send us some milk."

In Atlanta, Carrie Berry chronicled: "Mama has been very busy today and I have been trying to help her all I could. We had to go in the cellar often out of the shells. How I wish the Federals would quit shelling us so that we could get out and get some fresh air."

Sergeant Graham was relieved at dark, "and about 9, regiment called into the pits to repel an attack on us. Retired and at 1 o'clock manned the pits and lay on our arms until about daylight."

At Trinity Methodist Church, a small knot of officers attended vespers for the memory of Andy Neal.

AUGUST 12

Southern Press Association

"*Atlanta*—There is a brisk skirmishing on the entire left. The batteries up Marietta Street and the East State road opened on the city at 1 o'clock this morning, and have continued to fire up to the present, striking a number of houses on McDonough Street. No casualties reported.

"The enemy are still massing on the left, but are making an effort to extend their right."

■ *The New York Times*

"Hood is a stubborn old stick, in whose nature the mule nature predominates, and he will not give up while a door is open for him to get out. . . . We have massed very heavily on the rebel line of retreat and the troops have become so impatient to enter Atlanta and have an end of the row for the present that it will be dangerous to restrain them. Should the enemy not evacuate after tonight's demonstration, look out for a crash tomorrow or the following day. . . . The city is now almost entirely evacuated and scarcely a family remains. The majority have gone south but a number are lurking about in a safe distance in the rear awaiting the occupation of the city by our forces to return. Deserters report the houses much shattered by the shells."

✉ *The Daily Intelligencer* (Atlanta)

"The enemy continues to perpetrate his practical jokes in the neighborhood of Atlanta. He amuses himself by shooting shot and shell over the entire surface of the city, so that no spot is sacred or safe. Many buildings have been torn and defaced by the missiles, but they will only remain as honorable scars to exhibit in the future the gratifying fact that Atlanta was defended even if it was destroyed in the effort. A great many women and children remain in its limits, and are exposed to the danger of the enemy's fire. They, however, do not seem to be much disturbed by their dangerous position for the women walk the streets as indifferently, even more so than the old soldiers do, and the children make a business of picking up the fragments of the impotent shells to keep for playthings, or perhaps for sale as relics.

"Several persons have been killed and wounded by explosions. On Friday a white man and a mule were killed and two negroes wounded on the street before the Franklin Printing Office. On the same day, whilst the sexton was engaged in burying the body of one of Mr. Crew's family, the enemy furiously shelled the funeral party whilst it remained in the cemetery. No one was hurt, but the monuments and gravestones were very much broken. This must have been exceedingly delightful amusement for the people who are trying to teach us Christianity and recover us from barbarism by effective force measures.

"A great many houses on Peachtree Street have been completely torn to pieces by the destructive shot that rained on it. This being the most prominent portion of the city and plainly exposed in view, the enemy has easy and accurate range of the place.

"On Saturday a soldier was walking in the passenger depot with a sack of corn on his back. A shell entered the sack and exploded without injury to the man. A friend remarked to us that shell went against the grain—dreadful!

"The armies in the vicinity of Atlanta seem to have remained very quiet . . . we retain the advantage of position at every point, and the indications are that we will hold Atlanta."

General Sherman, held in check by the "stubborn defense of Atlanta," concluded that "our enemy would hold fast, even though every house in the town should be battered down by our artillery."

He ordered General John M. Brannan, chief of artillery of the Army of the Cumberland, to produce "more rapidity of firing, both for effect and that time may be allowed to remove the guns back to a safe place in case the whole army is required to move quick."

Soldiers, such as Andy Rose, still were impressed by the great barrage of August 9. "Gen. Shurmin opened 100 guns on Atlanta a few days ago," Andy wrote his parents, sisters, and brothers, "and they fired 50 shots apiece, that made 5,000 cannon shots that we fired into Atlanta in a short time. I guess that it made some rough work in the town. It made it hot for the rebs to stay in there and our guns are firing at the town most all the time last night. They kept shelling it all night. We have got some big guns up here now. There were four 100-pound Parrott guns. They are the things to throw the shells into Atlanta. We have got a great many other large guns besides them."

Friday morning had dawned "foggy . . . quite still." Graham

could not draw his rations of salt pork "because the men are said to be getting scurvy." As far as he was concerned, it was "all bosh."

There was commotion in Atlanta as nearly 1,700 steers were driven, bellowing, through the streets. They had been captured, said the men who were whipping them ahead in their shambling gait, in Joe Wheeler's raid yesterday at Marietta, where he had cut several miles of railroad track.

Several supply wagons, with United States Government markings plainly on their sides, rolled southward along the dusty thoroughfares in the midst of the noisy, odorous herd. Citizens, hopes suddenly raised, were as quickly disillusioned when Confederate quartermasters announced that all the beef was earmarked for the army.

"After a sleepless night," Joe Semmes wrote to "Eo," "disturbed by clouds of mosquitoes and the bursting of 20-pound Parrott shells every minute during the night, I feel hardly equal to my usual daily duty, but cannot refrain longer from writing to my own darling Eo my regular letter. Today my heart is very loving and my very arms yearn to press to my heart the living, breathing form of my beloved wife. Yes, darling, so kind are you with me, that I fancy I can almost feel you by my side, even looking over my shoulder with that mischievous and yet loving look peculiar to you at times.

"The murderous and vindictive Yankee guns which have thundered through the night and all morning are just now quiet for awhile, as it were in respect for the sweet communion I am having with the being whom I so tenderly love and who it appears hovers over and around me, protecting me by her love and prayers. Thus you see my beloved Eo, I have you constantly in my thoughts, especially in the hour of danger. And when the toil of the day is over, with my weary head resting on your bosom, in thought my heart overflows with love and I am happy until the truth rushes upon me, that it is not so, that you are many miles from me and then, but I must say no more.

"Your last letter of the 24th of July was rec'd two days ago, and I now trust that there will be no further interruption in our correspondence. Do you know that not only are your letters the only great comfort I now have, but they are to me a real treat, the oftener I read them the more I admire the style and contents. I don't say this to flatter but because it is the truth. I have seen and heard many letters read from all kinds of writers during the war and I have known none to compare to yours, as you say, put that in your pipe and smoke it. You might do with me what you please now, I will never again care whether 'you spoil my collar or not.'

"I was glad to learn that Myra and Clara had not started for Europe. I have not heard from them since the 11th of July, and supposed they had already gone. If Tom calls to see you try to prevail upon him not to go to Louisiana. I dread his being caught by some roving band of Yankees, and imprisoned for the remainder of the war.

"You speak of having no light after dark. Have you never yet rec'd the ten pounds of beautiful candles Tom took for you to Montgomery? I deprived myself of them for your sake and sole use, and I trust Alphonso or Ben have taken them to you. I was very much amused last night at Harper's Illustrated Weekly for Aug. 13th just brought in from the enemy. They make out a great victory on the 22d of July when McPherson was killed and we took 22 guns and over 200 prisoners, brought them to the rear, sure. They say we lost 6,000 killed and wounded, 18 standard colors and 3,200 prisoners and were driven back; whilst the truth is Hardee turned their right, captured the guns and prisoners, and held all their works for several days, until he was ordered to withdraw. The paper admits a great defeat at Petersburg, and heavy loss. It is filled with fine pictures of the impossible Yankee achievements in very picturesque style, and is very bloody and bitter against us.

"The Yankees keep up a constant fire now, day and night and are evidently getting tired of our holding Atlanta in spite of their promises to have it. They are very hard at work and pressing closer and closer though we are not by any means besieged—plenty of rations etc. on hand and are well guarded. You may however look for some important movements I think which may even take place before this reaches you.

"We are confident of winning the campaign in the long run, happen what may, Dawson writes me that he will go to Gainesville as soon as he is able. Now I must stop, my next letter I will write to Malcolm. Give my love to all and a kiss to the little ones, two for little Eo, for yourself I kiss you.

"With God bless you."

Just beyond the outer limits of Peachtree Street, beyond the vidette pits and the treetop signal platform where Lieutenant Edge still perched and tapped out intelligence, Captain Joe Vale and his men were having a treat—"houtzells" as his fellow Pennsylvanians called them, dried pears gathered about the countryside.

"Fruit of all kinds being in constant demand, and a rarity, the company concluded to cook all the pears at one time, and, inviting the company officers, have a feast. Accordingly, the captain and Lieutenant A. D. Parker ('Don Parker,') gathered with the boys around the camp-fire at the company cook shelter. After disposing of a short ration of pork, hard-tack and coffee, the grand dish of the occasion was brought in, or rather off, for in the informal fashion of ours . . . the camp-kettle containing the pears was yanked off the fire, placed on the ground near by, and each one approached at his convenience or opportunity, took a stick, fork or knife, as the exigencies of the service may have enabled him to supply himself with, and fished up a pear, which he took by the stem, put into his mouth, and ate. The pears were extolled, the cook praised for the perfection with which they were done up, and the foragers complimented as the best in the army.

"The feast was progressing, and it really was a treat to officers and men, when attention was directed to the frantic efforts Don Parker was making to pull the stem out of one he had in his mouth. He had seemingly got hold of a pear that was not cooked enough, at least the stem appeared unusually well fastened; in fact, as he muttered while holding between his teeth, it was 'clinched in the other end.' Holding it in his mouth, declaring with desperation that it would take a six-mule team to pull the stem out, but out it would have to come, or he would—just what, he did not say, but his determined countenance expressed unutterable things. The captain suggested a requisition on the quartermaster as a good thing to 'draw,' but Sam Duncan thought the best 'draw' was an 'ace high straight flush!' This fortunate suggestion of Sam's seemed to tranquilize Don, for he ceased his desperate efforts to pull the 'stem' out and proceeded to investigate when—lo! he pulled from his mouth a nice, full-grown, fat mouse, which he had mistaken for a pear and, holding on to the tail, had been trying to pull the stem out!"

In the afternoon, Sergeant Graham took part in "quite an artillery duel between two or three of our forts and those of the enemy with no injury on our side. One man was brought from the pits badly wounded, don't know what regiment."

Some pears found their way into the empty larders of Atlanta. "Mary came home yesterday," wrote Carrie Berry, "and we have not had so much wirk to do so I have ben knitting on my stocking. We had a present today of a bag of nice pears from our friend Mrs. Green. We enjoyed them very much. We do not get any nice fruit since the Army has ben here."

AUGUST 13

✉ *The Daily Intelligencer* (Atlanta)

"The enemy yesterday evening advanced his right about one mile, at the same time extending his left a short distance, but hurriedly withdrew this morning, from what cause is not yet known, to their original position. The Yankee officers attempted frequently at different places along the line today to communicate with ours. In several instances they proposed a cessation of picket firing, which was not authorized on consequence of the proposition not coming through the proper channel.

"No shells were thrown into the city during the night or

today, with the exception of slight artillery firing in front of Bates' gun."

■ *The New York Times*

"We are within about 2 miles of the city. The road that runs in front of the tent in which I am writing enters the main street of Atlanta just that far distant. Save on our extreme left, however, we can see nothing of Atlanta for the intervening forests and broken country. Being so near one of the largest cities in the South, we might reasonably expect to emerge from the primitive forests, which have been our habitation for so many weeks. But neither villas nor gardens, country seats nor pleasant drives are encountered. Dirt roads, an occasional loghouse and unshorn old forests are alone what we see two miles from the famous Gate City."

■ *Boston Daily Evening Transcript*

"Gen. Hooker is described as looking very much like a soldier. Well, he acts like one, too.

"Gen. McCook's cavalry loss in Georgia does not exceed 500. It was first reported to be 2,700 by runaways, who have a fine faculty at making figures lie."

Chief of Staff Shoup sent a "circular" order at 11:30 A.M. to the defending forces in and near Atlanta:

"Gen. Hood desires that you impress upon your officers and men the absolute necessity of holding the lines they occupy, to the very last. He feels perfectly confident that, with the obstruction in their front, and the artillery to break his masses, the enemy cannot carry our works, however many lines he may advance against them, and however determined may be his assaults, so long as the men occupy the trenches and use their rifles. Let every man remember he is individually responsible for his few feet of line, and that the destiny of Atlanta hangs upon the issue."

Sergeant Graham awoke to a "warm and somewhat cloudy" Saturday. Occasionally he heard "a big gun and picket firing constant." A certain tension had come over the men around him since they were "now within 80 rods of the Rebs works."

The never-ending allegro of skirmishing, like constant, nervous conversation, kept the hospitals on both sides filled at all times.

The 15th Army Corps, with headquarters a mile east of Heron's Mill and a few hundred yards north of the Sandtown road, had converted a "house on the hill" to medical usages.

"Six surgeons are in attendance," wrote Captain George W. Pepper of Ohio, "they receive and operate upon each case upon the instant. A wound is dressed in from two to 15 minutes. Amputations are performed in a trice, chloroform being administered. Pools of blood upon the floor are mixed up with the mud that is tracked in. The house's family dining table makes a good dissecting bench. Drawers from a bureau are laid upon the floor, bottoms up, for a couch to be spread. In a bed in one small room lay three terribly wounded men, side by side, the family bedding saturated with their blood. A lieutenant lies in a corner, dead—died before his wound could be dressed. A private sits upon a table, naked to the hips, a musket ball having passed through his body, from side to side, three inches below the armpits—he talks, is very pale and ghastly, but will live. Another sits on a chair, his leg cut off below the knee with a shell, as clean as with a knife. A Kentucky Captain, shot through the thigh, is seized with a spasm of pain while being taken from the ambulance into the house. He catches the sleeve of his coat near the shoulder with his teeth and bites, as would a mad-dog.

"Such scenes I witnessed during an hour—and our army was only skirmishing."

Barely a mile east of the hospital, and exactly two miles from downtown Atlanta, Graham, with his 16th Corps, stripped to the waist at noon as the weather "cleared up . . . hot." Then, "the batteries on both sides opened and we had another lively time. Musket balls came into our lines in a great plenty but no one was hurt." He listened to a report that three hundred Confederates had "delivered themselves up to us."

Within the city a soldier, gloomy but still of no inclination to surrender, wrote his sister in Chapel Hill.

"Sister (a resident of Atlanta), has heard nothing from any of you since I received your first," began Colin Dunlap. "She, Mr. Freeman and family were well about two weeks ago. I shall try and visit her tomorrow. I wrote to Major John Severance a few days ago asking him if he knew anything of our family as I had written so many letters and could get no answers that I had despaired of hearing except through him. It is no use for you to write to Sister as there is no Post Office. Everything of value has been removed, Stores all closed, the Yankees throw shells into the City every day most of the familys have caves to go into. Several fragments of shells fell into Susan's Yard. She and Mr. Freeman & Fannie stay with a Mrs. Ormond about two miles from the centre of Town. Mrs. O. has a cave. Mr. Freeman & the Catholic Priest are the only Clergy in Town. We have had several battles & skirmishes since I last wrote by the blessing of God I have escaped. John McVea of whom you have heard me speak was killed on the 22d July. He had only been elected Lieutenant 1st July. He leaves a wife and two children. Lady Allsup is well. We have only eighteen men in our Company. We left Dalton with 40 men three months ago. My Lieut. commanded the Regiment, being senior officer. Genl. Hood commands in place of Genl. Johnston, you have no idea what gloom is cast over the Army when we heard of the change."

A story about General Sherman filtered, apocryphally, through opposing lines into Atlanta. The Federal commander was said to have passed a mule teamster unmercifully beating his animal. It had stumbled into one part of Georgia's waffle-pattern of ditches and could not extricate itself.

"Stop pounding that mule!" shouted the equally quick-tempered general.

The soldier told him to mind his own business.

"I tell you again to stop!" snapped Sherman. "I am General Sherman."

"That's played out," the teamster allegedly scoffed. "Every man who comes along here with an old brown coat and slouched hat claims to be General Sherman."

His careless dress was already legend in Atlanta. Officers and civilians of the South—and much of the North—believed him to be the country's worst-dressed officer.

"We have had a very quiet day today," wrote Carrie Berry. "We have all ben very buisy trying to work some while we could get out in safety. We fear that we will have shells tonight. We can hear the muskets so plane."

AUGUST 14

✉ *Southern Press Association*

"*Atlanta*—The enemy opened fire upon the city with six batteries at 8 o'clock last night, their batteries being stationed on the Marietta, Peachtree and Williams Mill roads and in front of the Medical College and the Rolling Mill. The fire was very heavy and Engine No. 3 replied promptly. The enemy immediately concentrated his fire on the point of fire, but our men nobly stood their ground, despite of the rain of the shells, and succeeded in saving a large warehouse.

"Kyle and Co.'s and other buildings on the square were consumed.

"Not a person was injured, the women and children having sought safety in bombproofs.

"But little shelling along the entire line today.

"No movements of the enemy have been reported."

✉ *The Daily Intelligencer* (Atlanta)

"We have had quite a still time from the shells of the enemy until about 8 o'clock tonight when the shells commenced falling in nearly every part of the city, striking many houses, and doing considerable damage. About 12 o'clock two shells struck Dr. Biggers' house on Marietta Street, setting it on fire, destroying it, also Dr. J. F. Alexander's brick house adjoining, the house on the east side of Dr. B.'s and several other small houses adjacent to these buildings. Mr. Kile's large brick building at the corner of the angle of the square was saved only by the energy of Fire Company No. 3 which was on the spot soon after the fire broke out, and worked with but little help and more energy than I have ever seen firemen work before—several citizens assisting them.

"The other Fire Companies could not get help enough to keep their engines at work. No. 1 went to the cistern but could not get help to work on the brakes, so they assisted No. 3, and succeeded in saving all the buildings fronting on Peachtree Street. The wooden house that Mr. Bulce did business in caught fire two or three times but it was got out and saved. While the fire was progressing, the shells of the enemy fell every half minute in and about us all the time the houses were burning. Solid shot were also fired, falling near the brakes, but the firemen continued to work as though utterly regardless of them. I do not think a man left the place until the fire was extinguished. I have but little idea of the loss. I learn that provisions (much needed here) in some of the houses were destroyed, but I think to no considerable amount. There was, in fact, and is but very little in the city, and since the 22d July last there has been scarcely any provision for sale here. The shelling continued after the fire, without any intermission until 3 o'clock this Sunday morning.

"What I mean by saying, in the first part of this letter, that we have had quite a still time until 8 o'clock tonight, is that no shells fell in the city the 13th instant, of any consequence, but the sharpshooting on the lines has been continual.

"There is quite a calm this morning (Sunday) in the city—not a shell nor a shot to be heard, but a continual firing of small arms at the front.

"Atlanta it seems is to be fired and battered to the ground, if it cannot be captured by Sherman. To the Fire Batteries which so nobly did their duty on Saturday night, great credit is due. We know most of them personally, and a braver set of men never lived. To them it seems is entrusted now all the guard duty of the city, as well as to protect it from fire. Verily they have the post of danger as well as of honor. May the fortunes of war soon relieve them of the danger and may they live long to enjoy the honor they have already won!"

S. P. Richards, the British-born bookseller, had increasingly less stomach for the war. His friends had remarked on it, even though he had not yet been directly accused of Unionist sympathies.

"Another week of anxiety and suspense has passed and the fate of Atlanta is still undecided," he observed. "We have had but one severe shelling on our side of town and that was on Wed. night and kept us awake from 12 o'clock until daylight. Our *humane* foes allowed us to get well to sleep before they began their work of destruction. Another shell entered our store or rather the rooms above while I was there examining the premises to see if any more had visited them. I was enveloped in the dust made by it. On Friday I was on a militia 'detail' which worked all day. There is no fun in working hard and 'finding' yourself. Last night we went to Mr. Roots and spent the evening but did not sing. An Army Band gave the party a serenade and Root invited them in to cakes and whiskey. The shells flew all night on the other side of town, but we slept pretty well. I was detailed for service today, and marched off to the *shelly* side of Whitehall Street and there kept for three hours doing nothing. We then were dismissed until 4½ o'clock this afternoon, so I joined the folks on the way to Epis. Church. I have been accustomed to being the disposer of my own time at least on Sunday, and this being ordered about by others as though we were niggers is not much to my mind. O this horrid war! When will it end?"

"This being the Sabbath," wrote Battery Captain Tom Key, "I turned my face toward Atlanta and arrived at the Trinity Church just as religious services were commencing. The pulpit was occupied by a man of low stature, dark hair, black eyes, heavy short beard, and broad forehead shaped like an old-fashioned hat—larger at the top than at the base, but well filled with brains. His text concerned Paul's devotedness to Christ, when he said that he was not only willing to be bound but to die at Jerusalem for the Lord Jesus Christ's sake. The minister portrayed the devotion of Paul in beautiful and truthful colors, and pictured his Christian character as admirable. The music was excellent—vocal especially so—the parts being sung by the choir. It was the first time for more than twelve months that I had been in a church, the last place having been Wartrace, Tennessee.

"The congregation was composed principally of officers, old citizens, and old and young ladies. The soldiers looked sunburned and hardy with colored shirts corresponding to their brown faces, while the gentlemen citizens were dressed in white and black suits. The latter nodded and napped during the service, but not so the soldiers who were all ears and eyes—ears to hear the glorious gospel and eyes to look with pleasure upon the neatly dressed and beautiful ladies. You may know that I appreciated all these things, for on the Holy Sabbath I delight to attend religious worship both because there is something elevating, noble, and sublime in singing praises to our Redeemer, and because I am a constitutional admirer of the female sex.

"The scene brought back to memory days of happiness and the early associations of life, especially the period when I gave my young heart to God and to the noble girl who afterwards became my companion for life. Trinity in Atlanta is of the same architecture as the Methodist Church at Helena, and amidst the surroundings and the revivings of memory my heart was softened and tears came as I wished for peace, home and the consolation of our sacred altars.

"Some may think my reflections were strange, but let them be thrown into the woods and not know what it is to see civil society for three years, or to be sheltered by a roof, or to have access to female society, or to be allowed the exalted privilege of seeing within a house of worship once in twelve months, and then they will understand the emotions that arise in a person's mind as they did in mine today."

And the revival continued. The Reverend J. B. McFerrin wrote to the *Southern Christian Advocate* that he had ridden from Atlanta "to the line of battle to see the soldiers as they were resting in a shady wood. To my great joy, a young captain whom I had baptized in his infancy approached me and said,

" 'I wish to join the Church, and I wish you to give me a certificate; the Lord has converted me.' I gave him the document with a glad heart.

" 'Now,' said he, 'if I fall in battle, let my mother know of this transaction. It will afford her great joy.' Oh it was good to be there and feel that God was in that place.

"Yesterday, I baptized Col. T., of Tennessee. He is a lawyer and statesman, and has been in the army from the beginning of the struggle. He became interested on the subject of religion months ago, sought Christ, found the pearl of great price, united with the Church, was baptized in the name of the Holy Trinity, and now sends home his letter to have his name recorded with his wife's on the Church Register, and I trust it is inscribed in the book of life."

The Reverend Neil Gillis added:

"I never heard or read of anything like the revival at this place. The conversions were powerful, and some of them very remarkable. One man told me that he was converted at the very hour in which his sister was writing him a letter on her knees praying that he might be saved at that moment. Another, who was a backslider, said to me at the altar that his case was hopeless. I tried to encourage him; discovered hope spring up in his countenance; then commenced to repeat such promises in the Scriptures I could remember, and while I repeated, 'Believe on the Lord Jesus Christ and thou shalt be saved,' he bounded to his feet and began to point others to the Cross with most remarkable success."

That clear, warm Sunday was excellent for Lieutenant Samuel Edge's signal work. From his treetop he telegraphed:

"Three trains of cars arrived at Atlanta during the day: No. 1, of four platform and 2 box-cars, used as a construction train; No. 2, of four passenger and five freight cars; No. 3, of fifteen freight cars, doors closed; could not see with what loaded, or whether loaded or not. Train ran slow, engine appeared to be working hard."

Carrie Berry wrote: "Sure enough we had shells in abundance last night. We averaged one every moment during the night. We expected every one would come through and hurt some of us but to our joy nothing on the lot was hurt. They have been throwing them at us all day today but they have not been dangerous. Papa has been at work all day making the cellar safe. Now we feel like we could stay at home in safety. I dislike to stay in the cellar so close but our soldiers have to stay in ditches."

Kate Cumming had expected to leave the hospital in Newnan, but the trains did not arrive from Atlanta. The stationmaster could not raise a murmur on his telegraph system. A few lean cows grazed undisturbed on the thistles between the tracks north of the depot.

"I have spent a portion of the day with the young lad who cried so much the first night I came over here," the Scottish-born nurse reported. "He is wounded in the foot, has gangrene and suffers excruciating pain. His name is Morgan and he is from Mississippi. A Mrs. Ross has kindly offered to take sole charge of him. He has begged Mrs. W. and me to take him with us.

"Mrs. W. has been very busy; she does not know what I have been doing, nor I of her doings.

"A Lieutenant Summerlin, from Covington, Georgia, is here, badly wounded; his wife, a lovely woman, is taking care of him.

"She told me she was in Covington when the raiders passed through there and that they committed some terrible outrages; among others was the shooting of a Captain Daniel, a cousin of Miss W., of whom I had heard her often speak. He was in the State service and the vandals made believe they thought him a bushwhacker. He has left a large family of motherless children to mourn for him. He was a man of a highly cultivated mind, and stood well in the estimation of all.

"They went to the house of an old man, and as he knew they had come with designs on his life, he sold it dearly. He fought manfully, and killed some half dozen before he fell.

"Several of our attendants have come back; they had been sent for the books and other things that our folks were not able to take with them.

"The hospitals went to Macon by Atlanta and one of the men

has informed me that while passing there the shells flew all around the train, and one struck within a few feet of them.

"Atlanta is closely besieged. General Hood is now in command of this army; I believe Johnston is in Macon. There have been many conjectures as to this change of commanders, but no one can tell exactly why or the wherefore.

"Last evening Mrs. Brooks and myself went up to the College Hospital in which are many of our wounded, besides the prisoners. Among our men I found two Scotchmen, very badly wounded. The wounded Federal captain that I had seen before was here, and looked badly. The prisoners are in much better quarters in this hospital than our men at the Coweta House.

"All have fared much better than they have with us, as Mr. Kellogg, the steward owns the building and has all of his own furniture. There are two ladies who take care of the patients— Mrs. Kellogg and Mrs. Alexander—both kind and excellent women.

"We have had a few false alarms about the enemy coming, but they have always turned out to be our own cavalry. . . .

"The people here seem to regret our leaving the post, though I am told the quartermaster owes many of them money for house rent, etc. I know that Mr. Dougherty has not received one dollar from the government, and we have cut down quantities of timber on his land."

That night, the muskets banged on the fringes of Atlanta. Having mailed a letter home, Sergeant Graham listened to "some artillery" rumbling in the distance like uncertain thunder.

AUGUST 15

Richmond Sentinel

"There is nothing additional from either Atlanta or Mobile. . . .

"It may be that even without orders from LINCOLN, SHERMAN, in a few days, may find his lines of communications fully and effectually cut, and himself reduced to the necessity of making a desperate assault on the strong fortifications of Hood, or of attempting a hopeless retreat, or surrendering at discretion. The prospect ahead and, almost at hand, is for us, even according to the showing of the Northern press, decidedly rich."

Cincinnati Gazette

"On the Banks of Utoy Creek Fulton County, Georgia August 10 (delayed)—It is somewhat absurd to call the combat taking place here the 'Siege of Atlanta.' Our fortifications extend in long lines from east to west and everywhere confronted by long lines of rebel works. To break or turn the latter is probably to insure us the entire possession of Atlanta, with the capture or destruction of a large part of the rebel army. In the meantime, let the loyal people of the North take courage. Atlanta, being the very heart of the Confederacy, and of such primary importance that, according to the rebels themselves its fall will ruin them, a desperate resistance was to be expected. . . . Some great stroke of generalship on our part may give us the rebel army. But even ordinary good management must sooner or later insure us the possession of Atlanta, and that I confidently expect."

Atlanta Appeal

"Yesterday afternoon our people were but little disturbed by the enemy's batteries, and nothing worthy of recording occurred. At dark, however, our citizens were notified of the proximity of the enemy by the fire from his guns and the shelling was kept up during the night. Most of the time five different batteries were in constant play—one located apparently about one mile west of the State Railroad, another on the Marietta road, another near the south side of the Peachtree road, another on the Williams' Mill road, and the fifth still further to the south. The firing was increased during the night."

It was a hot Monday morning. Skirmishing crackled "constant."

Carrie Berry, when she awoke, was thankful there had been no shells. "And we thought that we would not have any today (but, my! when will they stop?) . . . but soon after breakfast Zuie and I were standing on the platform between the house and dining room and a very large shell filled with balls fell by the garden gate and bursted. The pieces flew in every direction. Two pieces went in the dining room. It made a very large hole in the garden and threw the dirt all over the yard.

"I never was so frightened in my life. Zuie was as pale as a corpse and I expect I was too. It did not take us long to fly to the cellar."

Rufus Mead, two miles outside of Atlanta, recognized similarities to his native Connecticut in the Georgia hills which seemed to flow toward Atlanta. Save for the thick pine forests, he felt that he could almost be on the pleasant low hilltop where he lived in Redding. After mail delivery, having received "the one I prize the most of all, i.e., from Home," he wrote:

He was glad "to have such good news in it as good visits, lots of rain &c &c for I feel just as much interested in all your affairs as if I was there with you.

"The suspenders came with the Standard last week and now before I forget I'll just hint about putting in a couple of nutmegs or a little cinnamon stick just to make a variety or spice. I think it would be a good idea. Dont you?

"I dont know but youll rather worry about what I wrote last time so Ill relieve your anxiety this time by telling you I am on duty again now and have improved my time of idleness in putting on 4 or 5 lbs of flesh to my not very emaciated form so now I can say Ruf is himself again. Our good weather still continues we have a shower nearly every day but it is not muddy, and the heat is so even we dont mind it at all. I cant say how

our siege is progressing but guess favorably—at least we meet
with no reverses, without you count Stonemans capture one. I
guess that might be called a draw game, especially as Kilpatrick
is now in the field again. It is reported that General Slocum is
to take command of our Corps. Nothing would suit our boys
better but it is not certain that he will yet. I am afraid to believe it or place too much confidence in it. It is reported too
that our Corps moves tomorrow to the right, near the Macon
R R but no orders yet. I am in hopes we might stay here till
Atlanta was taken. By the way there was tremendous fire there
last night. I cant see the lines so I wait till after supper, and
finish by candlelight.

"7:00 P.M. Had a supper of flapjacks and cold beef-tongue
but I dont see as it helps me to finish this letter—dont bring any
new ideas. It is trying to rain—begins to sprinkle right smart,
with a prospect of rainy night. We have lots of flies to bother us
yet daytimes, but so far our nights are unmolested. I saw one
mosquito yesterday but they dont trouble us at all.

"Today I hope the good men of Conn have given the soldiers
a right to vote by a good rousing majority, and will do still better for Uncle Abe next Nov. I hate to see party strife so high
at this time as it is but still I can but believe Uncle Abe stands
the best chance of any. One would think by reading the N Y
Herald or World that he was the most ignorant tyrant that ever
lived. Oh that Grant & Sherman could each have one good vic·
tory, then Id have no fears. Has any one enlisted yet from Redding or how does she fill her quota? I hope not by draft, though
I would like to see some of them out here right well.

"How do you like collecting taxes? How much did you get
on those 2 days?

"Ill try and get home to help you eat those blackberries, but
you needn't let them spoil if I dont. My sheet is full nearly so
Good Night. Your ever Afft. Son & Brother."

The Berry family stayed in the cellar until dinner time. "No
more fell so we came out again and stayed out till night though
we had them all day, but they did not come so near us again."

Kate Cumming arrived in West Point, and was quartered at
the Exchange Hotel, near the depot. She wrote:

"The landlord was moving but informed us we might lodge there for the night, as we had provisions with us; that was all for which we cared. He gave us a room without even a wash-bowl or pitcher in it; for the privilege of remaining in this delightful room we paid the moderate sum of two dollars.

"There was a large brick hotel in the place, but as we had such a short time to remain we thought it would be useless to change."

Before retiring, the Scotch nurse walked about the town which she found in a "forlorn" condition. She attempted to buy milk at a farmhouse but succeeded only in obtaining a watermelon. At the hospitals she met many badly wounded and sick, including cases of the dread infection erysipelas in an isolation ward. "If the enemy should attack the place I do not know what would become of all these poor fellows."

An evening rain settled the dust and the stench in Atlanta. By midnight, skies cleared and the moon and stars shone down on a quiet, dark city.

Dr. Calhoun was still unable to leave his sickbed. His family had retired early. Mrs. Calhoun had been vaguely uneasy because of troop movements crossing the city from west to east during the evening, accompanied by the usual bands of stragglers and sprinkling of thieves masquerading in uniform. She was awake and had heard the pendulum clock in the hall strike every hour. Eleven had echoed through the sleeping household some minutes ago when she was startled by a loud knocking at the back outer door.

Lucy Calhoun touched her husband to see if he was awake. When she discovered he was not, she decided not to disturb him. As Noble wrote:

"She quietly passed from her room into the rear one, at which door the knocking was heard; she crept cautiously to the door and demanded to know who was there. The response came,

" 'Open the door and let us in!'

"She then asked what was wanted, and the same voices still repeated,

" 'Let us in or we will break the door down!'

"As the Federals were momentarily expected and were greatly

feared, she asked if they were Federals or Confederates. The terrible answer came, 'Federals, and if you do not surrender at once we will burn your house down.'

"The threats were not very pleasant to her, so she, not then knowing what was best to do, informed them that if as gentlemen they would come to the front door she would surrender. In passing through the room, she spied a large dinner-bell, which she seized as she passed into the hall, then mounted the stairway and aroused her daughters, Indiana and Carolina, and the little grandson, who were sleeping in a front room upstairs.

"She, clad only in her night-robes, opened the front door upstairs which opened out on a balcony which was walled up on all sides about three feet, the tin roof of which was deeply covered with a cold dew. Upon this she stood barefooted and thinly clad, bell in hand, vigorously ringing in hopes of arousing some of their near neighbors.

"While she was ringing the bell, her daughters, who were terror-stricken, opened the front windows and screamed at the top of their voices. Six or eight armed men could be seen moving around in the front yard; the leader took such a position as to enable him to see and be seen by Mrs. Calhoun. He commanded in a stern voice,

" 'Madame, stop ringing that bell,' but she paid no attention to the villain's command. A second time he called,

" 'Madame, desist at once, or I will shoot!' at the same time bringing his rifle to his shoulder and taking direct aim at her; but her contemptuous answer was given by the increased number of strokes of the bell as it pealed forth on the midnight air. A more heroically grand woman as she stood, expecting each moment to be her last, would take the searchlight of years to discover.

"The daughters had descended to the room where the father was now not only awake and up, but, sick as he was, he had his trusty rifle pushed through the window, and had a perfect aim at the heart of one of the men, and was in the very act of firing, when his daughters stayed the hand that would have sent the villain face to face with his Maker. His daughters pleaded with him and insisted that if he were a Federal and should be killed by him, that in retaliation they would not spare a member of the family.

"By this time one of the neighbors, Mr. H., was aroused and came over to ascertain what was the matter; he had a pistol in his belt around his waist, but he was quickly commanded to surrender, which he did, giving up his pistol and his belt at the same time. Soon after another citizen, who lived a short distance beyond, was passing by on his way home, and he met with a similar fate, the only difference being he had no weapons to lose. The majority of the plunderers were then in the streets, where they actually bade the two citizens to march ten paces to the rear, which was obeyed with great fear, for, in army language, its meaning was to be shot. Soon after a belated home-guard, known as a militiaman, chanced to be passing by; he was halted and closely questioned, and stated that he belonged to Joe Brown's (the Governor's) 'malish.'

"They soon relieved him of his coat and hat and sent him on his way sorrowing. About the time the militiaman was out of sight a fearless young soldier by the name of Roscoe Ryan, who was a friend of Dr. Calhoun and family, but who knew nothing of the trouble, as the bell-ringing and screaming had ceased when the first two citizens had been detained, came by on his way home, and they attempted to play the same game on him, but in him they had met their master. He informed them in language too plain to be misunderstood that they were villains and scoundrels, and threatened to see that they were severely dealt with, and then passed on without further molestation.

"All of the prisoners were then released, and the would-be robbers and murderers slunk out of sight and hearing. Soon after a soldier was seen passing by, and, fearing that the men might return, Lucy Calhoun requested him to guard the house until morning.

"He stated that it would be impossible for him to do so, but insisted on leaving a gun for their protection in case of further trouble. She thanked him very kindly, but instead of going out to take it she requested him to lay it on the lawn, for she was suspicious of him, not knowing but what he might belong to the same gang who had just caused them much uneasiness. The gun

which had been placed on the lawn by the soldier remained
there until morning, when it was taken up."

AUGUST 16

The New York Herald

"Near Atlanta—The Union Army still threatens the fated city,
and is gradually though slowly advancing its works up to its
very walls. In some points our lines are so close to the enemy's that it is impossible to advance further without making
an assault. . . . There is one continual artillery fire kept up
along the lines, and as it is all converging on Atlanta it must
be rather a hot place to live in now. Parts of the town were set
on fire on the nights of the 13th and 14th. We could see the
thick volumes of smoke and then the lurid flames shooting
along the horizon. We could also hear the fire bells ringing.
Some of our batteries are pouring red hot shot on the town.
Captain Bradley, Sixth Ohio Battery, has established a furnace
for heating his shot. Most likely some of these fired the houses.
Again, they fill shells with fuses, and these spit and scatter fire
enough about to ignite timber work. I suppose the rebels will
soon accuse us of raining Greek fire upon them."

The Daily Intelligencer (Atlanta)

"The party of the enemy's cavalry that passed through Decatur last evening after reaching Cobb's Mills, returned last
night, and is supposed to have been only a reconnaissance. Another which moved simultaneously from Owl Creek Church,
struck the Atlanta and West Point Railroad at Fairburn,
burned the depot, tore up the tracks in several places, and then
withdrew about three miles and went into camp where they remained. Their force is variously estimated at from 2,000-5,000.

"The track has since been repaired, but trains are not allowed to run in consequence of the proximity of the enemy.

"Last night and today was unusually quiet along the lines. The enemy's artillery were remarkably quiet, which is generally attributed to the scarcity of ammunition, caused by interruptions of his communications.

"But few shells were thrown into the city last night. One set fire to a frame house on Peachtree Street. The loss was small.

"Advices from Washington to the 10th to the '*Chattanooga Gazette*' of the 11th says an official dispatch from Sherman to Halleck says, 'although the number of dead rebels seems excessive I am disposed to give full credit to the report. Although our loss is only 3,521 killed, wounded and missing, the enemy's dead, on the field alone, amounted to 3,221. The total amount of prisoners sent North is 1,017, wounded prisoners in our hands, 1,000 and the estimated losses of the enemy are at least 10,000.' "

Carrie Berry had not slept much more than the Calhouns. "We had shells all night," she wrote. "There was a large piece came through Mama's room directly after we went to bed and fell on the little bed and I expect if we had been sleeping there some of us would have been hurt."

Dr. Calhoun theorized that Tuesday morning, that the housebreakers must have visited his drugstore in the past. At the end of each day, it had been his custom to wrap up his cash—bills, gold, and silver—place the bundle under his arm and walk home, after locking the store. When the thieves had learned of his sickness, he reasoned, they had probably thought this was a good time to rob his house—since he could do nothing to overpower them.

However, as his friends remarked when they came to inquire of his health, the intruders had not reckoned either with the "heroism" of Lucy Calhoun or "that gallant young soldier, Roscoe Ryan."

Cousin Henry and Cousin Eddy later came to visit Maxwell Berry, "They told us that they did not think the Federals would be here much longer to torment us and I hope that it may be so for we are getting very tired of living so."

And Thomas Jefferson Newberry wrote his sisters in Mississippi to reassure they were "not forgotten by your Brother. I am glad to hear you both keep well and hearty. I have no news to write worth your attention only we have a very good band in our Regiment. We have dress parade every week end. The band goes out and plays and a heap of little girls come to see us about your size every evening on dress parade. You both must be good little sisters and be smart and grow fast. You both must write often and tell me the news. Tell all howdy.

> Goodbye little sisters,
> Your Brother"

Continuing south at 4:00 P.M., Kate Cumming was aware of a "jolt" a few miles beyond Opelika, as the locomotive catapulted from the track in a shower of wood sparks and clouds of escaping steam.

"I was reading and knew nothing of it until I heard some ladies scream. I then felt a motion as if the train was about to upset. I saw several of the cars ahead of us plunge off the road, and men jumping from them; many took to the woods, as they were fearful of an explosion." She remained in the car all night, not knowing what else to do.

Private John Dyer of Kentucky, who had left Newnan just before Kate Cumming, now was a purchasing agent for hospital supplies. His lumbago virtually cured, he was not certified as ready to return to combat. Today he was en route to Macon. Dyer had read of a Federal spy "treed" at Selma, Alabama, only to give his pursuers the slip and disappear "as if by magic."

While he was waiting for the Macon train the "spy business" had been running through his head, "and I found myself scanning closely the movements of everyone about.

"After boarding the train the same feeling took possession of me and in the course of my scrutiny my eyes fell on a very fine looking lady just across the aisle from my seat.

"She was elegantly dressed, in fact overdressed for the time and occasion and this was what attracted my attention to her. Moving my seat and riding backwards so as to face her, I settled myself to wait developments having no idea what they would bring forth, yet all the time my mind was on the escaped spy. The woman wore a thick veil and kept it closely drawn down which was of itself a little odd for a Southern lady at that time. Growing thirsty she went to the cooler near where I sat and drew a cup of water. As she pushed her veil aside I discovered what appeared like about a two days old beard on the edge of her chin. She had her back to me and I could see the beard plainly between me and the light on the other side of her.

"When she turned I was straight in my seat looking toward the rear end of the car as though nothing had happened out of the ordinary but I kept my hand on the butt of my revolver and determined to keep my eye on that woman.

"When we reached Fort Valley she stepped off the train and so did I. She started immediately up town and I to the Provost Marshall who was standing on the platform, where about this conversation took place between us. I will confess that I was a little excited.

" 'Captain, arrest that woman,' said I.

" 'What for?' said the Captain.

" 'Why! she's a man,' said I.

" 'That's a h—ll of an idea,' said the Captain, 'how can a woman be a man? are you crazy?' And he was proceeding to give me a piece of his mind when I broke in on him and convinced him that I was sane and very much in earnest. Beckoning to a squad of soldiers to follow, we started in pursuit and walked fast enough to gain a little on her. I, at the same time giving the Captain a history of my observations and impressions, soon had him convinced that the trail was pretty hot and he hurried up a little.

"The woman entered a cottage which was immediately surrounded by our force and the Captain and I entered. We found no one in the front room but pushing on came upon our suspect in the kitchen talking to the lady of the house and still closely veiled. Walking up to her the Captain removed her veil from over her face and there was the telltale beard and other evidences of the masculine gender, and we found enough evidences on his person and in his pockets to prove him to be the man we wanted."

In Atlanta, Sergeant Graham wrote: "We had one man (Norton of our company) wounded, while in the outside works and our orderly (Renne) was also struck but not hurt much. Firing continues through the day and the balls flying through the camp and at about 3 in the morning the enemy commenced again and four (sic) an hour there was firing. A few cannon shot were thrown at us. Received a letter from home today dated August 5."

AUGUST 17

The Daily Intelligencer (Atlanta)

"The enemy's cavalry retired from the vicinity of Fairburn, a portion crossing the river near Campbellton. The trains are running as usual.

"The enemy are busily engaged in fortifying on the North side of the Chattahoochee, principally along the Powder Springs and Campbellton roads in the vicinity of Sweet Water.

"Everything remarkably quiet along the front.

"The enemy opened fire upon the city from another gun, supposed to be a sixty-four pounder, planted on the Marietta road. Slow fire kept up all night, resulting in killing one citizen.

"It is generally believed that the Western & Atlantic Railroad was cut at Acworth by a portion of our cavalry on the 14th. News from that quarter anxiously looked for.

"Sherman and Thomas, the two great lights of the Western Yankee army, the terrible hydrae of the present destructive campaign, the demigods of the Western press, dispatched to the king Ape of the Washington menagerie that—Atlanta had fallen!

"With what utter astonishment they must have been confounded when they found General Hood's strategy, and the ubiquitous veterans of the Army of Tennessee, confronting them and disputing their advance at all points."

The New York Herald

"We had yesterday and today the average amount of skirmishing, and artillery firing and we are so used to this that a little firing is necessary recreation for us. Artillery firing is rather unpleasant at night, though, for when you lie down on your rude camp bed it will not help to compose you much to reflect that a huge 64-pound camp kettle might slip through you while asleep, such things happen.

"Toward the left of our lines is Howard's House, so called after the owner, Colonel Howard, now in the rebel service. This is a general observatory from which we have a fine view of the town and rebel works. With a good glass we could see the holes pierced by our shots through the houses, and troops passing and repassing.

"The town is much damaged, several houses having been burned down, others sadly dilapidated. In the rebel works I could see a group of rebels assembled around a fire, with one man ladling some pottage to the rest, all of which the poor fellows seemed to enjoy very much."

It was "a fine morning." As Sergeant Graham was ordered into the works in front of his camp he was met with "plenty of balls whistling through the camp . . . but no one hurt."

In the opposite fortifications, General French was visited by General Stewart at 6:00 A.M. "We went along the line. We returned and had breakfast. Then the artillery, as usual, began at the redoubt in front of the house. As the shells crossed the road on both sides of the house, it was dangerous to leave, and he remained an hour or more."

Maintenance gangs from Opelika arrived to clear the train wreck. Kate Cumming, noting that every car but hers was off the track, despaired of the men's job as "an endless one." When she walked ahead on the track she observed "quite a precipice," which made her believe that many of the passengers would have been "sent into eternity" had the accident occurred a few hundred yards farther.

Later, one of her former patients brewed coffee, "and we, like all the rest, ate our breakfast on the roadside. We were in the woods, and no sign of a habitation near. As there was little or no hope of our leaving there for some time, a gentleman who had found an empty house a little ways back came and took his party, Mrs. W. and myself, to it. We found it quite a nice retreat. It had been a schoolhouse and the benches and desks were left standing. We had books, and altogether had quite a pleasant day.

"Our gentleman friend was Senator Hill, of LaGrange, Georgia. With him were two nice young ladies, the Misses Leach, who were on their way to their homes in New York. They had been spending some few years in the South. Senator Hill informed us that the ladies of LaGrange had undertaken the care of the wounded left there, and his daughter, a girl of 16, had special charge of six. I was pleased to hear this, and only hope the ladies of Newnan will do the same. Mr. Hill gave us some nice biscuit and ham, his servant made our coffee for dinner, and altogether we had a most delightful repast.

"Miss Evans, the authoress, was on the train, going to Columbus, where she has a badly wounded brother. From her I learned that all was quiet in Mobile, although we have had a naval battle, and Forts Morgan, Powell, and Gaines were taken. . . .

"About 3:00 P.M. a woodcar came from Columbus, on which we all got. We cut branches of trees and held them over us for protection from the sun, and I have no doubt, as we went along, that many thought 'Birnam Wood' was coming. We reached Columbus without further accident in time to catch the Macon train."

Carrie Berry's day was dull by contrast. Her father had been troubled by his recurrent ailment, dyspepsia and more of the chickens had been stolen.

"But nothing of interest happened today," she recorded. "We

have stayed very close in the cellar. Mama ran up to Aunties to see how a shell had ruined her house yesterday."

Some citizens noted exceptional activity around the railroad depot, roundhouses, and other property. Captain William A. Fuller, twenty-eigth-year-old conductor with the W. & A. Railroad, had been ordered to start moving rolling stock and other equipment south to safe keeping. Fuller had gained recognition two years before by capturing the Andrews locomotive raiders. He played his role as nemesis until he saw James J. Andrews, the leader, hang from a gallows (a mile and a half from the center of the city on Peachtree Street). Fuller was also packing the remaining State papers out of Atlanta.

Lieutenant L. B. McFarland, Adjutant of the Atlanta Post Headquarters, published an order forbidding the sale of all "intoxicating liquors" in the city, "except under an order from these headquarters." Confiscation and arrest were set as penalties for violation.

"In the evening," General French wrote, "I was sitting on the fence enjoying my pipe watching the explosion of the shells, when who should ride up but Gen. M. Jeff Thompson, and he was invited to our quarters. I could not keep from laughing. I have an illustrated copy of the illustrious Don Quixote and here was a duplicate picture, or rather here before me was the Don himself, in form and features, and if Sancho had seen Jeff he would have called him 'Master.' He passed the night with us, entertaining us with his adventures in the West."

Later that same evening Graham left camp for the pits. "And at about midnight the enemy commenced on us with rifles and artillery and drove in one of our picket lines and then all quiet till daylight."

AUGUST 18

The Daily Intelligencer (Atlanta)

"All last night the Yankees kept up a constant shelling of the city. The firing was steady and our batteries replied regularly during the night, but as daylight approached the cannonading on both sides became more furious, and, to use a common phrase, the shells came into the city as thick as hail, doing a great deal of damage to everything which lay in the section of the city which the enemy seemed to have a particular spite at, and has continued all day up to this writing, twelve o'clock at night.

"Last night about 10 o'clock there was very heavy skirmishing on the left, which lasted for about two hours. The casualties on our side was very light, but is supposed to have been very heavy on the enemy's side. These beautiful moonlight nights are splendid for sharpshooting and skirmishing, and there is more or less skirmishing going on all along our lines every night.

"Very heavy skirmishing and cannonading has been going on on the left all day and up to the present time of writing, and from indications will continue until daylight. All the advantages which have been gained by either army has been by our troops. It was thought at one time today that a general engagement had commenced but it has not up to this time, though it may come off tomorrow, as no one knows what the enemy may bring forth. Everybody, both soldiers and citizens, are anxious for the big fight to take place, and when it does come, Sherman will suffer the greatest defeat that any Yankee General has suffered during the war. The longer the battle is delayed the stronger Atlanta will be.

"We have received information of a raid on the Western & Atlantic Railroad, which struck the road at Etowah, burning the Etowah bridge and tearing up 29 miles of the railway. . . .

"There has been several persons wounded in the city today

by fragments of shells, but I have been unable to learn their names, though I will do so by the time I write you again."

(Pilgrim)

At daylight, shells which chattered like freight trains over Sergeant Graham's head, "stirred us up some but no one hurt." The men then "commenced building cross the works to protect us from the fire.

"Fine morning but at 7 cloudy with prospect of rain. Cleared off and went in to camp at 8. About daylight three men who left their rifle pits last night marched through the camp with placards on their backs with the words 'left their picket post without cause.'

"There is also heavy cannoning on north sides and shells exploding every minute."

Nearby, Andy Rose fumed because he had received no mail. The day grew warm.

Carrie Berry was conscious of the artillery, noting that, "when I woke this morning I thought the hole town would be torn up. The cannons were so near and so loud but we soon found out that it was our guns so we have ben very well and content all day."

At 10:15 A.M. Sherman sent a dispatch to Thomas:

"General Barry says your big guns were ordered to stop firing as soon as the ammunition then on hand was exhausted. You understand of course that I have suspended the movement contemplated for tonight . . . keep the big guns going and damage Atlanta all that is possible."

Sam French recorded his belief that "the Yankees must be angry . . . because my batteries dared to wake them up with a few shells they raised—well—(I begin with a 'W') and never ceased until 2 P.M. and they threw not less than 2,000 shot at us and accomplished nothing, only one shell went by accident through our house."

By 11:00 A.M. Sergeant Graham noted that "hell was raised on the right of the 15th Corps for a charge on the enemy pits and we immediately fell on our works. Shot and shell fell from both sides for a half hour." Then Graham went back to help cook noon dinner.

At 11:55 A.M. Sherman telegraphed Thomas again:

"Signal officer at Howard's House reports at 10 A.M. a heavy cannonading for about half an hour previous in direction south 20 degrees east from his position. Some of the shells burst over the northern part of Atlanta."

And at 1:15 P.M. Thomas replied:

"The shots that go deep into the city are from 10-pounder Parrotts in General Ransom's front."

"Jabez," wrote the bookseller, S. P. Richards, "has just left us. He came to town on Monday to pack up and send off our stock of books etc. to Macon in a hired car. I got off militia duty and we packed up the books in the store drawers, boxes, etc., but changed our minds about sending it off as we preferred going to Augusta if we move the stock at all and Jabez is going first to see if a store can be obtained there. It *may* be many a day before we see him again. The 'Friend' has been suspended now for six weeks and it is time it was going again. I wonder if *I* shall assist in its resumption. The future is very dark and uncertain, truly a *sealed book* to our finite minds. But God reigns and the inhabitants of the earth are but as grasshoppers in his sight as far as their power and might are concerned."

From Macon, Dr. William P. Harden, surgeon-in-charge of the Empire Hospital reestablished at nearby Vineville, sent out a plea for rags. They were needed, he stated, for a special gangrene ward which "necessarily requires a large quantity of rags. We are in great need of them at this time. They will be most thankfully received from those who can spare them."

Kate Cumming arrived at Macon at four in the morning. After a few hours' sleep in the depot hotel, where she paid ten dollars for her room "and as much more for breakfast," she called on Dr. Stout, the director of hospitals, to find out where her hospital had relocated.

She found the doctor "low-spirited" at the thought of the sick and wounded being moved so far south in summer time, fearing the heat would be "deleterious" to them. He then revealed that her hospital was in Americus, seventy miles to the

southwest, and just as close to Opelika, her hometown. Since
the train did not leave until morning, she called on a friend,
Dr. Cannon, hoping he could recommend a boarding house.

"His two daughters were with him, and were keeping house
in two rooms, refugee style; one of the rooms was parlor, bedroom and dining-room, the other a kind of dressing room. It
astonished me to see how well everybody manages nowadays;
they put up with inconveniences as if they had been used to
them all their lives. The war seems to have raised the minds
of many above common every-day annoyances. Dr. C. insisted
on us remaining with his family and as Mrs. W. was half sick,
and we were both worn out, we were only too thankful to
accept the kind invitation. The family seem to be perfectly
happy, as much so, I expect, as they ever were in their home in
Tennessee. I shall never forget the cup of coffee I drank there;
it put me in mind of New Orleans.

"Dr. Nagle and an officer who is stationed at Andersonville,
where the prisoners are kept, spent the evening with us. The
prisoners and their behavior was the principal topic of conversation, and from all we could learn we did not like the prospect of
being so near them. (Americus is 10 miles below Andersonville.)
This officer informed us that no less than a hundred died daily.
He said they were the most desperate set of men that he had
ever seen. There are two parties among them, the black re-
publicans and the copperheads and they often have desperate
fights, and kill each other. This officer said it was revolting to
be near such men and did not like his position."

By supper, Carrie Berry concluded, "we have had less shells
today than we have had in a week."

But, at the same time, Graham noted that "the same scare
took place again." A soldier badly wounded in the back
was brought into camp and as the constant build-up of the
picket firing gave promise of a "noisy night."

Into the Provost Marshal General's office walked the Federal
scout, J. Milton Glass, just returned from a visit to the city.
The Provost summarized Glass's report and dispatched it to
Sherman:

"Went into Atlanta past our left flank at 13th instant; saw

one brigade of Martin's division of cavalry between the cemetery and Decatur . . . did not see or hear of any reserves along their lines; says their lines are very thin. The country between the enemy and Fairburn is open; nothing there but a few cavalry pickets and scouts. Saw large squads of negroes along the railroad from East Point to Fairburn, felling timber and throwing up breastworks . . . says that a large block of buildings near the center of Marietta and Woodley Streets was fired by our shells Saturday night and destroyed. The buildings contained cotton and a large drug store. Another building in same part of town was destroyed Sunday evening. Visited several camps. The men appear to have plently of rations and foraging from day to day, but there is no supply on hand."

AUGUST 19

✕ *Richmond Sentinel*

"*Atlanta*—There was heavy artillery firing on the center last night. This morning the enemy's batteries in front of the city opened a heavy fire, which exceeded anything yet witnessed. A forty-two pounder Sawyer shell exploded in a house, killing Captain Jarson, of the 14th Texas cavalry. Two children and several ladies were wounded. No further damage was done."

✕ *Atlanta Appeal*

"Another 24 hours passed, with comparatively little disturbance from the enemy. A few shells were occasionally thrown into our midst during the day yesterday, and during the night a slow but regular fire was kept up. The enemy seemed to be operating with only a single gun, which was fired about every 15 minutes. We have heard of no personal injuries sustained.

"For several days and nights good order has prevailed in the city, at least as much as could be expected under the circumstances. The stragglers have nearly all been picked up and taken to their commanders, and the effect of their absence is apparent. We again advise our citizens to refuse to feed the few that continue to prowl around, and their necessities will soon drive them to the trenches, where they ought to be, and where they will be well fed."

The Daily Intelligencer (Atlanta)

"During one of the intensely hot days of last week more than 300 sick and wounded Yankees died at Andersonville. We thank Heaven for such blessings. . . .

"We find that this would make 1800 feet equal to 600 yards or more than a quarter of a mile of dead Yankees. . . .

"To bury them side by side would require a trench 600 feet long equal to 200 yards, 7 feet wide and five feet deep.

It would require 120 men to dig the graves . . . 200 carpenters to make boxes . . . 25 wagons to haul them. . . .

"To the funeral cortege we will allow, for charity's sake, 0000000000 mourners."

The New York Times

"It was telegraphed last week to all the country newspapers, as an item of considerable importance, that one of our contemporaries in this city had received intelligence from Washington 'that Sherman's success at Atlanta was not at all problematical.' . . . Sherman's success at Atlanta *is* 'problematical' and decidedly 'problematical.' All military operations are 'problematical,' that is to say the issue of them is never certain.

"Everything about war is uncertain, and proverbially uncertain. 'The Fortune of War' has, in all ages, been regarded as the most fickle and inconstant of all the gods. If the public would only keep this constantly in mind, as it ought, we should have fewer of these terrible fits of despondency, into which we all plunge after each of our reverses and disappointments.

"In all speculations about Atlanta, it must not be forgotten that Sherman, so far from having no 'problem' before him is really engaged in the solution of the most difficult problem of war —the forcing of an entrenched camp, open in the rear and defended by a large army. It is an operation in which he has already several times succeeded and there is the strongest possibility that he will succeed again, but there is no certainty. It is only when a place is 'invested' that is, surrounded on every side, that its capture is, in a military sense, sure. . . .

"Probably the most hopeful indication at Atlanta at present is the enormous force of militia which, according to Southern accounts, the rebels are collecting at that place. 'Militia' in Georgia means very old men, and sickly men, and very young boys and such fighting material may be pronounced as worse than worthless, when opposed to such an army as Sherman's. They are useless for attack in the open field, they defend works very feebly; they sicken and die very fast when exposed to the hardships of war, and they eat as much and require as much food and ammunition as veterans of a hundred battles, and they are peculiarly liable to panic in action. We do not think much of our Northern militia, when embodied, like that of Pennsylvania, in the actual presence of the enemy; but bad as it is, it is a *corps d'elite* compared to the unfortunates whom Gov. Brown is now dragging to the fray."

It was a bright, warm Friday morning. Sergeant Graham, after an early breakfast, was detailed "on fatigue duty, cutting timber and building a bridge." While he was on this duty, and hardly before the beads of sweat had begun to stand out on his forehead and shoulders, "a yell was made by our men and a charge made. Shells flying and musketry rolling for one hour when all was quiet. A shot struck a tree in camp and cut it in the middle but it did not fall."

During this time, Brigadier General Grenville Dodge, commanding the 16th Corps, exposed himself to enemy fire by walking far out into the skirmish line. He had wanted a better look not only at the Confederates' defenses but at the rooftops of Atlanta. They had been silhouetted tantalizingly close over the treetops for weeks.

A sharpshooter, hidden in a vidette pit, obscured by twigs and logs, aimed for the general's head—and hit him. The bullet deflected over his forehead and plowed a furrow through his scalp, leaving the general apparently dead. But while the newspaper correspondents filed his obituaries, surgeons in an advanced hospital looked him over and decided he would recover.

Fenwick Hedley, noting that his 32d Illinois Infantry had "demonstrated," observed that "Schofield does not seem to be able to reach the railroad."

Within the Confederate lines, Taylor Beatty, too, was thinking about the railroad. He wondered if Wheeler would cut it in Sherman's rear. "If he succeeds as well as report says I think it will cause Sherman to fall back. If he does a peace candidate will be nominated on the 29th at Chicago. If this is done, there will be a glimmering of peace. As yet, I see no prospects for anything but a long war. . . . I am not as sanguine as most people seem to be about peace. Another assault on our lines Virginia —on North side of James has been disastrously repulsed—just as the one on the 6 inst. at Petersburg. We have rumors this evening that a Yankee raid 3,000 strong has cut the Macon road again. On the last raids we captured about 3,000. Hope we may be able to destroy this also."

Not a day had gone by, it seemed to David Conyngham, without skirmishing, artillery duels, assault and repulse, all making up the amalgam of a "regular siege." The rather short, good-natured Federal soldier-correspondent wrote:

"Like another Troy, the enemy fought outside their walls and intrenchments, and many an amusing combat took place, particularly between the skirmishers. I have often seen a rebel and a Federal soldier making right for the same rifle-pit, their friends on both sides loudly cheering them on. As they would not have time to fight, they reserved their fire until they got into the pit, when woe betide the laggard, for the other was sure to pop him as soon as he got into cover. Sometimes they got in together, and then came the tug of war; for they fought for possession with their bayonets and closed fists. In some cases, however, they made a truce, and took joint possession of it.

"It was no unusual thing to see our pickets and skirmishers enjoying themselves very comfortably with the rebels, drinking bad whiskey, smoking and chewing worse tobacco, and trading coffee and other little articles. The rebels had no coffee, and our men plenty, while the rebels had plenty of whiskey; so they very soon came to an understanding. It was strange to see these men, who had been just pitted in deadly conflict, trading, and bantering, and chatting, as if they were the best friends in the world. They discussed a battle with the same gusto they would a cock-fight, or horse-race, and made inquiries about their friends, as to who was killed, and who not, in the respective armies. Friends that have been separated for years have met in this way. Brothers who parted to try their fortune have often met on the picket line, or on the battle-field. I once met a German soldier with the head of a dying rebel on his lap. The stern veteran was weeping, whilst the boy on his knee looked pityingly into his face. They were speaking in German, and from my poor knowledge of the language, all I could make out was, that they were brothers; that the elder had come out here several years before; the younger followed him, and being informed that he was in Macon, he went in search of him, and got conscripted; while the elder brother, who was in the north all the time, joined our army. The young boy was scarcely twenty, with light hair, and a soft, fair complexion. The pallor of death was on his brow, and the blood was flowing from his breast, and gurgled in his throat and mouth, which the other wiped away with his handkerchief. When he could speak, the dying youth's conversation was of the old home in Germany, of his brothers and sisters, and dear father and mother, who were never to see him again.

"In those improvised truces, the best possible faith was observed by the men. These truces were brought about chiefly in the following manner. A rebel, who was heartily tired of his crippled position in his pit, would call out, 'I say, Yank!'

" 'Well, Johnny Reb,' would echo from another hole or tree.

" 'I'm going to put out my head; don't shoot.'

" 'Well, I won't.'

"The reb would pop up his head; the Yank would do the same.

" 'Hain't you got any coffee, Johnny?'

" 'Na'r a bit, but plenty of rot-gut.'

" 'All right; we'll have a trade.'

"They would meet, while several others would follow the example, until there would be a regular bartering mart established. In some cases the men would come to know each other so well, that they would often call out,—

" 'Look out, reb; we're going to shoot,' or 'Look out, Yank, we're going to shoot,' as the case may be.

"On one occasion the men were holding a friendly *reunion* of this sort, when a rebel major came down in a great fury, and ordered the men back. As they were going back, he ordered them to fire on the Federals. They refused, as they had made a truce. The major swore and stormed, and in his rage he snatched the gun from one of the men, and fired at a Federal soldier, wounding him. A cry of execration at such a breach of faith rose from all the men, and they called out, 'Yanks, we couldn't help it.' At night these men deserted into our lines, assigning as a reason, that they could not with honor serve any longer in an army that thus violated private truces . . . the rebels seemed to lose heart altogether, and the desertions were very numerous. While on the Chattahoochee, a camp of rebel conscripts on the Hendersonville road, seven miles from Atlanta, was abandoned, and nearly five hundred of them came into our lines.

"As I have said before, we had now settled down to a regular siege, pounding away at the beleaguered city on every side. Hood had his intrenchments and forts garrisoned with militia, convalescents, and some worthless conscripts, and had kept the veteran troops on hand to operate when required; they, having the arc of a circle to act on, could hurriedly move from point to point.

"Our heavy shelling was regularly replied to by the enemy, who revealed some heavy guns. I weighed one projectile; it weighed sixty-four pounds. It had plunged in among our tents at General Thomas J. Wood's headquarters, but fortunately did not burst, but made a regular fuss and a scare, kicking up a whole lot of puddle; in fact, conducting itself like a miniature volcano."

Kate Cumming was sent to the Macon depot in an ambulance. The train arrived almost on schedule and then chugged south, with few stops, the twenty-six miles to Fort Valley, the location of the Gamble and Buckner hospitals—where the Union spy, who had masqueraded as a woman, was being questioned. Kate recorded:

"There we saw a few familiar faces. The train remained about a half an hour at Andersonville, so we had time for a good view of the prisoners' quarters. I must say that my antipathy for prison life was anything but removed by the sight. My heart sank within me at seeing so many human beings crowded so closely together. I asked a gentleman near why we had so many in one place. He answered that we would not have men enough to guard them were they scattered. O, how I thought of him who is the cause of all this woe on his fellow-countrymen—Abraham Lincoln. What kind of a heart can he have, to leave these poor wretches here? It is truly awful to think about.

"But, as sure as there is a just God, his day of reckoning will come for the crimes of which he has been guilty against his own countrymen alone. To think of how often we have begged for exchange; but this unfeeling man knows what a terrible punishment it is for our men to be in northern prisons, and how valuable every one of them is to us. For this reason he sacrifices thousands of his own. May Heaven help us all! But war is terrible."

Later in the day, she finally reached her destination—Americus—"quite a large village . . . the weather is very warm."

Dyer was visiting Andersonville, admittedly from "curiosity." The first fact which puzzled the hospital purchasing agent was the very name:

"It would take a big stretch of the imagination to discover any town. A railroad depot and platform, the quartermaster's store hospital, a few shanties, for the officers, and guards, and the prison pen were all the signs of a town to be seen and these were surrounded by a big pine forest.

"But being more interested in the prison and prisoners than in anything else I devoted my whole attention to them. I arrived on the morning train and was present when rations were issued. I discovered that the prisoners received the same allowance as our soldiers in the field, who were then on half rations.

The only difference being that we were issued cornmeal while the prisoners drew cornbread of like quantity. In this they had the advantage as we had no skillets and had to bake our 'Johnny' cakes on slabs split out of pine trees and by the time the baking was done the corncake and rosin were pretty well mixed. But that was all right when we got used to it and then it was healthy.

"The prison stockade inclosed about thirty acres of ground situated in the end of a beautiful valley some two hundred yards wide and surrounded on three sides by heavily wooded hills. A stream of clear water fed by a spring ran diagonally across the prison near the south end, which with the cleanly appearance of every part of the grounds gave it—to an outsider—an appearance of comfort.

"The only drawback was the absence of shelter of any kind from the hot sun and to the thirty thousand prisoners inside these walls this was the worst punishment they had to endure. They only had their little 'flies' (or as we called them 'dog tents') holding two men, under which they would crawl in the heat of the day only, to suffer almost as much as if out in the sun and contract the naturally resultant diseases of this manner of living. The wonder is that the mortality was not greater than it was and indeed it appears large enough as on the day I was there one hundred and twenty were buried. But this day I learned was a record breaker. Had the prisoners been treated as badly by the prison managers as they were given credit for by some prejudiced and irresponsible writers nearly the whole lot would be planted right now on the Andersonville hills. But everything was done that could be done to ameliorate their condition. The sick were cared for in the hospitals as well as our own and had their own nurses to boot. Those who were growing weak were marched in large squads out into the woods to get exercise and rest in the shade.

"Fruit and vegetables were furnished them to prevent scurvy, in fact everything possible was done to alleviate their suffering. The Confederate authorities offered to allow the Federal government to send its own surgeons, medicines and provisions and administer them themselves, at the same time pleading for an exchange of prisoners and even sending a delegation of the prisoners to Washington to beg their government to relieve them in this way. This delegation was refused a hearing and had to return to prison and despair."

In Atlanta, Carrie Berry's day had been marked by departure. "Auntie went down to Grandpa's this morning and I missed her so much. That is the only place I had to run to. I have ben knitting on my stocking some today and sewing some today."

Sergeant William Graham was back on picket duty. His command "advanced the picket line and took a new pit near the enemy." The night turned "rainy and cool," but Graham could not roll up in his blanket. Midnight approached and passed, the firing stabbed the darkness, spasmodically, the rain drops beat down, and he crouched there in the mud—waiting.

AUGUST 20

✄ *The Daily Intelligencer* (Atlanta)

"The following official dispatch was addressed to Major Dawson:

" '*Atlanta, August 19*—A raid this morning on our left, in the direction of Fairburn—supposed to be intended for the Macon Road.

F. A. Shoup
Chief of Staff' "

✄ *Richmond Sentinel*

"From intimations in Georgia papers we expect to hear good news from Sherman's army very soon. To cut his communications so far from his base of supplies will be fatal to him."

▬ *Cincinnati Commercial*

"*One and a half miles Southwest of East Point*—At present the situation is greatly devoid of interest, except when regarded prophetically. The army has at length stretched its great length about 'the doomed city,' extending itself to the utmost extent; and yet the enemy confront us the entire length—nearly fourteen miles—with a defiant line, of whatever strength, and the huge walls of their earth and timber still keep at bay all our thrusts and passes at Atlanta. Not only this but, as I have said previously, their lines extend beyond our own to, and probably around East Point, and behind this, in comparative safety, their railroad pulsates with the bread and bacon of life to the rebel armies and we have not yet been able to raid it in two so that it would stay thus.

"Since reaching the confines of Atlanta, the rebels have grown strangely profuse of their artillery in comparison with their former caution and reserve. Of solid shot they throw more than we, and of shells fully as many. The former, in the circumstances which surround us, are particularly pestiferous. When aimed at the works (and the rebel gunners have grown fearfully accurate in their aim) they demolished them much more effectually than shells, and imperil the men in trenches by throwing down upon them the 'headlogs' and other timbers of the works. Besides this, our men are compelled to camp, almost without interruption, in dense woods, and the rebels know well that by smashing those balls through the thick trees, they can harrass us almost without limit with falling limbs and jagged splinters.

"It is described to me as something absolutely infernal to be compelled to pass a clear, moonlit night in a tent near the line in woods through which these howling devils go thwacking among the trees, battering limbs promiscuously, and sometimes sweeping low enough to rake through a whole row of tents. An officer of the 11th Ohio told me that as he lay one night, sleepless in his tent, listening to the shot which came every fifteen minutes, he heard a solid ball strike a tree over another regiment, and glancing from it, pass through the tent of a poor fellow who, wearing with long watching on the skirmish line, was sleeping, despite the noise, and carrying away his leg, plunge deep into the ground. The unfortunate man uttered a long, moaning wail, which told his startled comrades of his intense agony, but after a few repetitions, it grew feebler and feebler, and almost before the next missile arrived, his plaintive cries were silenced forever—Such is a single glimpse into the chilling terrors which are strewn through all this bloody siege of Atlanta.

"From their great siege guns, the rebels throw many 84-pound shells into our lines, and to these we cannot reply in kind. A majority of them never burst, but are carried off by the boys as trophies; but the peculiar deep-voiced 'n-o-o-o-o-o' has a demoralizing effect on the nerves. S'blood! how it makes one's blood thick about his liver, and his knees grow suddenly weak! The smaller shells, however, are more dangerous, since they give less warning of their approach, and almost invariably burst. The miseries to which these missiles have reduced our lads are set in a ludicrous and, at the same time, pathetic light by the remark of a veteran, when comparing with his comrades their respective experiences in campaigning, that 'he never before had to build breastworks to cook behind.' It is a thing greatly affecting a man's happiness when he is compelled not only to sleep, but also to cook and eat in a strictly horizontal position."

The Reverend W. T. Hall, chaplain of the 30th Mississippi Regiment, completed and sealed one of a growing number of letters he had written in recent days.

"It is my painful duty," he told Mr. Newberry in Coffeeville, Mississippi, "to inform you of the death of your son (Thomas Jefferson) a member of the 29th Miss. Regt. I presume, however, that it will be a satisfaction to you and your family to know by letter what you will necessarily learn in some way. Your son fell in the discharge of his duty to his country. He was on picket duty when the fatal shot (a rifle ball) struck him. As far as I know he was killed instantly. His body was brought back to the field hospital and intered [sic] as respectably as the circumstances would allow. He lies near the West Point Rail Road about four miles from Atlanta. This grave is marked by a board bearing his name. I wish that I was able to offer you such consolation as a friend and acquaintance might be able to suggest. I trust that the Lord may sustain you by his Grace."

At daylight, "north lines commenced to blaze away and kept it up all through morning. Rainy day, in the middle of mud and pit all day." It was, Graham continued, "very disagreeable."

Colonel Taylor Beatty was also impressed by the cloudburst of the previous night, "the first we have had in five or six days." He received reports that the Confederate forces had captured "1500 of the Yankee raiders, that 300 others escaped around our right. They burned a little town called Jonesboro, about 20 miles from here."

And Rufus Mead of Connecticut wrote from "near Atlanta" to his "Dear Folks at Home," though he had been without mail for three days, "owing to the track being torn up near Dalton, but now the train comes again, and as it brought a mail I suppose it will take mine out tomorrow. On my regular day I wrote on the 15th just about the time of the raid, and it may possibly get lost but I can't hear as any mail was lost, so I guess it has gone safely.

"We are here yet, neither losing or gaining ground as I know of, but I hear other corps are gaining little on our right. It is pretty evident the Rebs are determined to hold Atlanta as long as possible and as they are so strongly fortified it will be a long time probably before we get there. You must not be over anxious to hear of our being in there. General Sherman knows what he is at, I think, at least I am willing to trust him a while longer at least. I find I had built my hopes too high. We are now in about the same situation as Grant is, i.e. can't get any further and don't want to go back although the campaign ought to be over and troops have rest. We hear good news from Mobile but hardly venture to believe it yet, only hope it is true, as it concerns us considerably.

"I feel quite anxious to hear how Conn. fills her quota, and especially the town of Redding. I hope not by draft, though there are some I want to see sent out.

"I am sorry the Presidential election comes off this fall. I fear that our want of decided victories will have a tendency to encourage the enemies of the Administration and possibly defeat Uncle Abe, though I can't hardly believe that yet.

"I occasionally get a N. Y. Herald and any one would think

by that, that Old Abe was the most ignorant, tyrannical and con-temptible president we ever had & his Cabinet all either knaves or fools. Of course it don't effect me, but I trouble to think how widely circulated & how pernicious an influence that paper al-ways has exerted.

"The weather is very favorable yet but we had a rainbow this morning and today it has showered several times. A forty days rain might suit you but I can't say as I desire it very much, but I won't borrow trouble yet a while. As I wrote before I am on duty now and perfectly well, have issued rations for 3 days to come except fresh beef tomorrow night. Now for wants.

"Two pair of woolen socks—if you have to buy them get small ones I can get them of the QM but Govt socks have a good deal of floss or something that wears up loose so in 3 or 4 weeks they are worn out.

"By the way cant you put in a little candy in them. You know I havent had any now in most 6 months & I think a little would taste good.

"The paper, envelopes, towels, shirts, thread, pins slippers and boots have not come yet, but I suppose will in a short time.

"I want you to keep an account and see if they cost more than the $42 that Govmt allows me for clothing. I am not going to draw any thing this year. Have you heard from Lt Titus or the $70, he was to send you Let me know when you do? All the Bethel boys are well Your ever afft Son & Brother."

Carrie Berry had heard shells all day, "they have not been hitting very close to us but they have been giving them to Uncle Markham. He like to had his house burnt up by one passing through the house and set some cotton on fire which they had layed on the flore. I expect if they had ben at home some of them would have ben hurt."

Kate Cumming found mail awaiting her in Americus. One letter was from an ex-patient now bivouacked "11 miles west of Atlanta." She concluded that the letters revealed that "with all our retreating our soldiers are not down-hearted." Soldier "J" informed her that "the Yankees are broken of charging rebel breastworks. They keep shelling all the time; but thanks be to God, there is not much damage done. It is astonishing to see two armies drawn up confronting each other for hours and hours; everything is as still as a mouse, when all at once, men rush to arms. Then commences the booming of artillery and the heavy roar of musketry.

"This kind of fighting has been going on for the last 86 or 87 days, more or less, much to the detriment of Sherman and his hirelings. Poor old Sherman! he has had a hard road to travel, and in my opinion he will never reach Atlanta, as long as *Sergeant* Hood intends keeping him out. . . .

"On the 26th or 27th, I have forgotten which, General Hood issued orders for every man on the line to have a musket in his hands, excepting only those who were needed to work the guns of artillery.

"I took a musket, and on the 28th the Yankees pitched into our pickets, and such another cheering and rattling of small arms I never heard for picketing. I gathered up my ammunition and took my gun and ran into the ditch along side of the infantry, expecting the Yankees to charge, but it was only a feint on their part.

"The sound of small arms to me has become monotonous."

AUGUST 21

■ *The New York Times*

"It is 'advance the skirmish line and take up a new position,' 'deploy the lines and hold the ridge,' 'refuse the flank,' 'make a demonstration and cover the advance,' 'reconnoiter and fall back,' and all that, from the beginning of the day to the end thereof. If there is one thing more than another which is odious and exasperating, it is to be compelled to make daily note of the petty jangles and frictions of two large armies facing each other in the woods, and endeavoring each to get the better of the other, without getting in the way of the bullets or spilling blood. The extreme length of this campaign and the numerous hard knocks which the armies have dealt out, at one time and another, upon each other, have produced a spirit of caution which will permit nothing to be done on hazard, or at least without the closest possible previous calculation. The contest has become that of two trained and wary giants of an hundred watchful eyes, sore and smarting from continued batterings, and making a thousand feints and passes before venturing the solid thrust which comes straight from the shoulder. Before every suspicious piece of woods, the cannon sit down and sound its depths carefully before men are sent in; skirmishers push about everywhere, beating all bushes, and when they have come into line, they lie for days in position glaring at each other from behind trees and fences, and rocks, before a regular advance is attempted. All this is well, because necessary, but it is very slow. . . .

"As a clue to the whole series of operations for the past week or two it is perhaps not too early to say that the aim is simply and alone to get possession of the railroad between Atlanta and East Point. This gives meaning and point to the whole business, else so muddled and senseless. This accomplished, and all the effort and sacrifice of these many days is fully repaid, for failure in this is a failure to take Atlanta—a failure in everything. Right there before us . . . beats this great artery of life to the rebel city . . . so long as the whetted knife of Federal expectation is held back from severing this jugular of treason, so long is delayed the hour when it shall utterly consume the whole rebellious carcass."

▨ *Columbus Enquirer* (Georgia)

"Gen. Hood is putting guns into the hands of every available man connected with the army. All of the cooks have been armed and returned to their respective commands, and the negroes connected with the army have been employed in that capacity. Quartermasters and commissaries have been made to disgorge the many superfluous men in their departments: surgeons, also. The result is that the army has received a considerable reinforcement. In Clayton's division alone the number of new men returned from the cooking detachments reached 300 which at this time is considered a good regiment. The increase from the cooks alone will reach 4,000 effective men.

"But Gen. Hood does not stop there. He has ordered the arming of every artillerist except from No. 1 to No. 4 who are absolutely necessary to handle a piece; thus this source of increase will be obtained amounting to near 3,000 men. I must say, however, that the order converting artillery into infantry caused considerable fluttering among the battery boys. True, many of them take the thing quite easy, being perfectly willing to serve the country in this critical juncture in any capacity that will aid in the overthrow of Sherman and his 'Hessians.' . . .

"I am proud to say thousands of Georgians are responding to the last call of Gov. Brown. If a general engagement can be delayed one week longer, and the enemy retain their present position, Sherman and his army will be routed.

"Sherman does not manifest a disposition to shell Atlanta. . . .

"Large quantities of tobacco continue to be unearthed and brought forth from its hiding places in and around Atlanta, which Gen. Hood promptly impresses for the use of the army. There is no doubt but what the owners thought that Atlanta would be evacuated, and then they and their tobacco would fall into the embrace of the Yankees."

Thomas McCauley, an orderly sergeant formerly with the 14th New York Cavalry, arrived in the Union lines at 11:00 P.M. the previous night with a saga of imprisonment and escape extending over a year since his capture in Tennessee. Confined first in Libby Prison, Richmond, McCauley was transferred to Andersonville, from which he eventually escaped, with four other men, by digging a sixty-five-foot long tunnel.

Weeks of struggling through swamps and woods, hunted by dogs and shot at by pickets, led to the wounding of his companions and his ultimate capture. Returned to Andersonville, he was manacled with a sixty-four-pound cannon ball on one leg, and a thirty-two-pound ball on the other. However, he obtained a file, and once more set himself free.

Recaptured at Macon, while saddling a horse on which he

hoped to make a dash north, he was again escorted back to Andersonville, under heavy guard.

"You damned Yankee son-of-a-bitch!" the Andersonville guards swore at him, "try to escape did you? We'll fix you!"

This time he was chained firmly to six other prisoners. And again he filed his way to freedom. His captors unexpectedly gave up. They offered him his parole. But at three o'clock of the afternoon on which he was to be set free, not convinced of the sincerity of the promise, he obtained a Confederate uniform and left for Macon with a group of conscripts.

By the end of July, the adventurous Sergeant McCauley, a Tower rifle—Confederate issue—in his hands, was helping man the inner defenses of Atlanta—and in the embarrassing position of aiming his sights at his own forces. To his horror, two of his trench buddies were among those who had aided in his capture after his first escape from Andersonville. A third was a former guard at the dread prison camp. However, none of the three recognized him.

At four o'clock one morning early in August, he crept unobserved out of the breastworks and walked across the city. He found the streets were so full of idlers, stragglers, and soldiers winding up a boisterous twenty-four-hour pass that no one challenged him.

He boarded a train to East Point, his undoing. Suspicious railroad police arrested him and took him before the Provost Marshal. Again McCauley talked his way out of return to Andersonville—and, this time, a possible noose—and was returned to the Atlanta trenches with a warning against straggling in the future—"The South needs every man in this hour!"

But McCauley's luck, courage, and dogged determination prevailed. Without, he said, ever once having to fire his rifle towards Federal positions, he arrived among the Union skirmishers on the Marietta road—and identified himself.

It was not an easy story to believe, but the Federal Adjutant was convinced. The correspondent for the *Washington Star,* for one, decided it was one of the greatest adventures he had heard in a long time and soon was putting it down on paper.

Meanwhile, the dismal rain in Atlanta continued into the

morning. The trenches were reminiscent of the muddy broth of June while the city itself became studded with myriad puddles —the shell holes in streets, sidewalks, and yards. Citizens could not walk half a block without being splattered by passing wagons. The smells of dusty brick, oozing earth, uncarted garbage, and—always—horses hung in a damp miasma from one extremity of Atlanta to the other.

It was a day that did not raise the spirits of the glum, hungry populace. The music boxes that people sometimes wound on Sundays rested silent on mantlepieces. Should the children attempt to turn the keys, the strains of the most familiar of all— "Home Sweet Home"—was enough to evoke tears.

The Berrys prepared dinner of onion stew (Carrie's least favorite vegetable) to be eaten in the cellar. Zuie was still sick. She shivered in the dampness.

"It was a dark, rainy morning," wrote Carrie, "and we thought we would have a quiet Sunday but we were disappointed. Papa says that we will have to move downtown somewhere. Our cellar is not safe."

There was no thought of church this Sunday, though in some respects it was a relief to Carrie. She had often noted in her diary how annoying it was when people would sit in church and stare at her.

Many of the enveloping Federal forces, including Graham, were issued dog tents "for the first time." The soldiers wondered whether this was because of the rain, and the approach of fall with its cooler nights—or because Sherman had despaired of marching into Atlanta for many more months to come.

On the picket line there was heavy musket firing, with "many rifle balls flying through the camp . . . but no one was hurt today as yet." Union batteries barked spasmodically behind the advanced lines and, strangely, there was no reply from the Confederates. This caused some optimism in men whose spirits were as sodden as their uniforms.

While the Berrys remained in their cellar eating onion stew, a sprinkling of inhabitants and defenders of Atlanta did attend church, including S. P. Richards, Joe Semmes, and Captain Tom Key.

"I went to Epis. Church this morning," Richards wrote, "as it was rather wet, Sallie did not go. Yesterday for the third time only the *shells* went by our house, and a fragment fell in our back yard. A large one entered our back store door on Friday and bursting as it passed through the floor, tore up the latter pretty badly. It is said that about twenty lives have been destroyed by these terrible missiles, since the enemy began to throw them into the city. It is like living in the midst of a pestilence, no one can tell but he may be the next victim. The news is that the enemy have cut the railroads again, and also, we are told that our cavalry has certainly cut off Sherman's communications by destroying the road and bridges and blowing up the *Tunnel*! We do not know what to believe."

Tom Key, the Battery Commander, revisited Trinity Church and listened to the Reverend Haygood preach again. He noticed a number of soldiers in the pews though the general attendance seemed smaller than on the previous Sunday. He attributed the attendance of the soldiers to the fact that it was a rainy morning and church offered one of the few shelters in Atlanta.

Joe Semmes had received Eo's "charming letter" of August 7 on Thursday, "just after the Yankee raid was known to have struck our railroads; consequently I almost expected it would be the last from you for some time to come Thanks to God, however, we have again frustrated the designs of the enemy and though they have torn up the roads in three places, we will have trains running over them again by night. For some 48 hours I felt very great uneasiness at the movement of the enemy, they were said to be some twenty miles in our rear with Cavalry and a strong force of Infantry and a large force of our Cavalry being off on a raid to their rear, I was afraid they might do considerable damage before we could prevent. Genl. Hood was, however, equal to the emergency and so promptly checkmated them, that they have abandoned the roads and retreated. All sorts of rumors are current of the extent of damage done by our forces in the rear of the enemy, but we have little reliable information, the most we have coming from prisoners taken in front of Atlanta. This we know, that their communications have been seriously impaired but to what extent we have not learned.

"The enemy kept up a spiteful fire all night last night which did not prevent me from sleeping as soundly as though I was at home, but last Saturday night commencing about 8 o'clock and continuing until after sunrise Sunday morning they kept up a furious fire. Over 2,000 shells were thrown into the city and it was really a beautiful sight to see so many shells coming through the air at the same time, looking precisely like Meteors or shooting stars. About midnight the fire was so hot at my quarters that I had to get up and vacate to another point 100 yards distant but after awhile I returned; the shells being as thick there as at my quarters. No one could sleep however and most everyone spent the night out of doors. But one soldier was killed and several women and children killed and wounded. No soldiers are in the town, except occasionally and of course nearly all the fatalities are confined to the few remaining residents. Many houses are struck and some in many places, and occasionally the houses are set on fire by the explosives. It is often very ridiculous even amidst so much danger to witness some scenes that recur and hear the remarks made, some of the shells make a noise like a railroad train flying through the air and are called 'through to Macon' or 'Augusta' as they go screaming overhead. They are only dangerous when they burst before reaching us or when striking a building. Some sing 'flibberty-gibberty' in a very loud and fearful manner as they are whirled along, and others again make a hissing noise and explode only on striking some object.

"On Saturday night seven to nine batteries played upon every part of the city, shooting high over our works and right into the heart of the city, and yet the Yankee prisoners when charged with it, swear they are shooting at our lines. Enough of this dastardly business.

"You ask if I go to mass and confession. On Assumption day, 15th, I went to confession, but having taken my usual drink of water, this morning I went again and also to communion. Until Sunday week I had no chance to go to mass since the week before we left Dalton, though mass was sometimes said in some of the Divisions of the Army too remote for me to attend.

"I regret that Tom has undertaken the journey to Louisiana,

and do not think he is aware of the perils and the exposure he will have to undergo. I hope he will not attempt to cross the river unless he has someone well acquainted with the country to accompany him. The vicinity of the river is infested by gangs of lawless men, deserters, etc., who have no regard for either side, and unless he has some trusty person with him, he will be deceived and perhaps robbed. He should have full direction where and how to proceed before he crosses the river. From the grand reception account you gave me I should judge he was delighted with his visit and will leave under the impression that you are all living as well as before the war. Ben is now I guess the honored guest, and is enjoying himself hugely. I feel envious in spite of myself when I think of Ben's good fortune, and of the long probation I am still to have, before I can realize the joys I dream and think of almost every moment of the day.

"Will the time ever come again which I shall have my beloved always with me or near me, is a question I ask myself many times, with a sigh too, when I consider that at one time when she was always with me I did not sometimes sip of the cup of happiness, which she always had ready for me. Not that it was distasteful but because I never knew its full value until the war had deprived me of it. I never knew the strength or fervor of my own love, until the precious object was separated from me.

"I have not received a letter from our darling daughter for a long time though she is indebted to me. When you hear from her again send me her letters, and tell her I would write again but it is very difficult for me to find a quiet hour to do so. I will write Malcom the first leisure I have after this. Tell him I am very much afraid he is losing valuable time and that when he does go to school, after the war, he will be so far behind other boys that it will mortify him.

"Col. Dawson is improving slowly, and as soon as he gets well enough, will pay a visit to the Terrills, who are related to the Dawsons of Georgia whom we used to know. They have sent him a pressing invitation. After a short visit he will go to Gainesville. I have to send rations to our raid hunters in the rear and must go. Good bye, darling, and God bless you."

The rain continued into the evening, and the shelling slackened somewhat.

AUGUST 22

Southern Press Association

"*Atlanta*—Kilpatrick's raid, composed of 2,500 men, crossed the Chattahoochee at Cambellton, and struck the road at Fairburn at 8 o'clock Friday morning, and destroyed the road for six miles. The raiders then crossed over to the Macon road, striking the road at Lovejoy's Friday evening, and moving towards Jonesboro. The Federal infantry support which accompanied Kilpatrick's cavalry to West Point, returned, and the cavalry proceeded along, towards the Macon road. . . .

"The raiders burned the depot and post office at Jonesboro, destroying all the papers.

"The city is very quiet today. There is no shelling. The enemy deny the charge of shelling the city, and claim that their shot are all aimed at our defences."

Cartersville, Georgia, August 17

"Editor, *The Daily Intelligencer*—I have just arrived here from near Calhoun, having left our cavalry command on yesterday, destroying the culverts and bridges along the State road. We have been unable to attack the larger and well fortified bridges over Etowah and the other streams between Dalton and Atlanta that are defended with triangular lunette forts, but we have torn up the road, burnt the ties and cut and destroyed the rails so that they cannot be used again, and so that Sherman will not be able to repair it, for some weeks. The destruction of the road has been very complete thus far, and our success is very great. We do not find any opposition from the small garrisons along the road and have captured a large number of prisoners and stores without any material loss to ourselves thus far. A great deal of the captured property, cattle & c. has been sent by a safe route under a strong escort of the Army of Tennessee. The larger portion of our command has gone northward and by this time must have destroyed communications between Dalton and Nashville. The work is expected to be thoroughly and well done this time, as daring officers and picked men are on the expedition.

"It is expected that a strong cavalry force is after us, but no fears are entertained that they will do our army damage, or show fight. The destruction we have effected on Sherman's line of communication and the stores and trains we have destroyed cannot be repaired and replaced in a long time. We are hopeful that it will force the Army of the Cumberland to retreat. . . .

"The country we have passed through and all through the country that intervenes between Atlanta and Dalton, is thoroughly desolate and devastated. The people have been driven away four miles on each side of the State road, and everything in the way of horses, cattle, forage and provisions have been taken away. The poor people are suffering very much, but as they have no place but their mountain homes to go to, they are obliged to remain and suffer. The people are all hopeful, however, that the Yankees will soon be driven out, and say that a general impression prevails amongst the Yankee soldiers that they will retreat before long. . . . 'Id Est Nihil.' "

Conyngham, like other correspondents and many of the troops, became increasingly convinced that Sherman had but one objective—the railroad south of Atlanta.

"Right before us," he wrote, "within a few miles of our lines, almost within reach of our guns, runs this great life artery of the rebel city. Once cut, this jugular vein and Atlanta speedily falls. Sherman knew this well, and therefore turned all his attention to it; the rebels knew it well, and therefore were exceedingly vigilant and active to resist all our attempts upon it. They left their strong works to be guarded by the militia and conscripts, and followed up our movements with the utmost promptness and daring. It was evident now that the battle would not come off before Atlanta. Perhaps Sherman could take it by direct assault; but we had learned that assaults were always costly, even when successful. Sherman was cautious and wary, pushing his skirmishers everywhere, beating all bushes, and suspicious nooks and dells. Hood, on the other hand, was watchful to counteract any movement of his wily foe. It was a great game of chess. Hood had castled, and Sherman moved to checkmate him."

It was a windy, warm morning. Carrie Berry had been up since dawn helping her mother pack to move to a safer cellar.

Sergeant Graham was enjoying a sense of well being this "fine day" even though he had to duck "plenty of balls flying through the camp." A Lieutenant Baldwin visited his regiment and informed him that the railroad was "cut to Macon and 12 miles destroyed."

As Monday wore on, Carrie accompanied the Berry family to her Aunt's cellar on Alabama Street, near Central Avenue. Her Aunt lived next to the railroad tracks, in a target area. The cellar was roomier, more "livable."

Carrie held Zuie in her arms, while Zuie clutched her older sister's knitting. "We were glad," Carrie wrote in her diary, "to get out of our small cellar. We have a nice large cellar here where we can run as much as we please and enjoy it. Mama says that we make so much noise that she can't hear the shells."

Carrie wondered if her pony were still grazing in the back yard, and if the few remaining chickens would be stolen before she returned.

Her father was unhappy, since his dyspepsia had returned. He had his business to tend to as well as his sentry duties with the city guard. When he was in the cellar he sat glumly, pale, half-sick, and silent.

Lucy Harvie Hull was dividing her own time between cellar and parlor of their home on Peachtree Street. Her colored Mammy was saying the Yankees were coming "sho nuff."

Lucy's family had doggedly clung to their house, even after the chimney was knocked off and the walls pierced and scarred by many fragments. "My father was away all day and all night at

"Chevaux de frise" barricades of spiked wood encircle the Ephraim Ponder estate, a heavily fortified post in the outer defenses of Atlanta. Much blood was spilled here before the Federals finally captured the works and put their siege guns in position to shell the city's heart. *(National Archives)*

Battered mansion on the Ponder estate. Strongly constructed of brick, stone, and **plaster**, the house absorbed literally tons of shells and rifle balls. *(National Archives)*

The Atlanta Medical College. *(Courtesy Atlanta Historical Society)*

Downtown Atlanta during the occupation. First building with peaked roof on the left was a slave mart. *(Courtesy Atlanta Historical Society)*

This abandoned Confederate camp was within sight of the houses and spires of Atlanta. Part of Hood's "inner defense line," it was situated about one mile southeast of Atlanta's business section, near the old Oakland Cemetery. (*National Archives*)

This Confederate fort, captured by Sherman's forces, was rebuilt and strengthened by Union Engineers (note especially the thick, wood-shored earthworks). (*Library of Congress*)

Federal soldiers occupy Confederate fortifications overlooking the Georgia Railroad tracks after the line was cut by Sherman *(National Archives)*

A small Confederate fort on the outskirts of Atlanta faces a shell-damaged farmhouse which stood in the direct line of fire between opposing forces. *(National Archives)*

This photograph of a roundhouse was apparently taken in September, 1864, after Federal troops occupied Atlanta. The fact that none of the locomotives appear to be damaged would indicate that they had been seized by Union forces earlier in the war and used in the advance from Chattanooga. *(Courtesy Association of American Railroads)*

The empty roundhouse in this railroad yard appears to be on the big curve where the tracks turned out of the city toward West Point. All structures shown in this photograph were demolished before Sherman marched out of Atlanta in mid-November. (*National Archives*)

the railroad, moving the troops and Mother would not leave him until she must," Lucy wrote. "When I recall all this, we seem to have lived this way a long time, though I know now that it was only a few days; but at last, one morning we were waked in the dark, dressed and hurried down to the depot, where we were put into a freight car, Mother weeping bitterly, for my father could not leave with us, and Mammy wrapping us up from the chill morning air as she prayed aloud, or talked to other Negroes around the depot. I remember hearing them say that this 'mus be de las' train outen Atlanta' and that the Yankees were 'dess a packin' into the other side of town and that 'Genl. Sherman would be sure to take our house to live in,' which in fact he did.

"Later in the morning when the air grew light and warm, Hattie and I enjoyed the journey and the novelty of the freight car with furniture in it, beds and chairs and bureaus to play on, and above all, the knowledge that at last we were 'going to Grandpa's.' "

Others, like Sarah Huff, whose house had just been commandeered for the new strongpoint on the city's inner defense line, were inspired to poetry as they fled in these dying days of sultry August. Sarah entitled hers, *What Mother Carried Along*:

> Home ties must break,
> But what could they take?
> As they hurried and scurried along?
> Sought my Mother to save the best
> Of the things that she possessed
> She could not carry much along.
> Grandfather's clock ticked in the hall,
> Grandmother's picture decked the wall,
> To these did cherished thoughts belong—
> But the battle roar entered her door,
> She could not carry these treasures along.
> Into her bookcase Mother did look,
> Dropping hot tears on each loved book
> She was a lover of learning and song,
> But the cannon's 'boom' rocked the room
> She could not carry her books along.
> As little children around her flocked,

She thought of the cradle in which they were rocked
Motherhood welled in her heart so strong.
Dire was need as she refugeed.
By wagon and train and back home again,
But she carried their cradle along!

From his treetop observation post, Lieutenant Sam Edge was watching people, as well as Army operations in Atlanta. He reported, "the enemy are busy strengthening their works and building new ones in front of the Twentieth Corps. The new casemate battery and six-gun fort south of big gun and in front of the left of the Sixteenth Corps appear to be temporarily abandoned, casemates and embrasures being thickly covered with brush. At 4:00 P.M., three ladies, two girls, and a citizen, with a black servant girl, all of them well dressed, took quite a promenade on the large work in front of the main part of town. The enemy issued green corn again to their men in the rifle pits this P.M. The boxcars reported by Lt. Fish appeared to be loaded."

Evening had settled over Atlanta when a shell exploded in the dirt street in front of the Express Office. A lady was torn and mangled, she died instantly. A soldier, several feet away from her, lost a leg and was carried bleeding to the Medical College. There, Dr. d'Avigny, working tirelessly as one of Atlanta's few surgeons, amputated what remained of the leg. But, in the dominating confusion, no one thought to obtain the name of the lady, or of the soldier.

The defenders of Atlanta watched the Federal forces once more inching their lines closer in. Breastworks and rifle pits were advanced in some sectors. The men, in opposing trenches, were in clear view of one another in many places.

The shelling from the big guns continued. David Conyngham, reporter-soldier, continued to be profoundly impressed by the fiery shells bursting over the "doomed city," the flames from burning houses and the dark smoke, against the night, "enveloping it in one black canopy, hanging over it like a funeral pall."

AUGUST 23

✉ *The Daily Intelligencer* (Atlanta)

We have been favored with the perusal of a letter addressed by the Chairman of the 'Committee in Atlanta to deal out rations to the Poor' to a high official of this State, the suggestion coming from proper authority, from which we gather the following facts:

" 'Gen.—thinks the poor had all better be removed to some point where they can be better fed and food procured for them than in Atlanta. I cannot see, he says, how they can possibly be removed and sheltered. There are, I think, one thousand families, averaging, say, four to the family. Gen. Hood is now furnishing 1,500 rations per day to supply their present wants. . . . Looking to the time when the Macon and Western Railroad may be cut, in such a contingency he would be obliged to feed the army in preference to the poor; the demand then for food would be nearly double what it is now. The writer suggests that the State should give this subject immediate consideration. This, we learn, has already been given, and attention to it is still being given by the proper officer to direct it: Col. Whitaker, the Commissary-General of the State, under the authority of the Governor. One thousand bushels of corn, to be ground into meal, has already been ordered there, and more will yet be done for these suffering poor.'

"From the letter we also learn that Gen. Hood is doing all he can to ameliorate the condition of the poor who are still in Atlanta, and who have not the means to leave that city, or other home, or place of refuge to flee to. The writer says:

" 'The shelling is so heavy and constant that we cannot get grinding of corn done. The question of wood is also one of vital importance. The stock has been nearly all impressed or removed. The white men are in the ditches, the Negroes have been sent off for safety, so that hauling or labor can scarcely be had, and in addition, the army are consuming all the wood near the city. There is absolutely nothing coming into the city from the country. Our Mayor is absent and only two members of the Council are in the city, who have no authority over its finances but are laboring with all energy for the best interests of it, and for the poor. Whatever is to be done should be done without delay.'

"We publish the foregoing in order to suggest that relief be sent to the poor of Atlanta, especially by those who are able and are refugees from it. There was a time when the people of Atlanta nobly and generously gave to other suffering communities. Will not other communities now help the poor of the city? Send them meal and bacon, if only bushel of the one, and a side or shoulder of the other, many from different sections of the State, thus contributing will do great good. Living in cellars, bomb-proofs and caves. Let them at least have bread and meat!"

▨ Memphis Appeal

"There seems to be at present no scarcity of provisions in the city (Atlanta) and from the quantity that had arrived by express we judge there is enough to meet the wants of our greatly reduced population. The prices of some articles are high, speculators holding all there is upon the market, but as a general thing our market is now but little ahead of those of other cities."

▬ The New York Times

"Matters at Atlanta are unchanged. The army is engaged in advancing parallels and strengthening works. . . .

"There are quite a good many heavy guns planted at given points along our works, all ranged for the city . . . a heavy fire broke out in the city, creating quite an alarm. Care was taken to rouse the citizens by the ringing of the fire bells. The alarm was distinctly heard all along our lines, and called out many of us to witness the conflagration. In this however we were disappointed. A dense fog had risen, filling the intervening space between us and the fire, allowing us only a glimpse of its crimson light, fringing the cloudy masses with a burning glare."

The people of Atlanta awoke from a disturbed night of fitful sleep. From western perimeters the 20-pound Parrotts barked through the dark hours into the dawn. Their shells had been lobbed into scattered sections of the Gate City. A few Confederate batteries made desultory reply at sunrise.

Federal soldiers, not in the picket line, started foraging for corn. They blinked in the brightening sunshine. It looked like another hot, Georgia day.

Carrie Berry had been "very comfortable" since they moved to the larger, deeper cellar, "but Mama is fretted to death all the time for fear of fire. There is a fire in town nearly every day. I get so tired of being housed up all the time. The shells get worse and worse every day. O that something would stop them!"

And Henry Richards, one of the few remaining wounded soldiers in Atlanta, wrote to his mother in Savannah that the box she sent him had finally arrived, and "everything was spoiled in it but the pound cake. Tell Sister her bag is beautiful. I cannot help admiring it. My gratitude to you and Sister need not be expressed. My hand is about the same. The air is quite cool today. Give my love to Dear Sister and all and take a good share for yourself. Remember me to all my friends and also the servants and . . . Mary. Well I must close as my hand's tired.

I remain your affec. Son."

To accentuate disappointment and hunger in Atlanta reports persisted that Sherman's commissaries in Marietta were stocked sufficiently for at least three more weeks. His army "continues well fed" was the official word Hood's scouts brought back.

There was a new and not wholly explicable lack of cats and dogs in the city. Pets had mysteriously vanished. Some had been killed by the shelling or by the reckless driving of military wagons, others had wandered into the country in search of more food. It was speculated that some might even have starved. But the suspicion lingered in many minds, a suspicion that obviously would never be confirmed, that a few impoverished and famished citizens had begun to eat their pets.

By this time "Confederate fricassee"—the Atlanta equivalent of Mobile's "blockade pudding"—was becoming a delicacy. Earlier in the summer it had been a source of humor; now it was just hash, a tedious amalgam of any odds and ends that could be found in the kitchen. It was sometimes accompanied by willow-bark tea, and dished up as "Sherman hash." The repetitious joke was that even Old Tecumseh's britches had gone into the recipe.

After dark, Graham went into camp and ate his supper. He watched two wounded soldiers being brought in, then settled down to read a letter from home.

AUGUST 24

✉ *Southern Press Association*

"*Atlanta*—Scouts report that another Federal raid, seven thousand strong with nine pieces of artillery, started from Decatur early this morning, and went in the direction of Covington. . . .

"The situation in Atlanta is still unchanged.

"The enemy shelled the city at intervals all night.

"All quiet this morning except occasional picket skirmishing on Maney's front on our right."

✉ *Memphis Appeal*

"The firing upon the city during the last 24 hours has been slowly but regularly kept up. The shots appear to be directed at no particular locality, but fall in every part of the city that can be reached occasionally. Yesterday afternoon a 64-pound shell entered a house occupied by a refugee, a Mr. Gibbs, and exploded in a room where his family had just gone to welcome a soldier friend, who had called upon them. The soldier had his leg torn off and died from the loss of blood before medical aid could be procured, and a little child was killed by splinters. Two ladies in the room were also injured. These are the only casualties we have heard reported within the last 24 hours. This morning about 4 o'clock while the heavy cannonading along the center was going on, a building on the outer end of Marietta street was fired from some cause, not reported, and burned."

The Daily Intelligencer (Atlanta)

"During the last few days that portion of Atlanta lying along Marietta street has been furiously bombarded, making the avenues of travel perfectly untenable and the destruction of property almost unprecedented; yet it only effects the ruin of property, nothing else is gained by all his furious work.

"The shelling process has been increased in intensity during the past four or five days. The enemy has located several large siege guns which cast their 64 and 72-pounder missiles over all portions of the city, but thus far they have rained their terrible contents down on the suffering non-combatants, however, without much fatality resulting.

"The city is very desolate. There are few people remaining who could get away, and almost every house bears marks of the vengeance of the ruthless enemy. The streets are deserted, the homes desolate and abandoned except by the casual denizens. All in all it is as sad as a ruin, and deserted as an ancient city of the plain. . . .

"The enemy shelled the center of the city steadily last night. McDaniel's warehouse on Hunter street between Pryor and Whitehall was destroyed by fire this morning at 5 o'clock. Five hundred bales of cotton were consumed.

"The City Fire Battalion was promptly on hand and checked the spread of the conflagration under a heavy fire from the enemy's batteries. A small frame building near the State Railroad Shop was also burned last night. Both buildings were fired by shells.

"No casualties resulted from the shells.

"The city is comparatively quiet this morning, save the usual skirmishing with artillery and small arms. The Yankee raids reported by scouts yesterday is not confirmed by the reports of this morning."

"Ike" Pilgrim, former printer and now the paper's correspondent in Atlanta, was up again, after a few hours' sleep, to attend the fire which razed P. E. McDaniel's warehouse. It was his belief that only "superhuman" efforts by the firemen saved the whole block from being levelled, even though cotton and tobacco valued at nearly a quarter of a million dollars was destroyed. In spite of the shelling, Pilgrim was not convinced that incendiarism could be altogether ruled out.

"Tuesday night," he wrote, "the dwelling house of Mr. Daniel Fiske, near the State Road shop, was consumed by fire, destroying nearly everything, Mr. Fiske being unable to save scarcely anything.

"This evening about four o'clock, the warehouse at the junction of Alabama street with the Macon & Western Railroad, was discovered to be on fire. It was but a few seconds before the flames spread to the residence of Mr. P. J. Immel, and the large wooden house and the adjoining was soon enveloped in flames. Here the fire was checked by the gallant firemen from spreading in the direction of Whitehall street. One house near the railroad engine house was consumed. It is impossible to calculate the loss at the present time. The shells were flying thick and fast around the burning buildings, but the firemen stood to their posts without flinching. Too much praise cannot be bestowed upon the Atlanta firemen.

"The Yankees have rained shell into the city for the last 24 hours, but I have not heard of any casualties.

"There is no change in the position of the army so far as I have been able to learn since my last letter."

Contributing to the combustible quality of Atlanta was a new menace—quantities of tobacco and cotton stored in attics and back parlors as well as warehouses. Almost everyone had begun irrational hoarding of these commodities, even though they knew such stocks would be valueless if Atlanta fell.

The W. & A. Locomotive, *Swiftsure,* was damaged by a shell while in its shed.

A lady, identified only as Mrs. Cook, was killed as she walked along Marietta Street in the early morning. Another pedestrian, also a woman, was wounded by shell fragments on Peachtree Street.

The flood of rumors that were started as a backwash of the shelling were, not that the city was about to fall, but that Sherman was falling back, while proposing a six-day armistice.

Taylor Beatty received news of the fall of Fort Morgan at Mobile, and it made him very angry. Not even the heavy rain shower which developed later could assuage his anger. He heard rumors of another raid aimed at the Macon railroad, and was inclined to give it credence.

Before noon General Howard informed Sherman that "a fire seems to be raging in Atlanta, direction 10 degrees south of east from my tree. Can see heated air rising in dense columns; seems to be spreading; town is filled with smoke. I have directed my heavy guns to fire on the town."

At 3:30 P.M. he communicated again: "Fire reported spreading in Atlanta." And at 4:00 P.M.: "It broke out in rear of large block. Eighteen box and one passenger cars arrived, empty."

Carrie Berry was frightened, in fact had been "fritened twice today by fire. I have ben wanting to go home all day to get some grapes but it has ben too dangerous."

She went back to chewing her sweet gum and knitting. Zuie was better. Carrie did not need to watch her so carefully.

At 6:00 P.M., Howard passed on a signal report to Sherman: "a train of eight freight cars, loaded with boxes, bundles of goods and other articles, just left Atlanta; about 40 men on the train. The fire is still burning and spreading."

General Sherman, returning at 7:15 P.M. from a horseback inspection of the Chattahoochee pontoon bridge "to see in person that it could be properly defended by the single corps proposed to be left there for that purpose," wired General Halleck in Washington:

"Heavy fires in Atlanta all day, caused by our artillery. I will be all ready, and will commence the movement around Atlanta by the south, tomorrow night, and for some time you will hear little of us. I will keep open a courier line back to the Chattahoochee bridge, by way of Sandtown. The Twentieth Corps will hold the railroad bridge, and I will move with the balance of the army, provisioned for twenty days."

AUGUST 25

◼ *Southern Press Association*

"*Atlanta*—For some cause the Yankee batteries are silent this morning. Last night, a shell struck the Presbyterian Church, on Marietta street, and exploded in the basement, where a number of citizens had sought shelter.

"A fragment of shell cut off the arm of a citizen lying in bed in the basement. No other casualties reported."

◼ *Columbus Times* (Georgia)

"On Wednesday night a large, 42-pound shell entered the Presbyterian Church on Marietta street and after passing through the pulpit exploded in the basement of Sunday School room. Several families living in the vicinity, having taken refuge there, were more or less stunned and injured by the explosion, and one man had his right arm taken off.

"The scene in the room was frightful. It was after midnight and all the inmates were sleeping peacefully, perfectly confident of security. Mothers caught up their children hurriedly, rushed frantically into the streets, screaming, though without any definite purpose in view, save that of escaping for the time from the scene which struck terror into their souls—and there and upon the open streets, they stood crouching with their little families clinging around them, and knowing not where to fly for safety. Shell after shell in rapid succession came screaming through the air, and as the light of each terrible explosion —like lightning flashes—quivered over them, the figure of one palefaced mother could be described, with bare outstretched arms, vainly hoping to shield her little child from the falling fragments. Oh! The heartless cruelty of the foe! Oh! The mighty depths of a mother's love!

"Assistance came at last, however, and the panic-stricken women and children were huddled off into the bombproofs of kind neighbors in more secure localities and the wounded properly cared for."

■ *Richmond Sentinel*

"Wheeler is at work on the enemy's communications, and Sherman is becoming uneasy before Atlanta. An officer who has just arrived from Atlanta gives a cheerful account of affairs at that point . . . our commander there no more intends to give up Atlanta and no more doubts his ability to hold it, than Gen. Lee does as to Richmond. . . .

"Gentlemen from Atlanta state that it is rumored that Sherman is fortifying along the Powder Spring road. If the report is true, it is evident that he intends to fall back beyond the Chattahoochee and hold the position until reinforcements arrive; or he intends to fall back through the lower route to Huntsville, Ala. If he retreats he can go by no other route as Wheeler holds the one to Chattanooga. Besides he cannot get subsistence by any other. And even if he succeeds in forcing his way by this he will be unable to collect from the surrounding country over half or quarter rations."

■ *The New York Times*

"Life in the trenches is growing monotonous. The men are getting rest from the fatigue of the active three months' campaign, and yet it is not rest that they need, for there is a constant state of expectancy, which is tiresome to the mind and, through sympathy, prevents the thorough recuperation of the physical energies so much needed. . . .

"The weather is exceedingly warm by day, but the nights refreshingly cool. Our sunsets are glorious, and would do for the representation of an Italian sky. The moon, now full, looks softly down through the rising mist, and rests with a pale light upon the forms of the brave heroes who, in sleep, forget grim-visaged war, yet remember in dreams the joys of the past. Sleep, coffee and hard bread are the soldier's main resources. He can dispense with anything else.

"This quiet cannot continue long. Sherman's energetic brain will bring forth something shortly, and then you will have an-

other report to add to the already too long list of bloody battles, for it seems probable that our next real engagement will
be severe."

It had been another bad night. The kerosene refinery burned
down, sending oily, noxious smoke over the city. The yellow-
red glare cast weird shadows for several hours after midnight.
A single shell, rumor had it, killed six ladies in one room of a
house on Peachtree Street.

Yet, an underlying normalcy persisted, the brassy music
from regimental bands still blared through the background
staccato of bursting shells and jangling fire bells, and, in the
soft moonlight, lovers dared walk hand-in-hand as far as the
city's defences.

There had been other quiet mornings. But the stillness this
hot Thursday—the stillness after the interminable banging of
the shells—seemed a presentiment. Whether it was of sudden
peace, or of worse punishment to come, none could say.

Had the Federals "skedaddled," Atlantans asked one another? The word was "Yankee talk." Many citizens crawled out
of their "shebangs," another Northern term which meant cellar, bombproof, hole in the hillside, any refuge.

Mrs. Berry believed some sort of lull had arrived. She de-
cided it was safe to send little Carrie over to check on her
"Aunt" Healey, whose husband was Maxwell Berry's partner.
"We had not heard from her in so long."

So Carrie put down her knitting, replenished her supply of
sweet gum, and started out from her cellar. She blinked at the
unaccustomed brilliance, then hurried down Alabama Street,
surprised that so many buildings remained standing after all
the shelling. She was happy to find her own home was where
she had left it. The pony grazed in the back yard, but the chickens were gone.

Atlanta had survived, but Carrie could see that it was a different Atlanta. Everything was dirty, worn, the people looked
at her out of deep, tired eyes; the air smelled stale and heavy
with the vague odors of ruin and neglect.

Joe Semmes, like many soldiers, North and South, was beginning to think of fall and the cool winds of winter that would follow the last dry leaves from the trees.

"Your last two letters," he wrote "Eo," "of August 12th and 16th, reached me yesterday together. I hasten to let you know that I really am in want of nothing but two good woollen or mixed cotton and wool overshirts, with pockets, like those you made for me of moreno. The moreno are too light for army use except for dress occasions, and the only ones I now have are ragged. I do not wear collars at all and have sufficient handkerchiefs.

"I have not seen Warfield for three weeks, though I hear from him every few days; he is very hard at work all the time. He really is shabby, but I believe has his clothes somewhere in the rear. I think at Mr. Knox.

"For the last 48 hours the enemy has shelled us terribly, tearing our houses, burning some and wounding a number of persons, chiefly citizens. Yesterday five of our commissary employes were wounded. The day before a fine young man from Manin, Ala., dined with us, and two hours after dinner his leg was amputated on the same table we dined from. This morning the enemy are quiet and our guns are noisy. The surgeon of the Post Hospital informed me he had performed 107 amputations on men, women and children since the enemy commenced shelling the city, all citizens. His account of the soldiers is separate and the number not as great of course as all the troops are at the lines 1½ miles outside of the city.

"Brad dined here yesterday, this morning his brigade started after another raiding force of the enemy, which is said to be en route for Andersonville to liberate the Yankee prisoners. Don't be surprised to hear in 10 days that we are advancing again, even if you should first hear that we have retreated. We are quite well. . . .

"Make Ben all that brandy he can carry. You did not say a word about the candles. I have asked now at least twenty times."

Showers pattered into the city dust in the afternoon. They caused mud and chocolate-covered puddles, but did not cool the air, which remained sultry. The utter hopelessness of life in the besieged, battered city was seemingly intensified by the rain.

Carrie spent the afternoon with Aunt Healey who proved well, despite Mrs. Berry's misgivings. She had her own bomb-proof in the back yard, and was tolerably comfortable and happy in it.

"I stayed till after dinner," wrote Carrie. "We had such a nice dinner and so many nice grapes, but best of all we had no shells all day."

It was almost dark when the little girl returned to the cellar on Alabama Street and reported on Aunt Healey. Zuie was asleep, but there was, as always, accumulated knitting. Carrie hurried to start her needles going before the low-burning candle flickered out for the night.

There was activity in the Federal lines, little of which, however, had been detected by Hood's defenders.

"The army," wrote Fenwick Hedley, Adjutant of the 32nd Illinois Infantry, "commenced a movement against the West Point Railroad. All artillery and wagon trains that could be moved without attracting attention were sent early in the day in the direction to be pursued; and, as soon as night fell, the guns from the front followed the muffled wheels. A slight skirmish line was left in the pits, with instructions to keep up sufficient firing to induce the belief that the ordinary force was present, and all other troops silently left their works."

Colonel Charles D. Kerr, of the 16th Illinois Cavalry, reported the "skedaddle" in much the same way. "It was a dark, sultry night . . . (we) packed up dog-tents and equipment and to keep up appearances, silently stole away."

AUGUST 26

Friday morning was clear and pleasant. The showers of yesterday had brought back fragrance to the drying, scorched foliage in the hills and valleys between Atlanta and Decatur. The honeysuckle smelled sweet along the Chattahoochee and the South Fork of Peachtree Creek where it wound languidly past Decatur.

A woman, known as the widow Grober, living on the fringe of the little town, not far from the creek, was up early, thinking she would gather an apronful of blackberries. She assumed her transients of several weeks, Federal soldiers, would grant permission.

But the widow had progressed hardly ten feet beyond her well when it became apparent that the tents had vanished. Even though the bivouacked troops had been unwelcome guests, a strange feeling of abandonment gripped her.

"Hello!" she cried out, "hello!"

Her only answer was the clucking-scratching of the remaining hens as they ruffled their feathers in the barnyard dust.

"Hello!"

From a second-story window her black girl poked her head out. Then she stared in disbelief.

In the center of Decatur, Mary Ann Harris Gay was also awake early. She would not go blackberrying, but rather, by habit to the post office. There was that Nth chance that the occupying army would pass a letter, addressed to herself or to her mother.

Mary, unlike Widow Grober, did not find all the tents gone. But those which remained "seemed to be vacant."

When she hastened around her grounds, lifting her skirts above the late August jungle of thistles, she noticed that "not a blue coat was to be seen. What could it mean? Had they given up the contest and ignominiously fled!

"The booming of cannon in direction of Atlanta seemed to be 'decreasing.'"

Then the thought occurred to her that the Federal wagon train had merely gone foraging, protected by the heavy escort of cavalry which had camped on the Gay lawns. She reflected how some of those very troops had solemnly explained they had to guard supplies against the "dashing, sanguinary attacks of the 'Rebels.'"

Decatur, she realized, had no troops this morning, Confederate or Federal. She wasn't sure whether that was a condition to be desired.

In Atlanta, the citizens were convinced that the cessation of shelling yesterday had been a true harbinger of what unexpectedly seemed like peace. They, and the defending Confederate soldiers alike, crept at first cautiously towards the Union works, then more boldly. Their ears still rang with the melody of the sharpshooters.

But it was true, the skirmish line was gone. So were the entrenched regiments behind. Only the crows and rats and occasional scavenging foxes were left. General Sam French quit his secure works and tramped over the scarred earth that once had been no-man's land. He was nauseated by what he saw.

"I found everything in their works horribly filthy and alive with 'dog flies' to such an extent that our horses could not be managed. The clothing, new and old, was covered with vermin. My servant boys carried some jackets home that had to be buried. Their line of works was very strong. I found the brick furnace where they made 'shot red hot,' to fire day and night at intervals to burn the city. At first little 'niggers' got their fingers burned picking them up to sell to the ordnance department. . . . From Decatur all the way around to the Turner's Ferry Road the enemy has moved to our left. . . . There are no flies or vermin in our camp—strange but true."

Atlanta, dirty, battered, and deathly tired, was the scene of spontaneous rejoicing by midmorning. The correspondent for the *Confederate Union* of Milledgeville, reported: "Men, women and children thronged the hitherto silent thoroughfares and exchanged congratulations on the blessed change in the situation. Cellars gave up their occupants; basement stories were evacuated; holes in the Rail Road cuts were suddenly left alone in their glory, and Atlanta was herself once more.

"One individual, who had been burrowing in the earth for six weeks poked his head out of a hole in the ground and with consternation still depicted on his countenance, inquired 'are they all gone?' "

Many Georgians were less repelled by the Union trenches than was Sam French. They filled their pockets with a bizarre assortment of souvenirs—from bent forks to cartridge casings—before they picked their way homeward.

Capt. Tom Key, the Battery Commander and newspaper publisher who had attended church in Atlanta every Sunday, thought the "significant thing is that for twenty-four hours they have ceased throwing shells into the city." After an inspection of the empty trenches, where "chairs and ammunition boxes as well as other kinds where strewn so thickly that it was difficult to ride through them," he became certain "the scales have turned in favor of the South, and the Abolitionists are moving to the rear toward their own homes."

He was disposed to postscript his on-the-spot diary entry, "thank Heaven for this and for the gallant soldiery who so nobly have fought against overpowering numbers."

Maxwell Berry, however, was more cautious. Cousin Henry Beatty looked into the cellar on Alabama Street and told the family that they "need not fear the shells any more."

As Carrie understood it, "the Yankees left there brest works and he hoped they were on the way back to Tennessee. We have had such a delightful day. We all wanted to move today, but we will wait till tomorrow and see if the Yankees have gone."

Mollie Smith, accompanied by friends, walked out the crowded, rutted Marietta Road. At a spot almost three miles from the center of the city they came upon the site of a large Federal encampment, "and saw where strips of plank had been nailed, ladder-fashion, in the tall pine trees, from which, with the aid of a spy glass, the men could see all over city."

Mollie returned and wrote a letter to her brother, fighting in the Army of Northern Virginia, "I told him I had been hunting Yanks but nary a Yank did I find. . . ."

At noon, Confederate scouts galloped into Decatur, "then suddenly and mysteriously left." But Mary Gay was thrilled at the sight, just the same—"what joy their presence gave us!"

In Vineville, Georgia, a patient, "H. L. W. C.," at Fair Ground Hospital No. 1 finished the final stanza of a long poem, which he had titled *No News From The Front,*

No news from the front, no thought of the brave.
Who are battling with freeman's might;
Baring their breasts to the leaden storm,
While struggling for freedom's right.
All's quiet in front; still they say,
Though we are losing them one by one—
And we only give a sigh of regret,
When we think of them that are gone.

By evening Confederate troops manned most of the abandoned Union works, as jubilant Southern newspapermen filed their stories. The *Southern Press Association* correspondent figured "Sherman was not progressing to his satisfaction," and therefore his "backstep is a confession of failure."

Members of his army, however, were not advised of such admissions. Graham, for example, only knew he was marching night and day westward, through showers and sunshine until his feet ached.

"It is supposed," he observed, "we are going to cut the Macon road."

Fenwick Hedley, the Adjutant from Illinois, completed a march of nineteen miles and was glad to have coffee and rest, "which was sorely needed."

Rufus Mead, the surveyor from Redding, Connecticut, had gone in a different direction. "I guess the mail was about as liberal to me as any one so I'll patronize it by sending one back," he wrote from a "wagon camp one mile north of R. R. bridge on the Chattahoochee River." "The shirts, slippers, and envelopes came safely and I have the pleasure of wearing the slippers. . . . The shirts I judge are large enough and good enough. I only want them to last till spring for I think I'll wear cotton or linen next summer if I stay out here. I cant see why it needed so many stamps on the shirts as I though postage was only ½ cent an ounce, or am I wrong about it.

"Sophia's letter, also one with the Photograph of 3 of my acquaintances came on Wednesday, all very welcome That Photo I think first rate, you cant imagine how I prize it, as I do all of mine. Often I get them out & have a little confab with them. It helps beguile many a weary hour. I can imagine just what a time you had collecting taxes, eating dinner on the camp ground &c. I was sorry to hear Emma is so feeble. I fear she never will be strong.

"You will see by the heading that we have moved. I dont know the why's & wherefore's about it, only I know on Wednesday we got orders to move the train at 3 P.M. got off a little after 4 and about 10 P.M. parked our train on this the north side of the river. Yesterday we moved a little to get a good spot, handy to water &c &c and here we are now. The Brigade are over the river yet and have built good strong works over there. Only our Corps fell back and rumor says we are to hold the bridges on this river while the rest of the army try to get around on the other side of Atlanta and take it if possible, if not to fall back here too and have their communication open to recross the river.

"I can't vouch for the truth of this report but give it to you as I get it. As events transpire I'll try and let you know of it. Genl. Slocum is here but not taken command yet, I presume he will soon now. The whole army has supplies with them for 15 days and I think something decisive will be done in that time.

"If successful, Atlanta must be ours if we are defeated, another retreat I don't wish to think of the latter but it may be our fate.

"Our 40 days' rain ended the second day and it is getting quite dusty again now and very warm. I have my 'fly' up in a nice cool, shady spot and today issued for 3 days so I guess I can stand it if it is hot. The flies haven't found us here yet and I hope they will remain with the Johnnies. I don't think of any wants not this time, in fact, I guess you'll think I am running in debt about enough already? Never mind, Uncle Sam owes me over 220 dollars now and it keeps gaining 22 every month."

AUGUST 27

An uneasiness returned to Atlanta during the night as gunfire rumbled audibly from the west. However, in the morning it was explained that Hood's artillery was barking adieu to the last of Sherman's withdrawing Army—or in the direction in which Confederate gunners assumed they were withdrawing.

Captain Tom Key kept his own battery working hotly. By dawn, the stentorian qualities of the barrage had inspired him to comment: "These loud-mouthed gun wagons made the night hideous with their bass voices, and no doubt caused many bluecoats to fall in the cold embrace of death."

Then, strengthened by breakfast, meager as rations were becoming, he added, "the ladies of Atlanta look relieved since those frightful shells no longer come singing their songs of death and consuming beautiful residences into ashes. The women have proven themselves to be heroines under the bombardment."

Colonel Taylor Beatty, General Hardee's military lawyer from Thibodaux, Louisiana, returned to his tent after an inspection of Atlanta's perimeters. He found that "the enemy has withdrawn from the front of all but Hardee's Corps. They abandoned a good deal of forage—sutler's stores, etc. also some ammunition and two guns (spiked). We have picked up several hundred prisoners. Spent the day in town."

It was a cool Saturday. The Berrys moved back to Fairlee Street. The grandfather's clock still ticked in the hall, though dust had settled sepulchrally on the furniture and on every flat surface in the little frame house. In back, the rain barrel at the corner of the smokehouse was full. Mrs. Berry would use the water to replenish the stock of lye. The barrel of wood ashes, also employed in the process, stood in the opposite corner. No one had pilfered its precious contents. Lye, in fact any kind of soap, was as vital in wartime as food or ammunition.

The sights and smells of home, particularly the pungence of

the smokehouse, made Carrie "feel so glad." It was also a relief to "have no shells around us."

Throughout Atlanta, there was a new lightness of spirit. Other households followed suit of the Berrys to start cleaning-up. Even those structures which hadn't been hit were shabby and dirty from the long weeks of mole-like existence of their inhabitants.

It was said that former residents of Atlanta, together with ladies in a festive mood, were arriving on the afternoon train from Macon to aid in celebrating what was telegraphed over the South as a "victory."

S. P. Richards, who had known disappointment as well as toil in his life, was not so ready for exultation. The English-born bookseller had deep-seated doubts that Sherman had gone permanently.

"The first three secular days of this week," he wrote, "the shells rained heavily upon our city and on Wednesday set three separate houses on fire, as is supposed, and in one of these fires our two Printing Presses, stored in McDaniels warehouse, were burnt. We have never yet had them in use but may need them 'ere long. On Thursday the shelling ceased altogether and it was rumored that the enemy was retreating and it is now known that they have destroyed their camps around the city and are going *some*where but what is their design it is hard to tell. I fear that we have not yet got rid of them finally, but that they have some other plan in view to molest and injure us. But in the meantime we can rest in security for a while. safe from shells. We began to remove our stock of books from the store to the house this morning, but when we had brought up two loads of drawers, we concluded to stop and await further developments. I had our *pit* dug three feet deeper this week and a barricade in front of boxes filled with dirt. A letter from Harriet gives us a kind invitation to go there and live with them if we do not wish to stay in Atlanta."

His foreign ancestory and his devout and practical nature were among the many elements in the serious-minded choir-singer's makeup that caused him to wish the war would end. Peace and normalcy seemed the most important objectives.

Meanwhile, the Union forces kept marching. Graham judged that he was traveling south.

"Our army," he wrote, "has left Atlanta on the north side. We are going to cut the railroad. Encamped towards night within 5 miles of the railroad. Good marching on a fine day, pleasant and cool night."

General Sherman himself noted that the Confederate batteries, like those commanded by Tom Key, had been used "pretty freely" against his last units as they pulled out of old positions.

"But I think he (Hood) supposed we were going to retreat altogether. An artillery-shot, fired at random, killed one man and wounded another."

AUGUST 28

Three days of peace continued to bolster Atlanta's sense of confidence, if not well-being. The city was half-ruined; it appeared nothing could be done to restore the damage for years to come. Food was scarce and prices were exorbitant. There were few men left in most families, many had gone forever. But the shelling, the terrible, depleting shelling had stopped.

General Hood had stumped nervously about the porch of his headquarters on Whitehall Street. He, for one, was aware that Sherman was indulging in no capricious retreat. Finally, he wrote Secretary of War Seddon in Richmond of the new situation:

"The enemy have changed their entire position—the left of their line resting near the Chattahoochee, about Sandtown and their right extending to a point opposite and near the West Point railroad, between East Point and Fairburn. They hold all the crossings on the Chattahoochee, but not with a continued line."

He noted for his own records, "Sherman had now been over one month continuously moving toward our left and thoroughly fortifying, step by step, as he advanced in the direction of the Macon railroad. On the night of the 25th he withdrew from our immediate front; his works, which at an early hour the following morning we discovered to be abandoned, were occupied an hour later by the corps of Stewart and Lee.

"On the 27th, Gen. G. W. Smith's division was ordered to occupy the position of Stevenson's division which, together with Maury's command, was held in reserve."

General Sam French continued to survey the ground recently held by Sherman's army. "To give you an idea of the terrible musketry fire, in an open field between their picket line and mine one brigade picked up about 5,000 pounds of lead balls that had been fired on the lines. The ground was literally covered with them—oxidized white like hailstones. Trees three and four inches in diameter in front of my lines were cut down by balls."

It was a warm Sunday and to Carrie Berry "everything seemed so quiet this morning." The world that she had known had changed, even though the shelling had stopped, and perhaps it would never again be the same.

"I wish the people would come back so we could have Church School," she wrote. "Mr. —— came in this morning and brought some shells which Cousin Henry sent us. He got them from the Yankees. Cousin Eddy came in this morning to tell us goodby. We feel sorry he was going to move so far. We all ways love to see him and Cousin Henry."

S. P. Richards was forced into involuntary defense work to the same degree as when the shells were falling. "I am on duty today and it is *hard* duty too," he complained. "We have been all the morning unloading cars of Army wagons and putting them together. At two o'clock I have to go on again for the rest of the day. O when shall we be free again and at liberty to spend our Sabbaths at least, in a manner more consonant with our feelings and habits. A shell has entered the roof of our church and passed through the back of the seat in the choir close to Sallie's usual place, and finally lodged somewhere in the front wall without exploding. Everything is quiet enough now, we hear no cannon or musketry."

Captain Tom Key, with no Union troops to shoot at, put on his "new uniform" and planned to go to church. However, when he learned of a lieutenant who was setting out this morning for Mississippi, he first rode to the extremity of his line with letters for the officer to take to his wife and "dear friends."

He warned the officer of his own difficulties in crossing the wide, swift river last year and his narrow escapes from the Yankees. Then, with a friend, Thomas Lambert, he continued toward church once more.

"As Mr. Lambert and I rode toward the church, our theme was home, peace, and what we hoped to do and enjoy when we should be allowed to live again in peace and independence. The minister should have been proud of his congregation, for it was the largest that had turned out in the three succeeding Sabbaths. This, however, arose from the fact that the Yankee batteries were not making the holy day awful by their horrible shells bursting in the streets, passing through houses, and singing their hissing tunes of death around the temples dedicated to the living God. The man in the pulpit delivered his lecture with force and emphasis, and it was received with marked attention.

"After leaving church I called at Major R. Lonford's where I met with Judge Wright of Tennessee and Mr. Norton of New Orleans with whom I spent several hours in interesting conversation. One question of much moment was discussed: whether, if there should be peace, there would be a treaty between the United and Confederate States, pledging both parties to protect and preserve the property of individuals living under the different governments who in the war had opposed those governments. This conversation arose from a threat by a certain individual that when he returned to Tennessee or Arkansas he, with like minded individuals, would drive from the soil those who had opposed the Confederates in their struggle for independence, and perhaps might deal more harshly with them than take their property. Judge Wright thought that this government would, after peace, be compelled to adopt the common law of England."

Col. Taylor Beatty was more concerned with inspecting than church-going. Accompanied by his friend, Major Douglas West, he continued his tour of the abandoned works. He discovered "the Yankees have four or five lines," though he did not consider any "as good as our *one*." On the other hand, he found the fortifications difficult to assess since they were "all very strong."

"I had no idea of the strength of our position, protected as it is by a lattis, etc.," he added. "The flies were so bad we could not go very far. Returned by way of Marietta Street. Every house is struck, more damage done there than elsewhere. The house where Mrs. Cohen lived is hit—the parlor chimney being almost knocked down.

"Dined with West. Introduced to Lt. Col. Stevens. Have news from Wheeler dated 19th. He says no trains had passed for a week or more, that he had burned the stores at Dalton and destroyed the road to Cleveland, as he found Sherman got his forage from E. Tennessee."

Federal forces were now encountering the first units of scattered Confederates guarding the southern approaches to Atlanta. Astride the narrow ribbon of rails which stretched across the scrubby flatlands to West Point were a scattering of soldiers. They seemed tired and half-hearted, according to Fenwick Hedley, who had marched eight miles to a whistle stop known as Red Oak Station.

"They were driven without great effort," he continued, "and a footing on the railroad gained, when the army went to work with a will to destroy it, burning the ties and twisting the rails to such an extent as to utterly preclude the possibility of their use again."

The increasingly confident Union troops then drained the locomotive water tank near the railroad station and set fire to it, as if in final degradation. With its filler arm stretching lower and lower over the already scorched roadbed as the flames mounted, the tank resembled a stricken, incinerated elephant.

The men marched on.

Graham had arrived on the rail line to Macon, a few miles east of Hedley's men at Red Oak. "The first division of our regiment was immediately put on the skirmish line," he wrote. "A few shots were fired at us but we had it quiet while a fort was built on the side of the railroad and the road destroyed."

Kate Cumming, the Scottish nurse, was at last well settled in the Foard hospital in Americus. Supplies were filtering in anew and this morning she had just distributed copies of the booklet, written by an acquaintance, the Reverend Dr. Charles Todd Quintard, "Balm for the Weary and Wounded."

She decided she was going to "like the place very well . . . I never had such a nice kitchen."

Dr. Welford followed her from Newnan. He assured her that comrades like Fannie Beers were working hard and in good health.

"He brought word that our patients were doing pretty well; a few of them had gone to their long homes," she wrote. "He had been sent back as it was a false alarm, and there are many wounded there yet.

"Dr. Reese has returned from the front. He is very sanguine of our success; says that the Yankee pickets exchange tobacco and newspapers with ours, and have told them that Sherman is nearly exhausted, and will have to give up soon.

"I should like to believe this, but am afraid it is too good to be true. I see by the papers that we have had a good deal of fighting in Missouri and Kentucky.

"Lt. Haskill of Garrety's battery was killed on the 7th. He is much regretted. We have had quite a number of sick. The ladies of the place have called on us, and seem very anxious to assist us. I am very glad of this, as we have little or nothing of our own to give the patients. The paymaster has not been around lately; so Dr. H., like all here, is entirely out of funds.

"This is said to be a very wealthy place; and were we to judge from the carriages and fine horses we see, I should think the impressing officer had not been down this way for some time."

AUGUST 29

Life was so much more normal in Atlanta that children were thinking about school. September was but two days off, a month evocative of the sights, sounds, and even the smells of classrooms.

Carrie Berry decided to hunt for her teacher, Miss Fannie Holmes. "Zuie and I went over to Aunt Hattie Smith's this morning to see if we could find our school teacher," she wrote. "We stayed all day with her. We had a very pleasant time playing with Ellen."

She did not locate Miss Holmes, although Aunt Hattie promised to try to pass word to her. Aunt Hattie had a lurking suspicion that the teacher had moved to Macon for the duration. Macon remained, somehow, the embodiment of peace and security.

With children once more moving freely in the streets and their mothers, market baskets slung from elbows, on the prowl for groceries, Atlanta presented an unaccustomed aspect. The women still had to step across or walk around shell holes and dirty, dusty soldiers continued to filter through like an addled colony of ants.

Correspondents, in the sum total of all the confusion, half-truths, and contradictions, became increasingly baffled. There were no communiques from Hood. He had taken refuge within the recesses of his handsome headquarters, and only the muzzles of his guards' rifles answered the persistent caller.

This Monday the *Southern Press Association* reporter, after a night of futile sorting through a hodge-podge of leads, finally filed his bulletin on the wires to Richmond, which, with further editing and interpretation, appeared: "We have no late official news . . . but there was a rumor last evening that a despatch had been received to the effect that Sherman was retreating and that Gen. Hood was pressing him."

He had sent it in desperation. And now, exhausted, he went to bed in the Trout House—even as editors, like those on the

Sentinel in Richmond, were seizing his words and taking hope from them, as a cripple would from a convincing charlatan.

Headlines were set in the composing rooms of Southern papers carrying the earlier reports of Sherman's withdrawal. Now, at last, the tide *had* turned. Sherman was whipped.

"Reports from Washington" printed in the same newspapers, substantiated such thinking. "Lincoln," ran the story, "has under consideration propositions for an armistice with the enemy, as a political maneuvre."

On the other hand, little confidence or optimism in the future of Atlanta was manifested by the city's business or professional men. Dr. James W. Price, his Atlanta offices closed and boarded, had already moved to Zeilin's drugstore on Cherry Street, in Macon, opposite the telegraph office. At night, his frank advertisement in the *Intelligencer* continued, he could be found nearby at "Mrs. C. C. Taylor's." N. Weed, a wholesaler of Macon, had 60 boxes of "cheap tobacco" for sale.

From the Johnston Hospital, in Forsyth, an attendant had a delayed seizure of conscience. He bought a two-inch ad in the *Intelligencer* to announce he had "taken by mistake," about July 12, a fully accoutred cavalry horse, complete with haversack and documents, which had been tethered in front of the Atlanta Hotel. He wanted, now, to return the animal to its original owner.

A wave of nervous humor was sweeping the South. A man, went one joke, was asked if his horse were timid. "Not at all," was the retort. "He frequently spends the whole night by himself in the stable."

But Brigadier Gen. Iverson was indulging in no horse laughs. Stragglers were an ever-increasing problem. He advertised that Griffin was a "cavalry rendezvous," and that those who failed to rejoin their commands, "stragglers and depredators," would surely be brought "to justice."

Colonel Beatty still had not satisfied himself with the sight of the abandoned Federal trenches. They held a compelling, almost morbid fascination for him.

"Rode out," he noted this Monday, "with Capt. Sale to see the enemy's works on Peachtree street and road. About same as elsewhere. The flies so bad could not go far. The houses on Peachtree are not much injured, very few being hit at all . . . a rumor that enemy have retreated, I can't believe it, but hope it is so. Very hot."

The Federal forces were marching hard, certain that God was with *them*. Hedley had pushed on twelve miles further until, with his 32d Illinois Infantry, he came upon more Confederate forces. They lined the banks of the Flint River near Jonesboro, their bayonets glinting in the rays of the afternoon sun.

This group had more spirit than the guards encountered at Red Oak Station the day before, and "they assaulted the Union lines, evidently hoping to catch them before they could get well straightened out for action, but were repulsed."

Sergeant Graham found the day bright and pleasant. He was encamped on the Macon Railroad. He admired the fortifications the engineers were putting up and was convinced that "we can make a good fight here."

General Sherman had arrived at the Red Oak Station to personally check on the wrecking of the railroad late the night before. The job, he ordered, had to be "thoroughly" accomplished.

"The track was heaved up in sections the length of a regiment, then separated rail by rail," he recorded; "bonfires were made of the ties and of fence-rails on which the rails were heated, carried to trees or telegraph-poles, wrapped around and left to cool. Such rails could not be used again; and, to be still more certain, we filled up many deep cuts with trees, brush and earth, and commingled them with loaded shells, so arranged that they would explode on an attempt to haul out the bushes. The explosion of one such shell would have demoralized a gang of negroes and thus would have prevented even the attempt to clear the road."

Old Tecumseh, especially unshaven and roughly attired now, was altogether satisfied with the operations. His mammoth Military Division of the Mississippi was shaping its great weight closer and closer about Atlanta. Before lighting his night's final cigar, or taking one last swig from his saddle-bag whiskey bottle, he confided to General Thomas: "I have Atlanta as certainly as if it were in my hand."

AUGUST 30

Every person in Major General Frank P. Blair's 17th U. S. Army Corps either helped rip up and burn the rails, or swelled the gallery of intrigued spectators. Among the audience near Red Oak Station was a thirty-eight-year-old physician attached to the 17th, Dr. James Comfort Patten of Princeton, Indiana.

Dr. Patten had received his commission as Assistant Surgeon but four months ago. He had then spent a month wandering the Midwest and the South until he finally found his regiment, the 58th Indiana Volunteers, at Ringgold, Georgia.

Patten, who assisted the Senior Surgeon, Dr. Samuel E. Holtzman, became a good-natured addition to the regiment, willingly launching boats for fording streams, clearing ground, and pitching tents in addition to his medical duties. Lending a hand to the men who were twisting heated rails was just another chore to the Indiana doctor.

"Dr. Holtzman and I carried some straight (fence) rails," he wrote today, "and made our beds on them and then plucked a Georgia Goose, as gathering pine brush is called here, and slept well . . . next morning all hands went to work to straighten up the camp, thinking probably we might stay for some time. While in the midst of this job, the order came to strike tents and fall in, which was done at once. Those who had not got their share of the work done could now laugh at those who had. We now moved on and camped near night on the Montgomery r.r. Our troops spent the next day, the 30th tearing up the road and burning the ties and bending the rails across the heaps of burning ties and as they became red hot in the middle the weight of the ends would bend them so as to be unfit for use."

The Federal army was burning so many ties, along different sections of Atlanta's southbound and westbound railroad tracks that a smoky haze settled over the countryside. It obscured the sky with its dense, woody pungence like a thick fog or mist. These fires were augmented by flaming fence rails—for roasting the long, ripe, golden ears of corn.

Sherman, who had paused with General Thomas for lunch beside Shoal-Creek Church, remarked on the heat that day—a day "otherwise very pleasant."

"The infantry column had halted in the road," he observed, "stacked their arms, and the men were scattered about—some lying in the shade of the trees, and others were bringing corn stalks from a large cornfield across the road to feed our horses, while still others had arms full of the roasting-ears, in their prime. Hundreds of fires were soon started with the fence-rails, and the men were busy roasting the ears. Thomas and I were walking up and down the road which led to the church, discussing the chances of the movement, which he thought were extra-hazardous, and our path carried us by a fire at which a soldier was roasting his corn. The fire was built artistically; the man was stripping ears of their husks, standing them in front of his fire, watching them carefully and turning each ear little by little, so as to roast it nicely. He was down on his knees intent on his business, paying little heed to the stately and serious deliberations of his leaders. . . .

"As we walked, we could hear Gen. Howard's guns at intervals, away off to our right front, but an ominous silence continued toward our left, where I was expecting at each moment to hear the sound of battle."

Meanwhile, Captain Tom Key rolled up his tent and left Atlanta along the Sandtown Road to the west. He waited temporarily near a spring "at Mrs. Connally's."

At 1:00 P.M., Hood's Chief of Staff, Shoup, telegraphed to Hardee, at East Point:

"Gen. Hood does not think the necessity will arise to send any more troops to Jonesboro today. Will send a map soon as one can be procured. Gen. Lee is instructed to move Patton Anderson's division near the railroad to assist you if need be. Please place yourself in communication with General Anderson."

At 2:00 P.M., he postscripted this message, at his commander's request, "Gen. Hood . . . does not think they will attack Jonesborough today."

But the longer he sat in his high-ceilinged frame house on Whitehall Street, mopped his brow against the afternoon's gathering humidity, and listened to the cricketing song of late August beyond the wide-open windows, the more worried Hood became. For one thing, he wanted to see Hardee, his veteran corps commander, who had once refused command of this very army.

At 3:20 P.M., he wired Hardee: "An engine will be at East Point for you at sunset. Please come to headquarters."

The dispatch reached Hardee at Rough and Ready, the tavern-refreshment stop near the railroad, before 4:00 P.M. It was handed to him by Colonel T. B. Roy, a member of his staff.

At this very time, a few miles north of Rough and Ready, Lizzie Perkerson, tall, slender twenty-seven-year-old daughter of Thomas Jefferson Perkerson, farmer and the first sheriff of Fulton County, was feeding a pony that had been given to her little brother Dannie. The animal was lame when a soldier left it at the farm a month before, and Lizzie felt responsible for its well-being. She was serious and methodical about most matters of daily life.

Aside from Dannie, the Perkerson home was a place of women —Lizzie's two sisters, Matilda ("Till") and Nan, in addition to her mother. Her brothers, both younger than she, Angus and Dempse, had been fighting for the Confederacy almost since the first day of Fort Sumter. Dempse, however, was temporarily home.

There was disquiet in the sultry air. Living so far on the fringes of Atlanta, Lizzie had never been under the shelling. She would not, therefore, be prey to false hopes when it ceased. But this afternoon, the troop movements across the dusty, dirt roads and fields carried a special foreboding.

When Dannie finally clambered onto the pony and rode in search of the two remaining cows (the rest of the herd had been sent south in compliance with official orders), cavalry units turned and entered the Perkerson yard. They were members of Brigadier General John T. Morgan's command.

"They had been on picket three days without drawing any rations," Lizzie wrote, "and just at night they drew some corn-meal and then they didn't have a thing to cook it in. And the last one of them wanted a little bread cooked. So Nan and I put out to the kitchen and got up every old skillet and oven that we could and let into cooking corn bread."

The exhausted, hungry cavalry fanned out across the corn-fields between Perkerson's farm and McCool's, farther down the road. Asserting the "Yankees" were on the prowl, they said that they were guarding Hood's flanks against a possible assault.

In Atlanta, however, the citizens were entirely ignorant of the situation. Women were obsessed with a fervor for cleaning and straightening their long-neglected households. Carrie Berry was greeting her school "marm," Miss Fannie Holmes, who had come to her house.

"I was so glad to see my old teacher once more," she confided to her diary. "I hope she will commence school. I am tired of staying home."

But all was not well elsewhere. Hood flashed another order to Hardee at 6:00 P.M.

"Gen. Armstrong telegraphs that there is a probability of the enemy striking the railroad tonight between Jonesborough and the left of our army. Please prevent it if possible."

But he was still ill at ease. At exactly 6:10 P.M., his telegrapher was tapping out the desperate entreaty to Hood's corps commander:

"Please come in tonight!"

A few minutes later Hood was advised that a Federal corps had crossed Flint River and was annihilating Brigadier General Joseph H. Lewis' infantry brigade. Hood wrote another dispatch.

"Hold your position at all hazards," he implored his General. "Help is ordered to you!"

All officers were being projected into action. Captain Key left Mrs. Connally's home and continued with Cleburne's division, "three miles to a position south of East Point and began temporary works to meet a flanking movement of the enemy."

"Some skirmishing," he continued, "occurred two miles from the line, but it was a feint while Sherman moved upon the railroad at Jonesboro. Three corps drove our cavalry within a mile of that place, as a result of which Gen. Hardee's corps was ordered to move for its defense."

Meanwhile, in Key's general area, Lizzie Perkerson and her sisters continued to bake corn bread at a furious clip. They were also trying to find a way to save their brother Dempse from capture. He had been fighting with the Georgia Militia around Atlanta, and he didn't know how to rejoin his unit.

At 8:30 P.M., in Marietta, J. C. Van Duzer of the Signal Corps telegraphed his commanding officer, Major Thomas T. Eckert, in Washington:

"No news from Sherman today. Slocum pushed reconnaissance within two miles of Atlanta, finding only cavalry and not much of that. He had only a brigade and moved slowly but will know by daylight whether enemy still occupies Atlanta or not."

Van Duzer, former commercial telegraph operator at Carlinville, Illinois, was sometimes referred to as "the only fighting officer of the Federal Telegraph Service." He had once been confined in the guard house by General Grant for his outspoken attitude in behalf of his service, but had more than exonerated himself by his bravery under fire at Chattanooga.

As they advanced through Georgia, Sherman had continually marveled at how Van Duzer managed to keep his telegraph tent functioning directly behind the commanding general's own headquarters.

Hood, meanwhile, roaring orders, had seemingly found a solution to the incipient catastrophe at Jonesboro. Hardee had but "to drive the enemy at all hazards" back into the Flint River. Hood intended to tell his General so when he arrived aboard the special locomotive.

AUGUST 31

Hood had barely seen Hardee off for the depot and the train
to Jonesboro when he dictated a dispatch to him, reiterating
what the two officers had just discussed:

"You must not fail to attack the enemy so soon as you can
get your troops up. I trust that God will give us victory!"

The time was 3:10 A.M., Wednesday, August 31, 1864.

Hood knew he would not sleep this early morning. As the
crisis mounted, he no longer knew when he would sleep again.

On the road to East Point, the Perkerson girls were still baking corn bread like overwound automatons. The kitchen, which
had been lit all the busy night by candles, brightened as dawn
poked into the eastern skies.

The horses of Morgan's cavalrymen whinnied at their tethers
in the yard. Their acrid, pungent odor filtered through the
kitchen, blanking out the sweeter smells of cornmeal. The soldiers would soon be on their way again.

Others had not slept that night. Mary Gay, at Decatur, had
heard distant cannon firing, interrupted by "occasional lulls."
"The suspense," she wrote, "became intolerable." Then, just
before dawn, "in the midst of this awful suspense, an apparition,
glorious and bright, appeared in our presence. It was my brother.
He had left Madison a few days before, where he had been allowed to spend a part of his furlough, instead of remaining at
the Augusta hospital, and where he had received the tender ministrations of his estimable cousin, Mrs. Tom Hillsman, and her
pretty young daughters, and the loving care of his sister Missouri, who was also at this time an inmate of her cousin's household. How I wished he could have remained there until restored
to health. One less patriotic and conscientious would have done
so. His mother's joy at meeting her beloved son, and under such
circumstances, was pathetic indeed, and I shall never forget the
effort she made to repress the tears and steady the voice, as she
sought to nerve him for the arduous and perilous duties before
him. Much of his conversation, though hurried, was regarding

his Mary, in Texas, and the dear little boy dropped down from heaven, whom he had never seen."

The bright beginnings of day were clouded over by 5:00 A.M. Sergeant Graham was "ready to march." Rain seemed imminent as he breakfasted at 6:00 A.M., remarking on "the sound of cannon heard in a northeast direction . . . at about 8 and 10 formed line of battle and put breastwork of rails."

Tom Key, "at day-dawn," was finally able to permit his men to rest briefly after an all-night march. They had reached "the designated position," bordering tiny Jonesboro. But the soldiers were too tired to care where they were. They slept where they fell, not even conscious of hunger. Even in deep slumber they reflexively clutched the rifles at their sides.

Key "ordered up (his) omnibus and ordnance train, but the courier neglected to deliver the message or could not find them."

Before long he realized that the Federals were already entrenched in strong rifle pits from which they began to fire "briskly." He roused his entire company with the idea of charging the Union lines, but "about 10 o'clock they attacked Gen. Lowrey's line and it was supposed that they would advance upon us; but it proved only a demonstration and Gen. Cleburne's division, supported by Cheatham's, moved out upon the enemy south of Jonesboro."

At 10:00 A.M., Shoup telegraphed to Hardee:

"Gen. Hood desires the men to go at the enemy with bayonets fixed, determined to drive everything they may come against."

Lizzie Perkerson let her ovens go cold at last. Morgan's horsemen thanked her and galloped off, taking her brother Dempse with them. Now, she thought, "there was nothing left for us but to get ready for the blue coats."

The clock had not struck ten in Jonesboro when fourteen-year-old Thomas Jefferson Vessel was loping in from Lovejoy's astride his small horse. He had left his father's farm, 3½ miles to the south, to fetch the mail, as was his custom. Everyone was aware that trouble was "brewing" in the neighborhood, but young Tom was sure that he could accomplish the round trip.

As he neared Jonesboro, he heard sporadic rifle shots. In the past months he had listened to these sounds from afar. But the shots were closer, mounting in volume, speaking with deeper authority. He eyed the Georgia Railroad tracks, wondering whether he should turn his horse and head south on the dirt road beside them again.

Then, as the Court House came into view, across the tracks and to his right, the shooting swelled to more frightening proportions. He thought he saw a shell explode in an empty field.

Tom Vessel wheeled his horse around and kicked its flanks with his heels as hard as he could. The steed lunged forward, throwing the boy off. He ran after it, jumped on again, and, in his excitement and terror, was tossed off a second time. "I liked to run that little horse to death," was the way he described his panicky ride.

Other citizens of besieged Jonesboro were not far behind Tom. More shells were whistling in when Mrs. A. F. Sears quit her house. Her husband, a conductor for the railroad, was somewhere en route from Macon, leaving only herself and her colored girl.

She took the girl by the hand, raced past the Court House and across the track. She too was headed for Lovejoy, to the south, where it seemed the Yankees would not be.

Others were torn between saving themselves, their household possessions, or their horses and mules. The men, for the most part, decided on the latter, and began to lead the animals towards secluded thickets south and east of Jonesboro. It seemed that there was no sanctuary from the barrage of shells and bullets.

Several residences, including the stately Warren House across the road from the depot, had already been converted to hospitals. All available beds were occupied by the wounded from previous skirmishes as well as from the hospitals which were being moved from Atlanta for they, with the nurses and the few doctors serving them, could not flee.

Sherman was advised in the early afternoon that his armies were converging on the railroad according to plan. "Schofield reached it near Rough and Ready, and Thomas at two points between there and Jonesboro. Howard found an intrenched foe

(Hardee's corps) covering Jonesboro, and his men began at once to dig their accustomed rifle pits. Orders were sent to Generals Thomas and Schofield to turn straight for Jonesboro, tearing up the railroad-track as they advanced.

"About 3 P.M. the enemy sallied from Jonesboro against the Fifteenth Corps, but was easily repulsed, and driven back within his lines. All hands were kept busy tearing up the railroad."

It was an action of position as Sergeant Graham saw it, with "skirmishing going on near the railroad. We are near the railroad. At 3 heavy cannoning on our right and men ready with traps on left . . . formed the line of battle and lay hereabouts half hour and then started again and went about 3/4 of a mile further south, then east 1/4 mile further when we formed another line."

Captain Key "ordered up Swett's, Key's, and Goldthwaite's batteries, but General Lee's forces attacked Sherman's fortified position before we struck him on our front. The batteries kept within one hundred yards of the line as it advanced, and as soon as the infantry engaged the enemy, my batteries also poured hot iron upon them. Two batteries from the enemy felt of us, but we were too stiff in the backbone for them and they yielded the argument. After firing several rounds, the batteries were advanced to the hills near Flint River, where we gave them a few more of the same sort. General Lowrey had orders not to cross the stream, but the men could not be checked. He, therefore, withdrew them as soon as possible to the east side of the creek, leaving no time for me to make an effort to bring off the captured guns. The enemy being routed on the south of Jonesboro and driven across, the two divisions on that portion of the line were re-established on their original positions."

David Conyngham obtained a measure of grim satisfaction when he heard that Hood had awakened "too late . . . from his fancied victory" in Atlanta following the Union evacuation. He had mentally compared the strategy to the Trojan wooden-horse deception.

"Howard," he wrote, "found the enemy in force at Jonesboro, and at once intrenched himself, extending a salient angle within a mile of the railroad.

"At about 4 o'clock in the afternoon the rebels attacked Howard's position. Their chief assault was on the 2d division, 15th corps, now commanded by Brigadier General Hazen. This officer formerly commanded a brigade in the 4th corps, but in the translation of Maj. Gen. Howard to the command of the army of the Tennessee, he, knowing his worth and great military acquirements, got him transferred to his command, and assigned him to a division. He fully justified his expectations, and, for his brilliant assault on Fort Pulaski, was made major general.

"Hazen's division met the assault with firmness, repulsed the enemy, and took possession of a hill which commanded Jonesboro, and might be justly called the key of the position. . . .

"In Hazen's front alone the dead and wounded were actually piled on one another. Hazen captured two flags and several prisoners."

Mrs. E. E. George of Fort Wayne, Indiana, was desperately busy in one of the field hospitals at Jonesboro, in charge of an ambulance belonging to the 15th Army Corps Hospital. When she had started her nursing service earlier in the war she had observed, "I am old," but protested that "my health is good."

A shell exploded near her ambulance, killing two soldiers on their stretchers as they waited their turn to enter the wagon with its crude, limited operating facilities.

"No, I was not alarmed," she told doctors, "for I looked upon it as simply the intention of Providence to test my courage."

Joe Semmes had been caught in the Jonesboro battle by accident. Writing his "beloved wife" to gather the children, fall on her knees, and thank God for his "protection" and "preservation from a most horrible death or most shocking wounds," the Confederate supply officer reported on his departure from Atlanta "with a large train of cars with stores . . . stopped with the train at a station 12 miles from Atlanta on the Macon Rail Road called Forrest Station (from being in the woods).

"There the engine left me. Hardee's and Lee's corps made a rapid march from Atlanta to attack the enemy at Jonesboro 8 miles further down the railroad, from Forrest Station, leaving no force between the enemy and my train except a small number of pickets . . . the enemy was pressing towards the railroad between me and Atlanta. Whilst the enemy's fire was approaching nearer and nearer, the Col. of the 11th La. in charge of the pickets came up and told me he could not keep track of the enemy and was leaving with his small squad for his main command, and that nothing was between me and the enemy. Having no means of sending the train off, the Engine not being able to return for that purpose because the enemy had torn up some of the track after it left me, my capture was inevitable. I prepared for the worst, sent off my most valuable and important public papers by passing horsemen, tore up others (and all your dear letters which I treasured so much) and prepared piles of brush and light wood to burn the train of 18 heavy loaded cars to prevent the enemy from using the stores, as soon as they should get in sight. When they were within 400 yards of me a train appeared. I made the engineman couple my train to his and I was moved off just 15 minutes before the enemy struck the road in force. We steamed rapidly towards Jonesboro and passed through the town whilst the battle was raging, which I expected, we escaped the shower of shot and shell which was thrown at our lines only a few yards distant. I remained at the edge of town during the whole battle and escaped unhurt though many balls struck our train and men were killed and wounded all around it.

"Hardee's Corps repulsed the enemy on the left and carried on his work driving them two miles and across Flint River, but all the advantage was lost because Lee's Corps on the right failed in their charge and were badly repulsed, causing us to lose all the ground we gained on the left. The fight was a furious one and our loss about 1,500 wounded alone."

A mile north of Jonesboro, another train slammed on the brakes, reversed gears, and backed into Atlanta as fast as it could.

"The retreating railway train which carried the news to Atlanta that Sherman's infantry were moving northward on Rough and Ready Station, carried consternation with it," observed General Cox. "Hood himself seems to have been bewildered and to have seized at once upon the idea that this was the beginning of a general attack upon Atlanta."

Indeed, at 6:00 P.M. Hood's aide, Shoup, telegraphed Hardee

for the General. "There are some indications that the enemy may make an attempt on Atlanta tomorrow!"

Bit by bit, assembling the tragic, scattered scraps, Hood was seeing the situation in its stark, true light: Hardee's Corps cut off at Jonesboro; Lee's Corps caught in between; Cleburne's Corps, all but annihilated, limping piecemeal to Lovejoy's. Hood, aside from the Georgia Militia, Stewart's Corps, and some scattered detachments, had almost nothing with which to defend Atlanta. He was faced with the ultimate nightmare of a General in command—the enemy had separated him from his most powerful units. Lashing out in the bitterness of defeat, he attributed the debacle to Hardee's "failure."

Several thousand young men of the South lay dead or seriously wounded in and near Jonesboro by late afternoon. Only the children and people of Atlanta who were blissfully unaware found any measure of satisfaction on that dark Wednesday. Carrie Berry, for one, had been quietly "knitting all the morning." At supper time she left, Zuie in tow, to spend the night with Aunt Healey: "I know we will enjoy our selves."

Lizzie Perkerson was hostess to new arrivals. Dannie had gone off on his evening quest for the cows. Her father, the sheriff, had come home. The heat of the day was abating inside the farmhouse, and Lizzie hoped to catch up on the sleep she had lost. Then, abruptly, "we heard a gun and in a few minutes we saw Dan coming at full speed. And next we saw two Yankees, but Dan had got round in the back yard before they got in sight. Pa was at the shop. They asked him how long since a man passed on horseback. Pa told them just a few minutes and on they dashed. By the time they were out of sight a squad of some twenty-five or thirty men made their appearance and Len and old Beck in the crowd. They rode up and asked the same question. Pa told them who it was and all about it. So they rode around in the yard and had the pony brought out to be sure he was telling the truth. Ma went out and begged them not to take the pony and they finally concluded to leave him and took old Pete and dismounted Len and rode on. Well, we saw nothing more of them that day. They were the first that had come up from Jonesborough to Atlanta."

There was another kind of holocaust in Americus—the fiery demolition of Foard Hospital and many other buildings of the town. Kate Cumming was making her routine early evening rounds when "a cry of fire was raised!"

She looked in the direction from which the shout had come and "saw a large cotton warehouse in a blaze. The sight was fearful, as it covered the whole square and the cotton seemed to have ignited all at the same time. Had I not known how inflammable cotton is, I should have thought it was covered with turpentine. The flames spread with great rapidity, and it was not long before the whole square was entirely consumed.

"We have saved very little. A number of buildings were blown up; by which we lost much more than we otherwise should have done.

"Our hospital occupied three sides of a square; out of this there is one two-story brick building saved."

Almost all of the Foard Hospital—and its sorely needed bed-space—lay in ashes. L. Warfield, a correspondent, reported to his newspaper:

"I write to you amid the expiring flames, crashing walls and sinking embers of burning Americus. At five o'clock this evening the dreadful signal sounded, and now at midnight the place is in ashes. The throngs of citizens are slowly turning from the glowing ruins, with anxious glances backward, as if doubtful whether the remorseless billows had spent their full fury or would yet sweep the entire circuit of the village and leave them all roofless. But a little more hesitation convinces them that the terrible monster has exhausted itself at last; and with sighs of relief and silent thanksgiving lifted to Providence that their homes were spared the awful destruction they have witnessed this night, they head their footsteps homeward like departing spirits in the dismal and sombre light . . . seldom does it chance to one to witness such a spectacle."

As night settled over Jonesboro, the Federal armies had encampments encircling the community. They taunted the remaining Confederate defenders with sporadic picket firing and the yellow of their campfires, like jungle eyes beyond a clearing.

Within battered Jonesboro, there was silence, heat, pain—

without the balm of anesthetic—and the fetid smells of death and the dying. Every house that remained habitable after the battle became a hospital.

The handsome Warren mansion, atop a hillock on the north side of the village, was filled to overflowing with wounded men. Two cleanly drilled holes in the walls were large enough to pass a leg or arm through. The town's two places of worship, the Baptist and Methodist churches, were stained red with the blood of their maimed and wounded congregation which was still being carried in as midnight approached.

The dead were heaped like so much cordwood in the pine woods a quarter of a mile above the Court House near the disputed railroad tracks. No one had time to identify, bury, or even count them. They lay there, in the sticky heat of a Georgia evening, in silent requiem to the day's carnage.

"Night closed the work of death and thousands of wearied men threw themselves upon the ground and slumbered sweetly without pillows or blankets," Tom Key wrote. "I accommodated my dimensions to the length of a cotton bale, which answered finely after I had pulled out some of the cotton to make an elevation for my head."

At 11:00 P.M., Sherman, from his tent which was almost within sight of the roofpeaks of Jonesboro, dispatched a formal order to Thomas:

"General, I wish you would instruct Gen. Slocum at the bridge to feel forward to Atlanta, as boldly as he can, by the direct road leading from the bridge and to send any cavalry force he can raise over toward Decatur to watch the movements of the enemy in that quarter. Advise him in full of the situation of affairs here and we assure him that we will fully occupy the attention of the rebel army outside of Atlanta."

September, 1864

Before 1:00 A.M., Hood, sleepless, dazed, a gaunt, single-legged, and utterly defeated officer, ordered his friend "Steve" Lee to extricate himself from Jonesboro and protect the flanks, from Rough and Ready, of Atlanta's remaining defenders. John Bell Hood did not have to specify that he was assembling his remnant forces to evacuate Atlanta.

At the same early hour, the hollow-eyed correspondent for the *Intelligencer* was filing this dispatch:

"Today the Yankees effected a lodgment on the Macon and Western Railroad, between Rough and Ready and East Point Station. They attacked our forces with six corps, and by a very fierce and obstinate effort succeeded in gaining the position which divides our army. Gen. Hardee's corps, under Cleburne and Lee's corps, all combined under the charge of Gen. Hardee's resisted the advance of the enemy with determined valor and unexampled bravery, from early this morning until night, when the enemy still held possession of the road.

"Gen. Hood, with Stewart's corps and the Georgia Militia, remains in Atlanta, and communication between the two positions is kept up only by couriers. It is supposed that the enemy will make a rapid and terrible onset on the defenses of Atlanta at the earliest moment they can reach the city.

"The battle was very heavy along the entire line today, and resulted in very considerable loss to us. A large number of the wounded were arriving on the train during the night."

At 2:00 A.M., Tom Key moved his battery out of camp and into the position just vacated by General Lee. By the first streaks of dawn his battery, along with five others, was in position, protecting the invasion route to Atlanta.

Colonel Taylor Beatty, trying to return inside the city,

paused at 1:00 A.M. when his goal was rendered almost impossible by the hazard of being caught by Federal forces or shot by his own pickets. He sat down by the road with the troops and dozed fitfully until five. Then he headed his command south.

"Keep marching!" he ordered.

Lizzie Perkerson was awakened early by the cry that more Yankees were coming. As he wrote to her brother Angus: "Till and I jumped out of bed and before we were half dressed, in popped one of the blue D——ls. I think the spectacle he beheld slightly shocked his modesty as he very quickly withdrew to your room. But after he had explored it to his satisfaction, he gave us another call. He came to the door and asked us in a very commanding tone what was in a trunk that was sitting in the hall. Till told him to look and see if he wanted to know, at the same time throwing him the keys. He commenced knocking the trunk around. Till told him not to break that trunk but to get out of her way and she opened it herself. He rummaged through it but didn't take anything at all. While he was upstairs there were several others in the house. They went into every room and pretended to be looking for guns. But they found none and they didn't bother anything else. One of them told Pa that he wanted some tobacco. Pa told him to get it if he wanted it. So he went on."

Wallace P. Reed, the young writer, noted that Atlanta seemed to be "almost in a state of anarchy." He was amazed that many citizens had the impression that Jonesboro had been a great victory. "But a few deserters who arrived during the day, seeking hiding places in the houses of their friends, told a different story.

"Throughout the day troops were moving in every direction and unusual bustle and activity prevailed. The citizens noticed that they were no longer halted and made to show their papers on the streets. Crowds of strange negroes also made their appearance but they acted with great caution, and spent most of their time in cellars and houses that had been abandoned by their owners. Something was up; but the citizens could not tell what was coming. They could not believe that the city was to be given up. Their idea was that the Confederate forces were being massed for another battle."

General Sam French waited all morning for word to evacuate Atlanta. "And before noon the order came. I became the rear guard. There is confusion in the city and some of the soldiers in the town are drunk. Common sense is wanted. The five heavy guns that I had ordered to be spiked by the rear guard at 11 P.M. were burned by order of the Chief of Ordnance at 5 P.M., a proclamation to the enemy in my front line that we were evacuating the place."

Major Charles W. Hubner, the former Illinois and Tennessee journalist, observed terror as well as confusion in Atlanta on that drenching hot first day of September. "The streets were filled with hurrying men, crying women, and children."

By mid-afternoon the sparring along the Macon Railroad had flared into violent conflict again.

"Gen. Davis formed his division in line about 4 P.M., swept forward over some old cotton-fields in full view, and went over the rebel parapet handsomely, capturing the whole of Govan's brigade, with two field-batteries of ten guns," Sherman reported. "Being on the spot, I checked Davis' movement, and ordered Gen. Howard to send the two divisions of the Seventeenth Corps (Blair) round by his right rear, to get below Jonesboro and to reach the railroad, so as to cut off retreat in that direction. I also dispatched orders after orders to hurry forward Stanley, so as to lap around Jonesboro on the east, hoping thus to capture the whole of Hardee's Corps. I sent first Capt. Audenried (aide-de-camp) then Col. Poe, of the Engineers, and lastly Gen. Thomas himself (and that is the only time during the campaign I can recall seeing Gen. Thomas urge his horse into a gallop).

"Night was approaching, and the country on the other side of the railroad was densely wooded. Gen. Stanley had come up on the left of Davis, and was deploying, though there could not have been on his front more than a skirmish line. Had he moved straight on by the flank, or by a slight circuit to his left, he would have inclosed the whole ground occupied by Hardee's corps, and that corps could not have escaped us; but night came on, and Hardee did escape.

"Meantime, Gen. Slocum had reached his corps (the Twentieth), stationed at the Chattahoochee bridge, had relieved Gen. A. S. Williams in command, and orders had been sent back to him to feel forward occasionally toward Atlanta, to observe the effect when we had reached the railroad."

Conyngham also reported on the action:

"The 14th corps was ordered to assault the enemy's intrenched position. Cavalry and infantry steadily advanced, under a surging fire of musketry and artillery. They had to cross a cornfield, then a deep ravine, and strike up a slope to the enemy's works. The 14th corps stood the ordeal well; swept over the valley, charged right on the works, where a regular hand-to-hand conflict ensued, which lasted for nearly two hours, but finally terminated by our men gaining the works and capturing two batteries. They turned these guns upon the flying rebels, mowing them down by wholesale. . . .

"They also captured another battery of four guns, several battle-flags, and a large number of prisoners, including many general officers, thus swelling our list of prisoners captured in the expedition to about two thousand. Gen. Govan and his adjutant general were among the prisoners, Gen. Cummings among the dead."

Tom Key witnessed the same action. After firing sporadically at "several hundred Yankee wagons in a field" in the early afternoon, he fought off a desperate desire for rest. The battle was joined in earnest by three o'clock.

"The enemy made an attack upon Gen. Govan's line which was facing to the north, and Key's and Swett's batteries opened such a deadly fire upon them that the line was broken. The Yankees then brought up three or four additional lines of batteries and concentrating for a desperate assault, they charged up in this massed condition upon Govan's lines and against a portion of General Lewis's forces which had just been thrown upon the right of Govan and, of course, had no defenses. Gen. Govan's works were fairly strong though manned very thinly, about a rank and a half. Their fire upon the advancing enemy

was steady, and that of Swett's and Key's batteries very destructive, but the immense numbers and overwhelming forces of the
Yankees ran upon the works, sweeping over the right of Govan's
fortifications, striking the lines at both batteries, and capturing
the general and several of his gallant Arkansans. . . .

"The defense of the Confederates was noble, but they were
too weak to contend with such numbers. Gen. Cleburne authorized me to bring up a battery from any position that one could
be found, and Capt. Bledsoe came up at a gallop to engage the
advancing Yanks, taking position near a large white house. The
enemy's loss, however, had been so terrible that they did not
advance. Night brought the bloody contest to a close, and in my
opinion our opponents lost ten men to our one. Indeed, we
had but few killed and wounded, if they were not foully dealt
with as was one of Key's batterymen who, after being taken
prisoner, was cut down by a Yankee officer and then pierced
with the sabre after he had fallen. I withdrew Captain Goldthwaite's battery after dark and Gen. Cleburne ordered me to
report to Gen. Hardee for instructions as to where to move.
All the artillery was withdrawn from the line, and we began to
retreat toward Griffin. About midnight we reached Lovejoy
Station where we halted for the night."

In Atlanta, Carrie Berry had returned at noon from her
night with Aunt Healey. "We had a very pleasant time and
everything seemed quiet. Directly after dinner Cousin Emma
came down and told us that Atlanta would be evacuated this
evening and we might look for the Federals in the morning. It
was not long till the hole town found it out and such excitement there was. We have ben looking for them all the evening
but they have not come yet. Mr. ——— came in to tell us that
dear Cousin Henry was wounded and he thought he would not
get well. We are so sorry to here it. We loved him so much. I
finished my stockings today."

A number of more adult observers, meanwhile, painfully recorded the dying breaths of the Gate City.

"The sun went down looking like a great ball of fire as it
shone through the thick haze of red dust," Wallace Reed chronicled. "It was a hot, stifling night, and the people found it im-

possible to sleep. Shortly after dark the streets resounded with the heavy tread of marching soldiers, but the dust and darkness made it difficult to estimate their number. It soon became evident that they were moving out of the city, taking all their field pieces and army wagons with them. Whenever the soldiers passed a garden several men would rush through it, stripping it in a minute of every stalk of corn, and every green thing that could be eaten by man or beast. Of course no citizen objected or attempted to defend his property. All knew that this raid on the gardens meant that the city was being evacuated."

"Near Decatur," a correspondent of the *Intelligencer* who signed himself "Rover," wrote to his editors in Macon. "The disaster on Wednesday evening was fully as serious as first reported . . . the forces of the enemy on the Macon road consisted of five full corps of infantry, with a large force of cavalry. It was also known that a large force was south of the Chattahoochee in the vicinity of the railroad bridge. Both of these were threatening the city, and as it would have been folly to attempt to resist both, an evacuation was promptly determined upon, while the forces of Gens. Hardee and Lee should make an attempt to reach a point where they would be joined by those that might be withdrawn from the city.

"The removal of all the supplies and ammunition that the transportation facilities of the army would permit commenced early Thursday and was continued throughout the day. Large quantities of provisions were also distributed to the people, and at nightfall all on hand stored in the Georgia railroad warehouse and cars on the track. Throughout the day, also, the several bodies of troops, as they were withdrawn from the defences and filed through the city, were permitted access to the public stores. The rolling stock of the railroads, consisting of about one hundred cars, six engines was concentrated near the rolling mill before dark, and by that hour all the troops had passed through, with the exception of the rear guard left to prevent straggling. And here I would mention a fact creditable to the State troops. Their withdrawal was accomplished in good order and without confusion or straggling. The regulars acted differently. The order was for the troops to mass in the

vicinity of McDonough and the wagon trains and all moved
out in that direction. Previous to my leaving the telegraph
office was closed, and at dark the evacuation was completed,
with the exception of the detailed guard before mentioned.

"Of course great excitement prevailed throughout the day,
but a moderate degree of good order obtained. A few licentious
citizens and soldiers embraced the occasion to display the wick-
edness of their natures, but the great mass of both classes acted
with the greatest decorum. The citizens who had suffered from
the malice of the enemy during the bombardment, looked on
sorrowingly, and indulged in conjectures as to what would be
their fate when once in the enemy's power; while the troops
filed through the streets, with a steady tread it is true, but
nevertheless with sorrow depicted on their weatherbeaten coun-
tenances. . . .

"Whether the Yankees yet occupy Atlanta I cannot say, but
presume the telegraph will inform you. . . . I only know there
was nothing to prevent their entry."

Lovely Mary Rawson, in "The Terraces" on Pryor Street,
turned to her own diary to record her day. Her father, E. E.
Rawson, well known wholesale merchant and councilman, was
faced with the loss of his city, his prosperous business, perhaps
even his showplace residence itself. Mary was sixteen. Her dark
brown hair, her smile, her parasol, her pony gig, were now part
of the memory of a better, more patrician Atlanta.

"The morning dawned," she wrote, "and the bright sun arose
which ushered in another eventful month, September, 1864. Although the commencement of the day was outwardly so pleasant, language falls short in expressing the suspense and anxiety
experienced by everyone. Time after time had we been told of
the severity of Gen. Sherman until we came to dread his approach as we would that of a mighty hurricane which sweeps all
before it, caring naught for justice or humanity. Our fear of
his coming, however, did not prevent it.

"The forenoon passed slowly with nothing of importance
transpiring except a visit from Mr. Tenny, informing us that
a few cavalry had been left to dispute every inch of ground
through the city, as he said. This news caused us a great deal

of uneasiness. . . . Gen. Hood commenced his evacuation of our city. The gentlemen who did not wish to fall into the hands of the Federals might have been seen in the afternoon of this day in company of the last of the soldiers, wending their way slowly out of the now desolate Atlanta; as night threw around our home its sable shadows, silence reigned broken only by pleasant converse with our now absent friends. How different from the few last nights preceding; the pleasure and repose of these evenings was disturbed by the noise of exploding shells and the sharp crack of the death-dealing musketry. OH! how much more pleasure there would have been had it not been for the expectation of the scene of the coming morrow. Nine o'clock comes and we retire for the night."

S. P. Richards seconded those who looked with trepidation upon the events of Thursday.

"This was a day of terror and a night of dread," he wrote. "About noon came the tidings of a severe fight on the Macon RR and that our forces were worsted and the city was to be evacuated at once. Then began a scramble among the inhabitants thereof to get away—others to procure supplies of food for their families. If there had been any doubt of the fact that Atlanta was about to be given up it would have been removed when they saw the depots of Government grain and food thrown open and the contents distributed among the citizens free gratis by the sackful and the cartload. The RR cars and engines were all run up to one place in order to be fired just as the army left. Five locomotives and 85 cars, Cousin Bill told me, were to be burned. Mr. West told me that the militia were ordered to be on hand to go out with the army, so I thought I would resign, as I was not bound to go. About midnight Mr. West came to our back gate and called to me and told me that the Battalion had gone to McDonough and that he had backed out. I then went to the Macon depot with him and secured three sacks of meal."

Residents of Atlanta, who lived closer to the McDonough Road, Hood's exit route, heard the weary singing of "Lorena" as the soldiers trudged south:

A hundred months have passed, Lorena,
Since last I held that hand in mine;
And felt the pulse beat fast, Lorena,
Tho' mine beat faster far than thine.
A hundred months, 'twas flow'ry May,
When up the hilly slope we climbed,
To watch the dying of the day
And hear the distant church bells chime.
To watch the dying of the day
And hear the distant church bells chime. . . .

'Tis dust to dust beneath the sod;
But there, *up there,* 'tis heart to heart.
'Tis dust to dust beneath the sod;
But there, *up there,* 'tis heart to heart.

SEPTEMBER 2

The clock in the Berry's front hall struck midnight. It was Friday. The weather was humid, but clear, with an expectant stillness in the air. Carrie was asleep after a restless evening.

On Pryor Street, in the "better" part of the now tattered city, Mary Rawson slept fitfully.

S. P. Richards was hoisting the sacks of meal onto his shoulders at the depot.

Sam French, delayed in clearing his works, had just given orders for his men to march out of Atlanta as fast as they could.

Hood was already well along the McDonough Road, thinking of breakfast—and sancturay—in Lovejoy's Station. He obtained a bitter satisfaction in the "strange" fact that his adversary Sherman had attacked Hardee "entrenched," while overlooking Hood's own exposed "main body."

Wallace P. Reed, the Atlanta writer, was roaming the city, ever-curious as to what would happen next.

In Decatur, Mary Gay, her mother, and step-brother, Tom Stokes, had not retired. They were still comparing experiences.

Major Hubner and another officer had made such good progress towards the Flat Shoals road from McDonough that they wandered into a thicket to catch a nap.

Sherman, camped in a field two miles northwest of Jonesboro, was "so restless and impatient that I could not sleep." In rumpled trousers, and half-unbuttoned shirt, he paced in front of his tent and scratched at the stiff stubble which thickened hourly on his chin.

David Conyngham slept.

Colonel John Coburn, commanding the 2d Brigade of the 33rd Indiana Regiment, Third Division, under General Slocum, was probing from Turner's Ferry on reconnaissance toward Atlanta. He was inching warily forward with the handful of officers and men with him.

Only a few cavalrymen, guiding their horses at an easy gait, interrupted Atlanta's midnight lull.

Then, explosions flamed in the southeast skies. The earth was rocked with one blast after another—and in their wake "a near panic among those who did not know the cause."

Carrie Berry awoke and thought of Zuie, whom she took out of her crib and held in her arms. To Carrie it was "a grate explosion! and unpleasantly reminded us of shells."

Mary Rawson's "sleep and dreams were soon interrupted by rapid and loud explosions. On arising a most beautiful spectacle greeted our sight. The Heavens were in a perfect glow while the atmosphere seemed full of flaming rockets, crash follows crash and the swift moving locomotives were rent in pieces and the never tiring metallic horse lay powerless while the sparks filled the air with innumerable spangles. The crashing had scarcely ceased when our attention was called in another direction by a bright light which proved to be the burning of some more Government provisions."

Richards was at the depot with his meal sacks. Having been forewarned, he knew what was happening. "The ammunition train was fired and for half an hour or more an incessant discharge was kept up that jarred the ground and broke the glass in the windows around. It was terrific to listen to and know the object."

French was quitting his works when he heard the eruptions. The General's orderly, military mind raged at what seemed poor timing, at very least.

"This should have been done last of all, when the rear guard or pickets were withdrawn," he wrote. "Who would extinguish an ordnance train of bursting shells? So, lighted by the glare of fires, flashes of powder and bursting shells, I slowly left Atlanta!"

Hood raged anew. It was "negligence," "unnecessary loss," in his estimation, since the engines and loaded cars had been "on the track and in readiness to move." However, he again found someone on whom to affix blame—this time, the chief quartermaster who "grossly neglected to send off" the sorely needed train of supplies.

He cloaked himself in this consoling thought as he jogged over the rutted road through the dark, sultry night, a city—and perhaps a war—lost, in his wake.

Wallace Reed estimated that the explosion was the violent result of seventy carloads of powder and shells being ignited, some ten cars less than Hood himself had conceded.

"The infernal din of the exploding shells sent a thrill of alarm through the city," he noted. "Many believed at first that the Federals were coming in, and that a desperate battle was going on in the streets. It took five long hours to blow up the seventy carloads of ammunition. The flames shot up to a tremendous height, and the exploding missiles scattered their red hot fragments right and left. The very earth trembled as if in the throes of a mighty earthquake. The houses rocked like cradles, and on every hand was heard the shattering of window glass and the fall of plastering and loose bricks. Thousands of people flocked to high places and watched with breathless excitement the volcanic scene on the Georgia Railroad.

"Fortunately all the citizens in the vicinity of the explosions had been ordered to leave their houses before the work of destruction commenced. Every building for a quarter of a mile around was either torn to pieces or perforated with hundreds of holes by fragments of the shells. Day was dawning when the last shell and the last keg of powder exploded. Clouds of heavy, sulphurous smoke swept the ground, and choked men when they gasped for breath."

Even in Decatur the effect was cataclysmic.

"The shades of night came on," Mary Gay noted, "and darker grew until complete blackness enveloped the face of the earth, and still the low subdued tones of conversation between mother, son and daughter mingled with unabated interest.

"Hark! Hark! An explosion! An earthquake?

"The angry, bellowing sound rises in deafening grandeur, and reverberates along the far-off valleys, and distant hill-tops. What is it? This mighty thunder that never ceases? The earth is ablaze—what can it be?

"Dumbfounded we stood, trying to realize the crushing fact. Woman's heart could bear no more in silence, and a wail over departed hopes mingled with the angry sounds without.

"Impelled by a stern resolve, and a spirit like to that of martyred saints, our brother said:

" 'This is no place for me. I must go.'

"As he walked away from his sobbing mother, through the war-illumined village, I never beheld mortal man so handsome, so heroically grand."

Major Hubner and his friends planned to rifle the knapsacks of two other soldiers sleeping in the woods and thus "aped 'the ways that are dark and the tricks that are in vain' of the heathen Chinese and 'borrowed' those plethoric knapsacks and ate the contents."

An owl hooted. In the distance, toward Atlanta, the sky rocketed in reds, oranges, and yellows—a fiery *gotterdammerung* of Hood's own unsought creation. They paid the spectacle little heed, but munched their booty as they "trudged onward."

After midnight, Sherman became conscious of sounds of "shells exploding and other sound like that of musketry." Soon, he walked to the house of a farmer living nearby, "called him out to listen to the reverberations which came from the direction of Atlanta (twenty miles to the north of us) and inquired of him if he had resided there long. He said he had, and that these sounds were just like those of a battle.

"An interval of quiet then ensued, when again, about 4 A.M., arose other similar explosions, but I still remained in doubt whether the enemy was engaged in blowing up his own magazines or whether Gen. Slocum had not felt forward, and become engaged in a real battle."

David Conyngham continued to sleep. But not Schofield, Commanding the Army of the Ohio. He disagreed with Sherman's conclusions, which he believed held back his armies from potential annihilation of Hood's entire command.

"An untutored farmer," he asserted, "may well have thought 'these sounds were just like those of a battle,' but a practiced ear could not have failed to note the difference. . . . There could have been no room for doubt that these lights and sounds meant the destruction in Atlanta of magazines or carloads of fixed ammunition, and hence that Hood was abandoning that place. I reported my observations to Gen. Sherman, but he 'still remained in doubt.' The doubt was to me incomprehensible."

The 8th Kansas Infantry, observing the fireballs cascading skyward, logged the time as about midnight. The regiment was in position between Sherman and Atlanta.

Graham remarked on the sounds somewhat later, and guessed the reason.

Lieutenant Colonel H. W. Perkins, assistant Adjutant General to Slocum, sent a message at 2:30 A.M. to Brigadier General A. S. Williams, leading the 1st Division:

"The Major-General Commanding desires that you send out as soon as possible this morning a reconnoitring party toward Atlanta to ascertain where and what the firing is. Parties have been ordered out from Second and Third divisions, but they will not get started as soon as you. The General desires to get as early information as possible."

Atlanta was alive with lurid flames until dawn. "The continuous noise of the exploding ammunition was more terrible and intense as a terrorizer than the greatest battle which had ever occurred," Wallace P. Reed wrote. "Its effect upon the sleeping citizens who had no knowledge of what was to transpire was extremely startling, as the noise was as that of a nearby, fiercely fought battle, and the brilliancy of the illumination was such as the burning of a city in the distance would produce."

Colonel Coburn, of General Slocum's Federal corps, neared Atlanta from Turner's Ferry to the northwest as the sun started to poke over the stumpy pine tops.

"Cavalry," he observed, "was found to be in the city, and we advanced cautiously."

From Pace's Ferry, Dr. Stephen Pierson, a Major with Slocum's 20th Corps, was also advancing toward the metropolis which he had studied so long from a distance. He had observed the early morning explosions and now "knew" without waiting for a message, of the battle won.

"The long roll was sounded and, with the first break of day, the 20th Corps was on its way, our Division in the lead," he wrote. "For us it was a glorious morning; just how glorious those who were not marching with us canot fully comprehend. It meant the end of the campaign of more than a hundred days of almost continuous fighting, upon each one of which, somewhere along those lines, could have been heard the sounds of war, the sharp crack of the rifle of the outpost, the rattle of the skirmish, or the roar of a full line of battle; the end of a campaign of more than a hundred miles of marching, maneuvering, struggling, scarcely one of which was made unopposed; the end of a campaign crowned with victory and honor for the one, closed by defeat, without dishonor, for the other. The end of a campaign fought to a finish by antagonists worthy of each other. . . .

"As we neared the city I turned in my saddle to look back at the Regiment. A fine and hardy lot of men they were; not an ounce of superfluous flesh upon any one of them; lean-visaged, bright-eyed, quick of step, power and vigor; joy and triumph all over them and their every movement. Schooled, trained, disciplined, hammered in the fiery College of War."

Wallace P. Reed watched smoke lift, the sun rise, "as it had set the evening before, a blood-red ball, magnified by clouds and mists that were the handiwork of man. In the dread silence of that memorable morning ten thousand helpless people looked into each others faces for some faint sign of hope and encouragement, but found none. A few squads of cavalry were clattering out of the city to join Hood's army. They were riding in hot haste and were in no mood to answer questions.

"Their replies were brief and unsatisfactory. Sherman was coming in at once. They believed that his vanguard was already on Marietta Street. The Federals were all drunk, and they would plunder the city, and spare neither age nor sex. In this way they answered the citizens, and then they put spurs to their horses and dashed off at the top of their speed.

"Then came the awful hours of waiting—waiting for the unknown! Delicate women, as well as stalwart men, looked after their weapons and put them in order. There was no thought of resisting insults and robbery, but some outrages they were resolved to defend themselves against to the death. Men with wives and daughters stayed at home, to be ready for any emergency. But the center of the town was filled with the riffraff, with stragglers and deserters, with negroes delirious over their strange sense of freedom, and with lean and haggard men and women of the lowest class, who were going through the stores, picking up such odds and ends as had been left behind by their owners.

"This was the state of affairs on the morning of the 2d of September, when Atlanta, worn out and shattered by the storm of war, lay panting between two flags, under the protection of neither, abandoned by one, and with no hope of mercy from the other.

"The evacuation of Atlanta by Hood's army left the city without police protection, without a municipal government, and practically without any law, except the mob-like rule of the majority. Under the circumstances, however, this state of anarchy could last only a few hours. The citizens know that when the Federals entered the place they would be compelled, in their own interest, to restore order, and they felt that even an oppressive government would be better than no government. But it was feared that the first day of the enemy's occupation of the city would be marked by lawlessness and violence. The mob continued to plunder the stores and vacant buildings. They did not find many articles of value, but for several hours the streets were filled with a ragged crowd of men, women and children, who were helping themselves to everything in sight. They picked up buckets, tinware, canteens, pieces of furniture, old tents, and all kinds of rubbish. Of course they found little or nothing in the shape of provisions. The Confederates had carried off everything that could be eaten.

"In the midst of all this confusion there was no drunkenness, and no violence. Men forgot their old quarrels and differences, and met in a friendly way.

"The Unionists suddenly loomed up into importance, and not a few of their Confederate neighbors hunted them up, and requested them to use their influence to secure the protection of their property. In no instance was this refused. The Union people felt as uneasy as anybody, and showed a disposition to keep on the best possible terms with their fellow-townsmen.

"The hours slipped by, and still there was no sign of the enemy's approach. Among the prominent citizens who had remained was the Hon. James M. Calhoun, the mayor of the city. Mr. Calhoun was a man of cool judgment and indomitable courage, and he was devoted to his people. He was unwilling, in such perilous times, to abandon Atlanta until the worst dangers were over, and he therefore remained at his post, regardless of his personal interests. As the Confederates had made no formal surrender of the town, Calhoun decided that it was necessary for the civil authorities to act in the matter.

"Without such action the Federals would be in ignorance of the real condition of affairs, and it would be natural for them to march in, prepared for a hostile reception. It was the paramount duty of the hour to avert bloodshed, if possible, and with this object in view the mayor and his friends agreed that it would be best to meet the invaders before they swarmed over the breastworks.

"During the morning Mayor Calhoun held a conference with several members of the council and other prominent men. Besides the mayor, Messrs. J. E. Williams, E. E. Rawson, Thomas G. Crusselle, William Markham, Thomas Kile, Julius Hayden and a number of others were present. They were all mounted on horses, and were prepared for a rough ride. The members of the committee could not disguise the fact that they were about to undertake a dangerous trip. They did not know exactly where to find Gen. Sherman, but it was thought that his camp was only a few miles out on the Marietta road.

" 'Shall we go armed?'

"When one of the committee asked this question, it created a genuine sensation.

" 'It will never do,' said Mayor Calhoun, 'for us to go with a white flag into the enemy's lines, carrying weapons with us. It would be violating the customs of war. Before an explanation could be made serious trouble might occur, and our mission would be a failure.'

" 'But we may be bushwhacked,' suggested several.

" 'Are we to run the risk of being shot down without having a single pistol in the crowd for our defense?'

" 'I admit there is danger,' replied the mayor, 'but we must face it. The trees have all been cut down for miles, and our ride will be through the open country in broad daylight. Our white flag will be our best protection. If we are fired upon we must take our chances.'

"After this talk several gentlemen produced their pistols and turned them over to their friends to keep until their return. One man reluctantly turned over four six-shooters, and his companions felt relieved. With such an arsenal in the party a battle could hardly have been avoided.

"The citizens, with the mayor at their head, rode out Marietta Street. Nearly every residence had been abandoned, and many of the houses had been knocked into piles of splintered timber by the shells. The sidewalk and the street were badly torn up, and even in daylight the riders sometimes found it difficult to thread their way through the scattered debris. In a short time the dismantled breastworks were reached. They were entirely deserted, and, with the exception of a spiked cannon here and there, no traces of recent occupation were left. A peaceful quiet brooded over the red redoubts and the empty trenches, and a bird, perched upon one of the big siege guns, looked inquisitively at the horsemen, and after a few prefatory flirts and

twitters, poured forth a flood of silver notes—a song of welcome
—a jubilee carol of peace.

"Beyond the red clay fortresses, over the fragments of army
wagons and caissons, with eyes averted from the skulls and bones
that gleamed like so many white horrors in the fierce sunlight,
the little band rode on. They passed the rifle-pits and entrenchments of the enemy. Not a human being, not a living thing, was
in sight. Two, three, four miles, and not a sign of the enemy."

At dawn Sherman found that Hardee "was gone," south to
Lovejoy's.

Jonesboro—what remained of it—was entered peacefully by
the Federal army. Not a shot was fired. Not one Confederate
soldier well enough to hold a rifle was in the scorched, ruined
village.

The critically wounded remained, with some few doctors and
nurses. The handsome Warren House looked—and smelled—
like a battlefield hospital. The 52d Illinois Regiment moved
into it as its own headquarters and hospital. The litters bearing
Northern wounded were carried in and put down on the floor
boards next to those of the Southern wounded.

The same procedure was carried out in the fetid air of the
Baptist and Methodist churches and in one or two other homes
with walls defiantly standing and which could be called a shelter.

In the pine grove, burial squads moved in. Beneath the scattered evergreens, the men, sweating in the day's heat, dug parallel rows of trenches, four feet deep. They buried the hundreds
of piled Confederate corpses. But there still was not time to
identify even one of them, or to plan for other than a lone
wooden cross for the entire stark, somehow frightening, burial
place.

Dr. James Comfort Patten of Princeton, Indiana, started for
Jonesboro, "occasionally meeting trains of ambulances, with
wounded men going to the hospitals. We crossed Flint River
near its head where it is not more than twenty feet wide and
soon came to the Battleground. Our dead and wounded were
all taken away but a detail of our men were busy burying the
rebels and had most of it done. Our line of march did not take
us over the worst of the field and I did not see any of them.

"Some of the men passed where the burying party were at work. It is said that 900 of them (the Confederates) lay in a space of less than two acres. A little further on we came to Jonesboro and went through, the band playing Hail Columbia, a tune that I suppose the inhabitants had not been much used to of late. Our men had torn up the r.r. here very badly. It had been a very pretty town but there is a look of Desolation on it now that is pitiful. . . . Some of the people were there but many had left. On the far end of the town we saw the ruins of a large mill. . . . We went on down the r.r. till we passed a mile post marked 25 miles to Atlanta and 78 miles to Macon, we went on a half a mile, and turned into an old field and camped."

Mayor Calhoun and his party met up with the object of their uneasy ride.

"A sudden turn in the road," Wallace Reed continued, "brought them face to face with a marching detachment of men in blue.

"A brief halt—a hurried explanation. A Federal colonel rode up to the spot and asked a few questions. The white flag, the appearance of the strangers in citizens' garb, and the calm, measured words of Mayor Calhoun satisfied the officer."

As the "satisfied officer," Colonel Coburn of Indiana, reported the meeting:

"He surrendered the city to me, saying he only asked for protection for citizens and property.

"I asked him if the Rebel cavalry were yet in town. He replied that Ferguson's brigade was there, but was on the point of leaving.

"I replied that my force was moving into the city, and that unless that force retired there would be a fight, in which neither persons nor property would be safe, and that if necessary I would burn the houses of citizens to dislodge the enemy, that I did not otherwise intend to injure persons or property of citizens unless used against us.

"I ordered my skirmishers to advance, and they moved through the city. The cavalry rapidly evacuated the place. I at once sent dispatches to Brig. Gen. Ward at Turner's Ferry and to Maj.

Gen. Slocum at the railroad bridge of the occupation of the city by my command."

Shortly before noon, the signed surrender from Mayor Calhoun was in the hands of Brigadier General W. T. Ward, commanding the 3rd Division, 20th Corps:

"Sir—the fortunes of war have placed the city of Atlanta in your hands. As Mayor of the city, I ask protection for non-combatants and private property."

Ward, in turn, flashed word to Slocum, timed 1:00 P.M.:

"The city authorities have surrendered to my reconnoitring party, and my troops now occupy the same (Atlanta)."

Slocum ordered a locomotive dispatched over the rusting Western and Atlantic rails into the center of the city—if possible.

Ward, aware of the historic implications, decided to send a request. "As my troops took Atlanta, courtesy if not justice to me demands that I may be permitted to occupy the same. If not inconsistent with the public interest, I desire to be permitted to move my divisions to Atlanta."

By noon, as the bell of Wesley Chapel tolled, advance couriers had planted the flag over the Court House. Some citizens reputedly witnessed the Federal soldiers trampling and burning the Confederate Stars and Bars.

"Some 200 small arms were found in the City Hall (Court House) and about 16 pieces of artillery," Colonel Coburn continued, "abandoned in the works and burnt with a train of cars.

"The ammunition abandoned had been fired in the night and continued to explode with loud reports after we had entered the city, in the forts and among the ruins of the burning shops and buildings where it had been deposited.

"The works of the enemy were left almost perfect, and there seemed to have been no attempt at the destruction of anything but the materials of war.

"As we passed through the streets many of the citizens ran gladly out to meet us, welcoming us as deliverers from the despotism of the Confederacy.

"Others regarded us with apprehension and begged to be spared from robbery.

"Many of the buildings we found to have been much injured by our artillery, but such as will be needed for public use can be taken at once with slight repairs."

A Union army chaplain, the Reverend G. S. Bradley of the 22d Wisconsin, reported that "it was a scene of destruction seldom witnessed. In the northern portion of the city, nearly every house is damaged by shell from Yankee guns, and some fine dwellings are nearly demolished, shade trees cut down and fences splintered.

"In nearly every yard is a bomb-proof, or 'gopher-hole' as the boys call them, in which the families fled for safety when shells came thickest. These 'holes' are about six or eight feet deep, and from eight to 12 feet square, planked over and covered with dirt to the depth of three or four feet, with a little doorway upon the south side. . . . One old Irish woman remarked in my hearing as we were passing her, 'an sure I'se belave ye's are bains after all.'

"At one door I noticed a card in large letters: 'United we stand, divided we fall' and white flags without number. Most of the citizens kept well out of sight, and but very little enthusiasm was manifest anywhere, save in the ranks.

"As the Old Flag caught the breeze from the spire of the Court House, such a cheer went up as only a conquering army, flushed with victory, can give. Commencing in the Gate City, it rings out loud and long as it spreads from regiment to regiment . . . alas! in this hour of the Nation's rejoicing, thousands of happy hearth stones are made desolate and places that knew our brave boys shall know them no more."

S. P. Richards wrote sadly of this fateful Friday:

"About noon today the Yankees came in sure enough, a party of five or six came riding by our house. A committee of our citizens went out early and met Gen. Slocum and got his word that private property should be respected, upon which the city was surrendered to them and in they came. The Stars and Stripes were soon floating aloft over the city.

"The private houses were not molested by the soldiers and I was therefore very much surprised when I went down town to see armsfull and baskets full of books and wall-paper going up the street in a continuous stream from our store; and when I reached the store the scene would have required the pencil of Hogarth to portray. Yankees, men, women, children and niggers were crowded into the store each one scrambled to get something to carry away, regardless, apparently, whether it was anything they needed, and still more heedless of the fact that they were stealing! Such a state of utter confusion and disorder as presented itself to my eyes then, I little dreamed of two hours before when I left it all quiet and, as I thought, safe. The soldiers in their mad hunt for tobacco had probably broken open the door and the rabble had then 'pitched in' thinking it a 'free fight.' At first I was so dismayed that I almost resolved to let them finish it, but finally I got them out and stood guard."

Sherman received the news while pursuing the retreating Confederates toward Lovejoy's.

"The artillery, meanwhile," wrote Brevet Major Lewis M. Hosea, of Ohio, "kept up a lively engagement and the screaming of shells and the rattle of musketry formed an imposing accompaniment to the scene. I delivered my message (on Atlanta's evacuation) to Sherman and Thomas while both stood together watching the charge of Howard's battle line, and they both gave extravagant vent to the joy of the announcement.

"After a rapid cross-questioning and assurances that I had personally seen the inside of the works, they let loose and actually danced and flung up their hats, and embraced each other, while I bore the brunt of hand-shaking that made my arms sore.

"Of course the news spread and with it a chorus of shouting and cheers that finally reached the battle-front, and spurred on the attack into a successful charge."

Between Jonesboro and Barnesville another disaster had been spawned, though overshadowed by the overwhelming major one. Joe Semmes, who had reached Barnesville safely, was returning to Jonesboro with supplies. Three miles north of Barnesville there was a resounding collision.

"Our train met at full speed a longer train," wrote Semmes, "loaded inside and out with our own suffering wounded. The shock was awful. Not expecting anything of the kind, I thought for an instant that a shell had exploded in the car and the enemy were on us. I was thrown naturally forward, injuring my arm and side but breaking no bones.

"Full of pain as I was, the terrible screams of the wounded drew me to the wreck of the trains where the most frightful scenes of the battlefield were surpassed in horror by the sight I met.

"Some 20 were killed instantly and others were in the agonies of death whilst the air was filled with the screams and moans of many others. With only one arm which I could use I did all I could. Many of the poor creatures when taken out had to be left in the broiling sun, for there was no shade for a quarter of a mile. No water . . . nothing.

"One poor lady with both legs smashed and her breast smashed in and the bones sticking out I helped as well as I could, got her some whiskey and water, covered her."

Isaac Pilgrim, also at Barnesville, telegraphed the *Intelligencer:*

"Today the passenger train coming down from Atlanta collided with the up freight train about two and a half miles from this place.

"The engines Governor and Dispatch are a perfect wreck.

"Seven cars are broken up.

"Four cars are completely demolished.

"The down train was loaded with wounded soldiers.

"About 22 persons were killed, including one woman, one Major, and Lt. Vaughan. About 50 were wounded. Amputation is necessary in severe cases. . . .

"Many are horribly mangled. . . .

"The road will be clear by morning."

In Atlanta, the Federal troops continued to march in an imponderable, rowdy avalanche. The streets were blue with their companies and regiments.

"They had marched down Marietta Street, and had scattered after reaching the center of the city," Wallace Reed noted. "With the exception of a few stray shots on Decatur street, fired by half a dozen Confederate cavalrymen, who immediately dashed off at a gallop, they encountered no opposition. By three o'clock the army wagons began to roll in, and with them came the sutlers, bringing immense stocks of goods. In another hour the streets were enlivened by the cries of the army newsboys, who were shouting: 'Here's your *New York Herald!* . . . Here's your *Harper's Weekly!*'

"Before the sun went down the quartermasters and sutlers had occupied most of the stores. A news agent filled the old post-office on Whitehall street with novels and newspapers. A sutler opened a store just below Trinity Church, and exhibited a tempting stock of canned goods. There were several clothing stores. The United States Sanitary Commission opened a big depot of supplies on Whitehall street. The McNaught & Ormond building was filled with quartermaster's stores, and Mr. E. E. Rawson's fine building was similarly utilized."

To Mary Rawson the occupation was "a relief." She confided to her diary: "I had expected them to enter in disorder exulting loudly in the success of their enterprise. Atlanta was taken possession of quietly . . . immediately upon entering the town, the Stars and Stripes were seen floating from the flag pole on the Franklin Building. Father's store was used as a signal station; the signals were given with a blue flag having a large white star in the center and in the evening they used beautiful lanterns which moved in different directions."

Carrie Berry had watched citizens such as S. P. Richards hurrying home with morsels of provisions abandoned by the retreating army of Hood. She wrote:

"Every one has been trying to get all they could before the Federals came," she wrote. "They have ben running with saques of meal, salt and tobacco. They did act ridiculous breaking open stores and robbing them. About 12 o'clock there were a few Federals came in. They were picketed. In about an hour the cavalry came dashing in. We were all frightened. We were afraid they were going to treat us badly. It was not long till the infantry came in. They were orderly and behaved very well.

"I think I shall like the Yankees very well."

The boy, Noble Williams, together with the sons of two Englishmen, Mr. Crankshaw and Mr. Richardson, was at the depot looking for fodder. A few milk cows still remained in Atlanta.

"As cattle feed was a very scarce commodity," Noble was

to record, "they were anxious to obtain anything in the shape of food for their cows, and knowing that the Confederate army had been compelled to leave a large supply of hardtack, a large but miserable imitation of a cracker, their boys had been given sacks and told to go and fill them, and as the boys were playmates of Doctor C.'s (Calhoun) grandson he went with them to assist in filling the sacks. They reached the depot, where they found a large supply of hardtack, and also a large number of boys engaged in moving them.

"While engaged in filling their sacks some one in the crowd announced that the Federals were already in the business portion of the city. The boys cast their eyes in that direction and discovered that the announcement was only too true, for they could plainly discern the blue-coats in the distance, who were rapidly moving toward them, which sent a thrill of terror to their young hearts; and then, as it seemed to them, their race for life began, and with a swiftness almost equal to that of a deer they sped onward to their homes in hopes of safety.

"The home of Doctor C. was soon reached, where the younger of Mr. Crankshaw's boys, and Mr. Richardson's accompanied Doctor C.'s grandson into the house, when he crawled under his grandmother's bed for concealment, and it took considerable persuasion under promise of protection to get him out. The negroes working on the place had pictured the Yankees, as they called them, to him in the most glowing colors, as beastly and bloodthirsty monsters, whose delight it was to catch men, women and innocent children for no other purpose than to murder them.

"Soon after the boy came out from his place of concealment, a Federal officer and his staff were seen riding down the street in front of the house, a fact which assured all that the enemy had taken possession of the city. An hour later the tramp, tramp, tramp, of the greater portion of Gen. Sherman's army could be heard as they passed down the street by the doctor's house. This continuous motion was kept up for several hours, when the command was given to halt and rest.

"No sooner had they broken ranks than hundreds of soldiers' faces could be seen peering through the fence, which separated the street from the garden, and as the grape arbor, filled with temptingly luscious grapes, appeared before their vision, their mouths fairly watered, and their stomachs seemed to contain an aching void that could only be filled by a speedy and vigorous assault upon them; which in less than five minutes was accomplished, greatly to the damage of both the grapes and the arbor. Perched as they were on every available inch of slat, they were reminders of a flock of hungry blue-birds, and, strange to relate, out of that vast number of men who enjoyed the privilege of feasting on those luscious grapes, all had taken them by force with the exception of one, whose gentlemanly instinct was so perfect that even the rough army life had failed to efface it.

"He came to the front door and gently knocked; some member of the family opened the door to find a pleasant-faced young soldier with cap in hand gracefully bowing, and at the same time in a pleasant tone of voice requesting permission to be allowed to gather a few grapes. His gentlemanly demeanor had come so unexpectedly that it gained for him the friendship of all of the doctor's family. His name was Kellog, and he came from Ohio. It was quite a fortunate occurrence, the meeting of this soldier, as the doctor was confined to his bed with a very serious illness, and was greatly in need of the services of a competent physician to attend him, and as there were no Southern physicians, all having left when the city was evacuated.

"The last Southern surgeon to leave the city was Doctor John Whitworth, a Mississippian who had been in constant attendance upon the doctor for a week or more, and stayed at great risk until the very last possible moment. He was a nephew of Doctor C.'s wife; and the family had to implore him to leave to avoid capture, and how anxiously they watched him as he put spurs to his horse and rapidly disappeared from view, apparently safe from the boys in blue.

"Mr. Kellog was requested to have a Federal surgeon visit the doctor, which he kindly did, and in response to his request Dr. Wm. C. Bennett, a very gentlemanly and eminent surgeon, called upon the doctor and found him very ill. He was suffering with a dangerous tumor on one side of his face, and the doctor decided that a surgical operation would be necessary; and he called in another surgeon to assist him."

As evening approached, troops and wagons pounded unceasingly into the city. Captain George Pepper of Zanesville, Ohio, observed the pandemonium:

"The black population acted in the wildest disorder. They pillaged every house in the town, ransacking the whole from garret to cellar, smashing the windows, doors and furniture of every description—and committed every possible species of outrage. They broke the chinaware, smashed the pianos and annihilated the chairs, tables and bedsteads. They cut open the beds and emptied the contents into the streets. They dashed into the cellars and drank all the liquors, so that the whole of them became a drunken, and furious mob. This infernal carnival was carried on."

Captain David Conyngham, *New York Herald* correspondent, reached Atlanta that night.

"As we approached the city," he reported, "troops were drawn up before us, not knowing but we were rebel cavalry. We floated a white handkerchief, and soon joined old comrades and were received with loud cheers, which were redoubled when we told them all about the victory at Jonesboro.

"I at once went to report events to Gen. Slocum, for we were the first to reach Atlanta from Sherman's army."

Sherman himself was not fully convinced. At 8:00 P.M. he hurried a note to Thomas:

"Until we hear from Atlanta the exact truth I do not care about your pushing your men against breast-works. Destroy the railroad well up to your lines; keep skirmishers up, and hold your troops in hand for anything that may turn up. As soon as I know positively that our troops are in Atlanta I will determine what to do."

The 2nd Massachusetts Volunteer Light Infantry was marching into Atlanta. Its two bands blared loudly. The regiment started to spread its tents on the grass of City Hall Park, as Colonel William Cogswell assumed duties of post-commandant of the conquered city. Other tents were popping up like infectious white blotches across the park behind the Trout House.

Mary Rawson watched and listened, then sadly postscripted her diary for Friday, September 2, 1864.

"This day has closed and is numbered with those past and gone and the moon once more shines over sleeping, silent Atlanta."

The War Department in Washington was ready after supper to release the long-awaited bulletin—that the Gate City of the Confederacy had fallen. There had been so many false reports since July that Halleck held up the news for an hour or more, waiting for a possible "correction" to come over the slender copper wires from Georgia.

The East's large cities, Baltimore, Philadelphia, New York, and Boston, were dark when the word reached newspaper offices:

"General Sherman has taken Atlanta. The Twentieth Corps occupies the city. The main army is on the Macon road, near East Point.

"A battle was fought near that point in which Gen. Sherman was successful. Particulars are not known."

It was simply Slocum's own flash to the Chief of Staff. Most editors, however, were saving their largest type—which they sacrilegiously dubbed "Second Coming"—for the fall of Richmond. They would keep their heads in the way they played the capture of Atlanta tomorrow.

SEPTEMBER 3

At 6:00 A.M., fully awake and keen, with a characteristic lightning quality, Sherman dictated a dispatch from "near Lovejoy's" to Chief of Staff Halleck in Washington. He summed up the past three days' operations, concluding:

"Atlanta is ours and fairly won. I shall not push more farther on this raid but in a day or so will move to Atlanta and give my men some rest." Then he ordered Slocum to "move all the stores forward from Allatoona and Marietta to Atlanta. Take possession of all good buildings for Government purposes, and see they are not used as quarters. Advise the people to quit now. There can be no trade or commerce now until the war is over. Let Union families go to the North with their effects, and secesh families move on. All cotton is tainted with treason, and no title in it will be respected."

Saturday commenced rainy, windy, and consummately cheerless for the citizens of Atlanta. The occupation was underscored in all sections of the city as houses were commandeered for staff headquarters.

At dawn, Colonel Henry A. Barnum of New York moved into Hood's recently evacuated headquarters. Barnum was distinguished among other New Yorkers as the man who had come back from the dead. Two years previously he had been so gravely wounded at the Battle of Malvern Hill that he gasped from his hospital cot: "tell my wife that in my last thoughts were blended herself, my boy, and my flag. . . . God bless the old Fla—" and with his unfinished fervor for the Stars and Stripes lapsed into a coma.

He was unconscious so long that word filtered home that he was dead. His stirring "last words" were parroted by editor and minister alike to spur lagging recruitment for the war.

It came as an equal anticlimax to Colonel Barnum as well as his friends and eulogizers when he recovered and returned to active service.

Young O. L. Braumuller was one of the first Atlantans to make Barnum's acquaintance that early, wet Saturday. With his mother beside him, he watched the Federals moving into the frame house next door. His father was still in Nashville trying to sell Tennessee bonds, and now it appeared as though the family would not be reunited for an indefinite period.

"We had been notified ahead of time," wrote Braumuller, "that the Confederates would have to evacuate and that it would be safer to leave the city, but our home contained many valuable things, such as paintings, rugs and draperies, and mother decided to stay and protect them."

It was not long this morning before a wagon drew in front of the Braumuller home, "and several soldiers jumped out. Without saying good morning, by your leave, or anything, they began tearing boards off the walls. They were going to use the wood to build a camp, they said, and then told me to get out of the way and quit bothering them with questions.

"Mother was nearly frantic, for all of her great bravery. Of course, I was scared at the thought that we would be left without a roof, and I was so mad I could hardly see.

" 'I don't believe these men have been authorized to tear down our house,' I assured her, 'and I'm gonna see that Yankee colonel and tell him about it.'

"I ran as hard as I could to Colonel Barnum's headquarters, and dashed right into his office.

"He looked up at me with a smile and said, 'Hello, sonny, what you want? What's your trouble?'

" 'Well, general,' I said as I tried to catch my breath after the run, 'I'm from the big house next door, and they're tearing it down over our heads. I didn't believe you gave them any such orders.'

" 'Well, I guess not,' the officer replied. He reached for his hat, took a big pistol from the top of his desk and shoved it under his coat, and called for a corporal's guard. Then he started home with me.

"I had to hurry to keep up with him, and I could see that he was angry. When we reached my house he stopped squarely in front of the leader of the soldiers and said, 'Let me see your authority to tear down this house.'

"The soldier drew a piece of paper from his pocket. Colonel Barnum glanced through the note, and tore it into tiny bits and threw them into the soldiers' face. Then he ordered his guard to arrest the men, and led the way to the house, where my mother was standing in the door.

" 'Now, Mrs. Braumuller,' he said as he removed his hat, 'you need not be afraid that this will be repeated, nor that you will be molested again. I have my orders to obey, of course, but we don't take any stock in this business of tearing houses down over people's heads. If you have any more trouble, you just send for me.' "

After watching the soldiers trooping past her gate in seemingly endless procession, Carrie Berry paid a visit to one of her aunts and learned "she had a Yankee officer to spend the night with her." Only two Federal soldiers called at the Berry home, "to beg something to eat."

The rain, the defeat, the presence of the conqueror in multiplying numbers impelled Carrie's conclusion, "we all feel gloomy."

The Rawsons, since "E. E." had been born in Craftsbury, Vermont, had reason to hope their house would not be requisitioned. But "The Terraces" was threatened.

"The sun and bright azure are shut out by lowering clouds from which the rain pours in torrents," Mary Rawson started her diary. "At ten this morning Father had a visit from the provost marshal and several other officers, who wished us to give up our beautiful home for headquarters for the general. This request Father told him it was impossible to comply with for where could we find another home of any kind? They finally gave up the idea of taking it from us and seemed much pleased with our old school house instead. Oh how I felt to see the beloved old playground in front of the school covered with tents and the beautiful little shade trees cut down.

"Besides how could I see Miss Maria's and Miss Anne's cherished pet flowers trampled down by those who could not appreciate their beauty and fragrance? Oh it was too much and Mattie and I shed tears to think of the desolation. We were the only ones left of the pleasant class of seven who used to assemble daily at the Pine Hill seminary. How many friends were scattered in the great stampeed previous to the desertion of Atlanta. Many of the girls had gone further south with their parents and one dear classmate left us for another and I hope better world, during the enclosure of our city by both armies. Yes, the much admired and beloved Gussie Clayton was dead (Joseph Semmes' relative). But I forget myself. I was speaking of the visit of the officers. When they prepared to leave I was amused as well as astonished to see the behavior of the grooms. One of them happening to be in our bombproof, his master called 'Jack come out of that proof and get my horse' and how he did fly to obey his orders, brought his horse and equipped him for his rainy journey by buttoning on his oilcloth coat and after much elaborate brushing he gently placed him on the saddle and they went away. All this I witnessed from the dining room window."

Wallace Reed found the city "crowded" by mid-Saturday. Billiard rooms and drinking saloons were opened or reopened by the Federal army "and bills were out advertising a minstrel show" for the evening. It seemed to him that nearly a dozen Federal generals already "occupied the best houses."

Though he found that the soldiers "at first took what they wanted," they soon settled down and "in the main behaved tolerably well."

The "good buildings," however, referred to by General Sherman, did not exclude churches. Horses were stabled in the Sunday school rooms of the Central Presbyterian, where Carrie Berry had read the Bible, and St. Luke's churches. Commissary stores were piled ceiling-high in smaller rooms as army wagons and boxcars rolled in from Allatoona and Marietta. Other churches were expected to suffer Central Presbyterian's degradation.

The well-known priest, Father Thomas O'Reilly, made it plain that the Immaculate Conception Church must not be desecrated. He talked determinedly of appealing to the Bishop —perhaps even higher holy authority—to forbid all Roman Catholics in the Confederacy to bear arms.

The bells of Wesley Chapel, which had tolled the news of the Federal entry, were nearly removed—to be shipped North for melting. The Reverend Houston pleaded successfully that some church bells must be left to warn of fires.

David Conyngham was satisfied with the "strong proofs of the military despotism of the Confederacy," now revealed. "We captured in the trenches," he reported, "feeble old men, with gray heads and tottering steps, and mere striplings, who were too young to be taken from their mothers' leading-strings.

Everything had been made subservient to the army. It swallowed up the blood and wealth of the land, leaving its poor, deluded dupes stripped of everything—of the enjoyments of life itself.

"The people, after awakening from the first shock inspired by the terrible barbarities they heard of the Federal soldiers, seemed to welcome the new order of things. They were now protected, and could walk abroad in security. Gen. Slocum's administration of Atlanta was so impartial and rigidly enforced, that life and property there were as secure as in the city of New York.

"Near the depot were several slave marts, with their glaring signs, announcing, 'Slaves bought and sold here,' 'Slave auction rooms,' 'The great slave mart,' and such like. As the soldiers passed these they read them with a mocking laugh. As the poor negro passed these human shambles of his former degradation, his heart became light, for he no longer dreaded the galling chains, or the lash, or the auctioneer's hammer that was to consign him to a new master, and separate him from his wife and children."

General Hood telegraphed an oblique appraisal of his own military effectiveness, or lack of it, to General Bragg, President Davis' military confidant, in Richmond:

"For the offensive, my troops at present are not more than equal to their own numbers. To prevent this country from being overrun, reinforcements are absolutely necessary."

He thought it over, then added a characteristic postscript, a few hours later.

"My telegram in cipher this morning is based on the supposition that the enemy will not content himself with Atlanta but will continue offensive movements. All the lieutenant-generals agree with me."

In Washington, a message was dispatched to Sherman:

"The national thanks are rendered . . . to Major-General W. T. Sherman and the gallant officers and soldiers of his command before Atlanta, for the distinguished ability and perseverance displayed in the campaign in Georgia which, under Divine favor, has resulted in the capture of Atlanta. The marches, battles, sieges and other military operations that have signalized the campaign, must render it famous in the annals of war, and have entitled those who have participated therein to the applause and thanks of the nation."

It was signed, "Abraham Lincoln, President of the United States."

Major Charles Hubner, the Illinois journalist, reached Newnan, where "a singular thing befell me. . . . Much of our headquarters baggage had been destroyed, together with the munitions and stores that had been burned, near the old rolling mills in Atlanta, as the railroad was in the hands of the enemy. My little trunk was among the baggage and I did not know that headquarters luggage had been destroyed. A straggling soldier stopped to examine the great mass of burnt and unburnt stuff, and among other things picked up a daguerrotype case, this he put in his pocket. Happening to mention his find to a group of soldiers of whom I was one, he pulled out the case, opened it to show us the picture of the pretty girl it contained. I glanced at it, then excitedly exclaimed,

" 'This is mine—it is the picture of the girl to whom I am engaged!'

"The case was slightly torn but the picture of Miss Southworth was uninjured."

At Lovejoy's, Captain Tom Key, "worn out for the want of rest and something to eat," prepared to dig in. He was so weak from a diet of one meal a day that "it was with pain that I could remain on my horse to carry out my duties." There was little doubt in his mind on whom to affix the blame.

"I believe," he asserted, "that if General Johnston had remained in command of this army there would have been 5,000 more men in it, and all these trains been saved."

Disheartened Southern soldiers, too soul-weary to record their thoughts, if they knew how to write at all, grumbled vocally. "Give us back old Joe," was a familiar embittered lament heard around the campfires.

Under swaying lanterns and torches, Major General John W. Geary, former Postmaster of San Francisco, moved into quarters near Mary Rawson's home to be Atlanta's civil administrator.

Mary had "a fine view of Gen. Geary's headquarters with the tents surrounding it—my window presenting a good prospect of the city. The house was illuminated from the basement to the attic and the camp fires spread all over the hills filling the atmosphere with a light smoke with the pyramid of lights issueing from the windows of the general's home. . . . It grows late and I must retire to bed, not having a very flattering anticipation of the coming Sabbath and carried to dreamland by the music of the bugle."

But it was not too late for General Sherman. Whiskey bottle on his field table, he scribbled further reports to Halleck. The Commander of the Military Division of the Mississippi summed up the casualties at Jonesboro in the flickering light of an oil lantern.

"The rebels have lost besides the important city of Atlanta and stores at least 500 dead and 500 wounded and 3,000 prisoners, whereas our aggregate loss will not foot 1,500.

"If that is not success I don't know what is."

SEPTEMBER 4

Sherman wrote into the night. A later dispatch outlined the Major General's future plans.

"I propose to remove all the inhabitants of Atlanta," he continued, "sending those committed to our cause to the rear, and the rebel families to the front. I will allow no trade, manufacture, nor any citizens there at all, so that we will have the entire use of railroad back, as also such corn and forage as may be reached by our troops. If the people raise a howl against my barbarity and cruelty I will answer that war is war, and not popularity seeking. If they want peace they and their relatives must stop war!"

The resonant peal of church bells in Atlanta came as a heartening surprise to those who believed the Federals had removed all the bells and stabled their horses in every house of worship. However, Mary Rawson was "made sad" when she heard "the familiar chimes." It caused her to think of happier times.

"How often has this been the signal to us for leaving our homes to hear the word of God expounded. Today these peals serve only to send innumerable squads of soldiers to our own loved churches. The hills as well as the once-crowded thoroughfares of Atlanta are covered with bluecoats wending their way to the different places of worship."

S. P. Richards had much the same reaction. He found it "strange to go about Atlanta now and see only Yankee uniforms." And it was no less odd to observe a Provost Guard in City Hall. He found that "the enemy behave themselves pretty well except in the scramble for tobacco and liquor during which every store in town nearly was broken into yesterday. We heard the Church bells ring this morning and went to the Epis. Church and heard Mr. (Andrew) Freeman preach and a Federal Chaplain read the prayers."

Rufus Mead settled down to write his "dear folks at home" in Connecticut. "The long looked for day has come, and I can now head my letters to suit me. Of course the news is old to you but I could not get time to write sooner after I got here in the city.

"Now you'll find me in the S. E. part of town, or nearly out of it, under 'fly' in the dooryard of a good Union family, who happen to be near our train.

"I have made the acquaintance of the whole family even to the dog, who now lies in one corner of the tent as contented as can be, in fact he is a thorough going Union dog. The children are playing around as happy as any children can be, while the whole family appear as cheerful as any family I have seen, quite a contrast to the generality of the citizens we have met hitherto. I suppose the rebel population have mostly moved out long ago.

"On the night of the 1st we heard great noise in the city and thought it to be cannonading, but on the 2d we moved in here and found out it was caused by burning up 80 cars loaded with ammunition and arms of all kind, also the arsenal, foundry, rolling mill, etc. etc.

"Our Regt. was the first that came into the city as Regt., but the cavalry skirmishers were ahead of us. The Regt. got in about noon on the 2nd but I didnt come till last night. Our boys helped themselves to tobacco . . . of which there was any quantity, in fact that was about all that was left. Yesterday there was a guard put on so all pilfering is stopped and all the citizens say our soldiers are not half so bad as the Rebs were when they found they were going, and even citizens themselves went in for their share along with our boys as long as they could. I have been awful busy all day, so have not seen much of the city, but I hear there is scarcely a house without a shell-hole in it and I have seen many literally riddled. Every one had their bombproof where they ran with the shelling began near them, but over 100 citizens were killed nevertheless I learn.

"The destruction of property by the Rebs exceeds everything I ever saw in my life, and I thought I had seen something of that work before, I cant begin to tell it tonight but if we stay here a day or two Ill write a good letter all about it as near as I can. We expect Genl. Sherman here tomorrow with 3000 prisoners & 11 pieces of artillery captured in the late battle near Jonesboro. In his congratulatory order he says Hood's army is nearly used up and he can take our army any where he pleases in this state. I suppose he will keep up the movement till he takes Macon at least. I must write to Martin & others now so I will close this and write longer next time."

While the Perkersons were cooking noon dinner, a Federal officer approached their kitchen "and," Lizzie noted, "told Ma if she had any chickens she had better put them out of sight for there was a large body of soldiers coming. And they did come. The ambulance train and the Wagon train was passing continually for three days.

"On Sunday they took pretty well all the chickens, all the bee gums and pretty near all our cooking vessels. We were cooking dinner in the kitchen and they took dinner, pots and all. All we saved was what we snatched from them and brought into the house. They didn't come in. I suppose several of the officers being on the porch all the while restrained them some."

S. P. Richards returned from church planning to attend later services also. His straying mule had reappeared and was grazing in the back yard. Shortly after his return, three soldiers arrived and asked for dinner. They informed Richards that "their rations had not come and they would pay."

"Sallie had some cooked for them," Richards continued. "They belonged to Co. E 2d. Mass. Vols. but their spokesman was a Scotsman. They think that McClellan will be next President as he has been nominated by the Chicago Convention.

"At Mrs. Root's request I accompanied herself and Mrs. West to our church this afternoon and we heard an *Abolition* preacher from Indiana preach on the 'home of the blessed.'

"Returning to our homes we heard that another big fight at Jonesboro had resulted disastrously to the Confederates, and in confirmation of this we saw 1,800 'rebel prisoners' marched into town. They filled the street from the Baptist Church to Whitehall St. It was a sad sight but the Yankees *cheered* it lustily of course."

After dinner, a Captain Seymore called on the Rawsons. "Pa told him of the frequent depredations committed on our potato patch," Mary continued in her day's entry, "and he immediately sent us a guard. This afternoon as we stood in the upper front veranda, we noticed a great dust and what appeared to be a vast number of soldiers marching; besides, for the first time since the city was taken we heard the air of Yankee-doodle. After watching the soldiers some time one of the guards came around the terrace and saluted his fellow with the interrogation did you see the Johnnies? They were bringing in some captured Confederates and by close observation we could distinguish the two bodies of infantry, prisoners and the victors. These men were taken to one of the freight depots where a great many of the ladies visited them carrying delicacies."

The Rawson's servant, Hansel, later brought word that the milch cows were gone. This caused "some uneasiness as Sidney positively demanded milk. While we were at tea we heard one of them lowing. We then thought they would both be returned by morning."

To Carrie Berry it was "another long and lonesome Sunday." The little punctuations of the day, which had been taken for granted before the siege, now loomed in exaggerated magnitude. The lack or denial of them contained the seeds of heartbreak.

"How I wish we could have Church and Sunday School," she wrote. "We have ben looking at the soldiers all day. They have come in by the thousand. They were playing bands and they seemed to be rejoiced. It has not seemed like Sunday."

Meanwhile, wounded Federal soldiers were arriving in Atlanta. Corporal J. W. Gaskill, of Company B, 104th Regiment, Ohio Volunteer Infantry, was among their number. But his wounds were comparatively slight.

"After the fall of Atlanta," he reported, "the sick and disabled are loaded into ambulances and government wagons and conveyed to that city, a distance of 22 miles. A battle-scarred hotel called the Empire House is fitted up as a hospital and here our train of exhausted, sick and wounded boys are taken. During this long trip over rough and dusty roads all who are unable to walk short distances must grin and bear the punishment. Boys able to do a little walking spend the time trying to determine which is the greater punishment, walking or riding in the wagons. After walking a short distance they seem fully determined that riding is easier. . . .

"Families are loading their household goods in wagons and carts and departing southward. . . . Wealthy southerners who are responsible for this great war of devastation and death leave homes as we invade their territory and thus in a great measure escape hardships and throw the burden of suffering upon helpless and innocent. . . .

"Army supplies are coming in by rail and wagon trains and

Atlanta is taking on the appearance of a great military camp now almost made up of soldiers and governmental employes."

Joe Semmes, feeling better, wrote from Barnesville:

"I am still here waiting orders to go to the Front from Headquarters. My arm and side are yet sore and somewhat painful but otherwise I am quite well, though I am oppressed with anxiety about the state of affairs with the Army, from which we get no authentic information and a thousand rumors. As I feared, the failure of Gen. Hardee's efforts, in the battle the 31st of August at Jonesboro, to hold the railroad, was followed by the necessary evacuation of Atlanta on the night of the 1st and morning of the 2d; all our ordnance trains, and a large number of cars and some engines had to be destroyed, also a considerable quantity of commissary stores, for we had left fully 27 days rations in the city the night I moved from there.

"The Army is again reunited at or near Jonesboro, some 20 miles southeast of Atlanta, which position was held after severe fighting on the 2nd and 3rd. I presume we will remain quiet now for some time, as the enemy having accomplished the main point of the campaign, the capture of Atlanta, will not repair the railroads, but accumulate a large amount of supplies preparatory to further active movement.

"The fall of Atlanta will, I fear, prolong war at least another year. It may have a depressing effect on the people for awhile, but I trust we will all soon make another strong effort to regain our lost ground. In this connection I will state now, what you may say to everyone. That Gen. Hood and the troops of his Army, who did their duty, may feel proud of their efforts, and point with satisfaction in the future, if not now, to the facts in the case. He and they have done all that self-sacrificing and brave men could do, with the means at hand, to save the city of Atlanta, and have lost it with honor and glory; not driven from it and no surrender, but after desperate and bloody fights with superior numbers, beating them back in any attempt to take it, they abandoned the desolate and empty city, in good order in the face of a powerful foe, because their lines of communication and of course subsistence could not be maintained and the city too.

"These are the facts, and when the public understands them, Gen. Hood will receive praise and not condemnation. Atlanta really fell when the strong positions more than 40 miles north of it were abandoned. I have spoken of conduct of some of the troops, that conduct I believe lost us some of the advantages expected to be gained in the battle of the 31st of August. A portion of the troops from Alabama and Georgia behaved badly, straggled so as not to come up in time for the action, or positively refused to advance in the enemy's works. . . .

"I wrote you day before yesterday of my narrow escape in the collision of that day, the dead were 24 soldiers and 1 lady, the wounded nearly 100, some of whom must die. The horrors of that scene are constantly before my eyes and in my dreams, and can never be forgot. All the terrible scenes of the battlefield combined are nothing to that. The lady whom I waited on was so badly mangled, was a refugee from Nashville and died a few hours after the accident. One of my old regiment was badly mangled and recognized me but I could not tell who he was.

"If Ben has not left, you had better send me the two heavy undershirts for winter which I think I left. My letter of the 2d was mailed at Macon and ought to reach you four days before this. I have nothing since that last sweet letter which I had to destroy. . . . God bless you, your devoted, J."

Dr. James Comfort Patten of Indiana, was heading for Atlanta. "Started at noon and marched back through Jonesboro, on to Rough and Ready station where we camped in a field, and the inevitable rail was as usual called into requisition, softened in my case as usual by the down of the Georgia Goose, alias pine brush. While I was plucking my goose an order came up to me and told me that Col. Buel wished me to see a sick woman in a house a little way back.

"I went of course, and found her very low with typhoid fever, of twenty one days standing. Her daughter informed me that they lived in Atlanta but that our shelling had driven them out and they came there and were unable to get her back, on account of her sickness. Some Dr. had been attending her, but he was now gone. I gave her some medicine but advised the girl not to promise herself too much as the prospect was by no means favorable. I did not see her again."

At Lovejoy's, Hood, still smarting, sent a dispatch to Bragg in Richmond:

"Owing to the wanton neglect of the chief quartermaster of this army, a large amount of ammunition and railroad stock had to be destroyed at Atlanta. He had more than ample time to remove the whole and had repeated instructions. I am reliably informed that he is too much addicted to drink of late to attend to his duties. Am greatly in want of an officer to take his place. Can you not send one?"

As night approached, Sherman, not many miles from Hood, in a mellow, expansive mood, wrote a personal message to Halleck.

"My Dear Friend: I owe you a private letter and believe one at this time will be acceptable to you. I confess I owe you all I now enjoy of fame . . . you alone seemed to be confident and opened to us the first avenue of success and hope. . . .

"George Thomas you know is slow, but as true as steel; Schofield is also slow and leaves too much to others; Howard is a Christian, elegant gentleman, and a conscientious soldier. . . . Hooker was a fool. Had he staid a couple of weeks he could have marched into Atlanta and claimed all the honors. . . . Grant has the perseverance of a Scotch terrier. Let him alone and he will overcome Lee by untiring and unceasing efforts."

Sherman expressed anger when someone nominated him for the Presidency at the Democratic convention in Chicago. "If forced to choose between the penitentiary and the White House for four years . . . I would say the penitentiary, thank you, sir!"

SEPTEMBER 5

Monday arrived, but there was still no sign of General Sherman, whom the citizens of Atlanta expected hourly.

There was little outward defiance of the conqueror, with a few piquant exceptions. One young lady was observed climbing through the ground-floor window of a house and out the opposite rather than walk under the United States flag which hung from the doorway over the sidewalk. With her lovely auburn hair, she became an object of considerable attention of the Federal soldiers—who allowed her to display her small contempt for Old Glory.

The food and medical aid brought by the occupying forces tended to outweigh inherent disadvantages. Dr. Calhoun, for one, continued to improve "very rapidly" after the Northern surgeons had operated on him.

On the other hand, there were those who had reason to mortally fear the Union troops. Among them were those involved in the execution of James J. Andrews and seven others of his group who two years previously had daringly stolen a locomotive, *The General,* at Big Shanty. Andrews, a Union spy, and his plain-clothes Federal soldiers hoped to tear up the rails and burn bridges as they sped north, severing the main line to Chattanooga.

William A. Fuller, the pursuing conductor who not only helped capture the "Andrews raiders," but followed Andrews to his execution, was in Macon with the equipment he had snatched to safety.

He was high on the list of the vengeance-minded Federal troops, especially since three of them had escaped prison and marched into Atlanta with Sherman's Army.

There was, David Conyngham believed, a "Mr. Jones," the executioner of the Andrews' group. His principal occupation was keeping a livery stable "in the rear of the mayor's." According to the *New York Herald* correspondent "he was a devil incarnate; kept bloodhounds for hunting up men skulking from the conscription, or Federal prisoners trying to make their escape. Woe betide the wretch that got into his hands. Like all tyrants and ruffians, he was a coward, and bought exemption by his valuable services as a spy and dogger. This black-hearted ruffian used all his influence to get the poor men executed who attempted to destroy the bridges and run off with the train on the Chattanooga line.

"He succeeded, and as the poor victims were dragged along to the place of execution by the halters on their necks, this foul scoundrel followed them, goading them on, and mocking them. He was also accompanied by his bloodhounds, as he said, 'to give them a smell of Yankee blood.'

"The executioner had to enjoy the exclusive privilege of tying up his victims, and then drawing the plank from their feet. As their bodies dangled in the air, he swung them round, knocking the convulsed breathing frames against one another. All this time his bloodhounds barked and jumped at the dangling feet of their victims, and as they caught them they swung from them until the flesh gave way.

"Honest men shuddered at such fiendish cruelty, but durst not resent it. They dreaded the tyrant's power. I hope this fellow has met his deserts before this; if not, that all honest men will treat him with scorn, and society exclude him from its circles. Such a fellow is only fit to associate with his brother demons."

The Rawsons were still without their missing cows. Inquiries brought forth no clues and by noon Mary was inclined to give up the family's milk supply "as lost." The day was cool, quiet, and not unpleasant at "The Terraces."

A friend, George Zimmerman, arrived "to request that Father would call the next morning to see his mother, and Gen. Sherman had ordered all ladies whose husbands in 'Rebel Service' as he said, to leave the city in five days."

Carrie Berry was helping her father "tack a mattress." It blistered her hands "but it was for my bed and I think I shall sleep so nice that it will pay me."

The morning passed peacefully at the Berry household and,

in Carrie's words, "we have seen nothing." When she finished with the mattress, Carrie started on another pair of socks. At least, she reflected, the enforced confinement in cellars during the bombardment had enabled her to knit many socks for the family.

In Decatur, Mary Gay had decided to remove the Confederate winter uniforms hidden in her dining room ceiling. With Telitha, who had helped her put the clothing above the lath and plaster, she started to disinter them.

"When the darkness of night fully enshrouded the earth, with no other light than that which found its way from the campfires of the enemy through the latticed shutters, I stepped into the chair and thence upon the table, and Telitha followed and drew the chair up after her. Then with her strong dusky hands she seized the wardrobe as if it had been a toy in her hands. I steadied the chair by the wardrobe and stepped into it, and another step landed me on top of the wardrobe.

"My fingers penetrated the crevice between the slats which I wanted to pull off, and to a slight effort they yielded. Lest the noise occasioned by dropping them might attract notice, I stooped and laid each piece down as I drew it off the joist. When the aperture thus made was sufficient, I began to draw from their hiding place the precious Confederate overcoats and other winter apparel confided to my keeping by soldiers of Gen. Joseph E. Johnston's army, when they were at Dalton. One by one each piece was taken out and dropped down upon the floor. But by a lamentable oversight we afterwards found that one article had been left—a woolen scarf for the neck, knitted for my brother by his loving young wife in Texas.

"Carefully I descended, and, with the aid of the girl, placed the chair, the table and the dear old wardrobe (which deserves to be immortalized in song and in story), in less suspicious positions, and then proceeded to fold and pack in the sacks, already mentioned, the precious articles. The thought occurred to me that my mother would like to have a hand in this labor of love, and I opened the door between us. I shall never forget her appearance as she stood as if riveted to the spot, near a window, watching the moving figures without. I approached her and in a cheerful whisper told her that I was now putting the things in the sacks, and I knew she would like to have an interest in the job. She tried to respond, but she was too nervous to do so. Slowly but surely she was yielding to the pressure upon nerve and upon brain.

"As each sack was filled, a threaded needle securely closed the mouth. In a short while a number of these sacks stood in a group, as erect as if on parade, and I verily believe that if the host of profane, Godless braggarts (with but few exceptions), who surrounded the house, could have seen them at that time and known their contents, they would have evacuated Decatur in mortal fear of the ghosts of 'Johnnie Rebs.'

"This important work having been accomplished without discovery, or even a shadow of suspicion, I felt vastly relieved, and thanked the Lord with all my heart for the health, strength and ingenuity which had enabled me to consummate it. My mother and I lay down upon the same bed, and were soon blest by the invigorating influence of 'tired nature's sweet restorer.' "

Meanwhile, other units were moving up from Jonesboro in a rainstorm, but Sherman was delaying his own entry.

Fenwick Hedley, Adjutant with the 32d. Illinois Infantry, said of the operations: "The Army of the Cumberland was to be grouped in and about Atlanta, the Army of the Tennessee at East Point and the Army of the Ohio at Decatur.

"This movement began September 5th, and proved to be a remarkable conclusion to an eventful campaign. It rather resembled the retreat of a defeated army, than a victorious march by conquerors.

"As the head of the column turned toward Atlanta, Hood's army was but a little distance behind it, and his cavalry was particularly active. It was necessary, therefore, that the artillery and supply wagons should precede the troops. A heavy rain had been falling all day, and, what with the unmeasurable mud in the roads, and the unserviceable condition of the animals, consequent upon long service and ill-feeding, it was 9 o'clock at night before the long train was straightened out, and the troops began to move.

"The march was spasmodic and painful. For a few minutes,

sometimes for a half-hour, caused by a portion of the wagon-train stalling or breaking down. Occasionally, a wagon irretrievably wrecked, or its team utterly worn out, was thrown to one side of the road, and burned. At one moment, startled by such a conflagration, the writer's horse made a sudden leap, and the rider, asleep in the saddle through sheer exhaustion, was awakened by falling into the mud.

"After a march of six miles, consuming 12 hours' time, a halt was called, and the wearied troops prepared such food and took such rest as the weather would permit."

William Graham was camped at East Point by late afternoon where "D. Reader and the 2 O'Leary boys were quartered in an old house opposite the water tank. . . . Corps not arrived yet."

Dr. James Comfort Patten arrived at the Confederate fortifications south of Atlanta. "Here," he wrote, "I saw the most pitiful sight I have ever witnessed. A young looking woman was at work by the roadside skinning a cow that had been killed and a little girl some six or seven years old had a piece of the raw bloody meat in both hands devouring it with the eagerness of a starving dog. I could see the leaders in this thing starve but the poor children. . . .

"We soon came in sight of Atlanta and here all of a sudden Col. Buel concluded that we must begin to put on style and show off. He began to scold because the men had their coats off. He wore a light linen one himself. The men naturally did not like it to be abused so unreasonably, when they were not in fault, and so when showing off time came they became very awkward. One who did not know might have thought them not half drilled.

"The Col. looking along the line had his anger stirred by the sight of a man going through the manual with his gun wrong end up. He was almost ready to burst. He fairly boiled over, and putting spurs to his horse went for him. When he got there he could not tell which man it was for all was right when he got there and no one knew anything about him. The Soldiers are all know-nothings. He was mad but how could he help himself?

"I am glad he did not ask me who it was for I would not have told him nor would I have denied knowing, and at the same time I did not want any fuss with him. We got in order at last and the Col. who would be a Brigadier, rode away with his staff as proud as a kitten with two tails. He rode straight on through the city and the regt. following in such order as pleased themselves and the officers could not see it for they sympathized with the men in the whole matter.

"My own opinion is that the Colonel had a canteen of something stronger than coffee.

"The City is about the size of Evansville and is terribly shattered. I had often heard of the terrors of a bombardment of a crowded city but I never realized it before. Houses were shattered and torn in every shape that can be imagined, some utterly destroyed and some but little injured. Some had shell through the doors, some places the shell had burst inside of a house and torn it all to pieces. After seeing the destruction I no longer wondered at the insane fury with which they charged our works, rushing on as they often did with their hats pulled down over their eyes so that they could not see the certain destruction that awaited them.

"I am glad that I have taken part in this campaign. I would not for a great deal have missed that ride through Atlanta. It almost paid me for the whole campaign."

SEPTEMBER 6

Mary Rawson's breakfast was interrupted as "Grand-father came and told us that Aunty (Mrs. Sidney Root, S. P. Richards' friend) had been ordered to leave her beautiful home to give place to a Yankee colonel who had given her only half a day to move all her property.

"O cruel soldier! Could you not be a little more lenient? I concluded I would go with Father and see Miss Delia and as Grand-pa urged me I would go to Grand-Mas on my return. I found Miss Delia indignant at the thought of being driven from home. 'O,' she said, 'I would not live among them and if I had had any idea of their coming I would have gone 'ere this.' But notwithstanding her anger I had a very pleasant visit.

"I went according to promise to see Grand-Ma. The house was all in confusion, occasioned by the bringing in of Aunty's furniture. Then I went to Aunty's to see if I could not render some assistance and by constant running to and fro we succeeded in getting most of her valuables removed. But all this time the officers were there dictating as to what should be carried away and what should remain and continually repeating the injunction of haste, haste, forgetting that haste makes waste.

"On returning to my home I found Mother in great anxiety, caused by the information derived from the guard first and confirmed by Mr. Tenny and Mr. Andrews that all citizens should be compelled to vacate the city, though they still had choice of which home they would prefer. We could be sent farther down in Dixie or we could attempt the ice and snow of the Northern winter. Father did not think the report at all reliable, but went to the provost marshal to inquire. On reaching the office the door was closed; and a notice tacked on the door, saying that no one would be admitted until the next day. He then called on Gen. Geary and asked him concerning the order but he had heard nothing of it. So, wearied out by walking and anxiety, he returned home without any cheering news. O! these days of suspense; dark days. May our path of life ne'er be overcast by your shadows again."

The Neal home, at the corner of Washington and Mitchell streets, bustled with activity through the cloudy morning. An elderly Irish woman, engaged as housekeeper by General Geary's civil administration staff, was cleaning in preparation for a distinguished new occupant—General Sherman. But the woman, unimpressed, scowled as she swept away dust and cobwebs from the closed rooms and denounced her master-to-be as a "savage." For Sherman, she swore, "the worst fate is none too good."

On the other hand, it was employment.

Occupants of the block, recalling the death of Andy Neal not more than a month ago, thought the Union commandeering of the house a desecration.

At East Point, Hedley and the Army of the Tennessee dug in for an indefinite encampment. There was still corn in the fields for soldiers on forage. But livestock and chickens on nearby farms—like that of the Perkersons'—were virtually "used up," as Sherman predicted.

In Decatur, Mary Gay, as usual, had started the day with the sun. "The song of the lark had ceased to be heard in this war stricken locality," wrote Mary. "Chanticleer had long since furnished a savory meal for camp followers, and the time pieces had either been spoiled or stolen; but there was a silent unerring chronometer within that never deviated, and needed no alarm attachment to arouse me from slumber. The dawn found me up and preparing for the duties, and perhaps the dangers of the day.

"Telitha had become quite an attraction to a bevy of men who occupied soldiers' quarters, and wore soldiers uniforms, and drew pay for doing so, from Uncle Sam's coffers; and as she had been trained to ideas of virtue and morality she often came in frowning and much ruffled in temper by their deportment towards her. Being almost entirely deaf and dumb, her limited vocabulary was inadequate to supply epithets expressive of the righteous indignation and contempt which she evidently felt,— she could only say, 'Devil Yank, devil,' and these words she used with telling effect both to the amusement and chagrin of the Yankees. This state of affairs convinced me, that for her protection she would have to be kept within doors, and I therefore assumed the task of drawing the water, and a few other jobs indispensable even in life's rudest state. On this occasion, when I went to the well for a bucket of water, before preparing our frugal breakfast, I was asked by early marauders why I did not let 'that young colored lady draw the water.' I candidly answered them, and told them I was going to ask the officers of the encampment to protect her while I was gone, and I also would ask them to report any misdemeanor towards her, that they might witness, to headquarters."

Mary Gay, in addition to the staples of bread and butter for breakfast, enjoyed that "luxurious beverage," coffee, "furnished by one whose heart was in touch with humanity." Considering her outspoken sentiments regarding the Northerners, she hesitated to speak further of the source of the coffee.

Later in the morning, Mary finished covering the hole in the dining room ceiling and putting the "contraband" uniforms in sacks. She was now ready, in case she decided to leave Decatur.

Sherman finally rode into Jonesboro, "and there inspected the rebel hospital, full of wounded officers and men left by Hardee in his retreat."

Colonel Beatty rested at Lovejoy's, hoping the situation would remain static at least "for a short time."

"We must nerve ourselves for a desperate struggle," he wrote. "A few more such blows as we have received here and we are gone. We lost five locomotives, 81 cars, 25 days rations and a large amount of ordnance at Atlanta. Gen. Hood is a failure. I think Sherman gave him a great chance to distinguish himself but he did not seize it."

But Hood, headquartered not far from Taylor Beatty, was relieved that the Federal army was withdrawing "from our immediate front" toward Atlanta. He expressed his feelings in his notes.

"General Sherman published orders stating that his army would retire to East Point, Decatur and Atlanta, and repose after the fatigue of the campaign through which it had passed. We were apprised of these instructions soon after their issuance —as well as of nigh every important movement of the enemy— through the vigilance of our cavalry, spies and scouts, and from information received through Federal prisoners. Upon this date it may be justly considered that the operations round Atlanta ceased. We had maintained a defense during 46 days, of an untenable position, and had battled almost incessantly, day and night, with a force of about 45,000 against an army of 106,000 effectives, flushed with victory upon victory from Dalton to Atlanta."

To Secretary of War Seddon, in Richmond, he transmitted information of a more official—if less credible—nature: "Sherman continues his retreat beyond Jonesboro."

SEPTEMBER 7

Strains of music had brightened the night at East Point. The bandsmen of the Army of the Tennessee had blown their lustiest "housewarmings" for several hours.

"Now that the troops fully recognized the import of their brilliant but wearisome and bloody three months' campaigning," Fenwick Hedley stated, "and learned with what joy the news was received at home, they gave way to a protracted jubilee. The brass and martial bands, which had been silent all the long way from Chattanooga to Atlanta, now played their most exultant airs; and the men vied with the instruments in making noise expressive of great joy. All were happy and smiling, from the commander-in-chief to the humblest private in the ranks, and even the bray of the half-starved government mule seemed mellow and melodious, as it added to the din.

"Better yet, the 'cracker-line,' as the railroad was called, was again in repair, after having been greatly disturbed by the enemy; and presently the troops enjoyed the novel experience of abundant rations and frequent meals."

This happiness was not shared by the Georgians. Carrie Berry wrote of feeling "gloomy" and of how "times get a little worse every day." She was knitting a pair of gloves now, "but I don't know when I will get them done." She couldn't even find time to visit "Grandma."

Their colored girl, Mary, had left, adding to Carrie's burden. "I don't expect that she will come back any more, but we can do very well without her. I will have to go to work and help Mama."

While Carrie reviewed her day, General Hood was confronted with a letter from his conqueror:

"General: I have deemed it to the interest of the United States that the citizens now residing in Atlanta should remove, those who prefer it to go south, and the rest north. For the latter I can provide food and transportation to points of their election in Tennessee, Kentucky or farther north. For the former I can provide transportation by cars as far as Rough and Ready, and also wagons; but, that their removal may be made with as little discomfort as possible, it will be necessary for you to help the families from Rough and Ready, with all their movable effects, viz., clothing, trunks, reasonable furniture, bedding, etc., with their servants, white and black, with the proviso that no force shall be used toward the blacks, one way or the other. If they want to go with their masters or mistresses, they may do so; otherwise they will be sent away, unless they be men, when they may be employed by our quartermaster. Atlanta is no place for families or non-combatants, and I have no desire to send them north if you will assist in conveying them south. If this proposition meets your views, I will consent to a truce in the neighborhood of Rough and Ready, stipulating that any wagons, horses, animals or persons sent there for the purposes herein stated, shall in no manner be harmed or molested; you in your turn agreeing that any cars, wagons, or carriages, persons or animals sent to the same point, shall not be interfered with. Each of us might send a guard of, say, one hundred men, to maintain order, and limit the truce to, say, two days after a certain time appointed.

"I have authorized the mayor to choose two citizens to convey to you this letter, with such documents as the mayor may forward in explanation, and shall await your reply. I have the honor to be your obedient servant.

W. T. Sherman, Major-General commanding."

Hood's "obedient servant," however, had not waited—Sherman's order was already being published in Atlanta. The Rawsons learned of it after breakfast.

"Father immediately set out for the headquarters of Gen. Slocum," Mary wrote, "and afterwards to the provost—afterwards, home again at noon, we gathered around Father to hear Gen. Sherman's order read. During the forenoon he had seen Gen. Geary, Col. Beckworth, Capt. Forbes and Capt. Seymore. These had all expressed it as their opinion that the command referred to these men who in some way had been in the Confederate service and that all others could remain quietly in their home.

"The question now was: what explanation to give to the order? There was also another law written forbidding any person to sell cotton or tobacco, as such commodities would be impressed for the government use. Pa was kept constantly moving to and fro trying to get authority to dispose of his tobacco for some mere pittance though this was finally proved to be impracticable, unless a special permit could be obtained from Sherman."

Mary Gay reacted to the news with her characteristically passionate expressions.

"After every morsel of food had been taken from the people," she recorded, "and every vestige of nutrition extracted from the earth, the following order, in substance, was proclaimed throughout the land held by the right of conquest:

" 'All who cannot support themselves without applying to the United States Commissary for assistance, must go outside of our lines, either North or South, within the period of time mentioned in this order, etc., etc.'

"And by this order, and by others even more oppressive and diabolical, the Nero of the nineteenth century, alias William Tecumseh Sherman, was put upon record as the born leader of the most ruthless, Godless band of men ever organized in the name of patriotism—a band which, but for a few noble spirits, who, by the power of mind over matter, exerted a restraining influence, would not have left a Southerner to tell the tale of its fiendishness."

Joe Semmes was camped near the front lines at Bear Creek Station on the Macon Railroad. He had noted the Federal pullback toward Atlanta.

"We moved after them, reoccupied Jonesboro last night," he wrote, "recapturing our wounded who fell into the enemy's hands at that point, when we retreated. The enemy destroyed the railroad as they fell back, thoroughly. What are their intentions or where they will march next no one can tell. I think they will rest awhile at or near Atlanta, reorganize their decimated ranks, accumulate a large stock of stores, and then advance toward either Montgomery or Augusta, perhaps both should they be able to get up a sufficient amount of reinforcements.

"The aspect of the future is threatening and will, I fear, discourage many. I am however confident as ever, and cannot believe for one moment that the enemy will succeed in penetrating the interior of the country to such an extent as is feared.

"History is witness against the success of such movements and I feel that we are able and ought to prevent it. Nothing but incompetence in superiors and cowardice in inferiors, and the people, will be cause of the enemies' success. I fear, however, that his possession of Atlanta will enable him, while confronting our army with a strong force to hold us in his front, to detach strong bodies which will strike us at every undefended point and ravage the country. This is their favorite mode of warfare and you may rely upon it they will do their worst.

"The Army post office was destroyed at Atlanta, and with it some 100,000 letters and I suppose some from me to you; a new post office is being prepared, it was on the car and you must write as long as you are not cut off from me, directing simply to Army of Tenn.

"No commissary stores were lost at Atlanta or destroyed; about 550,000 pounds of meal were distributed to the people, but we lost heavily in ordnance stores, engine and cars, 81 cars and 5 engines, 25 cars of ammunition, and some quartermasters stores. All there should have been brought off and someone is to blame. Col. McMieken is blamed and is now having the matter investigated by a Court of Inquiry. In the 2nd battle of Jonesboro Hardee's Corps fought the whole Yankee Army, and of course was compelled to retreat. We lost several hundred prisoners and 8 guns, the Yankees admit a very heavy loss. I had a long chat with Henry Robinson the day I left Atlanta; he is looking very well and seems satisfied to wait for his wife, whom he describes as very charming and very like Bena. He was very much disgusted with Maggie's match, and the people generally in Washington and Georgetown. He is Loring's Asst. Adjutant Genl. with rank of Major and stands well. By the way Ben is not a Captain, he is only commissioned a Lieut. and Genl. Smith calls him a Lieut. officially. He is Captain by courtesy only, but if he gets the promotion under the new staff now, he will be a Major. This is between us, don't allude to it.

"I am living very lonesomely, no companions in my tent, and am as uncomfortable as possible. My clothes are in the rear, and I am not even clean, that is for me. Raph. Semmes book, 'The Cruise of the Sumter and Alabama, from the Private Journal of the Captain,' is published in New York republished from English editions. It will sell like wild fire. He is on his way home, and if successful in his voyage will be due the last of the month.

"Goodbye darling and God bless you. . . ."

The tragic story of Atlanta had reached Americus.

"Atlanta was important on account of its position," wrote Nurse Kate Cumming. "I hear few regret the loss of the city itself, not even Georgians, as they say it was the most wicked place in the world.

"A lady writes from Newnan that the wounded are all doing well, and that the ladies are very kind to them. She says Newnan is almost entirely deserted—everybody having left for fear of the enemy; many of them are here. . . .

"We have numbers of wounded men, who have been sent home on furloughs; while there, their wounds break out again, and as there were no experienced surgeons to attend them, they are worse than ever. A great deal of mischief is done in this way. This is one of the reasons why surgeons are so unwilling to give furloughs.

"The public square opposite to us is filled with tents, which are full of gangrene cases. One lad suffers so much we can hear him scream for two squares off!"

climate was much more congenial in the South. That that would
have undoubtedly have been our choice had not one great bar-
rier here presented itself. This was that all the men of the Confederacy were conscripted and were compelled to serve in the
Army. This we knew Father could stand only a short time and
he had no inclination to enter the Army. But a difficulty equally
as great debarred us from entering a life in the 'Yankee land of
Canaan,' the difference in the currency occasioned this embar-
rassment. Father's property mostly consisted in lands and Confederate money so we had not means enough to venture North;
unless Pa could get something for his tobacco. So we were in a
vacillating condition."

Mary Gay, after Sherman's "pronunciamento," was swept up
in general "bustle and rapid movement in every household
within the boundaries of usurpation."

"Under the strong arm of military power," she continued,
"delay was not permitted. Homes were to be abandoned, and
household goods and household gods to be left for the enemy,
or destroyed; and liberty under our own vine and fig tree was
to be a thing of the past, and dependence upon strangers a thing
of the future. In preparation for this enforced change, much
that should have been done was left undone, but there was no
time to correct mistakes—the armistice was only for ten days.

"What were we to do, my mother and myself, was a question
which presented itself with startling seriousness, and had to be
answered without delay. Our farm in Gordon county had already been devastated by the invading army, and every improve-
ment destroyed, and if we should lose our home in Decatur we
would be poor indeed. But what were we to do? If we left our
home, we knew it would share the fate of all other 'abandoned'
property, and furnish material for a bonfire for Nero to fiddle
by; and if we remained, by grace of better men than he, what
assurance had we that by any means within our grasp we could
obtain even a scanty subsistence, or be protected from personal
abuse and insult by an alien army whose gentlemen were vastly
in the minority?

"We learned that our neighbors and friends, Mrs. Ammi Williams and her estimable son, Mr. Frederick Williams (an in-

valid from paralysis), whose influence over General Schofield prevented my banishment from Decatur the very first night of its occupancy by the Federal army—and the venerable Mr. and Mrs. Buchanan (the latter a Bostonian and educated in Emerson's celebrated school for young ladies), and other families as true to the South as the needle to the pole, were going to remain and take their chances within the enemy's lines, and we determined to do so too."

The Federal troops were catching up on the mail. Rufus Mead wrote again to his "Dear Folks at Home."

"Nothing to do till most night I guess—I'll commence a long letter to you. I received your letter of the 25th on the 5th but since then we have had no mail. I believe the road is nearly if not wholly repaired so we will get news through soon. We hear all sorts of rumors from Richmond but don't fairly believe any thing just yet.

"Sherman issued an order & had it read off on parade last night, that 'he had accomplished his desire in this campaign— now he should make his headquarters in this city, while the army went into camp for 30 days to recruit their health, get fed, clothed & paid off, and every preparation made for an active winter campaign.'

"Our Corps are yet in the city while the others are outside but how long it will be so I don't know, but we rather expect to be sent out on the RR or as some think to the army of the Potomac, but this is all surmise.

"The city is scattered over a circle of 4 miles diameter but no two houses hardly meet, no street is graded or building lot leveled off. It resembles Waterbury somewhat in that respect only there is fewer factories and the houses are further apart and larger yards. On Whitehall St nearly all the stores are situated and all the business done except a rolling mill & foundry in the S E part of the city near the RR. This mill was owned & carried on by northern men, till within a few weeks when the Govt. seized all the machinery and carried it to Augusta, and when the Rebs left the mill was burnt in the general conflagation.

"The Macon Depot is in the centre of the city and has been

a good target for all our batteries. I should judge by the way things are splintered up. A large round house capable of holding 40 Locomotives with a turntable in the centre is fairly riddled both by shells passing through and also by bursting inside, while wooden buildings near by are splintered ties shivered & rails broken by them. Shade trees a foot through are cut off, fences broken down in short every kind of mischief is done by those iron missiles. I dont see how any one ever ventured to live there yet some did and escaped too Of course every one had his bombproof burrow dug & covered over from 3 to 6 ft with timber and dirt where they ran to in case of danger or furious shelling but 100 or so were killed nevertheless.

"I hope you will never know such horrors in your life.

"The city is completely void of all dry goods or groceries, but there was a few drugstores, as well as hardware tobacco & a few liquor shops. Citizens say the Rebs began the work of devastation before they left, and for one day our soldiers as well as citizens and more especially darkies continued the pillage—till the city is nearly empty. We put a guard and patrol on the next day and the best of order prevails now. Our boys who use the weed laid in large quantities of it, while a few got drunk of course but on the whole behaved very well so I hear all the citizens affirm; much better than their own men. I am now living in the dooryard where 3 families live, all strong union or northern descent quite intelligent, using more of the peculiar southern expressions and from them I learn many facts, at least I credit them as such. There are 2 men here who can talk pretty fast, but one young widow can beat them both. I believe she would talk a man blind if such a thing is possible. I thought her quite pretty & charming—not over 22 or 23 years old at first, but when I found that she had 3 children and the oldest one 13 it took away the romance considerably But she is good company and well informed nevertheless. She knows all the Rebels in the city as well as union and tells of the Ladies union meetings which they have held in secret all the while yet.

"She has seen 17 union men hung at one time for bridge-burning, after only a mock trial with no positive proof at all. One man by the names of Barnes formerely of New York was very conspicuous for his zeal in hanging Yankees and one time she says she saw him as they were hanging one in particular. The frame was so low that the man's toes touched the ground and Barnes took a shovel and dug a hole under him and then pulled his feet and kept them over the hole. She said she had him spotted but the fellow left with the army. . . .

"I send a list of prices here before we came, Sugar $20, Coffee, $35, Syrup $50, butter, $20, Eggs $12 per dozen, Milk $5 per quart, while drygoods were not to be had at any price for 6 months past."

The Berry family was working "in glad spirits." Carrie ironed and "Mama was buisy regulating things." Then, "Papa came and told us that Gen. Sherman had ordered us to move. It broke all into our arrangements."

The Massachusetts 2nd and 33rd regiments, both encamped on the Court House square, gave a concert that evening. These bands were "a source of infinite pleasure" to Sherman, who believed them "two of the finest bands of the army."

A group of Federal officers sponsored a ball at the Trout House and the young ladies of Atlanta attended, in spite of a warning ditty:

> Don't flirt with Yankee officers
>   Or meet them bright with smiles
> Or allow your tender hearts to be
>   Won by their tempting wiles:
> The time will come when we'll be home
>   And oh! how sad 'twill be
> To hear that you've been captured
>   By Yankee subtlety.

SEPTEMBER 9

General Hood replied to General Sherman's letter.

"Your letter of yesterday's date, borne by James M. Ball and James R. Crew, citizens of Atlanta, is received. You say therein, 'I deem it to be of the interest of the United States that the citizens now residing in Atlanta should remove,' etc. I do not consider that I have any alternative in this matter. I therefore accept your proposition to declare a truce of two days, or such time as may be necessary to accomplish the purpose mentioned, and shall render all assistance in my power to expedite the transportation of citizens in this direction. I suggest that a staff-officer be appointed by you to superintend the removal from the city to Rough and Ready, while I appoint a like officer to control their removal farther south; that a guard of one hundred men be sent by either party as you propose, to maintain order at that place, and that the removal begin on Monday next.

"And now, sir, permit me to say that the unprecedented measure you propose transcends, in studied and ingenious cruelty, all acts ever before brought to my attention in the dark history of war.

"In the name of God and humanity, I protest, believing that you will find that you are expelling from their homes and firesides the wives and children of a brave people. I am, general, very respectfully, your obedient servant."

At 10:00 A.M. Sherman dispatched a message to Halleck in Washington.

"All our troops are now in position, comfortable and well. In a day or two I will have telegraphic communication with Roswell round to Sandtown and can act promptly. A few of the enemy's cavalry followed us as far as Rough and Ready and last evening Gen. Hood sent in a flag of truce asking to exchange prisoners. I have about 2,000 in hand, and will exchange if he will make a fair deal. . . . weather beautiful, and all things seem bright."

It was a bleak Friday in Atlanta. E. E. Rawson, under the shadow of evacuation, was still wrestling with the added complication of selling his tobacco.

"Ill-fated weed," deplored Mary, "though much loved and longed for by Yankee soldiery, you seem as ever to be only a source of trouble to those who possess and use you! No success was experienced and evening found us as undecided as in the morning."

S. P. Richards was preparing for abandoning his bookstore and Atlanta.

"We have had several days of great excitement as it was understood that 'orders' had been or were about to be issued to the effect that *every* body not belonging to the army must leave the city going North or South as they saw fit, except the families of those men who had left the city before the Yankees came, and such *must go south*," Richards noted. "Mrs. Root was the first one to feel the storm as her husband has been quite a secessionist and large blockade-runner, two heinous crimes in the Federal Calendar. But as yet no orders have been published specifying anything and we do not know what we have to do. We have determined upon going to New York if we are sent off, as we want to get away from the war and the fighting if we can. The news is published today in the Yankee paper that Gen. John H. Morgan is killed.

"The Yankees have not molested us much at the house, they have generally behaved pretty well. One unpleasant feature of present circumstances is the important airs the negroes put on, and their indifference to the wants of their former masters. Of course they are all free and the Yankee soldiers don't fail to assure them of that fact. Jabe's 'Sally' has come out of her hole now and is as independent as can be. 'George' and 'Clem' are said to be in the city too. So our negro property has all vanished into air.

"Henry's baby died last night, little Katie, age 15 mos. Mr. Bohnefield the undertaker was clever enough to give him a plain coffin worth six dollars in greenbacks and Joe and I dug a grave under a small oak in Henry's garden, and Rev. Mr.

Freeman the Epis. Minister officiated; and so the little one has passed away from the present evil and 'evil to come.'

"Yesterday was Dora's birthday; she is 10 years old. I wrote her a long letter upon the importance to her giving early attention to the interests of her soul. Mr. Seymour agreed yesterday to let me have $75 in gold out of $250 that he was prudent enough to secure in time, so that I shall have enough to get to New York with, at any rate, I hope. How I wish I had the value of our city lots and negroes in gold at this juncture."

Maxwell Berry did not intend to dispute Sherman's order.

"We all commenced this morning to prepare for moving," Carrie wrote. "We don't know how long we will get to stay here. We are all in so much trouble."

There was confusion everywhere. Conyngham observed the preparations by Atlanta families who were "merely joining their friends." Their plight seemed as nothing compared to "the men who had concealed themselves from conscription, who had been persecuted by rebel authority, whose friends had been shot down or hung up for their Union sentiments, who concealed our wounded men and fed them, and who screened our prisoners and aided their flight, who longed for us as their friends, (for they) did not well know what to do. They found our friendship as destructive as the rebels' enmity. Some few went north; the most of them remained, hoping, like Mr. Micawber, that something better would turn up.

" 'Could you tell me who are our friends?' said an old, respectable citizen to me.

" 'If you tell me your politics, I will,' said I.

" 'At the breaking out of the war I owed large sums to northern merchants, and I paid them. I had neither hand nor voice in bringing on this war; I wanted to live under the old flag. During the war I gave every assistance in my power to relieve Union prisoners, and my only son was caught aiding one of them to escape, and shot. The rebels then stripped me of my property, and called me a d—d Yank. Only for my age, they'd hang me.'

" 'Well, I think you are a Union man,' I replied.

" 'I have given proofs enough, at least; and now what's my

reward? You hunt me from my house and place in my old age. Do you think but I am suffering for my country? I have the alternative of going north and starve, or going into the rebel lines and being hung.' "

Women like Mary Gay and Lizzie Perkerson had no fear of "rebel" wrath. Mary Gay, who had acquired a taste for intrigue and danger during the investment of Atlanta and Decatur and the see-saw presence of Federal and Confederate cavalry, now had another inspiration. She would take advantage of the armistice to "evacuate" to Rough and Ready. But she would have the uniforms with her; when she had delivered them, she would return home.

Her friendship with Major Campbell earlier in the summer paid further dividends. She received a letter from him in Decatur, mailed September 1, 1864.

"Miss Gay—It was hard for me to reconcile my conscience to giving the enclosed recommendation to one whose sentiments I cannot approve, but if I have committed an arror it has been on the side of mercy, and I hope I'll be forgiven. Hereafter I hope you will not think of Yankees as all being bad, and beyond the pale of redemption.

"Tomorrow I leave for my own home in the 'frozen north,' and when I return it will be to fight for my country, and against your friends, so that I suppose I shall not have the pleasure of again meeting you.

                                        Very respectfully,
                                        J. W. Campbell."

The recommendation she had requested had been forwarded to General Schofield. The Major hoped her "case" would obtain "favorable consideration," and that "her desires" would be granted.

While Mary Gay was congratulating herself, Lizzie Perkerson was having affairs far less her own way, "shut up here in the house, hardly able to breathe" because of the Federals.

"On Wednesday the Infantry began to build their works and camps." "And on Thursday," Lizzie wrote, "they tore down the Ginn house, Screws, stables, crib, shuck house, the cook kitchen, the shop, garden and yard palings. I do reckon there was five hundred here, knocking, cursing, ripping and staving all day, swearing they would tear the house down from over us if we didn't get out of it. They gave us one man to guard us and he poked about and whispered and encouraged them until they got everything they wanted and then they gave us three men every day while they stayed here. They prevented them coming into the house. That was all the good they did us. And that was a great deal. The house never was plundered by them except the ones that came in first. They were for a whole week picking up board to build their camps and when they got done you never saw a place as nicely cleaned up as ours was. You couldn't have found a board or a piece of plank as large as your hand on the place. And Till's place they didn't leave a symptom of a house or anything else.

"The breastworks extended from East Point up the railroad to Stokes. There they built a large fort across from that right through McCool's yard, the ditch right at the chimney of his house and the abattis at the other end over by Uncle Ellis's house and on to the top of the hill this side of the Lee houses, at that point towards them. By this you may know how close we were to them. Their picket line was at the top of the hill this side of Terry's. So you see we had a full benefit of them. A great many of them tried to be very friendly. The house was full of the officers day and night, or that is till bedtime. None of them boarded with us. They would walk down after supper with their shoulder straps shining like new money and their black boots and paper collars ever so fine. Think I had like to have had a *beau* in the crowd?

"He was Capt. Williams of the 68th Ohio Regt. and is the hatefullest old scamp that has ever made a track on Georgia soil. I want you to look out for him if you ever come in contact with Sherman's army, and lay down your gun and take him by the back of the neck and shake him till he hollers and then tell him it was done at my request.

"They didn't interrupt Pa or Dan in any way. Never asked Pa to take the oath at all. Nan and I was no ways particular how we talked to them at all. I talked to them of our army and

my brothers that was in our army all the time. It would ag-
gravate some of them, others seemed to think it all right."

SEPTEMBER 10

Sherman sent a reply to Hood's letter before breakfast.

The high ceilings of the Neal home echoed with expletives
as he dictated his angry rebuttal. The cherubs on the bedroom
wallpaper all but blushed, while the elderly housekeeper smiled
as she supervised the cooks in the kitchen.

"I have the honor," he commenced, "to acknowledge the
receipt of your letter of this date, at the hands of Messrs. Ball
and Crew, consenting to the arrangement I had proposed to
facilitate the removal South of the people of Atlanta, who prefer to go in that direction. I enclose you a copy of my orders,
which will, I am satisfied, accomplish my purpose perfectly.
You style the measures proposed 'unprecedented' and appeal to
the dark history of war for a parallel, as an act of 'studied and
ingenious cruelty.' It is not unprecedented for Gen. Johnston
himself, very wisely and properly, removed the families all the
way from Dalton down, and I see no reason why Atlanta should
be excepted.

"Nor is it necessary to appeal to the dark history of war
when recent and modern examples are so handy. You yourself
burned dwelling houses along your parapet, and I have seen
today fifty houses that you have rendered uninhabitable because they stood in the way of your forts and men. You defended
Atlanta on a line so close to town that every cannon shot and
many musket balls from our lines of investment that overshot
their mark went into the habitations of women and children.
Gen. Hardee did the same at Jonesboro, and Gen. Johnston did
the same last summer at Jackson, Mississippi. I have not accused

you of heartless cruelty, but merely instance these cases of very recent occurrence, and could go on and enumerate hundreds of others, and challenge any fair man to judge which of us has the heart of pity for the families of a brave people.

"I say that it is a kindness to these families of Atlanta to remove them now, at once from the scenes that women and children should not be exposed to, and the 'brave people' should scorn to commit their wives to the rude barbarians who thus, as you say, violate the laws of war, as illustrated in the pages of its dark history.

"In the name of common sense, I ask you not to appeal to a just God in such a sacrilegious manner. You, who in the midst of peace and prosperity have plunged a nation into war, dark and cruel war, who dared and badgered us to battle, insulted our flag, seized our arsenals and forts that were left in the honorable custody of a peaceful ordnance sergeant, and seized and made prisoners of war the very garrisons sent to protect your people against negroes and Indians.

"Long before any overt act was committed by the, to you, hateful Lincoln Government, you tried to force Kentucky and Missouri into the rebellion in spite of themselves, falsified the vote of Louisiana, turned loose your pirates to plunder unarmed ships, expelled Union families by thousands, burned their houses, and declared by act of your Congress the confiscation of all debts due Northern men for goods had and received.

"Talk thus to the Marines, but not to me, who have seen these things, and who will this day make as much sacrifice for the people and honor of the South as the best born Southerner among you. If we must be enemies, let us be men, and fight it out as we propose to do, and not indulge in such hypocritical appeals to God and humanity. God will judge us in due time, and He will pronounce whether it will be more humane to fight with a town full of women and the families of a brave people at our backs, or to remove them in time to places of safety among their own friends and people."

His housekeeper, far from shocked at the vocabularly of this violent, red-haired general, was now telling her friends he was "the nicest man in the world . . . had been shamefully slandered."

For Mary Rawson it was "another day of continued exertion and restless anxiety . . . wasting our precious fifteen days. Another appeal was made today to Col. Beckworth and he promised to see Gen. Sherman and obtain a written paper allowing us to dispose of our provisions and tobacco if he could. With this assurance we prepared to spend the approaching Sabbath."

To Carrie Berry "every one I see seems sad. The citizens all think that it is the most cruel thing to drive us from our home but I think it would be so funny to move. Mama seems so troubled and she can't do anything. Papa says he don't know where on earth to go."

O. L. Braumuller and his mother decided to go to Nashville, where they could hope to be reunited with the senior Braumuller. The boy already had glimpsed the force behind their northward migration. "I saw Gen. Sherman at Five Points, talking to several officers. . . . I was some distance away, but I recognized him, and he appeared to be the villain in the play."

He noted that his mother speedily realized "we would have to leave, and that we would do well to get away with what we could. The conquerors promised us transportation out of town, and that was about all they would promise.

"Each family could have a fourth of a box car, they said. Freight cars were very small, not much larger than a wagon. Mother decided that she would try to save two pianos we had in the house, for these would be easier to convert into ready cash than the valuable paintings and rugs we had.

"She told the officers that she would like to have a whole car, so that she could move the pianos to Nashville. There was no use trying to save the pictures and rugs, she said, but she would dearly love to keep the pianos.

"The officers took the hint and provided the car, sending men to help move the bulky music boxes. By letting her go with them, the men could help themselves to the other valuables without any questions being asked."

Trinity Methodist Church was designated a temporary storage place for most pianos and other articles of furniture belonging to the dispossessed. The Provost Marshal assigned a guard to stand at the front door of this peculiarly inappropriate warehouse.

Mary Gay was now readying for her trip in another direction. Never wanting for plans or the physical means for their execution, she had obtained a wagon, complete with a span of "fine horses," and an Irish driver.

"Put those sacks into the wagon," she commanded briskly, pointing to the bulky containers of the Confederate uniforms. "When the last one of them was stored away safely in that moving repository, one of those feelings of relief and security came over me that had more than once given me courage to brave successfully impending danger—and I donned my hat, and bade my mother and the faithful girl an almost cheerful 'Good-bye,' and took my seat by the driver, en route for Dixie.

"I asked him to drive under my direction to the residence of my estimable friends, Mr. and Mrs. Posey Maddox, the parents of the accomplished and erudite, Charles K. Maddox of Atlanta. To my great joy I saw wagons in their yard, already laden with their household goods, to be carried to the depot and turned over to Federal authorities, who assumed the transportation of them to Jonesboro and the safe delivery of them to the Confederate authorities, who in turn assumed the transportation and delivery of them to the nearest Confederate station. Mr. Maddox had secured the use of an entire freight car, and gladly consented to take me and my baggage in with theirs.

"Curses and imprecations too vile to repeat, and boisterous laughter, and vulgar jests resounded through the streets of Atlanta. Federal wagons followed in the tracks of Confederate wagons, and after a few light articles were placed in the latter for Southern destination, the former unblushingly moved up to receive pianos and other expensive furniture which found its way into every section of the North. And this highway robbery was permitted by William Tecumseh Sherman, the grand Mogul of the Army of the Republic. Truly had the city of Atlanta been turned into a veritable pandemonium."

Mary would tarry a night or two in Atlanta until the processions of human misery got under way.

SEPTEMBER 11

In the North, it was a day of Thanksgiving, which Lincoln had proclaimed after the fall of Atlanta.

In Georgia, it was a Sunday of renewed sorrow and penance. The streets were lined with laden wagons ready to move households north or south. For the former, their immediate destination was no farther than the depot.

"This morning," wrote Mary Rawson, "Mother concluded that although we had not the slightest idea of our future home, we had better commence the task of packing.

"Scarcely was the work begun when we heard that all those who went South would have their trunks searched and all goods not ready made be removed. Now came the question as to how we could secrete them and so take them with us. We finally prepared two trunks to go either way by folding pieces of goods between ready made clothes and by tearing the cloth into pieces of sufficient length to make dress skirts and a great many other ways we found of hiding our goods. While we were in the midst of our work Aunt Charlotte came over from Grandma's and told us they had already opened Aunty's trunks twice and came to perform the same detestable office again. When Aunty refused decidedly to open her baggage any more and Col. Beckworth coming in at that moment gave him a sound cudgening. Aunt Charlotte expressed her determination to follow her master and mistress wherever they go. Dear old Granny may you be well protected and carefully nursed during your old age and when life is over be laid gently to rest by those who can and do appreciate you.

"This afternoon on hearing martial music, we looked up from the front porch where we were sitting to see the street filled with cavalry and infantry pack mules and army wagons and cattle crowded promiscuously together, the cavalry and infantry ensigns floating in unison together. The musicians all riding on white horses. After making the signal for the march to commence they rode silently along until they passed in front of Gen. Geary's headquarters when simultaneously they broke into the old soul stirring 'Hail Columbia'; the suddenness of the music startled me.

"They then, (after finishing this piece) slowly and silently marched through the city. A few minutes after this Mother went over to see my Grandparents and Aunty; and I went to have a little talk with Mattie; her father had determined to go to the North and so it seemed probable that the friends of seven years would be separated. We finally parted, I with a beautiful sprig of honeysuckle in my hair, placed there by Mr. Andrews who remarked that this would be the last time he would deck my hair for me."

Joe Semmes was "quite well" though "almost out of doors, being located in a miserable hut, all my baggage and comforts being in the rear." His quarters, Semmes added, were located near Sam French's.

"The country is uninviting and made desolate by the troops of both armies; consequently, I get nothing to eat, but corn bread or bacon or beef. Before this reaches you the news will be read of the short armistice between the two Armies and the cause of it. The fiend Sherman has done what not even the Czar of Russia had done in Poland; he is going to transport the entire population of Atlanta from their homes, to go where they can and live as they may. We left them enough to eat for the moment at least, but he has taken that and all else they had from them and sends them out to starve or do worse.

"Tomorrow the truce begins and all the wagons of the Army go forward this evening to receive the unfortunate people. The wretch, after raining shell fire among them for 50 days, now drives them forth like the people of Isreal were driven from Jerusalem. None but niggers remain, they are the beloved equals and fit associates of the debased Yankee.

"We have no mail as yet but I hope tomorrow to hear from you as the Army Post Office will be opened again tomorrow. Warfield has gone to the rear with an attack of rheumatism, as usual he went off without seeing me, though this time he sent me word. Stragglers are being brought to the front at the rate of at least 1,000 a day. Do you wonder that Hood had to give up Atlanta. . . . The 30 miles of country which the Yankee occupied has been left a perfect desert. The whole population, rich and poor, are utterly ruined and they are pouring in to our Chief Commissary for their daily food. The Yankees did this thing in cold blood, for they were not in want of anything they destroyed.

"The wagons, four and six muleteams, are now collected in front of my quarters, to go forward to bring down the unfortunate people of Atlanta. They will come with nothing but their clothing. All their household property and provisions will be taken by the enemy.

"We expect to do nothing during the armistice but wash up bodies and clothes and rest. Even the work on the railroad which was destroyed by the Yankees must be suspended though I have no doubt they will work to repair whatever damages they have."

Dr. James Comfort Patten attended church.

"Had preaching by Bryant, who gave us a pretty good discourse," he wrote afterward. "It is a lovely day rather hot but still pleasant. I sat in the shade on a pine box and listened to the discourse as well as I could but somehow I would still catch my mind running off to the church in Princeton and then the group of blue coats around me would fade away and instead of them would come up the familiar faces of the congregation at home and I could almost feel Morgan leaning his head on my knee to go to sleep. I can't help wishing many a time that I could be back at such times in the old congregation. But then I think again this is all wrong. . . . If God had intended me to stay there he would have left me there instead of sending me out here. And so I will try and await patiently the result, but I hope that it will not be long delayed and that our next news may come to us as good as that which we have been able to send from here. I hope that Grant in his place may have as good success as Sherman the crazy has here.

"He may be very crazy but I guess the rebs think by this time that there is almost too much method in his madness and that if he is crazy, save them from the grasp of one who is sane."

Meanwhile, Mayor Calhoun and councilmen E. E. Rawson and S. C. Wells were writing an eleventh hour plea to Sherman.

"At first view, it struck us that the measure would involve extraordinary hardship and loss but since we have seen the practical execution of it so far as it has progressed, and the individual condition of the people, and heard their statements as to the inconveniences, loss and suffering attending it, we are satisfied that the amount of it will involve in the aggregate consequences appalling and heart-rending.

"Many poor women are in advanced state of pregnancy, others now having young children, and whose husbands for the greater part are either in the army, prisoners, or dead. Some say, 'I have such a one sick at my house; who will wait on them when I am gone?'

"Others say, 'What are we to do? We have no house to go to, and no means to buy, build, or rent any; no parents, relatives, or friends to go to!'

"Another says, 'I will try and take this or that article of property, but such and such things I must leave behind, though I need them much.'

"We reply to them: 'Gen. Sherman will carry your property to Rough and Ready, and Gen. Hood will take it thence on. . . .

"This being so, how is it possible for the people still here (mostly women and children) to find any shelter? And how can they live through the winter in the woods—no shelter or subsistence, in the midst of strangers who know them not, and without the power to assist them much, if they were willing to do so?

"This is but a feeble picture of the consequences of the measure . . . we most earnestly and solemnly petition you to reconsider this order, or modify it, and suffer this unfortunate people to remain at home, and enjoy what little means they have."

The Reverend Mr. Freeman, minister of St. Philip's, whose church was already being used as a stable, attempted to add his plea on behalf of the people.

"Fortune of war, sir, fortune of war!" Sherman barked. "I want this place for a citadel, and want no white citizens in it!"

SEPTEMBER 12

The evacuation from Atlanta began.

"On leaving the breakfast table," wrote Mary Rawson, "I hastily tied on my hat and veil previous to going to bid my dear kindred goodbye, for this was the day appointed for them to go. Arriving at the house I found two huge Army wagons and two ambulances at the gate and men hurrying to and fro with trunks and other baggage. At last they all came out and took their places in the ambulance and after a sad adieu they slowly departed. Then I returned home and all along the street in front of Mrs. Zimmermans I noticed many vehicles for taking them away and even more sadly than at first if possible I continued my walk."

Conyngham suspected that those moving south "seemed to enjoy the thing."

"The cars taking them down were loaded with a miscellaneous cargo," he reported. "In some were crowded together tottering old age and maidens in their youthful bloom. The former fretted very much at being thus rudely torn away, root and branch, from the soil on which they grew, and in which they hoped soon to rest their wearied hearts. As for their young companions, they seemed to treat the thing as a kind of sentimental journey. I fully understood this when we reached the rebel quarters, when I saw with what a warm greeting the rebel officers and soldiers received them. Some even carried their enthusiasm so far as to welcome them with warm kisses and embraces. In addition, the wagons were crowded with a heterogeneous medley of poodle dogs, tabby cats, asthmatic pianos, household furniture, cross old maids, squalling, wondering children, all of which, huddled together, made anything but a pleasant travelling party, which I accompained."

At the same time, Sherman was replying to Mayor Calhoun.

"We must have peace, not only in Atlanta, but in all America. To secure this, we must stop the war that now desolates our once happy and favored country. To stop war, we must defeat the rebel armies which are arrayed against the laws and Constitution that all must respect and obey. To defeat those armies, we must prepare the way to reach them in their recesses, provided with the arms and instruments which enable us to accomplish our purpose . . . the use of Atlanta for warlike purposes is inconsistent with its character as a home for families. . . . Why not go now, when all the arrangements are completed for the transfer, instead of waiting till the plunging shot of contending armies will renew the scenes of the past month? . . .

"You cannot qualify war in harsher terms than I will. War is cruelty and you cannot refine it; and those who brought war into our country deserve all the curses and maledictions a people can pour out. I know I had no hand in making this war, and I know I will make more sacrifices today than any of you to secure peace. But you cannot have peace and a division of our country. . . .

"You might as well appeal against the thunderstorm as against these terrible hardships of war. They are inevitable, and the only way the people of Atlanta can hope once more to live in peace and quiet at home is to stop the war, which can only be done by admitting that it began in error and is perpetuated in pride. . . . I want peace, and believe it can only be reached through union and war, and I will ever conduct war with a view to perfect and early success.

"But, my dear sirs, when peace does come, you may call on me for anything. Then will I share with you the last cracker, and watch with you to shield your homes and families against danger from every quarter.

"Now you must go, and take with you the old and feeble, feed and nurse them, and build for them, in more quiet places, proper habitations to shield them against the weather until the mad passions of men cool down, and allow the Union and peace once more to settle over your old homes at Atlanta. Yours in haste."

Mary Gay continued her journey, by boxcar.

"At length our time came to move in the worse then death-like processions going Southward, and in a short while we were at Jonesboro, our destination, so far as Federal aid extended.

"As soon as I stepped from the car I wended my way to the Confederate officer of the day, whom I recognized by his regalia, and told him of my success in concealing and bringing out of Federal lines the winter clothing of our soldiers. He listened with polite attention and said it was a wonderfully interesting story, but altogether improbable.

" 'Go with me and I will prove to you the truthfulness of it,' I eagerly said.

"As it was a bleak equinoctial day, and drizzling rain, Mr. and Mrs. Maddox had not yet left their car, (by way of parenthesis, I would say that the favors shown to these excellent people was in consideration of Mr. Maddox being a very prudent minister of the gospel) and, when we reached it, I asked Mr. Maddox to roll one of my sacks to the door. He did so, and I then asked the officer to examine its contents. A blade of a pen knife severed the twine with which the edges of the mouth had been sewed together, and the loved familiar gray and brass buttons, and other articles, verified the truth of my statement. He looked amazed, and exhausted his vocabulary of flattering encomiums upon me, and, what was more desirable and to the point, he asked what he could do in the matter, and assured me that there was nothing within the range of his jurisdiction that he would not do. I told him that the object of my coming to him was to ask that he send me and my precious charge to Gen. Granbury's headquarters, as among other overcoats I had one of his in charge, as well as many other things belonging to his staff officers. He told me the finest span of Confederate horses and the best ambulance on the grounds should be at my service as soon as possible.

"During the interim, I opened wide my eyes and took in the situation in all its horrible details. The entire Southern population of Atlanta, with but an occasional exception, and that of many miles in its vicinity, were dumped out upon the cold ground without shelter and without any of the comforts of home, and an autumnal mist of drizzle slowly but surely saturating every article of clothing upon them; and pulmonary diseases in all stages admonishing them of the danger of such exposure. Aged grandmother's tottering upon the verge of the grave, and tender maidens in the first bloom of young womanhood, and little babes not three days old in the arms of sick mothers, driven from their homes, were all out upon the cold charity of the world. . . .

"When one of the long trains from Atlanta rolled in with its living pulsing freight and stopped at the terminus, a queenly girl, tall and lithe in figure and willowy in motion, emerged from one of the cars, and stood, the embodiment of feminine grace, for a moment upon the platform. In less time than it takes to chronicle the impression, her Grecian beauty, classic expression and nobility of manner, had dageurreotyped themselves upon the tablets of my memory, never to be effaced by mortal alchemy.

"The pretty plain beige dress, trimmed with Confederate buttons and corresponding ribbon, all conspired to make her appear, even to a casual observer, just what she was—a typical Southern girl who gloried in that honor. She stood only a moment, and then, as if moved by some divine inspiration, she stepped from the car, and falling upon her knees, bent forward and kissed the ground. This silent demonstration of affection for the land of Dixie touched a vibrating chord, and a score or more of beautiful girlish voices blended in sweetest harmony while they told in song their love for Dixie.

"I listened spell-bound, and was not the only one thus enchanted. A United States officer listened and was touched to tears. Approaching me, he asked if I would do him the favor to tell him the name of the young lady who kissed the ground.

" 'I do not think she would approve of my telling you her name, and I decline to do so,' I said in reply.

"Not in the least daunted by this rebuff he responded:

" 'I shall learn it; and if she has not already become the wife or the affianced of another, I shall offer her the devotion of my life.'

"The Confederate officer of the day, God forever bless him! came for me. The army wagon was ready and standing by Mr. Posy Maddox's car, waiting to receive its precious freight, and a few minutes, sufficient to transfer it from car t. wagon, and after waiting to see the last sack securely placed in the wagon, I too got in, and took my seat by the driver. A long cold drive was before us, but I was so robust I had no fear of the result.

"The driver was a veritable young Jehu, and we got over the ground rapidly; but, owing to a mistake in following directions, it was a long time before we reached our destination, the course of which must have been due west from Jonesboro, and through a dense forest. And oh, the beauty of that forest! It will remain a living, vivid memory, as long as life endures. Its rich, varied and heavy foliage had been but slightly tinged by the frosts of autumn, and it was rendered more beautiful by the constant dripping of rain drops from every leaf and blossom. As the evening came on, dense, impenetrable clouds canopied the earth, and shut out every ray of sunlight, and almost every ray of hope. At length night came on, dark and weird, and silent, and we were still in the woods without compass or star.

"Just as my brave heart was about to succumb to despair, a vision of delight burst upon me—a beacon light, yea, hundreds of beacon lights, appeared before me, and filled my soul with joy. The camp fires of Gen. Cleburne's brave men beckoned us onward, and gave us friendly greetings. Every revolution of the wagon wheels brought us perceptibly nearer the haven of rest. Sabbath-like quiet reigned throughout the encampment. No boisterous sounds nor profane imprecations broke the stillness. But there was a sound that reached my ear, filling my soul with joy, unspeakable.

"A human voice it was.

"I had heard it before in the slight wail of infancy; in the merry prattle of childhood; in the melodious songs of youth; in the tender, well-modulated tones of manhood; and now; there was no mistaking it—in the solemn, earnest invocation to the Lord of Hosts, for the salvation of the world, for the millenial dawn, and that 'peace on earth, and good will to men,' which would never again be broken by the clarion of war, or earth's rude alarms. No sweeter voice ever entered the courts of Heaven.

"My obliging young driver stopped the horses at a favorable

distance, and I heard the greater part of that grand prayer, and wept for joy."

Conyngham passed the afternoon and evening conversing with his erstwhile enemies, noting how "kindly" he was received by Maj. William Clare, in charge of the Confederate Guard, and counterpart of Col. Willard Warner, of Sherman's staff.

"Everything," reported the Irish soldier-correspondent, "went on in the most friendly way—visits paid between Federals and Confederates, exchanges made, friendly intercourse kept on. One could scarcely realize that these laughing, chatting groups were deadly enemies, who tomorrow would strive for one another's blood."

In Atlanta, the remainder of Mary Rawson's day drifted "slowly and sadly by with no certainty of our journey."

Life was the same for Carrie Berry, who was helping her mother pack. Maxwell Berry had been informed that he might remain in Atlanta "if he could get into business."

Hood was writing to Sherman once again:

"You order into exile the whole population of a city; drive men, women and children from their homes at the point of the bayonet, under the plea that it is to the interest of your government, and on the claim that it is an act of 'kindness' to those families of Atlanta! . . . and because I characterize what you call a kindness as being real cruelty, you presume to sit in judgment between me and my God; and you decide that my earnest prayer to the Almighty Father to save our women and children from what you call kindness, is a 'sacrilegious, hypocritical appeal.' . . .

"You say 'Let us fight it out like men.' To this my reply is—for myself and I believe for all the true men, ay, and women and children, in my country—we will fight you to the death! Better die a thousand deaths than submit to live under you or your government and your negro allies!"

In the privacy of their diaries or letters, some Union soldiers were inclined to agree with Hood. One of them, Colonel J. H. Keatley, wrote:

"If war simply means killing, and is nothing more than to

do the greatest and speediest harm to the enemy, then its modern methods are indefensible, and the giving and taking of quarter, a false refinement. Claverhouse taught the maxim that 'war is war' and invested the story of Glencoe with a tragic intent and at which history will never cease to blush. The order to depopulate Atlanta was obeyed amid agonies and sorrows indescribable, and the city, but for the presence of the soldiers, who had captured it, was as desolate as the ruins of Nineveh."

The *Intelligencer* postscripted the subject with its own Philippic, ". . . of all the remorseless, hard-hearted, unfeeling brutes that Yankeedom has sent forth to waste the South, this man is the most remorseless, the most hard-hearted, and the most brutal."

The writer was referring to General Sherman, but the *Macon Telegraph* was not in agreement since it found the "refugees report generally kind personal treatment from Gen. Sherman and his officers. Whatever exceptions may have occurred have been in violation of orders—instances of individual pilfering, which cannot always be prevented in an army and in many cases have been detected and punished.

"A friend whose wife was left an invalid in Atlanta and came within our lines a day or two since, says that at her request Gen. Sherman came to see her and finding her unable to attend to the arrangements of her moveables for transportation, had them all bound up nicely and transported to our lines, even to her washtubs."

SEPTEMBER 13

Mary Gay finally met her brother, Lieutenant Tom Stokes, at the encampment. He provided her with a "brand new tent," a buffalo robe for mattress, a folded coat for a pillow, and a

This scene of desolation marks the site where several ammunition trains were blown up by the retreating Confederates in the early morning hours of September 1, 1864. Gaunt chimneys are all that remain of Schofield and Markham's great rolling mill beside the railroad tracks. (*Library of Congress*)

Union troops destroy railroad tracks in Atlanta. When time permitted,
Sherman's soldiers heated the tracks red hot in improvised ovens like
these, then bent them around trees. So fascinated did some of the Union
generals become with this assignment that they even planned the breakfast menus (always including a whole chicken per man) for "rail-busting"
squads, who were then supposedly able to wreck five or six miles of track
before sundown. *(Library of Congress)*

Railroad wrecking was elevated to a science in Sherman's army. The lever being used on these tracks was developed especially for his troops by his own Engineers. By means of this lever, the rails, which were much lighter than those in use today, were pried up as easily as though they were held down by carpet tacks. *(Library of Congress)*

The last train to leave Atlanta is piled high with refugees and their household goods. *(Library of Congress)*

The Atlanta railroad depot after it was blown up by Federal demolition squads. The Concert Hall in the right background was used as a hospital until July 28 when all the hospitals in Atlanta were evacuated south. *(Library of Congress)*

OFFICE OF TRANSPORTATION DEPARTMENT.

U. S. MILITARY RAILROAD,

Atlanta Sept 12 1864.

'Will Transport

John Stewart

Capt. & A. Q. M.

A ticket for railroad transportation from Atlanta to Rough & Ready, dated September 12, 1864. Federal troops conducted citizens to this tavern stop on the Georgia Railroad (five miles south of Atlanta), where Confederate forces met them under a flag of truce. *(Courtesy Atlanta Historical Society)*

This dispatch to Georgia's Governor Brown was sent by Major General Howell Cobb in Griffin (forty miles south of Atlanta on November 16, as soon as his scouts brought him word that Sherman was destroying Atlanta and moving his army out of the city. *(Courtesy University of Georgia Library)*

View of Atlanta in 1866 showing the railroad crossing between Whitehall and Peachtree Streets. The National Hotel is on the left; beyond it is the Norcross Building on the lot where the First National Bank now stands. The saloon and billiard parlor, the ruins, and Hagan & Co. to the north occupy ground now covered by the Peters Building. (*National Archives*)

Andy Neal is buried in Oakland Cemetery beside his brother James, who survived him by only seven months. Close by is the grave of Carrie Berry.

After the bloody fighting at Jonesboro which preceded the fall of Atlanta by only a few hours, hundreds of Confederate dead could not be identified. This memorial stone marks their mass grave.

The National Cemetery in Marietta where most of the Union soldiers who fell in the Atlanta campaign are buried.

gray blanket for covering. She had slept minus only the skirt of her dress "that it might not be wrinkled."

Refreshed from her sleep "under the protecting care of these noble men," she washed with the aid of a pan of water, a towel and "a mirror about the size of a silver dollar." Even a comb and brush had been provided. Her own brother's voice had awakened her:

" 'Get up, sister, or you will not be ready for the roll call!' "

Her breakfast included a "decoction which he called coffee." Afterward, she started for Lovejoy's, in a wagon train. She herself rode in an ambulance, seated opposite two young Lieutenants, with Tom next to her. He sang "Auld Lang Syne" and reminisced on their childhood. He spoke of his wife Mary in Texas and his boy.

"He took from his vest pocket the impression of the foot and hand of his only child, a dear little boy whom he had never seen, and kissed them, and then folded them carefully and put them back in his pocket and said:

" 'I must hurry back to Texas!' "

At a large, square house, "which appeared to be full of people," she said goodbye to her half brother.

"Thomie and I advanced toward it a few steps. Suddenly, as if admonished that a soldier's duties should have precedence over everything else, he took me in his arms and kissed me fervently once, twice, thrice. I understood for whom they were intended. . . . I felt intuitively that I should never look upon his face again."

But Sherman was satisfied, now that the potential that would "oblige officers to listen to everlasting complaints that aren't military" was being removed.

The trains continued to roll south. On one, sharing space with the refugees, or "exiles" as they preferred to call themselves, was Major George Ward Nichols, aide-de-camp of Sherman, en route to assist Colonel Warner.

"Our engineer was a young man," he wrote, "who pleasantly informed me that it was not the best policy to jump from the engine in the event of an upset.

" 'Always stick to the machine,' he said, 'I have been overturned three times in the course of my experience and never was injured beyond a light scratch on the nose. Always stick to the machine.'

"With all respect to your opinion, I thought to myself, I shall jump at the first indications of danger; and I proceeded to impress upon the mind of Col. Warner the fact of the superior management of railroads in England and on the Continent. . . . I was busily engaged in digging the cinders out of my eyes, when we turned a sharp curve in the woods, and beheld a man by the embankment frantically waving a red flag, while a party of men not ten rods distant, who had just taken up a rail from the track, were waving their hats and shouting for us to stop.

"Our engine-driver—keen-eyed, alert, and clear-headed—at once saw the dangers, reversed the machinery, put the tender-brake in operation, and the huge monster in an instant was quiet as a sleeping child.

" 'A close rub, sir!' said my friend the engineer. 'Six feet more and we should have pitched into the ravine there. . . .'

"Twenty minutes of travel carried us over the ten miles which intervened between Atlanta and the neutral ground, where the banished citizens are handed over to the Rebel officers, and the exchange of prisoners takes place. Rough and Ready as completely answers to the first part of its name as one could imagine and perhaps to the latter half; for it appears to have been getting ready to be a town since its foundation, and is likely to remain in that condition for an indefinite length of time. Two miserable shanties, the respective quarters of the Federal and Rebel guards, separated for a distance of about 200 yards, constitute the burgh of Rough and Ready.

"Dismounting from our engine, we approached the hut nearest the Confederate lines. It was a characteristic specimen of the habitations of the poor class of whites at the South. A few refuse boards fastened upon an irregular frame; a disjointed window in a shattered sill; a battered door swinging upon a single hinge, formed its striking features; while several swords and pistols, hanging upon the side of the house, indicated the presence of soldiers. The single room was half filled with smoke.

puffing lazily from a fireplace around which were scattered sundry dilapidated pots and pans; but we had little time and it was not our business to take an inventory of the goods and chattels in the establishment. A pale, sickly woman, seated in the rickety porch answered our question as to the whereabouts of Maj. Clare, a staff officer of Gen. Hood, who represents the Rebel party in the truce.

" 'He's h'yar somewhar, round the corner of the yard, I reckon. Say, Betsy, whar's Maj. Clare?'

"We made the circuit of the corner and found the major; a handsome, polite gentleman, by the way, who was seated near some ladies, in the midst of a collection of baskets and household goods. We were presented to the ladies, when the two officers stepped aside for the discussion of the business which had brought them together, leaving me to attempt the somewhat difficult task of entertaining persons who had evidently just been evicted from their homes in Atlanta. . . . The youngest, a lady of refinement, remarked:

" 'It is very hard to be obliged to leave our home. We have not felt the war before, except in the cost of the luxuries of life. We did not believe your army would ever penetrate so far south; but I suppose our removal is one of the necessities of the situation, and we would much rather give up our homes than live near the Yankees . . . there are not two nations on the face of this earth . . . who hate each other more . . . we will never live with you again . . . anything rather than become subject to the North.'

"During this conversation, which I have written out because it is a fair picture of the opinions of the Georgians frequently expressed to me, a long train of wagons and ambulances from Atlanta provided by Gen. Sherman had driven into the space between the outposts, and deposited their freight of women and children with their household furniture. These people seemed to be almost entirely of the lower class. The wealthier citizens removed from Atlanta when the firing began; those only remaining who were willing to take the risk of shot and shell, and the possibility of Federal occupation.

"The dust from our wagons had barely subsided when the

sharp crack of the whip and the loud cries of train-master and mule-drivers announced the arrival of the Rebel convoy to remove the people whom General Sherman had refused to permit Hood to throw upon him as a burden. Bidding adieu to the ladies, and with a kindly grasp of the hand from Maj. Clare, we departed from Rough and Ready. . . . The afternoon was slowing waning into evening."

There were additional problems, including the teamsters themselves. Already six Confederate teamsters were suspected of deserting to the Union lines, and twelve Federals were supposedly on their way south. Each truce team promised to return the errant horse and mule drivers if found.

About this time, Mary Gay was reaching Lovejoy's.

"Here as at Jonesboro," she wrote, "the face of the earth was literally covered with rude tents, and sidetracked cars, which were occupied by exiles from home—defenceless women and children, and an occasional old man tottering on the verge of the grave, awaiting their turn to be transported by over-taxed railroads farther into the constantly diminishing land of their love. During the afternoon I boarded an already well-filled southern train and moved about among its occupants as if at home. For were we not one people—the mothers, wives and sisters of Confederates? The diversity of mind, disposition and temper of this long train of representative women and children of Atlanta, and of many miles contiguous, who were carrying minds and hearts brimful of memories never to be obliterated, but rather to harden into asphalt preservation, was illustrated in many ways. Some laughed and talked and jested, and infused the light and warmth of their own sunny natures into others less hopeful; some were morose and churlish and saw no hope in the future and were impatient with those who did see the silver lining beyond the dark clouds suspended over us; and some very plainly indicated that if our cause failed they would lose all faith in a prayer-answering God."

Mary Gay continued on towards Griswoldsville, as part of her roundabout route to Decatur. She figured it would be several days before she arrived home.

Hood was writing "His Excellency Jefferson Davis:

"In the Battle of July 20 we failed on account of General Hardee . . . our failure of August 31 I am now convinced was greatly owing to him. Please confer with Lieutenant-Generals Stewart and S. D. Lee as to operations around Atlanta. It is of the utmost importance that Hardee should be relieved at once. He commands the best troops of this army. I must have another commander."

He then addressed a dispatch to Brigadier General A. R. Lawton, Quartermaster General in Richmond.

"It is very important that funds for the payment of this army should be sent without delay to prevent dissatisfaction and desertion in consequence of the non-payment of the troops."

. . . and to Governor Brown in Milledgeville, who had just ordered back his own State militia from Hood's army.

"The enemy having robbed the people in the vicinity of Jonesboro, I have about 1,000 applications daily for rations in that quarter. I cannot subsist them. Can you not make arrangements and send food for them?"

Sherman, on the other hand, exulting in a relative plenty, quipped to a friend, "we prefer Illinois beef, but Georgia mutton will have to answer in certain contingencies."

Mary Rawson, meanwhile, learned that her family would sign the pledge of allegiance and migrate north.

"This morning," she wrote, "Father concluded to go himself to see Gen. Sherman and ask if he could get a written order permitting him to sell his provisions. About 10 o'clock he came back bringing the papers signed by the General, then came a long conversation with Mother which terminated in the resolve to brave the severities of the cold North West. We immediately prepared to emigrate to the prairies of Iowa. We had no time to spare and now began the work of packing in earnest, and from morning till night we were running up and down stairs assisting Mother in her work."

Maxwell Berry, however, had steered into quite the opposite situation.

"Papa got into business today," Carrie recorded "and the rest of us went to wirk in good earnest thinking that we will get to stay. I hope that we will get to stay. Mama dislikes to move so much."

Rufus Mead wrote home again—"Sherman is sending citizens each way now as fast as possible. We now feed 2 or 3,000 and he says he cant afford it. Sixty wagons went from our Division today to carry stuff south to Rough & Ready—twelve miles south of here, while as many went from each other Div. He intends to hold this as a military base of supplies & cant afford to keep either friend or foe unless connected with the army. We are now in camp, and at quiet again, while furloughs are granted for 2 out of 40 men in a Co I guess it wont pay me to go so far and stay so short time, only 30 days in all and 10 or 15 on the road most probably.

"Irad Williams bid me Good Bye today. He intends to go via L B Lantons &c so I sent nothing by him. Last Sunday I went to water the horse & take a short ride when I heard the church bell, so I hurried back, went up there & sure enough the organ was playing and on entering I found them singing the first hymn.

"The chaplain of the 2nd Mass preached an excellent sermon from the words 'What wilt thou have me to do?' It is the first sermon Ive heard since April last. It is to be open every sabbath while we stay here. It is the 2nd Presbyterian. The Methodist & Roman Catholic are open also. It really did me good to go to church once more.

"This is about all the benefit we get from living in a city. We live a little better now than on a campaign, get soft bread also can get our victals cooked in better style, but so far I get nothing outside from the commissarys. I see a few tomatoes peanuts, sweetpotatoes, &c but get none yet. I see figs but they are not ripe yet. It is getting late so Good night all. Your ever Afft Son & Brother."

SEPTEMBER 14

Others, along with the Rawsons, had resolved to return to the Union. S. P. Richards, sick of the Confederacy, was packing for New York, by way of Louisville. The Braumullers, mother and son, left for Nashville in a boxcar. "Sitting on the pianos . . . the world seemed a dreary place for me just then, but she cheered me up. I believe she was the bravest and most competent person I ever knew."

After they met Mr. Braumuller in Nashville, they hoped to continue still farther north, "we had every faith in the Confederacy, but there was no way we could help the cause, so my parents decided to go to New York and remain until after the war was over."

Mrs. Braumuller hoped to realize a few hundred dollars from the sale of the pianos. But travel at best was hazardous, even under army protection.

"I wanted myself," wrote David Conyngham, "to get a poor soldier, who was going home to die, inside on one of the cars. Though they were full of strapping, healthy negroes, who were either servants to the extortioners, or had the almighty dollars to pay their way, I could not gain admittance for the poor fellow. A few dollars in a conductor's pocket were of more importance than his comfort or safety. I gave him my blanket and oil-cloth, but I have since learned he never reached home, for when taken off the top of the cars at Chattanooga he was found dead.

"I simply mention these facts as a caution to generals not to place too much confidence in employees, unless they are well tried and tested."

Rufus Mead had been watching the tedious, glum process. Each day he had counted one hundred six-mule teams going south "as far as Rough & Ready and there they meet the Rebel teams.

"The wagons carry the stuff only, while the citizens walk or the women & children ride in Ambulances. It makes an odd looking train when they all get together, ready to start. The armistice lasts till 9 P.M. on the 21st Inst. It raises quite a commotion among this community, some are raving mad of course for they calculated to stay here and live on the Govmt. while they could act as spy or smuggler, &c just as they have done for a long time back. But Sherman intends to put a damper on such operations in future. There are some families here whose husband & father is in the Militia against his will and it seems harsh to send them away from home, but they must suffer the penalty of poor Tray. Many of them want to go & would have done so before if Hood would let them. This makes the Rebel officers mad, and they say that Sherman will repent this order of his. That is what a few of the rabid ones say but I am told most of them are nearly discouraged.

"Three or four nights ago, our officers & theirs had a regular jolly time of it and our Brig Q M who had charge of the train says they all agreed to come back with him, and would have done so if it had not been contrary to the rules of the armistice. Some swore they'd desert as soon as it ended at any rate. Our teamsters say the same of their teamsters too.

"Next time you send a paper you may put a lot of matches in it. They are scarce and poor out here. Wrap them up so they won't set the mail on fire & so burn up my other letters. I cant think of any thing else now. So Good Bye."

Dr. Patten watched troop as well as civilian movements.

"The cars run by us here just in sight of our camp," he noted. "We can see that they are swarming with men moving to the front. Gen. Sherman is evidently strengthening himself for some important movement, but what it is, or where he is going to take us is more than we can guess. We may go to Mobile or Charleston or Richmond. We would like to know, and I doubt not that gen Hood would like it better than even we would. . . .

"We have almost daily visits from the women from a good many miles round bringing in vegetables to barter for something to eat. They will not take money but want *bread* or flour or meat. They say that money would be worthless to them as there is no place that they would be able to buy anything with it. They tell some pitiful stories of starving children, and the worst is that they are true. I have seen some things that I never expected to see and I hope I may see no more such. . . .

"We still hear occasionally from home and the news is rather more cheerful. Our work here at Atlanta has had a good effect on the traitors at home, they begin to think that we will soon have the rebellion crushed here, and then for the traitors at home. They already begin to shake in their shoes for they feel that they have lost the game on which they have staked their country and the Birthright of their children. And they even now begin to feel the weight of that infamy that will ever be a traitor's doom, knowing full well that their names will go down to posterity so blackened that Arnold will pass for a patriot and Iscariot for an honest man by comparison with them."

But Georgians such as Lizzie Perkerson were too involved with urgent concerns, such as health, to evaluate accusations of treason. At the "Yankee-infested" Perkerson farm, Lizzie's sister Till and a servant Black Jim had been deathly ill with the "billious fever."

"Our chance for a Dr. was the Yankees. Dr. McCook, a brother of the noted Genl. McCook treated them both. He seemed to be a very good physician but they both like to have died. When Till was just getting so she could begin to sit up, Nan took Typhoid Fever. She had been sick a week and Ma and Alice (another sister) both took it. When they got sick we were right between the two picket lines and we could get a Dr. from neither side, so here we were. We sent after every Dr. that we had any hope of getting and could get none. We started Len after Dr. Lowen. He met him and he said he could not possibly get here under two days and Mother looking like she would die every day. Well, we waited two days and he still didn't come so we sent for him again and his family had not seen nor heard from him since Len saw him and didn't know what had become of him.

"The next day Aunt Flora came to see us, driving an old broken down Yankee horse. I told her if she would stay with them and let me have her horse and buggy that I would go down below and see if I could get a Dr. So I took Dan soon in the morning and started after Dr. M. Parker who lived at Morrow's Station this side of Jonesborough. When I got to Rough and Ready I found a vidette who said that I could go no further. I told him my business and also told him that I was going on. Well, he told me to go on some distance and I would find the pickets on the road and to tell them to go with me to the Lieut. I told them what he said. One of them said they thought from my looks I could go to the Lieut. as well without him as with him. I told him that I was of the same opinion, so on I went.

"Directly I came to a camp of some ten or a dozen men. They halted me. I told them my business and after asking me a hundred questions about the Yankees he ordered a man to mount and take me to the Capt. who was still further down the road. Well, on we went, came to the Capt., answered all the questions he could ask, told him what I wanted and where I wanted to go and got for an answer 'You can go no further.' I told him that I could and would go on. Well, he said that he could do no better for me than send a guard with me to headquarters near Fayetteville. I told him all right and drove on under guard.

"Well, we traveled on faithfully until three o'clock to get to Hd Qrs. The Commander after asking all the questions he could think of, gave me a pass and dismissed the guard. So there I was. My horse tired down, me twelve miles from the Drs. and twenty from home and my horse tired down. But I put on a bold front and started again. At dark I was at Jonesboro and the horse so badly tired that I had to walk from there to Dr. Parker, six miles. We got there at ten o'clock. Next day at twelve we got home. Dr. Parker thought he had to do something and didn't know what, so he gave Ma a dose of medicine that like to have killed her and went off and left her worse than he found her. Well, she just remained in that condition five days. When the Yankees commenced passing Pa told some of the officers what a condition we were in and they sent three Drs. in and they gave her medicine that relieved her almost immediately, and she has been mending slowly ever since and now she can begin to sit up a little and I think is out of danger. Nan is about well, so is Alice. All this while Aunt Flora was down sick and not able to do one thing."

General Sam French wrote President Davis in response to a request by "several officers" and "in regard to a feeling of depression more or less apparent in parts of this army." Although at first he had "declined doing so," he now deemed it advisable: ". . . for your own satisfaction it might be well that you send one or two intelligent officers here to visit the different divisions and brigades and ascertain if that spirit of confidence so necessary for success has not been impaired within the past month or two. They might further inquire into the cause if they find in this army any want of enthusiasm."

And Sherman, in smoldering rage, informed Hood that their correspondence had been "out of place and profitless. . . . I was not bound by the laws of war to give notice of the shelling of Atlanta, a 'fortified town, with magazines, arsenals, founderies, and public stores;' you were bound to take notice. See the books.

"This is the conclusion of our correspondence, which I did not begin, and terminate with satisfaction."

Hood, deciding not to reply, resumed correspondence with Bragg, in Richmond. His mood was optimistic. "I am very much gratified at the feeling now existing among the officers of this army," he wrote. "All mortified at their feeble efforts on the 31st ultimo. I think we will make a better fight the next time than we could have done any time since we left Resaca."

SEPTEMBER 15

"All well," Sherman wired Halleck, "and troops in fine, healthy camps, and supplies coming forward finely. Governor Brown has disbanded his militia to gather the corn and sorghum of the State. I have reason to believe that he and Stephens want to visit me, and I have sent them a hearty invitation. I will exchange 2,000 prisoners with Hood, but no more."

Carrie Berry had been troubled by mosquitoes among other annoyances. Yesterday had been tiring since she had washed clothes all afternoon and then "got dinner by myself . . . but I suppose I will have to learn to wirk."

This morning work continued with "a general cleaning up . . . everything seems so clean and I hope that it would stay so."

The women traders were still visiting Dr. Patten's camp. "Some of them bring in beans, some chinkapins and muscadines, while some I have reason to believe resort to more questionable means of obtaining the desired food. But who shall blame them, when their children are starving. Shame on the man who will take this advantage. But I have no doubt it is done every day, and that too by men whose position should be the guarantee of their good conduct. There is whiskey in camp again and such a time as we will have while it lasts. I wish our commanding officers could once get it beat into their heads that whiskey is an unmitigated nuisance. . . .

"Our stock is rather short and we will soon have nothing to trade. A little girl wanted to sell me some muscadines yesterday. I offered her the money for them but she said she could not eat money, and as I had nothing else, we did not trade. I shall be glad when we get out of this for I am tired of war and all its sights and sounds. I don't think I shall ever want to hear another Bugle Call, or to see another six mule team. Some of the men are making a little speculation in tobacco. John Clark bought a hundred dollars worth yesterday and today sold out for one hundred and forty, a pretty good move for one day. Some of the others have done equally as well. (Sergeant) John Farmer, I suppose has made more money out here than he could possibly have done at home. . . .

"Some women are in camp trading. They have a little boy about three years old along. As they start out he sings out 'goodbye Yankee!' These natives are known among the soldiers by the name of Elm Peelers . . . One of our officers asked one of them if there were any rebels near where she lived.

" 'If there were I would not tell you,' was the reply.

"They are venomous. We give them not much comfort for we don't like to furnish them with bread and divide with bushwhackers who lie around to pick off our men and I don't see the propriety of feeding them while they starve our men in prison."

Meanwhile, Fannie Beers had been evacuated from Newnan to Fort Valley, "a pleasant and very hospitable town, where new and excellent hospital buildings had been erected."

Her husband had been wounded at Jonesboro and for the first time in the war was forced "to claim my care." She took him to Fort Valley, where he made a fast recovery and was ordered back to his command.

"The day of his departure," Mrs. Beers wrote, "was marked by hours of intense anguish. . . . The train which stopped at the hospital camp to take up men returning to the front was crowded with soldiers,—reinforcements. I had scarcely recovered from the fit of bitter weeping which followed the parting, when, noticing an unusual commotion outside, I went to the door to discover the cause. Men were running up the railroad track in the direction taken by the train which had just left. A crowd had collected near the surgeon's office, in the midst of which stood an almost breathless messenger. His tidings seemed to have the effect of sending off succeeding groups of men in the direction taken by those I had first seen running up the road. Among them I discovered several surgeons. Something was wrong!

"Wild with apprehension, I sped over to the office, and there learned that the train of cars loaded and crowded with soldiers had been thrown down a steep embankment, about three miles up the road, and that many lives were lost. Waiting for nothing, I ran bareheaded and frantic up the track, for more than a mile never stopping, then hearing the slow approach of an engine, sunk down by the side of the track to await its coming.

"Soon the engine appeared, drawing very slowly a few plat-form-and baggage-cars loaded with groaning, shrieking men, carrying, also, many silent forms which would never again feel pain or sorrow. The surgeons upon the first car upon descrying me crouching by the roadside, halted the train and lifted me upon the last car, where, among the 'slightly hurt,' I found my husband, terribly bruised and shaken, but in no danger.

"Arrived at camp, where tents had been hastily pitched, the wounded and dying were laid out side by side in some of the largest, while others received the dead. The sights and sounds were awful in the extreme. At first I could not muster courage (shaken as I had been) to go among them. But it was necessary for purposes of identification, so I examined every one, dying and dead, feeling that *certainty,* however dreadful, might be better borne by loving hearts than prolonged suspense.

"Among these dreadful scenes came a minister of God, whose youthful face, pale and horror-stricken, yet all alight with heavenly pity and love, I can never forget. Tenderly he bent above these dying men, his trembling lips touched by divine inspiration, whispering words precious to parting souls. Unshrinkingly he performed his mission to those who yet lived; then, passing among the dead, lovingly composed and prepared for decent burial the mutilated bodies."

In Fort Valley, two weeks after the end of the fighting at Atlanta, the war continued without letup for Nurse Beers, her husband, and the hospital staff.

In Atlanta, the Rawsons were finally about to make a train trip of their own. The day had been one of activity, since General Geary had decided to move his headquarters into the beautiful "Terraces." Soldiers were tramping through the rooms with the general's own furniture, while outside there was the incongruous spectacle of other soldiers sweeping grass lawns preparatory to spreading tents.

Mary spent the afternoon in the garden "among the flowers," then ate supper "in sadness." Afterward, "everything was in confusion. The wagons had arrived and the baggage was being rapidly stowed away for transportation. Then came the parting from loved home servants and kindly associations. There was mammy who had been living with us ever since I can remember. Mother used to leave me in her care when I was a wee child and her kind ebony face looked down upon me then. There was Charlotte with her little ones around her tearfully shook my hand. There were many others with whom it proved a hard trial to part, and it shall be my earnest prayer that this shall not be a lasting separation . . . taking a sad farewell from servants and friends, we seated ourselves in the ambulance which slowly moved out of the yard. In a few moments we found ourselves on the hill on which stood our school house and from which a fine view of our place could be obtained. Never never did this hill look so pleasant in the setting sun as it now did and now as I look upon the groups of oaks and hedges of arboreta I for the first time could appreciate the words of the song which offers such a beautiful sentiment, 'the dearest spot of earth to me is home sweet home.'

"But I must not linger as we passed our old play ground and the street along which I used to walk so often on my way to meet so many cheerful faces in the singing meetings at the music rooms of Mr. and Mrs. Sharpe. Dear dear Atlanta! City of hills, with your bright blue sky, southern constellations, innumerable bright flowers and birds and clear sparkling water, your wells of which were never insufficient. When oh when shall I again tread your pavement and breathe your exhilarating atmosphere?

"It seems *so* sad that our beautiful stores and the fine passenger depot, where so many gay companies of young persons on pleasure parties have been accommodated by finding seats under the protection of your roof from the heat of summer and where so many poor sick soldiers have found shelter and kindness should be levelled to the ground. And old churches whose isles our feet have so often traversed gladly. May your spires never be brought low!

"But I must hasten. Now we pass in front of the park and here we stop. Father goes right away to see about the car that had been promised us but finds the train full and no box reserved. He now goes to the manager of the train and complains that he did not keep his word. He then said as he said he would provide one tonight he will have one brought directly.

"We waited some half hour when we received the intelligence that the box was made fast to the train and they were storing the baggage in the two ends of it. Then we left the ambulance and walked under the shed . . . the last time that we will ever stand under its broad arch.

"The word was finally given for us to get on board and one by one we were placed in our rough, temporary home. There were ten of us, then came Mr. Andrew's family of six and lastly a little pet dog, 16 refugees in a box as Mr. Andrews said on getting in. We were scarcely seated when the shrill whistle of the engine told us we were about leaving. Then in a few seconds we received a sudden jerk that nearly seated us on the floor, then we went dashing and clattering along, and soon Atlanta—and with it home—was not distinguishable in the distance.

"After we were well on the way we had sufficient leisure to inspect our novel abode. The roof of which was draped in handsome sable hangings (I will not say cob-webs) that swayed to and fro in the breeze. The two ends of our house were blocked up with baggage and as it became dark had it not been for the rapid return of the cars we might have been taken for a band of gypsies.

"From dusk the darkness gathers until, as Milton says 'no light but rather darkness visible' caused a deliberation as to how we could better our condition. Mr. Andrews handed each a lantern which after some parley they concluded to suspend by a nail over our heads. This answered our purpose finely for a time but the motion of the cars made the lanterns swing back and forth, while its constant click-click kept time with the noise of the wheels as they rumbled along the iron rail.

"We had not been riding long when the little ones became sleepy, when came the tugging at the mattresses until we had a very comfortable bed. The children now tumbled down to sleep and Mother and Mrs. Andrews had a nice nap too, while Mattie and I sat in the door watching the dark shadows as they swiftly passed us and talking of bygones. We sat here until we became unable to resist the effects of the varied motions and much fatigue we rested our sleepy heads on a corner of the bed and slept soundly until I was startled by a crash—and raising my head could not distinguish from what cause the sound proceeded until I heard Mrs. Andrews ask, 'did it hurt you Laura?' And sis Laura said,

" 'It fell right on my head.'

"Then I knew that our lantern had fallen suddenly, and when we again found the light we saw the remains of it scattered on the floor."

The engine whistled with testy persistence. The car clattered and swayed. The Rawsons and fellow refugees were borne through the night, northward, farther and farther from a way of life they would never, never know again.

Much more than a city had fallen.

Autumn, 1864

The leaves brittled on the oaks of Atlanta. Chinkapins were falling. The winds whistled through the countryside at night with a chill presentiment. The midday haze and the sun's drenching heat were gone. For autumn was coming, unmistakably, to Georgia.

Exhausted from summer's armageddon, men and women shared the opinion of an editorial writer "a strange calm is mantling the land." They were glad that it was.

Sherman claimed he was "perfectly at home," serenaded by nightly band concerts and sometimes entertained by theatrical performances. Though he confided to no one, his heart ached with a loneliness and sorrow that could not be readily mitigated. His seventh child, Charles Celestine, born in the General's absence in May, was ailing, and doctors could not promise that he would live out the year. Willy, his nine-year-old namesake, had died of typhoid shortly after the fall of Vicksburg— Willy whom Sherman's associates well remembered, dressed in a boy's uniform, with sergeant's stripes, walking beside his father at dress parade.

The gruffly ebullient Sherman had been despondent for weeks afterward. He had castigated himself for bringing his family to the Mississippi swamp country. Light and song had for the moment been extinguished in Tecumseh's life, and his friends wished with a nameless impotency that they could comfort this distant, hard-bitten man.

Now, facing the loss of perhaps another son, Sherman was nonetheless able to chronicle the daily events with objectivity.

"Gen. Thomas occupied a house on Marietta Street, which had a veranda with high pillars. We were sitting there one evening, talking about things generally, when Gen. Thomas asked leave to send his trains back to Chattanooga for the convenience and economy of forage. . . . I insisted on his retaining all trains, and on keeping all his divisions ready to move at a moment's warning. All the army, officers and men, seemed to relax more or less, and sink into a condition of idleness. . . .

"The telegraph and railroads were repaired, and we had uninterrupted communications to the rear. The trains arrived with regularity and dispatch, and brought us ample supplies. Gen. Wheeler had been driven out of Middle Tennessee, escaping south across the Tennessee River at Bainbridge; and things looked as though we were to have a period of repose.

"One day, two citizens, Messrs. Hill and Nelson, came into our lines at Decatur, and were sent to my headquarters. They represented themselves as former members of Congress, and particular friends of my brother John Sherman; that Mr. Hill had a son killed in the rebel army as it fell back before us somewhere near Cassville, and they wanted to obtain the body, having learned from a comrade where it was buried. I gave them permission to go by rail to the rear, with a note to the commanding officer, Gen. John E. Smith, at Cartersville, requiring him to furnish them an escort and an ambulance for the purpose. I invited them to take dinner with our mess, and we naturally ran into a general conversation about politics and the devastation and ruin caused by the war. They had seen a part of the country over which the army had passed, and could easily apply its measure of desolation to the remainder of the State, if necessity should compel us to go ahead.

"Mr. Hill resided at Madison, on the main road to Augusta, and seemed to realize fully the danger; said that further resistance on the part of the South was madness, that he hoped Gov. Brown, of Georgia, would so proclaim it, and withdraw his people from the rebellion, in pursuance of what was known as the policy of 'separate State action.'

"I told him, if he saw Gov. Brown, to describe to him fully what he had seen, and to say that if he remained inert, I would be compelled to go ahead, devastating the State in its whole length and breadth; that there was no adequate force to stop us, etc.; but if he would issue his proclamation withdrawing his

troops from the armies of the Confederacy, I would spare the
State, and in our passage across it confine the troops to the main
roads, and would, moreover, pay for all the corn and food we
needed. I also told Mr. Hill that he might, in my name, invite
Gov. Brown to visit Atlanta; that I would give him a safeguard,
and that if he wanted to make a speech, I would guarantee him
as full and respectable an audience as any he had ever spoken
to."

Senator Joshua Hill later wrote to James R. Crew in West
Point (one of the messengers for the Sherman-Hood exchange
and with whom Hill had corresponded in June and July relative to locating the body of his son): "I saw a great deal of
Atlanta—houses and people. There had been no wanton destruction of property to any extent beyond fencing and outbuildings
which in some parts of the city had suffered. If I could see you
I could tell you much more than I can undertake to write. I can
say of a truth that Gen. Sherman was right in his arbitrary order.
Those who remained were generally in a pitiable condition—
with small available means and no market they were faring
badly. . . . I was treated with marked kindness wherever I went.
I spent a week nearly about Cartersville & Kingston and several
days at Rome. From Kingston to Atlanta the country as far as
the eye can reach is one prolonged scene of desolation. The
silence that reigns is only broken by the sound of moving. . . .
men, teams of wagons, squadrons of cavalry and occasionally a
railway train. I wish it could be seen by every war man in
Georgia. But I doubt if it would do any good—so visionary and
fanatical have they grown."

Sherman received a growing list of callers, including men of
less political stature than Hill. One day, General Howard recalled, a "courteous gentleman" presented Old Tecumseh with
a "superb" box of cigars.

"To each army commander," Howard continued, "he presented something, my share being some table furniture.

"Sherman was greatly pleased and expressed his gratitude in
unusual terms.

" 'You could not have pleased me more,' he said.

"Two days afterwards the same gentleman visited Sherman

again at his Atlanta home and asked for a permit to bring sut lers' stores from Nashville to the front. Several officers were present. Sherman then displayed the terrible anger that was in him,

" 'Leave, sir! Leave at once, you scoundrel! Would you bribe me?' he said.

"The trader did not wait for a blow but rushed out in hot haste."

Another caller was Bishop Henry C. Lay, of Arkansas. The clergyman, who had baptized Hood in August, had been visiting with his close friend General Hardee, in Jonesboro. He now wished to cross Federal lines "to visit an old lady who has been as a mother to him," as Hardee himself wrote in his request to Sherman. Bishop Lay started out with a group of Federal prisoners about to be exchanged.

"We carried 149 Federal officers, not under guard, and most of them on foot. In the ambulance with me was Capt. Buel, who informed me that he was a nephew of Bishop Wilmer's. He is also a relative (brother-in-law, I believe) of Gen. Adams of our cavalry.

"Reaching Rough and Ready at midday, we hung out our white flag. Presently the train from Atlanta came down, the flag bearer seated on the cowcatcher of the engine. The officers, headed by Col. Henry on our side and Col. Warner on the enemy's, met and saluted. The exchange occupied some hours. We gave 149 officers and received 473 privates, with 16 surgeons and 4 chaplains thrown in without equivalent.

"After the prisoners had been transferred, some time was occupied by the officers in settling up their accounts. Some sick soldiers came for shelter into the porch of a deserted house where I was sitting. I said to them,

" 'We hear some of your Georgians have deserted in Atlanta.'

"One of them replied that they were men from Georgia regiments, but not all Georgians. They were urged to take the oath of allegiance, with permission to go North and reside during the war. Many had yielded. But this was not the worst. Not a few had enlisted, receiving a bounty of as much as $1000 each. A Georgia battalion had been formed of such. . . .

"At length the signal was given for departure. Col. Warner introduced me into the 'caboose' car provided for the officers and told me that he would take charge of me and convey me to Gen. Sherman.

"After proceeding a mile or so, there was a cry, and an excitement. The train stopped and many hands were extended to help in a sheepish-looking deserter. A little further, we reached the camps; a fine band mounted on the roof of the cars and played the 'Star Spangled Banner.' The men rushed out and lined the road, cheering, and we entered Atlanta in a jubilee.

"I was entirely overlooked, Col. Warner formed the prisoners into line, with the band, and marched them up to headquarters. I shouldered my saddlebags and followed in the distance. I could perceive that Gen. Sherman was making a speech which was received with enthusiasm.

"When all this was over, I approached and inquired of Col. Warner to whom I should report. He apologized for his neglect and carried me at once to Gen. Sherman.

"I found him most comfortably established in a fine house near the City Hall. The furniture seemed to be that of the owners. There was a parlor handsomely furnished, and opening into this another used as an office.

"Gen. Sherman greeted me very cordially. He was in slippers and easy in manner. He has that military sort of courtesy which puts one at ease. He read a private letter from Gen. Hardee with much satisfaction and asked if I proposed to write to him. When I assented, he said that it was perhaps not well to extend the correspondence further; but to say to Gen. Hardee that he was gratified by his letter, and should always be happy in any matter—such as my own, for instance—to extend to him any courtesy consistent with his duty.

"He carried me into a private room and provided water. My attire needed apology, for I was in homespun and unshaven, but he cut short my apology, saying everyone knew I was just off a march. I was introduced to Gen. Stanley, an old acquaintance at Fort Smith before the war, and gave him a private letter from Gen. Hardee.

"About six he invited me down to dinner. Mrs. General Rousseau and a married daughter and sundry of the staff were at table. We had pea soup in tin plates, some roast beef and vegetables afterwards; no drinkables. Gen. Sherman did the talking, which was mostly addressed to me. It was so casual that I cannot recollect much of it. Something was said about McPherson, and I remarked that he was considered in the South the kindest of their Generals. He assented, but said he made people behave themselves; for instance, he expelled certain women from Vicksburg for interrupting divine service by leaving church when the prayer for the President of the United States was used. He branched off here to say that he was for letting people pray as they chose, but could not see why people could not pray for Lincoln or 'even for me.'

"I replied that there was no objection to praying for any individual, but the use of the prayer in question was the acknowledgment of a political fact.

"To this he rejoined with some vague declamation about the clergy handling politics, which I thought not quite civil, and to which I made no reply. He spoke presently of the excess of officers in the armies, remarking that it was greater in our armies than in theirs. He complained that we had many officers without employment who had become guerillas, and declared his purpose to hang all such officers whom he found engaged in partisan warfare without commands suited to their rank; whereat the ladies seemed highly pleased.

"Dinner over, he invited me out on the piazza and offered me a cigar. His conversation for an hour or two was very interesting, and he assumed a tone which led me to speak quite openly on some points.

"He complained that Gen. Hood had treated him ungenerously in their late correspondence. It was Hood's part to refer it to his government and they could publish it if they chose; in sending it to the papers there was an effort to excite unreasonable prejudice against him.

" 'To be sure, I have made war vindictively; war is war, and you can make nothing else of it; but Hood knows as well as anyone I am not brutal or inhuman. . . .'

"As to the shelling of Atlanta, he denied that this was intended. He threw no shot at private dwellings. It was our fault in putting our lines close to the city. He was shelling the lines and the depot. After all, there was no damage in this part of the city (near the City Hall). I reminded him that I was in Atlanta all through the siege; the shells fell everywhere; the hottest fire I had been in was at private houses; shells struck St. Philip's Church near by and passed over the city. . . .

"I mentioned that we at Gen. Hood's headquarters thought he had a special grudge against us. He said no; he knew the house was on Whitehall street, but not in what part of it.

"On the second point, the exiling of the citizens, he said that it was the most merciful thing he could do. He held Atlanta as a fortress in the enemy's country. . . .

"Presently he began to speak of the campaign which had just ended in the capture of Atlanta. I remarked that General Johns(t)on was reported to have said that his move upon Jonesboro was the only mistake he had committed in all his advance; although he gained Atlanta, he could have been struck while in motion.

"To this Gen. Sherman answered: 'If I could talk with Johns(t)on after the war is over with the map between us, I could show him I did not risk too much. But I was very anxious all of the first day. When night came, however, and I found Hood had not divined my movement, I said to General Thomas, "I have Atlanta as certainly as if it were in my hand." '

"I told him that he was criticized freely by military men for allowing our army to escape intact when its corps were so widely separated. 'Ah,' said he, 'if I had known what that explosion in Atlanta meant, I would have fallen on you. I heard it and went out to look, but I thought that Slocum (?), whom I had left to watch you, had become impatient and made an assault. I ought to have taken Hardee's corps.' . . .

"He passed hence to speak of the war in general. He observed that it was an artificial war brought about by the ambition of individual men; that it was impossible for two nations to exist side by side on the continent. The case was like the effervescence of a soda powder; agitation could be ended only by union. . . .

"He went on to say, 'Your people had much the advantage in

the beginning of this war. You were a military people, respected the profession of arms and cultivated military education. If I went to New York and was introduced as Capt. or Maj. Sherman, U. S. A., the people passed me by as a useless man; but if I went to Charleston, my profession was a passport into society and caused my acquaintance to be sought. You took to arms naturally and easily; we had to acquire the military profession against our tastes.

" 'But you made a great mistake in organizing a Confederacy. Had you clung to the Union and claimed to be legitimate exponents of the American ideas, the true representatives of the American Constitution, you would have had better success. As it was, you surrendered at once into our hands the most valuable of the common property—the memories and traditions, the flags and emblems, the songs and national airs. These are invaluable in sustaining the popular enthusiasm.

" 'This war ought to be arrested. It is intensifying the greatest fault and danger in our social system. It daily increases the influence of the masses, already too great for safety. The man of intelligence and education is depressed in value far below the man of mere physical strength. These common soldiers will feel their value and seek to control affairs hereafter to the prejudice of the intelligent classes.'

"I asked him just here if he believed it possible to have a stable government in which property was not represented in the legislature. He replied no, emphatically, but added that the North had always recognized that principle, especially in giving the South a representation in Congress for slave property. The rage for universal suffrage prevailed in the South far more than in the North.

"I told him that thinking people in the South were very generally convinced of the necessity of introducing some conservative features into our system of government; for my own part, I regarded the present as a crisis in the great American experiment, and believed changes would be developed, approximating our condition more nearly to that of European powers. I mentioned an article from one of the English reviews which in its title well described our future: *Resurrection through Dissolution.*

"As I rose to take my leave, Gen. Sherman apologized for not having a bed to offer me. He said he would forward me to-morrow under Gen. Thomas's protection, and he would see to it that I should return within our lines without inconvenience. He then sent a staff officer with me to the hotel with directions to see that I was comfortably accommodated.

"In person, Gen. Sherman is spare and of good height. His hair is (not unpleasantly) red; his forehead very fine, his eye clear and restless. He impressed me as a man of active temper, who must needs be doing. His face is somewhat dyspeptic in its expression. He would be accounted ordinarily a kind-hearted man; but when aroused, severe and utterly unrelenting. His manner is very frank and outspoken. He does not seem to keep a large staff about him, and told me that he threw the business of the army into the staff of the corps, so that he keeps himself unembarrassed with details. At Gen. Hardee's headquarters the officers had been much amused by a sarcastic letter of his in reply to a Confederate chaplain who had lost a horse and claimed indemnity. It was in Gen. Sherman's own handwriting, two pages long. I judge him to be forty-five or forty-six years old."

Sherman was the object of attention and interest by all in Atlanta, even his soldiers. Rufus Mead penned many a word about the great victor.

"Have you seen Genl Shermans letter in reply to the Mayor & others asking him to revoke his order sending the citizens out of the city? It is a capital thing, a little of the best of the kind I have seen yet In short we begin to think Genl Sherman is a little ahead of any body in the U S not excepting Grant now. You ought to see him as he rides along, most always alone, and never faster than a walk. He reminds you of a circuit preacher so sober & thoughtful, apparently not noting any body or thing He is the least pretending of any of our Generals. . . .

"Everything in camp goes on in its usual routine day after day just the same unvaried duty. The paymaster still keeps away much to the sorrow of very many, in fact I dont see why it is so. Many families sorely need the money and much grumbling would be stopped if the Govmt would pay. I cant think it is for want of funds, if it is how do they expect to carry on the war 2 years longer as they may have to, though I hope not. For my own part I am unconcerned for I have plenty yet & my expenses are light I went to Church last sunday again, so I have one privilege as long as we lay here They have evening meetings but it is nearly 2 miles off so I dont go now, when the moon shines evenings I guess Ill try & attend sometimes. Yesterday I took a ride out to the S W of the city to see the works of the Rebs. It is astonishing to see what fortifications they had every side of the city, but all in vain for them, but quite convenient now for us."

Churches such as the one Rufus Mead attended were diminishing in number with respect to spiritual functions. A slaughter house was now operating in the basement of the Central Presbyterian. A portion of Father O'Reilly's Immaculate Conception had been converted to hospital wards. But this usage the cleric from Drumcora County, Ireland, could not protest.

Atlanta passed into the fall of 1864 with but a sprinkling of her original inhabitants. Residents had been leaving all summer. The September evacuation had witnessed the exit of 446 more families, consisting of 705 adults and 860 children, accompanied by 79 Negro servants. A trickling northward continued on the daily trains to Chattanooga.

Progress of those who had already departed for Tennessee was occasionally attended by continuing misfortune and peril. The Braumullers, reunited, lingered in Chattanooga several weeks before boarding another train for Louisville. They had found Mr. Braumuller in "poor health," but he was heartened by the sale of his Tennessee bonds and the pianos for $2,000.

"As we approached Bowling Green, Kentucky," wrote O. L. Braumuller, "we were startled by a fusillade of shots outside the windows. The train came to a stop and the shots continued, so we knew we were being held up by a band of guerillas, fighting men who aided neither side, but preyed upon everybody.

"The bandits set fire to the train and yelled for everybody to get out or be burned up. It was raining hard, and the blazing train was standing in a deep cut. We had to climb up the muddy bank unaided. Then the guerillas took the $2,000 out of father's clothes, and accepted $25 from Mother's purse.

"However, they did not leave us totally stranded. Mother had $800 hidden in her clothes. When the war started she showed a peculiar attachment for gold. Her faith in the Confederacy had never dwindled, but she said she preferred gold, and every time she got hold of a gold piece she put it away. Father was a little angry, and often chided her about it. He said it showed poor faith to prefer gold to Confederate money.

"However, their playful quarrel was settled by the robbery. Mother had won, but she never mentioned it again.

"After we had climbed up the bank, everybody lined up to be robbed. Then we stood or sat on the wet ground. Father was seated on a stone, and was wearing an old-fashioned shawl, when a ruffian came along and took the garment from him. My blood boiled, for I feared Father might catch his death of cold, but there was nothing an eleven-year-old boy could do.

"After the guerrillas left we went to a farmhouse where we were fed. We had to wait there a couple of days until the railroad was built back. The heat from the burning train had buckled the tracks.

"Another train took us to Louisville. Then father said that we were not in any hurry, and that we might as well get what enjoyment we could out of the trip. We went to Cincinnati on a river boat, and then got passage on another boat to Pittsburgh. It seemed wonderfully peaceful chugging up the quiet river on a steamer, with green hills on either side, and no shells or bullets to dodge. It was also more comfortable to sleep in a stateroom than on a seat on a day coach, or on a piano in the box car.

"From Pittsburgh we proceeded to New York by train. We were considered curiosities all along the line, for we wore clothes that had been made before the war, and they were now four years out of style. New styles hadn't penetrated into the Confederacy."

Dwellings, such as those vacated by the Braumullers, were now "home" to Federal officers, settled in as though they had always lived in them.

"Judge Erskine's residence and other fine houses," reported Wallace Reed, "were torn down, and the lumber was used in building cabins for the troops.

"Thus were the people of Atlanta driven from their homes into exile. Their city was turned into a vast camp, occupied by 80,000 soldiers, and a new line of fortifications was erected to defend it from a possible Confederate siege. Atlanta's fame as one of the historic cities of the continent will grow as time rolls on, and future generations will pronounce her heroic defense in a siege of forty days, one of the most glorious chapters in the history of the war. To those generations must be left the task of raising monuments on our battlefields, and on the spots where our heroes fell; and to their historians must be left the work of writing the complete story of the bloody struggle for the Gate City."

While the Union armies rested and prepared for their winter campaign by salting great quantities of beef and accumulating stores of ammunition, the people gradually picked up the threads of their former lives. Some composed poems to assuage their heavy hearts:

> Take O take back Atlanta, now marred by shells
> Of the Foe who possess and destroy;
> O we then shall be free midst the ringing of bells,
> We will sound loud our proud nation's joy.

The song became popular in the privacy of Southern parlors and by late fall had multiplied into uncounted stanzas. Music among the negroes, however, had not changed. Those who had not shuffled north or south could still be heard humming:

> Rabbit take his pipe to smoke
> 'Coon eat turkey hash;
> Possum try to crack a joke,
> But wolf run off wid de cash.

President Jefferson Davis paid a visit to Macon and later Hood's headquarters at Palmetto. Major Hubner, of Illinois, was shocked at some soldiers, "almost mutinous," refusing to listen to speeches as they cried:

"We don't want any talk, give us back old Joe!"

Sherman, who followed the daily developments in the camps of his enemy through spy reports and by the accounts in the Southern newspapers, commented:

"Davis seemed to be perfectly upset by the fall of Atlanta and to have lost all sense and reason. . . . He denounced Gen. Johnston and Gov. Brown as traitors and the cause of all the trouble, and prophesied that the Yankee army was doomed to a retreat worse than that of Napoleon from Moscow."

The Southern press felt much the same way. The *Montgomery Mail* sniffed at the "rambling, desultory character" of Davis' remarks and added, relative to his "meddling" in the selection of generals, "The President is again on his travels to 'confer with the generals.' May God deliver us this time from that dispensation which the past teaches us to anticipate."

Fall drew to a close and the days shortened. Troops huddled around campfires at night. Heavy coats and blankets were issued by quartermasters.

Winter was coming.

Outside of Atlanta, the refugees wondered whether to continue south or belatedly accept the Federal offer of transportation north. Georgia newspapers printed appeals for food and clothing. Relatives of the homeless could barely subsist themselves. They could not help.

Sherman received Hood's permission to attempt to alleviate another problem of humanity—the infested prison camp at Andersonville. The Confederate General agreed to allow a train of food and medical supplies to pass through his lines.

However, Hood himself was swinging back onto the march, moving ponderously toward Tennessee, and harassing the W. A. railroad to Chattanooga. At Allatoona, Brigadier General John M. Corse made history with his defense of the important stores center and railroad switch point.

Sherman, who had been obliged to quit his comfortable Atlanta headquarters and take to the field, positioned himself atop Kennesaw Mountain. From its heights, he observed the cannon smoke puffing upward from distant Allatoona, now surrounded by French's troops.

"Hold the fort, for I am coming!" Sherman signaled.

At a bloody price the fort was held and General Sam French was forced to record yet another frustration. Sherman, when he saw his haggard commander, face scarred by a Minie ball, remarked, "Corse they came damn near missing you didn't they?"

The incident was too obvious an inspiration for P. P. Bliss, the evangelist, to resist. Soon he was lustily singing his own composition:

> Ho! my comrades see the signal
> Waving in the sky,
> Reinforcements now appearing
> Victory is nigh. . . .
> Hold the fort, for I am coming
> Jesus signals still!
> Wave the answer back to heaven
> By the grace we will!

The Allatoona fight also added further documentations to Sherman's growing reputation for invincibility and foresight. Two Confederate pickets were overhead discussing the blasting of a tunnel further along the railroad, near Dalton.

"Now the Yanks will have to git or starve," opined one.

"Oh, hell," replied his companion, "old Sherman carried a duplicate tunnel along."

In Jonesboro, an elderly widow, Mrs. Allie McPeek, had completed a claim against the United States Government—for exactly six hundred dollars. She had nursed wounded soldiers of both sides during the bloody fighting, and had so touched General Schofield's heart that he wrote approval in advance of whatever bill she might later forward to Washington. She was unable to explain how she had arrived at the exact figure.

In Atlanta, the Massachusetts 33rd Infantry band was making civic history by its concerts and theatrical benefits—mostly to raise money for Mrs. Rebecca S. Welch, formerly of Columbus, whose husband and son both had fallen in Virginia. With two other children in addition to four young ones of her recently deceased sister, Mrs. Welch was living at the home of a friend, Colonel George Adair.

The season had opened in late September with a vocal and

instrumental concert in the long-empty Athenaeum. Admission was one dollar. Mrs. Welch herself, entering into the spirit, offered a piano solo, sang *Then You'll Remember Me,* and joined in a quartet, which included her daughter, Miss S. Welch, to render *Come Where My Love Lies Dreaming.*

Heartened by the night's receipts of two hundred dollars, the band climbed into their horse hacks the next morning for the short ride and started practicing for a repeat performance. Mrs. Welch was in accord, having unexpectedly acquired a taste for footlights. However, a twenty-one-year-old pianist from Stoneham, Massachusetts, A. P. Hazard, decided to embellish his band's usual repertoire. He initiated a series of plays and dramatic sketches, himself serving as actor, manager, bill-poster, printer and property man. Superintending the overall project was Colonel William G. Le Duc, quartermaster of the 20th Corps.

Printing his programs on the back of old discharge papers, he arranged such ambitious presentations as *The Cobbler's Frolic,* which he labeled as a "laughable pantomime." Mrs. Welch and her daughter joined the cast, and asked Musician Hazard for a part in the next scheduled production, *The Lover's Serenade.*

The Athanaeum was packed for seventeen nights. Privates, whose pay was thirteen dollars a month, sat next to officers and the well-dressed, theater-minded men and women of Atlanta. Mrs. Welch was presented with two thousand dollars, and the band at least "cleared expenses."

Atlanta's impromptu fall theater season was a success.

But otherwise, life during the occupation was uneventful. Carrie Berry was "lonesom" with no school, at times she was sick and shivered through the cold, rainy days of October. She hemmed towels and sheets, knitted socks and sweaters. One day she reported, "I made me an apron . . . and my doll a dress."

Cow's brains became a delicacy, dumplings a staple. Once a pig was bought from a country friend and slaughtered by "Papa." Aunt Healey finally left for Chattanooga, and almost broke Carrie's heart . . . "everything seems so quiet."

The Union forces, too, had a surfeit of inactivity, and of chill fall weather.

"It rains about half the time," Rufus Mead wrote, "and that together with the suspense makes it lonesome enough. Meat is scarce so they cut down on meat but we have any quantity of hardbread, coffee and sugar and tomorrow I hear we get more hardbread to make up deficiency in meat." But the weather, even more than food, dominated the thoughts of the troops.

"The wind began to blow about midnight from the N W and blew harder & harder till noon than a regular gale till night," Rufus continued. "It reminded me of a day in Conn 4 or 5 years ago when the wind blew so and not a cloud to be seen all day. No further news yet. Every one is kept busy on the forts yet. The plan is to build a line of forts just around the very center of the city so as to make that almost impregnable. Sherman means to make this his base of supplies and goes to work as if he thought the war might last for years yet . . . Very cold night but too windy for frost. We had to fix our tent over & put a stove in it to keep comfortable. No work on the forts today. Officers had to register all their colored servants otherwise they would be taken up and sent to work at digging. All other negroes in the city are to be employed in that way. I guess Slocum is of the opinion that negroes must do something to earn their freedom that Uncle Abe gives. One of the finest & most prominent buildings in the city is a Female Seminary, situated on a very high hill about ¾ of a mile from the Depot. It is built of brick about 60 x 100 feet, 3 stories high and about 20 feet to a story. From the cupola is the prettiest sight in the city. The country for miles in every direction is as plain as can be. It seems a pity to destroy such buildings but such a commanding position cannot be overlooked in war times, so down comes the Seminary and soon the sword will rule over where the pen held the sceptre of power, although in consideration of the adage, that the pen is mightier than the sword. The boys are tearing up floors and carrying off windows to build shanties for themselves. I felt quite angry at first to see the destruction of such valuable property and public property too, but when I learned why it was done I acquiesced at once. Property is dear to us but life is much more so. Monday . . . A very cold night and a heavy frost this morning. Heard lots of cheering and hurrahing in camp long before light, & on getting out found that Slocum had notice from Sherman that Richmond is ours. We have no communication yet to Chattanooga either by rail or telegraph, but they signal from one point to another so we gets news after a while.

"This news has been told so many times that we hardly credit it yet, so dont let off half the enthusiasm we would if we knew it to be true. In fact not over half believe a lot of it and even they have many doubts. We fixed up our tent &c just the same as if no such news had come, still we keep thinking, 'Oh if it true' and how earnestly we long for further particulars. Tom & I had to draw rations, get 1½ pounds bread & ½ lb. beef yet, but a guard is going to Marietta after cattle tomorrow. Chattahoochee bridge repaired so trains run over that now. Rumor says the road will be done to Chattanooga by Thursday, then will get a mail & newspaper. We miss them wonderfully."

The countryside around Atlanta presented an ever more poignant scene of desolation.

"Many trees had fallen by the army-woodman's ax," as young Noble Williams saw it, "and those left standing were but the shattered remnants of their former selves, for cannonball, shell and Minie had vied with each other in their attempts at relieving the mighty oaks and pines of their limbs and trunks. The woods and fields were strewn with the carcasses of dead and decaying animals, most of which had performed valuable service, but becoming disabled were shot or left to die of starvation, and the sickening stench of their dead bodies attracted numbers of buzzards which fattened on the dead and decaying remnants of war. Many hungry and half wild dogs made night hideous with their howling, and frightened the women and children greatly, as they could be seen at almost any hour daily running wildly about the streets, seemingly seeking whom they might devour."

As November approached, word reached Atlanta that General G. T. Beauregard, supplanting Hood in executive favor, was actually giving orders to the Army of Tennessee. According to De B. Randolph Keim, a correspondent for the *New York Herald,* "the new commander opened his campaign in a proclamatory denunciation of everything in sight, sparing no terms in chastisement of the invaders and spending the balance of his effort in an appeal to honor stimulated by horrors of all kinds, including rape, arson and other sorts in stock to reignite the slumbering enthusiasm of the southern people."

Sherman, unimpressed by oratory, was endeavoring to convince Grant at City Point, Virginia, of the necessity for ravaging Georgia by a march to the sea:

"Until we can repopulate Georgia, it is useless to occupy it, but the utter destruction of its roads, houses and people will cripple their military resources."

Lizzie Perkerson had obtained vicarious satisfaction at Hood's escape to the north. The Yankees were "the maddest set when they found that Hood was in their rear and they had to leave you ever saw, I reckon," she wrote to her brother.

"They thought that Hood had moved to Macon until he was clean across the river. They moved off then, all except the garrison at Atlanta and we saw but few afterward. They didn't bother us any more. The picket line was at the Loften place. We knew nothing more what they were doing until they left for good. We kept hoping that they would leave and when we failed to hear their drum for a day or two we would think they were gone but to our sorrow we would hear it again. After they had been in town about six weeks one night someone called Pa up and when he went out he found that it was some southern soldiers and they told him that the Yankees were leaving and they were going into Atlanta.

"Next morning early a woman that is living in Jim McCool's house sent for some of us to come over, that her child was dying. I went and when I got there she wanted me to go up after Mrs. Sylvie, so I put out and directly heard cannonading in the direction of town and when I got up in sight of the Holland crossing I could see the guns. Our soldiers were firing from the hill at Sally Whits place. So I began to feel sort of squeamish but I ran up to the house and while I was there they began to bring out our wounded to Sylvie's to dress their wounds. The fight continued for two hours. But finding the Yankees in strong force, our men withdrew. But not until they had driven them in the works round the city. We lost three killed and eleven wounded. Two of our men were buried in Loften's yard. The Yankees lost three killed and twenty wounded. Our men then went back to Fayetteville and settled down. Finding that they were mistaken, they concluded to let the Yankees have their way."

Lizzie also noted the inevitable and widespread Negro problem. "Ed Taliaferro went down into Henry County and all his negro men ran away from him and . . . the Yankees got all his horses and mules and destroyed pretty near all his household goods and came so near getting him they shot him in the back. But he says he escaped by good running. . . . Every Negro Terry had went but Kit and he was with Taliaferro and they caught him in this last trip but Kit got away from them and came back. . . . Ours are all at home and they are all the negroes in the neighborhood. Stokes left old Bess up here to take care of his place and he moved into town before the Yankees got here. When Dan went to leave he marched up to the door and made a polite bow and said 'I now bid adieu to you and slavery' and off he went. He came to the kitchen once after he left but he tryed to slip around the house to keep any of us from seeing him. . . .

"Dr. William Gilbert moved down in Henry and about time the Yankees came in here he went to South Carolina and got him a place to move to and started and the second day after he started he fell off his horse dead in the road. His family buried him by the road side and went on. Some of his negroes left. I saw old Reese go by. You can't imagine how it would take the Yankees down to see a whole gang of negroes and children go straggling along. We would tell them to look out yonder is some more of Sherman's reinforcements. Some of them would cuss, others would laugh, but they all acknowledge that the Georgians had played off on them by sending off all their negroes that were valuable and leaving those that were nothing but an expense. . . .

"The Yankees burned Will's houses and took all the stock.

They are all well. Grandma says Indeed she gave one of them three very good licks. He was taking the wheat out of the wheat house and the paddling stick was close by and she just put it to him. They took pretty well all the grain Grandma had. Uncle Will looks a little cross but I think he will live and do well yet. Aunt Lizzie Hearn was here yesterday. They never got to her house at all. She seems to be getting on finely. Uncle Ang was here last week. They burned his mills and workshop but he says he will build them again and will probably be able to make some improvements on the old plan. He says that they treated Aunt Mary pretty badly. They tore up her black silk dress and in fact pretty near all her clothes. John and Jim both went North. The last news Jim was in Ky and John in Indiana. Don't you reckon John will make a fortune up north where people all work for what they get? The last I heard from Ben Brewster he was well and fixing to go back to his command."

The Perkersons started November with a meager barnyard— one hog, four chickens, two "old Yankee mules," and ten dogs. This was, Lizzie commented ruefully. "the sum total of our livestock."

Soldiers in Atlanta received a flood of mail following the repair of the tracks temporarily torn up by the Confederate raiders, and "many thousand hearts beat quicker, happier" at the spate of family news. To Rufus Mead, hastening to reply to his "dear folks at home" in Redding, Connecticut, it appeared as though he would spend Christmas in Georgia.

"We had orders to prepare winter quarters which looks as if we might stay here some time, but of course no one knows. My winter quarters are built now yet I can get ready to move in half an hour any time. Our beef cattle got through safe so tomorrow we get full rations of beef again. The greatest want now is forage for the mules, & horses, that are dying off fast from actual starvation. In our Brigade about 10 a day for the past week have died. They got some forage out in the country south here today, and tomorrow they expect a train from Chattanooga so we will fare much better I hope.

"It seems so pitiful to see a fine large mule worth $200, lie

down and die just because he is too weak from starvation to
stand up, but it was far worse at Chattanooga last fall.

"Some of our prisoners excaped from Macon say our prisoners there are living on an ear of corn a day. It dont seem
hardly possible yet I fear it is so. . . .

"The paymasters were just too late to get here before the
R R was torn up but expect them on soon now.

"I have but little doubt now of Uncle Abes election, but yet
one cant help feeling a little anxious about it, especially as soldiers who have so much at stake. My second sheet is full so I
will wait till next time & close now. As ever your Afft Son &
Brother."

By the first week in November, trainloads of conscripts were
pouring into Atlanta to strengthen an army weakened by the
expiration of thousands of enlistments. Dr. Patten, for one,
found the new soldiers of better quality than he had anticipated.

"Some of our conscripts are coming in daily and I think
before long they will all be here," he reported. "They are as a
general rule a better set of men than we looked for and look
well. There is one old fellow among them who is over age but
some time back he wanted to get a young wife, and represented himself as being several years younger than he really
was. This did very well then but when the draft came he did
not find it quite so funny for the authorities took him at his
own valuation, and sent him down here to meditate at his leisure on the benefits of misrepresentation and the other conscripts are having more fun out of him than if he was a circus."

Sherman watched trains "whirling by" in the opposite direction, their engineers waving him "an affectionate adieu."
They were laden with "an immense amount of stores which
had accumulated at Atlanta" and the sick, the wounded, the
over-age, and even the weary soldiers—all of whom had been
lumped together by the commanding general as "trash." They
had no place in his fast-materializing plans.

Sherman started for Atlanta from field headquarters in Kingston. "It was surely a strange event—two hostile armies marching in opposite directions, each in the full belief that it was

achieving a final and conclusive result in a great war; and I was strongly inspired with the feeling that the movement on our part was a direct attack upon the rebel army and the rebel capital at Richmond, and that, for better or worse, it would end the war."

Old Tecumseh was convined that, at the very least, he could "make Georgia howl!"

NOVEMBER 12

From his field headquarters at Kingston, General Sherman wired Thomas shortly before 8:00 A.M.:

"The trains are well up and I will start this morning. Telegraph me at Allatoona tonight."

It had been a day of menace and violence in Atlanta.

"We were fritened almost to death," wrote Carrie Berry. "Some mean soldiers set several houses on fire in different parts of the town. I could not go to sleep for fear that they would set our house on fire. We all dred the next few days to come for they said that they would set the last house on fire if they had to leave this place."

Sherman was perturbed at the premature attempt to fire the city. The plan, David Conyngham reported, was to destroy Atlanta by the rear-guard of the army once in motion toward the Atlantic Ocean:

"The first fire burst out on the night of Friday, the 11th of November, in a block of wooden tenements on Decatur Street, where eight buildings were destroyed," he continued.

"Soon after, fires burst out in other parts of the city. These certainly were the works of some of the soldiers, who expected to get some booty under cover of the fires.

"The fire engines were about being shipped for Chattanooga, but were soon brought in, and brought to bear on the burning districts.

"The patrol guards were doubled, and orders issued to shoot down any person seen firing buildings. Very little effort had been made to rescue the city from the devouring elements, for they knew that the fiat had gone forth consigning it to destruction. Over twenty houses were burned that night, and a dense cloud of smoke, like a funeral pall, hung over the ruins next morning.

"Gen. Slocum offered a reward of five hundred dollars for the apprehension of any soldier caught in the act of incendiarism. Though Slocum knew that the city was doomed, according to his just notions of things it should be done officially. No officer or soldier had a right to fire it without orders.

"It was hard to restrain the soldiers from burning it down. With that licentiousness that characterizes an army, they wanted a bonfire."

During the night, Major General Henry W. Slocum, from his suite in the Trout House, had scribbled a letter to his wife Clara in Syracuse. A little, pinched man with an incongruously large mustache, Slocum was, like his more famous Commanding General, a confusing synthesis of brusque, hard-bitten soldier and soft-hearted emotionalist.

He had shut the balcony door and windows against the city din: the shouts from Decatur Street below and the military comings and goings from the long-since commandeered Masonic Hall next door.

"The last train for the north leaves here tomorrow morning," Slocum scrawled in the yellow glow from the oil lamp. "Our soldiers are scattered along the railroad a hundred miles north, and as soon as that train passes, the work of destruction will commence. The railroad will be completely destroyed and every bridge burned. Then both armies (the armies of the Tennessee and Georgia) will assemble here, and after destroying the city will comence the march. I fear their track will be one of desolation.

"I have been to the railroad depot for the past three days several times and have witnessed many sad and some ludicrous scenes. All citizens (white and black) begin to apprehend that something is about to happen. The few white people remaining after their families were sent away are alarmed and many are leaving the city, giving up horses, lands, furniture, negroes and all. The black want to go North, and the Car House is surrounded by them. Hundreds of cars are literally packed with them and their dirty bundles, inside and outside. Old toothless hags, little pickaninnies, fat wenches of all shades, from light brown to jet black, are piled up together with their old bags, bundles, broken chairs, etc. Some are gnawing old bones, some squatted by the cars making hoecakes, some crying for food which we cannot supply. Many of the white people are as anxious to get north as the darks, and gladly accept a place in a car reeking with the odor peculiar to the 'American of African descent.' It is a sad sight and I anticipate seeing many such before spring.

"I wish for humanity's sake that this sad war could be brought to a close. While laboring to make it successful I shall do all in my power to mitigate its horrors."

The burning of those parts of Atlanta which might have military significance had been blueprinted by Sherman. On Friday morning he had informed his Chief of Engineers, Captain Orlando M. Poe, that he "may commence the work of destruction at once, but don't use fire until toward the last moment."

For more than a week, Lieutenant Colonel Charles F. Morse, twenty-five-year-old Boston architect attached to the Atlanta post headquarters, had been planning for the massive demolition. His squads had inspected houses, undermined walls and chimneys of buildings earmarked for destruction, and had even planted powder bags.

By the time Poe arrived to take over the project, Colonel Morse could report that he had destroyed one small house successfully as an "experiment." Inwardly he fumed that he could not continue with his task, and told his associates of his disappointment.

Late that Saturday afternoon, the scenes Slocum had viewed at the passenger depot came to an end. The last train from Atlanta chugged northward, through pitted, red clay streets, past skeletons of buildings and grotesque rubble heaps.

It carried the military as well as the "exiles." Fenwick Hedley watched its progress past Big Shanty. Soldiers whose service had expired sat or stood beside officers who had resigned.

"Large sums of money," wrote Hedley, "were committed to them by their comrades, for delivery to families or friends at home. One, a surgeon, had not less than $12,000 in his valise enclosed in ordinary envelopes. . . . hearty cheers and 'God Bless you!' came from scores of the homeward bound; as hearty cheers and fervent 'good-byes' from those left behind."

"By midnight a glare of light reached from Atlanta as far northward as the eye could reach," Hedley added.

It was the burning of Sherman's lifeline to Chattanooga as he prepared to cut loose for Savannah. "For miles back of Atlanta. . . . the track of destruction was marked by day by a line of curling smoke and by night by a broad streak of light that seemed like the Aurora Borealis."

These southern skies commenced to flame as red, seemingly, as Georgia earth.

NOVEMBER 13

In the wake of Sherman's scourging return to Atlanta, depots, bridges, public buildings, stores, barns, in fact even the major sections of cities and towns, lay smoldering.

Rome, Kingston, and already-mauled Marietta were burned and broken. Federal officers lost no chance to remind Georgia that these latter day Carthages were a portent for whatever or whomsoever obstructed this invincible of armies.

"An immense amount of government property," wrote Conyngham, "which we could not transport to the rear, or carry along with us, had been destroyed at the different depots. Coffee sacks, cracker boxes, sugar and pork barrels, bales of blankets and boxes of clothing, were burst open and strewn about and burned. Soldiers were loaded with blankets and supplies, which they got tired of before night, and flung away. It is said that about three million of dollars worth of property had been destroyed in this way. . . .

"The Michigan engineers had been detailed to destroy the depots and public buildings in Atlanta. Everything in the way of destruction was now considered legalized. The workmen tore up the rails and piled them on the smoking fires. Winship's iron foundry and machine shops were early set on fire. This valuable property was calculated to be worth about half a million of dollars.

"An oil refinery near by next got on fire, and was soon in a fierce blaze. Next followed a freight warehouse, in which were stored several bales of cotton. The depot, turning-tables, freight sheds, and stores around, were soon a fiery mass. The heart was burning out of beautiful Atlanta.

The few people that had remained in the city fled, scared by the conflagration and the dread of violence."

Major Ward Nichols, Sherman's aide-de-camp, was in agreement: "Atlanta is entirely deserted by human beings, excepting a few soldiers here and there," he wrote. "The houses are vacant; there is no trade or traffic or any kind; the streets are empty. Beautiful roses bloom in the gardens of fine houses, but a terrible stillness and solitude cover all, depressing the hearts even of those who are glad to destroy it. In the peaceful homes at the North there can be no conception how these people have suffered for their crimes."

Yet, Nichols was not wholly correct about the desertion of Atlanta. For even as he took pen in hand, Carrie Berry, one of those "human beings," was writing: "The Federal soldiers have ben coming today and burning houses and I have ben looking at them come in nearly all day."

Outside of the city, "human beings" like Lizzie Perkerson clung tenaciously to their parcels of earth.

"They all fear that I am taking the Fever now but I hope

not," she continued in her letter to her brother Angus. "I feel very badly but I have gone through enough to make a stouter person than me feel badly. I haven't undressed to go to bed in a month until last night. But I am taking medicine and hope that I will not get down. I don't want you to be uneasy about mother for I think she will be up in another week. There has been a great deal of sickness in this country since the army came in here. But I don't think strange of it. The whole country is full of dead horses and mules and the ditches standing full of stagnant water, enough to kill anything."

It was Sunday.

After Mass, Father O'Reilly, apprehensive about the churches, considered another visit to Federal headquarters. Must he, the thought bore in, again threaten higher intervention? He decided to wait one more day.

Major Henry Hitchcock, thirty-five-year-old St. Louis lawyer and Sherman's Assistant Adjutant General of volunteers, arrived in the city. He went to Judge Lyon's "fine house—large, double brick, very handsome." There he met Colonel Amos Beckwith, "Plain, very rough, vigorous, indefatigable—largely entitled to credit of Atlanta campaign as to commissary supplies. Army of 120,000 never on half rations! B. gave us lunch, very welcome.

"Met also General Easton, C. Q. M., and Capt. O. M. Poe, Ch. Eng.," he continued. "Poe this A.M. *rammed down* big stone and brick depot, no fire or powder applied. N. B. Saw at Kingston joint letter of E. and B. to General, recommending that the destruction here be specially in Poe's charge—'to prevent irregularities, he having reliable men under him.' So ordered at once by telegraph.

"Rode by the depot ruins in entering town: *perfect smash*. The big Railroad bridge—very fine, on several stone piers over the Chattahoochee—was destroyed early today, before we got there: we crossed on Poe's truss bridge.

"Haven't seen fifteen citizens here—all soldiers, and *plenty of them*. Even part of an army of 120,000 men makes a big show: some corps are outside of the city, some below, some above, camped or arriving.

"Discussion at lunch about destruction, retaliation, etc. Even McCoy was warmed up, and Col. E. boiled over in recalling the summons of the reb. commander to our men at Resaca, and at Dalton, and at Tilton, 'to surrender, or *no prisoners would be taken.*' None were taken, nor those places either. But I don't wonder that such things infuriate our men."

At 6:30 P.M., a military telegraph operator in Nashville flashed the telltale news to Washington: "Ceased to communicate with Sherman yesterday. . . . rivers still swelling but rain stopped."

In Tennessee, Bishop Lay, impeded by the same torrential downfalls, washed out bridges, train wrecks, and a Pandora's warborn assortment, was struggling to reach Chattanooga.

"I telegraphed and wrote to Gen. Thomas at Nashville," he wrote, "and each time received in reply an assurance that the way would be open in three or four days to Atlanta.

"At last, on the 7th of November, I set out again and reached Chattanooga on the 8th.

"It rained dismally; the streets were a sea of mud and filth; the hotel was so crowded that a bed or a meal had to be almost fought for; interminable trains of cars covered the tracks. For two days I splashed through the mire from one office to another. It now became revealed that Atlanta and the roads leading to it were to be abandoned. Sherman was about to advance into the interior of Georgia; it was doubtful whether any train would go to the front.

"On the morning of the 10th of November I found myself in a freight car laden with bags of oats. One door was torn off so that the car could not be closed, and as a special favor three officers and myself were allowed to ride inside. We spent two days and two nights in this car, making 70 miles."

NOVEMBER 14

Dr. James Comfort Patten "started on the grand raid. We were astir early in the morning, packed up what we intended to carry along and left the rest in our huts. We then set fire to them and at 12 all our houses, shops and stables were in ashes."

Captain George W. Pepper of Zanesville, Ohio, with the 15th Corps, was passing through Atlanta while Dr. Patten's regiment had skirted the southern fringes of the city.

"Here are luxurious homes now the scenes of no domestic joys," Pepper reported, "stately warehouses where no wealthy merchants congregate; beautiful temples where resound no more the organ's swell or the notes of praise. All is solemnly desolate. The destruction caused by bombardment was great. Whole buildings were shattered by artillery. Clouds of smoke, as we passed through, were bursting from several princely mansions. Every house of importance was burned on Whitehall street. Railroad depots, rebel factories, foundries and mills were destroyed. This is the penalty of rebellion. Heaven and earth both agree in decreeing a terrible punishment to those perfidious wretches who concocted this wasting and desolating war.

"There is one spot of sacred interest, the cemetery a lovely city of the dead. Here nature has her trees, her verdant slopes. Art has added beauty to the already beautiful walks of nature. Ah! how many brave sons of the Union sleep here . . . and so, with sorrow and pity we pass the Gate City, breathing a prayer that the all-powerful will grant forgiveness to the miserable ingrates, whose love of slavery inaugurated this terrible rebellion. Once more the march. We adapt ourselves to circumstances, our baggage consisting of a towel, a cracker, a Testament and a late Southern paper announcing Sherman's retreat from Hood."

Carrie, in terror, did not stray far from her yard. She observed the continuing destruction. "They came burning Atlanta today. We all dread it because they say that they will burn the last house before they stop. We will dread it."

Sherman arrived at his headquarters in mid-afternoon, gratified that "all preparations had been made." Colonel Beckwith was ready with his report: 1,200,000 rations had been distributed to the sixty thousand troops, enough for a twenty days' march even assuming the countryside did not provide its own nourishment; there was a "good supply" of beef cattle, to be driven on the hoof, although an exact count was lacking; forty rounds of ammunition per man; twenty-five hundred wagons, each drawn by six mules, and six hundred ambulances would make up the caravan, now beginning to leave the Atlanta staging area. It would wind eastward over the Georgia countryside, a procession at least five miles long.

Federal spies reported that corn had been stored in cribs by Governor Brown's militia, in such convenient locations and in such quantity that Sherman concluded it was "seemingly for our use."

Before supper, the Commanding General watched Poe's scientific destruction.

"He had a large force at work," Sherman recorded, "had leveled the great depot, round-house and the machine shops of the Georgia Railroad, and had applied fire to the wreck. One of these machine shops had been used by the rebels as an arsenal, and in it were stored piles of shot and shell, some of which proved to be loaded, and that night was made hideous by the bursting of shells, whose fragments came uncomfortably near Judge Lyon's house, in which I was quartered. The fire also reached the block of stores near the depot, and the heart of the city was in flames all night, but the fire did not reach the parts of Atlanta where the court-house was, or the great mass of dwelling-houses."

Even from the outskirts of Atlanta, the spectacle of destruction was vivid. Lizzie Perkerson watched, and concluded great operations were in the making. "We were sure they were going to leave . . . The fires continued until Monday night and we discovered several large fires in the country. Till and I were on the porch looking at the fires when we heard the clanking of swords and spurs coming up the road. Well, if I had seen them building the fire to this house, I would never have felt more certain that we were gone up. But they came up to the poplar tree and turned out in this road and stood a few minutes and went back. In about two hours we heard them coming again. This time they rode up in front of the house and hallowed. Till went to the door. They asked her what them dogs was making such a fuss about. She told them that she didn't know, but supposed from what she had heard herself that they were barking at soldiers that was riding around here, so they turned and went off and we soon discovered that they were on picket on top of the hill and next morning by sun-up the whole road was full of them and we found they were leaving sure enough but going down the country instead of up. Well, they were passing all day and until eleven o'clock next day, and since then I have felt free as a bird turned out of a cage. They didn't bother us much in passing. They sent in a guard without being asked for it. They told us they were going to play smash with the Confederacy, just going to sweep it out at one lick."

Colonel Adin Underwood, of the Massachusetts 33rd Infantry Regiment, believed the night "was one to be remembered."

"No darkness—in place of it a great glare of light from acres of burning buildings. This strange light, and the roaring of the flames that licked up everything habitable, the intermittent explosions of powder, stored ammo. and projectiles, streams of fire that shot up here and there from heaps of cotton bales and oil factories, the crash of falling buildings, and the change, as if by a turn of the kaleidoscope, of strong walls and proud structures into heaps of desolation; all this made a dreadful picture of the havoc of war, and of its unrelenting horrors.

"As the band was playing in the theater that night, the flaming red light from the approaching fire which flooded the building, the roar of the flames and the noises of the intermittent explosions added scenic effects which were not down in the bills, and will never be forgotten. And when later in the night it serenaded Sherman and played in the light of the flames *John Brown's Soul Goes Marching On* the members must have appeared to the crest-fallen civilians like so many Neroes fiddling with delight at the burning of Rome. It seemed like a demoniacal triumph over the fate of the city that had so long defied Sherman's armies."

Dr. Patten, by now ten miles east of the city with his regiment, looked at his watch and found that the glow from the burning buildings even at such a distance enabled him to "see the time very plainly."

But he had little opportunity for reflections: "the trains kept halting and starting and Gen. Ward being in liquor and out of patience, came and abused Col. Moore for stopping."

Dr. Patten wondered if they would ever pause for breakfast.

NOVEMBER 15

Atlantans awoke "to gaze upon the most awful and sickening sights it had ever been their misfortune to witness."

As Noble Williams was to note: "their own beloved city was enveloped on all sides in a seething mass of smoke and flame, madly curling upward to the blue skies above, and leaving behind only blackened ruins and heaps of ashes. Gen. Sherman's men had applied the match, and the flames completed the work which it had begun; but not until it had brought many innocent owners of property to the very verge of, and in many cases absolute poverty.

"Unfortunately for the doctor, his entire stock of drugs, notes, accounts and valuable papers all went up in smoke. Just opposite the doctor's residence stood the handsome home of Mr. H., which was one among the very last to be fired. Some Union soldiers had been observed as they left the building, and a few moments later the house was one solid sheet of flame. The heat from the fire was so intense that it drew the rosin from Doctor C.'s front door. His family were living in the center of a circle, the edges of which were emitting flame, smoke and heat, as one of the wicked incidents of war. Descriptive power is almost inadequate to vividly portray the real horrors of such a conflagration."

By 7:00 A.M., Capt. Poe's staff estimated that 37 per cent of the city was already in ashes. The fires had spread impersonally beyond military objectives, consuming most of the churches. These included ill-starred St. Luke's which had seen so few services since its consecration.

Furiously, Father O'Reilly demanded that the Federal troops give protection to the houses of worship. Thus aroused, their bucket brigades saved the Central Presbyterian Church and adjoining Second Baptist Church, the Trinity Methodist and St. Philip's churches, in addition to the Immaculate Conception. Father O'Reilly believed that his intervention saved, as well, the City Hall, though a resident nearby, Mrs. Holcombe, insisted it was her plea which reprieved the municipal structure.

Major Hitchcock, the St. Louis lawyer and Sherman's staff assistant, breathed the cinder-laden air and observed "clouds of heavy smoke rise and hang like pall over doomed city."

To Carrie Berry the day was especially "dreadful. . . . things have been burning all around us." She feared the approaching night "because we do not know what moment that they will set our house on fire."

By mid-afternoon, the city was a furnace. No citizens ventured outside of their houses. Most were back in the basements or bombproofs which had afforded refuge from shells. Some read those portions of the Bible which predicted a fiery end of the world, certain that the prophecy was close to realization.

"The air was resonant with explosions," Conyngham reported, "while flames were mounting to the sky from burning depots and factories all over the city. . . . men were cheering and singing patriotic songs, and fairly revelling in the excitement and novelty of the situation."

At dusk, Major Ward Nichols, aide-de-camp of Sherman, watched a "grand and awful spectacle—this beautiful city now in flames. The heaven is one expanse of lurid fire; the air is filled with flying, burning cinders; buildings covering two hundred acres are in ruins or in flames; every instant there is the sharp detonation or the smothered booming sound of exploding shells and powder concealed in the buildings, and then the sparks and flame shoot away up into the black red roof, scattering cinders far and wide."

Yet Carrie Berry was comforted since the provost marshal had sent a guard to their property "a little while after dinner and we felt a little more protected."

Captain J. C. Van Duzer, having acquainted his town of Carlinville, Illinois, with the war's opening days as telegraph operator, now believed he was witnessing its closing counterparts. He watched the smashing of the depot across the street from his office in fascination.

"The implement used for this purpose," he wrote to his family, "was the battering ram, a large sawhorse about 10 feet high, a chain swinging down from the center with a 21-foot bar of railroad iron poised with the chain in its center, has caused more destruction in one day than I ever heard of before. . . . The stone depot had been previously mined and packages of powder buried under its walls. The object I suppose is to set the woodwork on fire as soon as we leave and let the powder do what we left undone. This afternoon 'BN' office and buildings all around it were set on fire. And now while I am writing you the Trout House, our office and the whole of the business portion of Whitehall street is in a perfect blaze, many private residences have also been destroyed but this is more an accident than intention. . . .

"Gen. Howard with the Army of Tennessee passed through town yesterday and this morning moved forward taking the Jonesboro Road. Gen. Slocum also pulled out this morning on the Augusta Road with a portion of the 'Army of Georgia,' leaving Gen. Jeff C. Davis to bring up the rear. I am now at Gen. Sherman's Headquarters and tomorrow morning early we start."

Major Hitchcock, also at Sherman's headquarters, reported the holocaust from the vantage point of high ground: "on parallel ridge, say 200 yards north, valley between, runs 'Whitehall St.' (principal business street) with fine blocks of warehouses, etc. running E to and by R.R. depots, etc. From our rear and E. windows, ½ of horizon shows immense and raging fires, lighting up whole heavens—probably, says Sherman, visible at Griffin, fifty miles off. First bursts of smoke, dense, black volumes, then tongues of flame, then huge waves of fire roll up into the sky: presently the skeletons of great warehouses stand out in relief against and amidst sheets of roaring, blazing, furious flames,—then the angry waves roll less high, and are of deeper color, then sink and cease, and only the fierce glow from the bare and blackened walls, etc.

"Now and then are heavy explosions, and as one fire sinks another rises, further along the horizon, till for say ⅓ of the circle, N. E. and E. of us, and some on the N. W., it is a line of fire and smoke, lurid, angry, dreadful to look upon. Went down to the corner and looked out over where the R.R. depots were—all covered with smoking and still blazing ruins. But was rejoiced to find on the way that sentries were posted in front of the two churches near our Headquarters, with orders so strict that on returning with other officers he would not let us go *by it* on the sidewalk, but ordered us out into the street: and soon after did same to two or three others going down cross street along west side of church. This is right. I note these and preceding facts because Gen. S. will hereafter be charged with indiscriminate burning, which is not true. His orders are to destroy only such buildings as are used or useful for war purposes, whether for producing, storing, or transporting materials, etc. of war: but all others are to be spared, and *no dwelling touched*. He talked to me again today about this, apparently because of the evidently painful impression I received at Marietta. Said nothing like excuse, but simply explained the facts. At table he remarked—'this city has done and contributed probably more to carry on and sustain the war than any other, save perhaps Richmond. We have been fighting *Atlanta* all the time, in the past: have been capturing guns, wagons, etc., etc., marked "Atlanta" and made here, all the time: and now since they have been doing so much to destroy us and our Government we have to destroy them, at least enough to prevent any more of that.' . . .

"Saw Poe's men at work yesterday with his new contrivance for quickly tearing up R.R.'d tracks: simply a large iron hook, hung on a chain whose other end has a ring to insert a crowbar or other lever. . . .

"As I write, 11:30 P.M., the fires are pretty much burnt out, and from my 2d story (S. W.) window I can no longer see the glare in the sky. No dwelling has been touched, nor the Court House, nor any church. The Masonic Hall is spared. The only danger yet is from stragglers and teamsters, after the guards are withdrawn, which they must be tomorrow. I see plainly how true it is that 'those are the men who do these things.'

"Quite a feature tonight was a serenade (early) by the splendid band formerly of 33d Mass. Vols.—now a brigade band. Always will the Miserere in *Trovatore* carry me back to this night's scenes and sounds. This band is celebrated, as also that of the 2d Mass., now kept up by the officers.

"We start tomorrow at 6:30 A.M. for the seashore. The movement commenced today—XV, XVII, and XX, Howard south and K(ilpatrick) dashing ahead. Perhaps the rebs will be puzzled to guess where the blow will fall.

"This campaign will be no joke in *any* point of view—but if successful, as we believe and expect, a splendid one now and hereafter. Doubtless it will be death to those of us who may fall into their hands—but if so, 'twill cost them dear."

Conyngham objectively kept count, with a reporter's eye, of the buildings consumed during the height of the conflagration. In some respects, he felt, it was like butter pats melting on a summer's day.

"The Atlanta Hotel," he wrote, "Washington Hall and all the square around the railroad depot were soon in one sheet of flame.

"Drug stores, dry goods stores, hotels, negro marts, theatres, and grog shops were all now feeding the fiery element. Worn-out wagons and camp equipage were piled up in the depot, and added to the fury of the flames.

"A stone warehouse was blown up by a mine. Quartermasters ran away, leaving large stores behind. The men plunged into the houses, broke windows and doors with their muskets, dragging out armfuls of clothes, tobacco, and whiskey, which was more welcome than all the rest. The men dressed themselves in new clothes, and then flung the rest into the fire.

"The streets were now in one fierce sheet of flame; houses were falling on all sides, and fiery flakes of cinders were whirled about. Occasionally shells exploded, and excited men rushed through the choking atmosphere, and hurried away from the city of ruins.

"Dr. Peter Paul Noel D'Alvigny, the only Confederate army surgeon left in Atlanta, barely saved his Medical College. He found, according to some reports, Federal soldiers stacking straw and broken furniture in the entrance hall. They had already ignited the pyre before he proved there were still sick and wounded soldiers in one rear ward.

"Look!" he shouted, throwing open the door. There were too many to be moved, and the troops extinguished the blaze, aided by Dr. D'Alvigny. His hands were scorched, his shirt blackened, but he saved the Medical College.

Even though the zenith was passed by midnight and individual fires burned with less intensity, the terror was unabated for those who lived through it.

"Oh what a night!" Carrie Berry said. "They came burning the store house. . . . it looked like the whole town was on fire. We all set up all night. If we had not set up our house would have ben burnt up for the fire was very near and the soldiers were going around setting houses on fire where they were not watched. They behaved very badly. . . . nobody knows what we have suffered!"

NOVEMBER 16

At 3:00 A.M. Major Ward Nichols, Sherman's aide-de-camp, was with his regiment, encamped east of the city. Ringing in his mind were the strains of *John Brown*. . . . that bands had played late into the night, even as the funeral flames for Atlanta leapt skyward and crackled. The music had sounded "so grand, so solemn, so inspiring."

He believed, when he left the downtown section, that White-hall and Alabama streets were in ruins, and not many buildings were standing on Pryor, Hunter, Mitchell and Loyd streets. Marietta Street was a ghastly "wasteland." He did not relish thinking about this onetime artery for a prosperous city.

He had heard it estimated that five thousand buildings had been consumed in two days, including every school. It made him agree that "General Sherman is kind of careless with fire."

Minutes past three o'clock, Nichols gazed upon watch-fires "burning dimly," and listened to "the occasional neighing of horses." Strangely, after the doomsday pandemonium of the night, "all is so silent that it is difficult to imagine that 20,000 men are within a radius of a few miles. The ripple of the brook can be distinctly heard as it breaks over the pebbles, or winds petulantly about the gnarled roots.

"The wind sweeping gently through the tall pines overhead only serves to lull to deeper repose the slumbering soldier who in his tent is dreaming of his far-off Northern home.

"But in an instant it is all changed. From some commanding elevation the clear-toned bugle sounds out the reveille and an-other and another responds, until the startled echoes double and treble the clarion calls. Intermingled with this comes the beating of drums, often rattling and jarring on unwilling ears. In a few minutes the peaceful quiet is replaced by noise and tumult, arising from hill and dale, from field and forest. Camp fires, hitherto extinct or smouldering in dull gray ashes, awaken to new life and brilliancy, and send forth their sparks high into the morning air. . . .

"The potatoes are frying nicely in the well-larded pan, the chicken is roasting delicately on the red-hot coals, and grateful fumes from steaming coffee-pots delight the nostrils. . . .

"Knapsacks are strapped, men seize their trusty weapons, and as again the bugles sound the note of command, the soldiers fall into line and file out upon the road."

As the eastern sky lightened, wagon trains and marching men were already snaking eastward out of Atlanta. It was an army of "little devils," in Sherman's own words. The older men had gone home to rest, now it could be considered an army of boys, "many not old enough to vote, many regimental commanders not 30."

David Conyngham was marching out with them. "At a distance the city seemed overshadowed by a cloud of black smoke, through which, now and then, darted a gushing flame of fire, or projectiles hurled from the burning ruin.

"The sun looked, through the hazy cloud, like a blood-red ball of fire; and the air, for miles around, felt oppressive and intolerable. The Tyre of the south was laid in ashes, and the 'Gate City' was a thing of the past."

Major Hitchcock checked his watch. It was 7:00 A.M. when the soldiers began to file eastward through the streets. "Weather fine for marching," he wrote, "cloudy but not threatening, air hardly cool. Going out of town, passed through burnt district, still smoking. Saw no dwelling destroyed, and outside of central business part of town comparatively little damage. Should say ¼ of area of town destroyed, but this the largest and best built business part.

"Passed through and along . . . struck with fine appearance and elastic step and bearing of the troops. At head of one brigade the old 79th Pa. band was playing same quick step as at Kingston serenade. One fellow very drunk, sitting on ground as we passed troops at a rest or halt. Cursed General loudly, evidently for drunken brag. General (Sherman) rode quietly by him, not 10 feet off—heard all—no notice."

Several soldiers called to their commanding general, "Uncle Billy, I guess Grant is waiting for us at Richmond!"

It was a "devil may care" feeling in his army that Sherman contemplated with mixed reactions. Responsibility weighed heavily on his lean shoulders "for success would be accepted as a matter of course, whereas, should we fail, this 'march' would be adjudged the wild adventure of a crazy fool."

Men and wagons of the 14th Corps clogged the narrow, wooded Decatur Road, along which Sherman guided his own horse. He jogged past the wasteland left by the explosion of Hood's ammunition train, past the tombstones of Oakland Cemetery on the other side of the twisted tracks until, shortly, as he was to chronicle, "reaching the hill, just outside of the old rebel works, we naturally paused to look back upon the scenes of our past battles.

"We stood upon the very ground whereon was fought the bloody battle of July 22d, and could see the copse of wood where McPherson fell. Behind us lay Atlanta, smouldering and in ruins, the black smoke rising high in air, and hanging like a pall over the ruined city. Away off in the distance, on the Mc-Donough road, was the rear of Howard's column, the gun-barrels glistening in the sun, the white-topped wagons stretching away to the south; and right before us the Fourteenth Corps, marching steadily and rapidly, with a cheery look and swinging pace, that made light of the thousand miles that lay between us and Richmond. Some band, by accident, struck up the anthem of *John Brown's soul goes marching on;* the men caught up the strain and never before or since have I heard the chorus of *Glory, glory hallelujah!* done with more spirit, or in better harmony of time and place.

"Then we turned our horses' head to the east; Atlanta was soon lost behind the screen of trees, and became a thing of the past. Around it clings many a thought of desperate battle, of hope and fear, and now seem like the memory of a dream."

EPILOGUE

The vines grow up the walls of the 1½-story wooden structure at 524 Marshall Street, Decatur, Georgia. Beside the front walk a tree stump hints of the shade it furnished on a distant yesterday, and of those it amply shaded. In back, a smokehouse tilts in crumbling abandonment.

And on the porch the lady smiles as she rocks back and forth, back and forth.

"Yes," she affirms, "yes, indeed. Miss Gay lived here. Why, many folks in Decatur remember Mary Ann Harris Gay."

The street turns a corner, past a filling station. Three blocks farther on, half-hidden in a grove of maples is another old house. In the parlor sits one of those who remember.

"Miss Gay was small," Wesley Hamilton Weeks recalls haltingly, "she was tiny. She wore black. . . . always." And then a pause while his daughter tucks his blanket about his legs. "I'd see her, walking towards the city hall, or to the Williams' place, or, or . . . ?" He looks for help at his daughter.

"Maybe to the railroad station?" she finishes.

He nods and then grows quiet, this immensely weary man of ninety-eight years. Memory, or the power to translate it, has dimmed again, and the momentary sparkle has faded from his eyes.

Others, somewhat younger, piece together the tragedy of Mary Gay's later years—a story of war-strain and human malice. While the South was humiliated in its defeat, Mary was meted an especial Calvary. She had been too "friendly" with the Yankees. Her neighbors shunned her.

The years moved on. The little woman, well into her middle years, found refuge in poetry after completing her autobiog-

541

raphy *Life in Dixie During the War*. Her mother was dead, and she lived alone in the frame house—except for infrequent visits from her early-widowed sister-in-law, Missouri Stokes.

Mary, by this time possessed with certainty only her memories, and to these she retreated with increasing compulsion. The components of her past, whether of her doing or undoing, were combining to crush the fragile Mary Gay, yet, the vindictiveness of the townspeople persisted with a smoldering fury.

She ventured out of the house, market basket in hand, only for necessary errands. She was aging, stooped, a heart-breaking spectacle.

But she did not break any hearts of the women of postwar Decatur, who had sat in their terrible judgment. It was as though they obtained satisfaction from her gradual disintegration.

At night, the past swept before her in a wild, uncontrollable flood until she screamed in terror. Neighbors awoke and remarked, in the darkness of their bedrooms: "It's that Gay woman again."

By now, another generation, not present at the condemnation of Mary Gay, was appearing. One man in particular would hurry into his bedroom slippers and bathrobe and run down the street to her house. There he would sit beside the frightened little figure, hold her bony, shaking hand.

"Everything's going to be all right, Miss Gay," he would soothe.

Finally, she would grow calm and push back the tangle of hair from her face. Sometimes, she would sit and stare, with a nostalgia deep in her eyes, at the ceilings—especially at a bulbous patch in the plaster above the dining table.

But Mary could not go back. The light-heartedness which had buoyed her through the War Between the States could not be resummoned any more than the ghosts of the men who had fallen in it. She lived in a haunted solitude.

Mary Gay endured into another century, even after her accusers were gone. She survived like an anachronism.

Mary lived through the greatest war the world had ever

known. Then, just after she had turned ninety, everything, perhaps belatedly, did become "all right." The year was 1918.

Next to her mother and Missouri, Mary Gay is at peace in old Decatur Cemetery. Never again will she have to hide Gen. Granbury's uniform or wheedle a bag of coffee or a pass from Federal officers—or worry about what the neighbors are whispering. Song and beauty have come back, forever.

Through the somnolent back streets of Decatur, past City Hall, past Ammi Williams' house and the railroad station, the old road winds eastward through Covington, as it did that morning Sherman's army tramped over it, to Savannah. Six miles in the opposite direction, on the eastern fringes of Atlanta, is a sprawling textile plant, where once stood Markham and Schofield's rolling mill. And a few hundred yards beyond that is Oakland Cemetery.

Beneath its gnarled trees rest many who shared the prelude to a type of terror that was to become commonplace to succeeding generations. Here lie the mortal remains of Mrs. William M. Crumley, who wrote a diary under the name, "Carrie Berry," of Mary Rawson, and Andy Neal, S. P. Richards. . . . in fact, almost enough souls to populate the old city of Atlanta.

"S. P." returned to resurrect his book and stationery business, which endures to this day. He had earned his remaining years of calm and prosperity, years in which neither fires, shells, nor the duties of a deputy militiaman interfered with the ordered tenor of his way. His grandchildren enjoyed several summers with the gentlemanly, solemn old man and his voice rang out in glory of his Lord in Sunday choir almost until the day that the Lord decided to answer him.

Braumuller and his father did what they had sworn they never would, as they journeyed back to Atlanta and reopened the music store. But for the wartime adjunct to his business there was no longer a market—drum manufacture. No one in the South even cared to hear a drum, with its connotations of pain, misery, defeat. . . .

Lizzie Perkerson took leave of the world at ninety-seven (in the old house which still stands). In spite of all the harsh words she had aimed at the Yankees, she married one. The sheriff's daughter from Fulton County who excelled in baking corn bread became Mrs. Sumner Butler of New York soon after the fighting ended.

In Memphis, Benedict Joseph Semmes had attained seventy-eight when a parish edict threatened to deny him and his "beloved Eo" the burial plot he had so long contemplated. Barely in time, "Joe" Semmes moved to another apartment and thereby satisfied church boundary requirements.

The front pew in St. Peter's he had occupied for the better part of seventy-five years had lost one of its worshipers.

But Eo was not ready. At ninety-eight, still active and healthy, she tripped over a lawn sprinkler at the start of what was to have been another busy day in her garden. After a score of years, she had gone to join Joe, Joe who had consumed the war era in worry for her and their children's well-being.

As a matter of fact, his only surviving child, Tom, now lives in New York, is past ninety and robust. A number of his grandchildren fought with distinction in World War II.

Fannie Beers, Kate Cumming, and Grandma Smith returned to the lives they had left to nurse the soldiers. But some did not enjoy the peace that had so belatedly arrived. Mrs. E. E. George, of Fort Wayne, who had survived the shelling at Jonesboro, succumbed a few months later at Wilmington, North Carolina, to typhoid fever. She was accorded a hero's funeral in her Indiana community, perhaps the first woman to be buried in Fort Wayne with military honors.

Rufus Mead gazed again over the Connecticut hills. He had a great deal to tell his "dear folks at home" about what happened in Georgia when he helped Old Tecumseh save the Union. Soon, he was awarded a Government contract to survey Bridgeport harbor and blueprint what is today's Seaside Park.

Later, Rufus forsook his native state for Orange, New Jersey. There he is remembered by a dwindling few as the kindly Sunday School teacher of the First Presbyterian Church. He was eighty-six years old when, one morning in 1922, the sexton draped the school room in black and prepared for a funeral.

The Reverend Quintard carried sad memories of his St. Luke's Church in Atlanta. Never again was a house of worship raised out of its ashes. Never again would a Nellie Peters drop her pocket handkerchief at her brother's—or sister's—funeral. Business structures took over the site, as they did Carrie Berry's home nearby.

Yet others needed Charles Todd Quintard as much as had the Confederacy. The Stamford-born surgeon-minister served the Union in postwar Nashville in his familiar capacities: doctor and chaplain. Later he became Bishop of Tennessee and presided over the growth of the University of the South, at Sewanee.

Many in the Episcopal Church speak of the versatile Dr. Quintard as though he were still in their midst—and leave any burden of proof, thereby, to the doubters.

General Pat Cleburne never found the horse for which he had advertised that July. Before the year was out, he was killed in the battle of Franklin, Tennessee. Gen. Granbury and Lieutenant Tom Stokes both perished in the same sanguinary action —wearing, presumably, the overcoats Mary Gay had so carefully guarded.

People like David Conyngham and Wallace Reed continued careers as writers, Tom Key, as a publisher, and Henry Watterson as an editor. Never losing his inherent belligerence, the latter was the "Marse Henry" in 1915 who thumped editorially that perhaps it was time for the United States to consider another war.

People . . . soldiers like Sergeant Graham, or Private Alonzo Miller, or Andy Rose . . . returned to the limbo whence they had sprung. They were never heard from again, these ephemeral punctuations in the book of time.

Many more, who had left not even as much record behind them as Graham, or Miller, or Rose, did not go home. In the National Cemetery, Marietta, for one, there are 10,158 graves. Here lie the boys from the North who in their wildest fancies would never have contemplated eternity at places like Buzzard's Roost, Pumpkin Vine Creek, Culp's Farm, Ezra Church, Rough and Ready, or along a dusty path called the Lick Skillet Road, or on the banks of a muddy, tepid stream with the improbable name of Ulcofauhatchee.

Shortly after the war, Major W. H. Chamberlin visited Marietta and noted the 3,100 graves marked "Unknown."

"Who can tell," he speculated, "how many of these nameless heroes met death on the skirmish lines? There is a world of pathos in their lost identity, and in the picture of the broken home-circles it suggests . . . if their voice could be heard it would say: 'we are content, for over us, and over the whole country, floats today, and forever, the flag of a preserved, united Nation!' "

Yet, the passions and bitterness persist in the nation, "United." Where, in Marietta, can the stranger find a sign pointing to the meticulously-tended National Cemetery, an Arlington in proportion? But, several blocks to the South the Confederate dead sleep in their own well-directed, placarded cemetery.

Perhaps the dead in Blue and Gray could wonder for what they perished?

Visitors come to look, but never more to weep, in either cemetery. There remain tears for the fathers, husbands, or sons who fell at the Marne, or Normandy Beach, Tarawa, or near the Yalu River, but who is there to remember the soldier who was killed nearly one hundred years ago?

Who can recall the little marks of personality, the nuances of voice, step, or even the smell of a rank but familiar cigar which can evoke the warmth of memory, the anguish of loss?

The past, too, is all but erased from Atlanta, as though the summer of 1864, as well as the fears of its inhabitants, had never existed but in the fancy of historians. The golf course which roams over the battleground of Peachtree Creek is itself symbolic of the transformation of the "Gate City of the Confederacy." It neither smells, feels, or looks the same.

The horses which once so pungently stamped the city have been replaced by gasoline-powered vehicles. The myriad attendant odors of masonry, pavements, sidewalks, and even of people themselves dominate a pulsing city which a third of a million call home—and a beautiful home.

The snowball bushes in lovingly-tended front yards, which to the slaves "looked like a week's wash hung out," have long since been swallowed in a sea of asphalt. "The Terraces" of Mary Rawson, on Pryor Street, or the home of Lucy Harvie Hull, on

Peachtree, where "Mommy made beat biscuits by the wheelbarrow full, have given way to business structures, and to utilitarian drabness.

The scent of magnolia blossoms is no more in downtown Atlanta, for the residential district has pushed far beyond its Edens of yesterday, all the way to the banks of the Chattahoochee. If the common well could be found at Five Points, under a matted jungle of steel, concrete, brick, piping, and electrical conduits, some citizens would still have to walk nine or ten miles from the city limits to reach it.

A new hotel rose on the site of the Atlanta. With elevators (or a sort) and running water (here and there) it was a showplace of the South. But the evil star which shone above its predecessor lingered at the Kimball House's own fated zenith. In a few years, the ornate hostelry, too, burned to the ground.

Reconstructed on a less pretentious scale, the second Kimball stands today on the corner of Pryor and Decatur streets, defying age, wear, and a changing clientele. Its clerks look with incredulity upon those who inquire about the old Atlanta, an almost legendary hotel whose sole surviving legacy is a billiard room and a persisting reek of tobacco.

That wounded officers could have lain bleeding in corridors and bedrooms above this same parcel of earth seems almost beyond the realm of comprehension.

But it happened, once.

At Ivy and Ellis streets the traffic shoulders noisily across the intersection, like a mechanized, miasmic avalanche. Who, however, has time to think about the little girl who was killed there on a Wednesday noontime by the first shell to crash onto Atlanta?

In the city rush, who has time to think?

The sumptuous Ponder estate is gone. The abodes which have mushroomed in its stead are something other than elegant. The project might cause Sam French to be even more anxious for relief from Atlanta duty.

In this same area, where Sherman's gunners kept hot shell batteries sizzling, heat of another sort continues. Hot music wails through the night, melding with fiery liquor and sweating bodies which rock and roll into the dawn.

Who, in the sweep of time, has heard of *Lorena?* Who can recall when an army marched out of the city, chorusing the melancholy verses? Or, who can care?

Dr. d'Alvigny's Medical College has fared better with respect to memory and significance. The old structure was torn down, but the ground remains sacred for its original purpose. One of the buildings of the large Grady Hospital occupies the original acreage.

The gas flame burns in the lamp post beside which Sol Luckie the barber was killed; the shell hole in its base has never been repaired. Perhaps beneath the asphalt of Forsyth's Alley (now Street) remains the wreckage of the two thousand sewing machines W. B. Young could not sell.

Atlanta University now furnishes higher education for Negroes on the site of Federal Fort No. 7. There, one morning, General Sherman, immaculately uniformed for the first time in months, posed for an army photographer.

Beyond Atlanta's city limits, communities such as Jonesboro, Newnan, Covington, and Oxford have not changed measurably. Many of the old houses survive along narrow, shaded streets which have witnessed little further excitement since the summer of 1864. In some the scars of shells or Minie balls are lovingly preserved.

In Covington, the pews are back in the First Methodist Church which Grandma Smith knew only as a hospital ward. The rear windows of the chapel at Oxford (belonging to Emory University) have been little altered, even to paint, since Walter Clark watched patients escaping through them to the sanctuary of adjacent woods.

In many an unmarked, shallow grave in those woods lies the dust of soldiers of both sides, buried and forgotten in the haste of skirmishing and fear of more cavalry raids.

At Social Circle, the railroad station has been replaced, but the trains operate with an infrequency reminiscent of Grandma Smith's tedious wait.

At Macon, the picnic grounds behind the Wesleyan College, where General Iverson was to have been feted, will entertain no one or ring with no voices other than those of customers in the shopping center which has been built upon them. The woman's college itself has moved to a new campus six miles west of Macon.

In other sections of the United States, the Atlanta campaign, obviously, is etched less acutely. Here and there a monument, a plaque, a statue recalls a battle, a regiment, or a leader. Joe Hooker, astride his horse, grimly guards the State House, in Boston. Sherman himself rides triumphantly on the greens of several cities.

At 75 West 71st Street, in New York City, weathered stone lions still flank the front door of the house in which the revered Tecumseh died that St. Valentine's Day, 1891. Editorial writers eulogized him as "the saviour of the Republic."

The greater portion of the United States was plunged into deep official mourning.

"Sherman?" asks the frowsy woman, pausing before one of the apartments of the converted dwelling. "Sherman?"

There is a look of defensive contempt in her eyes.

"Well, ain't that somethin'? Ain't that somethin'. . . !" With a cackle of disbelief, she slams the door.

Yet, the present was resummoned, suddenly, cruelly.

His once handsome house, the generation, the cause General Sherman personified, and all the "little people" whose lives he involuntarily affected now seemed, even as Atlanta had to him, "the memory of a dream."

BIBLIOGRAPHY
AND ACKNOWLEDGMENTS

The author expresses deep appreciation to many who personally helped the *Last Train From Atlanta* get under way, and faithfully continued to further its headlong but often halting progress. These names come to mind:

Peter A. Brannon, Mrs. Allen B. Burrus, Arthur B. Chitty, E. Merton Coulter, Mrs. J. E. Dance, Isabel Erlich, Charles Dwoskin, Mrs. R. L. Foreman, Mrs. J. H. Franklin, Franklin P. Garrett, Mrs. Dorothy Candler Hamilton, Colonel Allen P. Julian, Myrna Lichtman, Charles O'Neill, Dr. James W. Patton, Mrs. Angus Perkerson, Dr. B. E. Powell, Charles Rawson, William H. Runge, Mrs. Mattie Russell, Mrs. B. J. Semmes, Mrs. Robert T. Sterrett, Ella Mae Thornton, Arthur B. Upshur, and —Thomas Yoseloff, without whose faith the documentary would still be, at most, a future idea.

There are, of course, many others who helped. The omission of their names must be attributed only to faulty memory.

Sincere thanks go to the patient staffs of these principal libraries: New York Public Library, Boston Public Library, Illinois State Historical Library, Widener Library, Houghton Library, Boston Athenaeum, Ferguson Library (Stamford, Connecticut), Atlanta Public Library, State Library of Virginia, Decatur-DeKalb Library (Georgia), and the libraries of these universities: Yale, Princeton, Virginia, Duke, North Carolina, Emory, and Georgia. Also, the National Archives and the Library of Congress made significant contributions in source material, general leads, and in rare old photographs.

Specific contributions from these libraries:

University of Georgia: files of the newspaper *Southern Confederacy,* the newspaper *The Confederate Union,* the letter home from Robert J. Wood, also files of *The Atlanta Journal* and *The Atlanta Constitution* containing recollections of O. L. Braumuller and Mollie Smith.

Atlanta Public Library: especially for the amazing completeness of the files, which furnished an eyewitness account of the death of Sol Luckie, the barber, beside the lamp post.

University of North Carolina: Benedict Joseph Semmes letters (herewith published for the first time); the Mrs. George Johnson Baldwin collection (Lucy Harvie Hull); Benjamin Yancey collection ("Gussie's" letter); Colonel Taylor Beatty diary; Elizabeth S. Wiggins letter, the Bishop Lay papers.

Emory University: the Andrew Jackson Neal letters; (published for the first time) *Georgia's Confederate Hospitals,* thesis of Mildred Jordan; Evan P. Howell letter; J. J. Miles letter; Henry Richards' letters.

Duke University: Andrew K. Rose collection. William Graham letters.

Princeton University: Andre deCoppet Collection, for John C. Van Duzer letter.

The University of the South, Sewanee: Quintard papers.

These historical societies:

Atlanta Historical Society—specifically for the Carrie Berry diary, the Mary Rawson diary, S. P. Richards diary, the James R. Crew collection, the Alonzo Miller letters, Colonel Barnett's and Hosea Garrett's and Colin Dunlop's letters, Mary Rushton's notes, Major Charles Hubner's recollections, Sarah Huff's poem and the song *Lorena.* Innumerable rare photographs, as credited elsewhere in the book, were furnished by the Atlanta Historical Society. Other hints, leads, and innumerable aids—including a night key to the society's headquarters and working room at the desk where Margaret Mitchell wrote much of *Gone With the Wind*—were willingly and without question generously provided the author through "Ned" Julian, the society's able director and eminent 1861–65 historian.

Western Reserve Historical Society—microfilm prints of two

invaluable newspapers of the summer of '64, *The Daily Intelligencer,* of Atlanta, *The Sentinel* of Richmond.

Georgia Historical Society—from various issues of its *Historical Quarterly,* the Rufus Mead letters, the Lizzie Perkerson letters.

Mississippi Historical Society (*Journal of Mississippi History*) —the letters of Matthew Andrew Dunn and Thomas Jefferson Newberry.

Southern Historical Society—Colonel Roy's comments on Hardee.

Indiana Magazine of History—Dr. James Comfort Patten's letters.

New Jersey Historical Society—the diary of Major Stephen Pierson.

Iowa Journal of History—Samuel Mahon quote.

Virginia State Historical Society, Massachusetts State Historical Society, Southern Historical Society, and the Pioneer Citizens' Society of Atlanta (*Pioneer History of Atlanta*).

A debt is owned many contemporary newspapers including *The Atlanta Journal and Constitution* for permission to quote freely from any of their excellently researched articles on the siege of Atlanta which have appeared this century; *The New York Times,* the *New York Herald,* the *New York Tribune,* the *Boston Transcript,* and any number, such as the *Commercial Appeal* of Memphis, with a lineage dating back to the Civil War (or War Between the States).

Many magazines, past and present, were helpful in the preparation of *Last Train from Atlanta*—including *Frank Leslie's Illustrated Weekly, Harper's,* and the *Atlantic Monthly,* to whom many thanks are owed for special permission to quote from the Bishop Lay recollections of his visit to General Sherman.

Because of the exhaustive research necessary, the author could not keep note of every single source consulted, nor even of all the business enterprises and organizations (such as the Association of American Railroads or even the Coca-Cola Company) which were helpful in one way or another. However, these books and pamphlets seem to have furnished a particularly valuable amount of "paydirt":

Archer, W. P., *History of The Siege and Battle of Atlanta,* Knoxville, Georgia, Moncrief Company, 1941 (special permission on Mrs. C. B. Moncrief).

Allen, Ivan E., *Atlanta From the Ashes,* Atlanta Ruralist Press, 1928.

Avery, Isaac Wheeler, *History of The State of Georgia,* New York, Brown & Derby, 1881.

Austin, J. P., *The Blue And The Gray,* Atlanta, Franklin Printing and Publishing Company, 1899.

Bennett, William W., *A Narrative of the Great Revival,* Philadelphia, Claxton, Remsen and Haffelfinger, 1877.

Beers, Fannie A., *Memories,* Philadelphia, J. B. Lippincott, 1889.

Bowman, S. M., "Sherman and His Campaign," *United States Service Magazine,* 1865.

Brown, Joseph M., *Mountain Campaigns in Georgia,* Buffalo, 1886.

Bradley, the Reverend G. S. (Chaplain 22d Wisconsin), *The Star Corps, or Notes of an Army Chaplain During Sherman's Famous March to The Sea,* Milwaukee, 1865.

Cate, Wirt A., *Two Soldiers, The Campaign Diaries of Thomas J. Key and Robert J. Campbell,* Chapel Hill, University of North Carolina Press (excerpts through special permission), 1938.

Copp, Elbridge J., *Reminiscences of the War of The Rebellion,* Nashua, New Hampshire, 1911.

Conyngham, Captain David P., *Sherman's March Through the South,* New York, Sheldon & Co., 1865.

Cox, Jacob D., *Atlanta,* New York, Charles Scribner's Sons, 1882.

Cox, Jacob D., *Military Reminiscences of The Civil War,* New York, Charles Scribner's Sons, 1900.

Catton, Bruce, *This Hallowed Ground,* New York, Doubleday & Company, 1955.

Commager, Henry Steele, *The Blue and the Gray,* New York-Indianapolis, The Bobbs-Merrill Company, Inc., 1950.

Clark, Walter A., *Under the Stars and Bars, or the Memories of Four Years Service,* Augusta, Georgia, Chronicle Printing Co., 1900.

Clarke, E. Y., *Illustrated History of Atlanta,* Atlanta, Dodson & Scott, 1922.

Clowell, James Debussey, *The Untold Story of Atlanta*, Chicago, Volunteer Press, 1871.

Cumming, Kate, *Gleanings From Southland*, Birmingham, Roberts and Son, 1895.

Battles and Leaders of the Civil War, New York, Thomas Yoseloff Edition, 1956 (Compiled).

Dowdey, Clifford, *The Land They Fought For*, Garden City, Doubleday & Company, Inc., 1955.

Dodge, Grenville M., *The Battle of Atlanta and Other Campaigns*, Council Bluffs, Iowa, Monarch Printing Co., 1910.

Dubose, John W., *General Wheeler and the Army of the Tennessee*, New York, Neale Publishing Co., 1912.

Dyer, John Will, *Reminiscences of Four Years in the Confederate Army*, Evansville, Indiana, Keller Printing Co., 1898.

Eckenrode, H. J., *Jefferson Davis*, New York, The Macmillan Company, 1923.

French, Samuel G. (General), *Two Wars, An Autobiography*, Nashville, Confederate Veteran, 1901.

Garrett, Franklin K., *Atlanta & Environs*, New York (By subscription).

Gay, Mary Ann Harris, *Life in Dixie During The War*, Atlanta, Constitution Job Office, 1892.

Gaskill, J. W., *Footprints Through Dixie*, Alliance, Ohio (*n.p.*), 1919.

Hedley, Fenwick Y., *Marching Through Georgia*, Chicago, Henneberry & Co., 1890.

Hitchcock, Henry, *Marching with Sherman*, Edited by M. W. deWolfe Howe, New Haven, Yale University Press (excerpts by special permission), 1927.

Howard, Oliver Otis, *Autobiography of Oliver Otis Howard*, New York, The Baker and Taylor Co., 1908.

Hosea, Lewis M., *Some Sidelights on The War for The Union*, Cleveland, Ohio, Commandery, Loyal Legion United States, 1912.

Hornady, John R., *Atlanta, Yesterday, Today and Tomorrow*, Atlanta, American Cities Book Co., 1922.

Hood, J. B., *Advance and Retreat*, New Orleans (Published for Hood Orphan Memorial Fund), G. T. Beauregard, 1880.

Howe, M. A. DeWolfe (ed.), *Home Letters of General Sherman*, New York, Charles Scribner's Sons, 1909.

Hunter, Robert, *Sketches of War History*, Cincinnati, Ohio, Commandery, Military Order of the Loyal Legion United States, Robert Clarke and Co., 1890.

Johnston, Isaac N., *Four Months in Libby and The Campaign Against Atlanta*, Cincinnati, Methodist Book Concern, 1864.

Jones, Charles Edgeworth, *Georgia in The War*, Atlanta, Foote and Davies, 1909.

Jones, Katharine M., *Heroines of Dixie*, Indianapolis, New York, The Bobbs-Merrill Company, Inc., 1955.

Keim, DeB. Randolph, *Sherman—A Memorial*, Washington, United States Government Printing Office (by Authority of Congress), 1904.

Kirwan, A. D. (ed.), *Johnny Green of The Orphan Brigade* ("The Journal of a Confederate Soldier"), University of Kentucky Press, 1956.

Knight, Lucian Lamar, *History of Fulton County, Georgia*, Atlanta, A. H. Cawson, 1930.

Lewis, Lloyd, *Sherman, Fighting Prophet*, New York, Harcourt, Brace & Co., 1939.

McCallie, Elizabeth Hanleiter, *The Atlanta Campaign*, 1939.

Mitchell, Margaret, *Gone With the Wind*, New York, The Macmillan Company, 1936.

Miers, Earl Schenck, *The General Who Marched To Hell*, New York, Alfred A. Knopf, Inc., 1951.

Morison, Samuel Eliot, *Oxford History of the United States*, Vol. II, London, 1927.

Morgan, Mrs. Irby, *How It Was, Four Years Among the Rebels*, Nashville, Publishing House M. E. Church South, 1867.

McElroy, Robert, *Jefferson Davis*, New York, Harper & Brothers, 1937.

Major, Duncan K., *Supply of Sherman's Army During the Atlanta Campaign*, Fort Leavenworth Army Service Schools Press, 1911.

McNeill, S. A., *Personal Recollections of Service in The Army of the Cumberland*.

Moore, Frank, *Women of The War*, Hartford, S. S. Scranton and Co., 1866.

Miller, Francis Trevelyan (ed.), *The Photographic History of the Civil War*, Thomas Yoseloff Edition, 1957.

Minnesota Commandery, M. O. L. L. U. S., *Glimpses of The Nation's Struggle*, St. Paul, 1887.

Noll, the Reverend Arthur Howard, *Doctor Quintard Chaplain, C S A, and Second Bishop of Tennessee*, Sewanee, Tennessee, Tennessee University Press, 1905.

Nichols, Major George Ward, *The Story of The Great March*, New York, Harper & Brothers, 1865.

Pepper, Captain George W., *Personal Recollections of Sherman's Campaign in Georgia and the Carolinas*, Zanesville, Ohio, Hugh Dunne Publishers, 1866.

Price, Samuel W., *The Skirmish Line in The Atlanta Campaign*, Washington, 1904.

Pollard, Edward A., *The Lost Cause*, New York, E. B. Treat Co., 1867.

Official Records War of The Rebellion, Government Printing Office, 1880.

Quint, Alonzo H., *The Record of the Second Massachusetts Infantry*, Boston, James P. Walker Co., 1867.

Ridley, Bromfield L., *Battles and Sketches of the Army of Tennessee*, Mexico, Missouri, Missouri Printing and Publishing Co., 1906.

Reed, Wallace P., *History of Atlanta, Georgia*, Syracuse, D. Mason & Co., 1889.

Randall, Charles W., *General Sherman's Campaign in Georgia*. (Type copy in Atlanta Public Library. No publisher. No date given.)

Smith, Mrs. S. E. D. ("Grandma"), *The Soldiers' Friend*, Memphis, The Bulletin Publishing Co., 1867.

Smith, Charles R., *Bill Arp, So-Called, A Side Show of the Southern Side of the War*, New York, Metropolitan Record Office, 1866.

Senour, F., *Major General William T. Sherman and His Campaigns*, Chicago, 1865.

Seward, William H., *Issues of the Conflict—Terms of Peace*, Washington, McGill & Witherow, 1864.

Sandburg, Carl, *Storm Over The Land*, New York, Harcourt, Brace & Co., 1939.

Schofield, John McA., *Forty-Six Years in The Army*, New York, Century Co., 1897.

Sherman, William T., *Memoirs*, Vol. II, New York, D. Appleton and Co., 1875.

Slocum, Charles E., *The Life and Services of Charles E. Slocum*, Major General Henry Warner Slocum, Toledo, Slocum Publishing Co., 1913.

Turner, George Edgar, *Victory Rode the Rails*, New York-Indianapolis, The Bobbs-Merrill Company, Inc., 1953.

Underwood, Adin B., *The Three Years Service of The Thirty-Third Massachusetts Infantry Regiment*, Boston, A. Williams and Co., 1880.

Vale, Joseph G., *Minty and The Cavalry*, Harrisburg, Edwin K. Meyers, Printer, 1887.

West, Granville C., *McCook's Raid in The Rear of Atlanta and Hood's Army*, Washington, M. O. L. L. U. S., Commandery of the District of Columbia, 1898.

Williams, Noble C., *Echoes From the Battlefield*, Atlanta, Franklin Printing Co., 1902.

Wiley, Bell Irvin, *The Life of Johnny Reb*, New York-Indianapolis, The Bobbs-Merrill Company, Inc., 1943.

Wilson, John Stainback, *Atlanta As It Is*, New York, Little, Rennie & Co., 1871.